Working With Words

A Handbook for Media Writers and Editors

EIGHTH EDITION

Working With Words

A Handbook for Media Writers and Editors

Brian S. Brooks
University of Missouri–Columbia

James L. Pinson
Eastern Michigan University

Jean Gaddy Wilson
Position the Future Consultants

Bedford / St. Martin's
Boston ◆ New York

FOR BEDFORD/ST.MARTIN'S

Publisher for Communication: Erika Gutierrez
Developmental Editors: Mae Klinger, Linda Stern
Editorial Asistant: Caitlin Crandell
Production Supervisor: Samuel Jones
Marketing Manager: Stacey Propps
Project Management: Books By Design, Inc.
Permissions Manager: Kalina K. Ingham
Text Design: Claire Seng-Niemoeller
Cover Design: Marine Miller
Composition: Books By Design, Inc.
Printing and Binding: RR Donnelley and Sons

President, Bedford/St. Martin's: Denise B. Wydra
Presidents, Macmillan Higher Education: Joan E. Feinberg and Tom Scotty
Director of Development: Erica T. Appel
Director of Marketing: Karen R. Soeltz
Production Director: Susan W. Brown
Associate Production Director: Elise S. Kaiser
Manager, Publishing Services: Andrea Cava

Library of Congress Control Number: 2012942172

Manufactured in the United States of America.

7 6 5 4 3 2
f e d c b a

For information, write: Bedford/St. Martin's, 75 Arlington Street, Boston, MA 02116 (617-399-4000)

ISBN 978-1-4576-0493-5

Preface

Working With Words had its beginnings in our own work as newspaper copy editors. We found the stylebook and dictionary didn't always answer the questions that came up every day about grammar, usage, punctuation, compound-word spellings and similar issues. Plus, changing attitudes forced writers to be more aware about avoiding racism, sexism and ageism, as well as dismissive language about the disabled, new immigrants, religious group members and so on. We kept a small shelf of books to consult at such times, but there was no single, comprehensive resource a member of the working press could turn to for such answers.

Later, when teaching editing to students at the University of Missouri and supervising their work on the daily *Columbia Missourian,* we realized that if professionals needed a book that addressed all these questions in one place, students needed it even more. Instructors across the country report that students are underprepared in grammar and style.

Grammar is not stressed in public schools today, and our students typically tell us the last time their teachers covered it at all was in middle school or even elementary school. Further, modern technologies such as texting, tweeting and IMing introduce a casualness in communication and confuse students' writing habits even more. The irony, of course, is that these modern technologies not only affect student writing but also demand adaptation and attention from all of us as writers and editors, whether we are students learning the ropes or experienced journalists.

Working With Words Today

With news outlets, both print and broadcast, continually cutting down on staff and stressing more and more their online presence, how do students and seasoned journalists adapt? What skills and principles lead to success with technology and media that are changing so rapidly?

Although knowing grammar, usage, style and tightening isn't the whole answer, it is an important part of the picture. Employers still complain that too many recent college graduates are deficient in language skills. And the rise of new technology requires students and working journalists to become better self-editors than ever before.

Journalists also need to know how different media should influence the way they write: Do the old language rules still apply? What adjustments help journalists use Facebook feeds or blogs to promote reader interest without sacrificing integrity or making embarrassing gaffes? As the way readers consume the news shifts, providing them with clear, compelling writing becomes more challenging and all the more important.

The Best Guidance for Writers and Editors

In this book, we try to meet the challenges of writing and editing in today's world, and that's part of what we think sets this book apart from others. We explain the issues as simply as possible by elaborating on the AP Stylebook rules and guidelines and giving plenty of examples. We even provide a summary in the appendix of the most essential style rules to help beginners get off to a faster start and more advanced students or professionals to fill in a few gaps.

But, at the same time, we haven't tried to make the subject look easier than it is, as many books do, by leaving out the harder, trickier questions that arise when you make your living working with words. Instead, we face these issues straight on in the main text as well as in the Journalism Tip boxes that provide more specific guidance on challenges confronting journalists on the job and in the ESL Tip boxes that help multilingual students deal with the vagaries of the English language.

And unlike other media-writing handbooks that only cover the rules, without providing guidance as to how to put them into action, *Working With Words* teaches the full spectrum of journalistic writing—from a mastery of English grammar and mechanics in the first half of the book to understanding different journalistic styles and writing methods in the second half.

Marginal tabs included in the page design help identify the parts of the book, "Grammar and Usage," "Mechanics," "Style" and "Writing Methods for Different Media," for easy access. In particular, Part Four, "Writing Methods for Different Media," recognizes how new technologies that increasingly marry print and electronic media call for us to learn how to write for different media and offers three chapters (14 through 16) on the key elements of writing for print, radio and television, and online media. These chapters build on the fundamentals of grammar, usage, mechanics and style laid out in Parts One through Three and show how word choice, word order, style and even story organization change with the medium.

Working With Words is more than just a grammar and usage manual. This brief but comprehensive text aims to fill the needs of students and professionals, providing a well-rounded, comprehensive resource that can be used from journalistic training through a professional career, no matter the medium.

New to This Edition

In the Eighth Edition, we've added cutting-edge advice about writing for online media, created navigational tools that make the book even more useful and tweaked coverage of grammar fundamentals to make this crucial coverage even more helpful to students.

More Advice That Students Need Now. We've updated the Eighth Edition to keep pace with the changing landscape—today's media writers need to be able to write well in traditional formats and in Twitter's 140 characters.

- **A Revised Introduction for Students.** We begin the book by outlining the massive changes that have recently hit journalism—from the decline of newspapers to the growth of online media and cable television—while maintaining the importance of grammar and explaining to students why it still matters.
- **Cutting-Edge Advice on Writing for Online Media.** A fully revised Chapter 16 presents the advice students *really* need for writing online, including guidance on blogging, search-engine optimization, promoting news using social media like Twitter and Facebook, and editing your own copy. The wire-service style summary now lists the preferred spelling for social media and computer terms.
- **Updated Tips for Writing With Fairness and Sensitivity.** The demands of writing with fairness and sensitivity evolve quickly, and writing for larger, more inclusive and more global audiences requires more sophistication and sensitivity than ever before. Therefore, in Chapter 13 and throughout the book, we provide the latest guidance and advice to ensure appropriate and fair language.

Better Navigation. New navigation tools help busy students and working professionals find important information on the fly.

- **Part-Opening "Quick References"** provide speedy access to the most commonly looked-up rules and tips in each part.
- **Useful "Lists at a Glance" Feature.** This table, found after the main Table of Contents, leads readers to the most important lists in *Working With Words*, from misused and confused words and phrases to words often misspelled, common compounds, and words and phrases to tighten.

More Writing Help. Instructors throughout the country tell us that students have trouble grasping the fundamentals of grammar and mechanics and applying these principles to their own writing. Because good journalists must first be good writers, we have provided even more help on writing fundamentals.

- **Even Better Coverage of Key Grammar Points.**   In response to instructor feedback, we have fine-tuned coverage and examples of grammar and mechanics that students find most challenging, including subjects and objects, noun forms, verb tense and mood, and modifiers.

- **New Diagrams Provide Visual Reinforcement.**   Visuals help students grasp key concepts like written formality, quoting sources and news-story structure.

- **Updated Examples in Every Section.**   As usual, we've updated material throughout the text, adding new examples — from coverage of the basketball player Jeremy Lin to convergence in the newsroom — and reflecting changes in the most recent edition of the AP Stylebook, including a list of the preferred spelling for social media and computer terms.

Media Resources.   Students can use these media tools to become better writers and editors.

- **Now Available as an e-Book.**   *Working With Words* is available in a variety of e-book options for use on a computer, tablet or e-reader. Visit bedfordstmartins.com/ebooks to learn more.

- **Online Writing and Grammar Help at News Central bedfordstmartins.com/newscentral.**   News Central is a free and open Web resource that contains *Exercise Central for AP Style*, with thousands of exercises addressing the most common errors students make in abbreviations, capitalization, numbers, attribution and copy-editing symbols. Students can also access up-to-the-moment RSS news feeds from a variety of media outlets and beats, and links to a variety of research tools.

- *VideoCentral: Journalism* **bedfordstmartins.com/newscentral.**   News Central is also the gateway to VideoCentral, our premium video collection for the journalism classroom, containing over two dozen clips of media insiders like Amy Goodman, Clarence Page, Jim Spencer and David Herzog, talking about the latest trends, from convergence to media entrepreneurship to real versus fake news sources, and more. In addition, several clips help students gain valuable insight into the interviewing process. Go to bedfordstmartins.com/workingwithwords/catalog to learn more or for packaging information.

Support for Students and Instructors

Ancillary materials help students and instructors get the most benefit from using the Eighth Edition. For more information on the student and instructor resources or to learn about package options, please visit the online catalog at bedfordstmartins.com/workingwithwords/catalog.

- *Exercise Book for Working With Words*, **Eighth Edition.**
Revised and updated, the exercise book gives students the opportunity to master the writing and editing skills covered in the main text, including grammar and mechanics guidelines, practicing proper copy-editing symbols, rewriting sentences for clarity and conciseness, learning how to write successful leads and recognizing the conventions of wire-service style.

- *Answer Key for Working With Words*, **Eighth Edition.**   An online answer key, available only to instructors through the book's catalog page (bedfordstmartins.com/workingwithwords/catalog), provides answers to all the questions in the exercise book.

Acknowledgments

In closing, we again want to thank our families for their love and support. Thanks also to the many faculty, students, professionals and others who have used previous editions of this book. Thanks especially to students, faculty and media professionals who have sent us suggestions for this new edition.

We are further grateful to the following reviewers who graciously offered comprehensive suggestions for this new edition: Sharon Bracken (Baylor University), Jim Brosemer (Bethune-Cookman University), Scott Brown (California State University, Northridge), Andrew W. Dilworth (Jackson State University), Betsy Edgerton (Columbia College Chicago), Kym Fox (Texas State University), Eddye Gallagher (Tarrant County College), Garry Gilbert (Oakland University), Kristyn Hunt (Lamar University), Cathy Johnson (Angelo State University), Suzanne McBride (Columbia College Chicago), Jodie Peeler (Newberry College), Zengjun Peng (St. Cloud State University), Gemma Puglisi (American University), Denise Barkis Richter (Palo Alto College), Felecia Jones Ross (The Ohio State University), Barbara Selvin (Stony Brook University), Joe Sheller (Mount Mercy University), Richard J. Toth (University of Maryland) and Carol Zuegner (Creighton University).

Thanks, too, to the staff at Bedford/St. Martin's, who have believed in this book and who have worked with us to make it what it is. We especially want to thank our editors this time, Linda Stern and Mae Klinger, for their well-considered suggestions for making this, once again, the best edition so far.

Good writing takes good, hard thinking. This book lives because writers, students, educators and journalists send us questions about each edition or suggestions for the next. Please write us with yours. Here are our email addresses:

Brian S. Brooks   BrooksBS@missouri.edu
James L. Pinson   jpinson@emich.edu
Jean Gaddy Wilson   jeangaddywilson@aol.com

Brief Contents

Contents

PART FOUR   Writing Methods for Different Media   319

Useful Lists at a Glance

Here's a guide to the most commonly referenced lists in the text.

Working With Words

A Handbook for Media Writers and Editors

Introduction for Students

> When written in Chinese, the word "crisis" is composed of two charac-
> ters. One represents danger, and the other represents opportunity.
> — President John F. Kennedy

Although some Chinese speakers say the linguistic analysis by President Kennedy in that quote is mistaken, the idea itself—often repeated by politicians, business people and motivational speakers—has truth to it. Certainly, it accurately describes the situation facing journalism today: not just danger for those who fail to make an effective transition into the digital world but also opportunity for those who figure out how to do it well.

The massive alterations that have hit journalism within the past decade continue to reverberate. Journalists and media organizations are still grappling with the changes they must make to preserve and advance journalism for themselves and, more important, for our nation as a whole because the public needs to stay well-informed for democracy to function.

The Influence of Digital Media

Historically, media companies often enjoyed profit margins two or three times those of most companies. But by 2008 profits had declined so much that broadcast stations and wire services began layoffs in response.

Various reasons have been offered for the sudden downturn in profitability. Most often blamed is the Internet. Why buy a newspaper when you can read the news free online and in a more timely manner than in your local paper? In addition, Internet sites like Craigslist offering free want ads, monster.com offering job listings and auction sites like eBay took away much of the profitable classified-ad business.

As a result, some daily newspapers either closed or went online only. Others cut back to a print edition just a few times a week and other days refer readers to their website.

Newspapers had long before established websites and seen them as the future, but the future arrived before media companies were clear as to how to adjust their business model to this new world. Larry Dignan

1

explains in his Kindle e-book "The Business of Media: A Survival Guide" that newspapers still make most of their income from the print editions, despite many readers canceling subscriptions and going for their news to the Web. But the Web also offers lower production costs and so greater potential profit margins to news providers. The industry's problem, Dignan says, is figuring out how to get the two to mesh—that is, to get to the point when most newspaper income comes from online, where the profit margin could also be higher.

Many ideas have been offered for new business models, including: online ads, which so far typically may bring in only about 5 percent of a newspaper's ad revenue; "crowd funding" through individual donations to projects the public chooses; a donation approach like the one National Public Radio has used for years with fund drives to raise money; and even government subsidies.

No one has yet come up with one magic solution, but more and more online news sites are deciding to charge for some or all of their content—about 100 newspapers as of summer 2011. One survey around that time found 60 percent of newspapers were considering charging for their Web content but that only 51 percent of them thought that would work.

Journalism and PR Jobs in the Future

Although the media are changing, the basic skills of journalism—interviewing, evaluating facts, and organizing and presenting information—remain the same.

Still, change brings with it the increased likelihood that you'll work not only at a variety of media outlets during your life but also in a variety of media careers. We in journalism are in fact just now catching up with others in the general public who for decades have changed *careers*—not just jobs—an average of seven times during their life.

As a journalist you will have to become a lifelong learner, adapting by mastering new knowledge and skills. And you will also face less job security and greater responsibility for your own health benefits and retirement plans.

On the positive side, though, you'll have the chance to influence the important changes facing journalism and experience the excitement and stimulation of this new journalism frontier. And many of you will take advantage of the opportunity to become entrepreneurs, creating your own blogs or other online publications, publishing your own e-books, writing Web applets, and so on.

In this changing climate, students studying journalism or public relations, as well as working journalists and PR professionals hoping to keep their jobs, ask themselves: Will writing and editing skills still be important in an increasingly online world? Or will the informal standards of blogs and other websites written by nonjournalists, of social networking sites like Facebook and Twitter, as well as email, instant messaging and text messaging, make style, grammar, usage and even spelling rules increasingly irrelevant?

We think there will be—indeed already *is*—an inevitable lessening of formality in the writing we read each day. But we also think sites that want to distinguish themselves by their professionalism will seek to establish their credibility by the quality of their writing as well as of their research and reporting. Further, with fewer gatekeepers between you and your audience to check your work, you'll be more and more responsible for editing yourself, which means that, even more than before, in this new world, we're all editors now.

This book teaches the language skills we think are still needed to be successful in this new era of journalism and, we should add, of public relations. Professional PR practitioners have long been trained to write like journalists to increase the chance that their announcements will be picked up as news.

Of course, the Web offers people in PR the exciting chance of reaching an audience directly through their own websites. But for now at least, PR students are best advised to learn and follow journalistic style in their writings, and when it comes to the Web, follow whatever new standards evolve in both fields.

Why Does Grammar Matter?

In this book, we focus on those underappreciated, misunderstood parts of writing and editing grouped together by many instructors under the name "mechanics" and by many in the media as the "micro," or detailed, part of the job—grammar, usage, style, punctuation, spelling, tightening and so on. Of course, these things don't strike most of us as nearly so much fun or so important as the more creative "macro" parts.

In fact, professionals may tell you they were hired for their creative skills rather than for their knowledge of mechanics. But they also appreciate that a strong knowledge of fundamentals is what separates pros from amateurs.

Many writers admit they still have things to learn about grammar, but they have a respect for the subject gained from experience. The novelist, journalist and essayist Joan Didion, for example, said, "All I know about grammar is its power." We don't pretend that mere knowledge of grammar and other mechanics can turn a mediocre writer into a great one, but we're convinced it can help empower any writer to strengthen whatever talent he or she has.

Of course, what you have to say and how freshly you say it are of the utmost importance. But if the word order is unclear, if the wrong word has been used or if the punctuation or spelling is incorrect, readers can become confused or distracted from the important points. Because of this carelessness, readers might even become distrustful of what you're trying to say. And in this faster-paced media world with people skimming Web articles for information, readers will close poorly written, wordy or unclear pages in search of something better.

For this reason, if you want to work as a professional writer or editor, your chances are better if you've mastered the power of such details. And remember, when you apply for media internships or jobs, potential employers almost always test you on mechanics.

We've tried to offer rules in this book not so much as "thou shalt not" commandments limiting your creativity but rather as the codified experience of writers and editors who, through the years, have noticed what works and what doesn't work. Although some of the specifics you learn here may change as the language, dictionaries and stylebooks change, the principles will remain basically the same, and this book can serve you as a guide throughout your career—even through different careers.

What Makes Good Writing Work?

Good writing can be summarized in what we call the *Three R's.*

Good writing is *reader-centered.* More than anything else, a piece of writing must appeal to its readers—give readers what they need or want in a way that is fresh and creative. That means, among other things: Don't just tell—show. Be concrete—give details, facts, figures, quotes, color. And where appropriate, use lively language. (See especially Chapters 14–16.)

Good writing is *readable.* Writing should be clear and concise so that readers can understand it easily and without wasting their time with unneeded material. Clear writing is conversational and uses short, simple, familiar words. Concise writing isn't simply brief. Rather, it's writing that says everything that needs to be said but doesn't use unnecessary words. (See especially Chapters 11–12.)

Good writing is *right.* That means it's correct in big ways and small: correct factually, legally and ethically, and also correct in its mechanics. (See especially Chapters 1–10, 13 and the appendix.)

How to Master Mechanics

In the length of one quarter or semester, no one is going to be able to master *all* the rules in this book. Realistically, what you *can* achieve is an overview of the issues and familiarity with the most important points. Once you have that general understanding, you'll find yourself thinking, "I don't remember the rule, but I remember there is one." Then, if you use this book as a reference and look things up as you run into them in your work, you'll find yourself effortlessly learning many more of the rules.

Here are some tips for those who want to accelerate the process:

1. Get excited.

The key to mastering anything is getting yourself excited about it.

Don't think you can get excited right now about grammar and usage and style? Then get excited about writing and editing. Get excited about the medium in which you plan to work. Get excited about your field: journalism, public relations, advertising or creative writing. But most important, get excited about language.

A big part of getting excited involves reading. For example, want to be a great political writer? Then read all the political writing you can, especially by the best in the field. Listen to all the political analysis you can, especially on 24-hour cable-news channels. And then read biographies of political reporters and commentators you admire to learn how they succeeded.

Reading not only is fun and informational in itself but also is a way of subconsciously absorbing good habits of thought, organizing patterns, language rhythms, vocabulary—and even grammar, usage, punctuation and spelling.

2. Get in the game.

Don't just read about it or take classes in it—do it. Most people find that until they have the experience of actually applying something, they don't really understand it—even if they think they do.

So, start using this material in real life by working for your college newspaper or radio station, applying for internships, freelancing articles, stringing for newspapers, getting a part-time job and so on. We've seen again and again that students find the advice here much more useful once they've had to grapple with mechanics at real media outlets.

And remember, getting in the game now means more than just improving your grammar skills—you'll improve your writing and professional skills and start collecting the clips, experience and contacts you need to land your first internship or job.

3. Practice reading as an editor does.

You're reading along and come across the word *hotline*. If you're reading as a typical reader does, the word could have been spelled *hot-line* or *hot line* and it wouldn't have made a difference. You'd just get the meaning and read on.

But an editor reads differently. She will see a compound word like *hotline* and stop and ask herself: "Is that right? Or should it be hyphenated or two words?" She'll then look it up and fix it. (It should be two words, according to the AP Stylebook.)

A good editor, then, is not necessarily someone who knows all the rules. A good editor is someone who has learned to read while constantly asking, "Do I know with certainty that this is right?"

Reading like an editor is also great practice for improving your own writing. It's easier for most of us to spot problems in others' work before we spot the same problems in our own. But when you start noticing what works and what doesn't in writing by others, your own writing will get better from the experience.

Again, as more journalists turn to blogging and use social media like Facebook and Twitter, skill at self-editing becomes more and more important because there's often no second set of eyes looking over your work.

4. Learn the joys of rewriting.

Writing is a three-stage process of *prewriting*, in which you decide what you want to write about, research it and come up with new ideas; *writing*, in which you sit down and crank it out; and *rewriting*, in which you reshape your work into publishable form.

In the rewriting, or revising, stage, you look more closely at both macro and micro issues. This is the stage at which some people focus on the micro issues for the first time because they find they have fewer problems with writer's block if they just let their writing flow during the writing stage without interruption. They then focus on the mechanics after they have their ideas down.

Too many beginning writers try to shortchange the final step, but no serious writer would turn in a rough draft as the final product.

5. Take fixing problems seriously, but shake off those you miss.

When you're editing, think of yourself like a goalie in hockey or soccer. Your job is to stop the mistakes that have made it this far. Good goalies are ones with a low goals-against average—that is, few goals are scored against them. But even the best goalies can't have a zero goals-against average for long.

No matter how good you are, you're going to miss some shots or let some mistakes slip through. And when that happens, you're likely to feel frustrated and wonder whether you're as good at this as you should be. The trick is in learning to treat each potential "scoring" opportunity against you more seriously as it happens, when there's still something you can do to stop it, rather than beating yourself up afterward if you missed.

When you *do* miss something—and everyone does—it may help to say to yourself, "Good thing I'm not a brain surgeon!" Take the miss as a challenge for next time, not as justification for self-flagellation now. As they say in hockey, "Keep your stick on the ice."

PART ONE

Grammar and Usage

Quick access to the most commonly looked-up items in this part . . .

(continued)

CHAPTER 1

Grammar Basics

> [T]he need to write well is greater than it has been in a long time. We're writing more often than people did twenty years ago because e-mail and text messaging have taken the place of phone calls, and blogging is a popular pastime. We're all "professional" writers these days because our coworkers, friends, and family judge us on our writing, and we all secretly fear that we could do a better job.
>
> — Mignon Fogarty, "Grammar Girl's Quick and Dirty Tips for Better Writing"

One of the biggest complaints we hear from media teachers and employers is that too many students aren't learning the grammar and usage they need to work at media jobs—whether in print, broadcast or online media, as well as in public relations or advertising. Yet, says Mignon Fogarty, host of the Grammar Girl podcast (http://grammar.quickanddirtytips .com), we're all writing more now.

But most often, today's writing is informal—personal communications between friends using email, instant messaging on the computer or text messaging on the cellphone.

Of course, there's nothing wrong with texting someone on your cellphone *CU L8ER* or IMing someone *R U there?* Such abbreviations save time and are fine as long as both you and your friend know them. But students wanting a media career need to master a way of writing for mass audiences that's more demanding and less casual than writing to a single close friend, just as you dress more formally for most jobs than you do for hanging out with friends on the weekend.

For people working in the media, knowledge of grammar is one of the most important skills of the trade. So, let's first understand what grammar is.

Grammar Basics

Using Standard English

Grammar is the study of the form of words and their arrangement in speech or writing. But the way we use words in speech often differs from the accepted standards in writing. As shown in the following figure, there are also different standards—ranging from most formal to least formal—for writing for a newspaper, magazine, book, Web page, or radio or TV station as opposed to writing an email message, an online instant message or a phone text message.

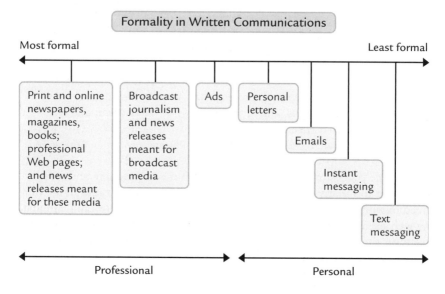

In this book, we mainly focus on the grammar and usage required for more formal media writing. For some situations—such as live broadcast reports, or personal columns or reviews in a newspaper or magazine, or blogs on the Web—a more relaxed standard is appropriate. But it's easier to lower your standards than it is to raise them. By learning the highest standards, you'll be preparing yourself for all occasions.

Don't worry if you haven't studied grammar since middle school or even never. Most students these days haven't been taught much grammar or usage, so you won't be alone. And you've probably successfully mastered subjects far more difficult.

Why Don't We Write How We Talk?

Most students easily understand on their own that writing for mass media is different from text messaging. But they often find it harder to understand why the informal English we use when speaking isn't appropriate for print, broadcast or online writing. Why can't we write how we talk? After all, isn't good writing conversational?

Conversation and written language—even written language meant to be read aloud—differ in many ways. What sounds right in conversation is often ineffective or inappropriate in writing.

According to a study by Albert Mehrabian, now a professor emeritus of psychology at UCLA, we get across up to 93 percent of our meaning in conversation in ways other than the words—tone of voice, pauses, stress, body language and gestures. That meaning can easily be lost when we record merely the words, as we do in writing.

But written language has its own advantages over conversation. One of the most important is that writing lets us reconsider and restate our thoughts and words. We normally speak much more loosely and informally than we would care to have recorded in writing. Although news sources often gripe about being misquoted by journalists, nobody insists that newspapers print all the *uh*s, *er*s, stammers and false starts that a recording would reveal.

If your writing relies on how you talk rather than on what is considered correct in writing, you're using the wrong tool for the job. For example, the words you learned by ear may not be what you thought you heard. Did you really hear that *d* in *supposed to*? Or the people around you may not have used words in the precise way considered correct in writing. They may have lacked the education. They may have spoken a regional dialect that differs from standard English. Or they simply may have spoken informally.

In daily conversation, for example, most people use *their* as a singular pronoun in a situation in which the person could be male or female, or use *lay* instead of *lie* to mean "rest." Either of these errors would probably go unnoticed in daily conversation but would be considered incorrect if written to be read in print or on the air.

Conventional Wisdom

When you get down to it, the basic reason for knowing grammar is to communicate better. The same can be said for knowing a topic we take up later in this book: *usage*, or the meaning and use of particular words. Knowing the precise meanings of words and the proper relationships between them—usage and grammar—makes us better writers and better journalists.

An astute reader may notice, however, that some of the rules seem more like arbitrary conventions than natural, logical guides. But conventions represent agreement, and agreement, too, opens doors to communication.

Actually, a bigger problem is that not everyone subscribes to the same rules of style, spelling and grammar. Among journalists, the most widely accepted standards for style are set by The Associated Press Stylebook and Briefing on Media Law and the most widely accepted spellings in the latest edition of Webster's New World College Dictionary. We have tried to conform as much as possible to these.

> ### ESL Tip
>
> Students for whom English is a second language should note that the better they are at conversational English, the more they, like native speakers, will need to be aware of how informal conversation differs from media writing.

Competing Grammars and Stylebooks

For grammar and usage not covered in the AP Stylebook, there is no single standard to consult next. We have gathered advice from many sources and have included here what we think are the most common, reasonable and useful standards.

A multitude of grammar and usage guides exist, and they take a variety of approaches. Of the two major current approaches to grammar—traditional (*prescriptive*) and *descriptive*—we mainly follow the older, and more traditional, prescriptive approach, while adopting ideas from the other when they are helpful. Traditional grammar says, "This way is the right way." The newer descriptivist grammar, taught in linguistic classes, says, "Anything is right if commonly said by native speakers."

The media prefer the consistency of traditional grammar's set prescriptive rules, and that is what journalists are expected to know when they take job tests. But we can't overlook the fact that a century of scientific and historical research by linguists has disproved a number of the rules that have been passed on by teachers and editors.

For example, we're often told not to use the word *hopefully* as a *sentence adverb* (a word that modifies an entire sentence)—as in *Hopefully, the snow will miss our area*—because it doesn't say who's doing the hoping. But there aren't comparable rules against other sentence adverbs, such as *frankly* or *strictly speaking*, which likewise don't say who's being frank or speaking strictly.

Our advice for *hopefully* has been not to use it except in the accepted sense of "in a hopeful manner"—*She says she looks to the future hopefully*—not because it's illogical to use it as a sentence adverb but because the usage is so universally condemned by convention. But AP has recently decided to accept *hopefully* in either sense.

But why do the media often cling to traditional grammar and its sometimes outdated rules? Inconsistencies in the style of a newspaper, online news site, magazine or book draw attention to themselves when readers should instead be concentrating on the content. Deviations from standard grammar or usage in the media industry may cause the audience to become confused, maybe even to misinterpret what was said. And when the audience discovers inconsistencies or misused words, credibility is undermined as seriously as if a factual error had been made. In fact, when language is misused, factual errors often get created.

Besides, consistency saves time and money. Without consistency, a writer might add a comma only to see it taken out by an editor and then put back by a proofreader. If we agree on conventions, we can avoid wasting each other's time—and time, as the saying goes, is money.

But the prescriptive rules, like the one for *hopefully*, have to be amended occasionally to reflect not only changes in the language but also research that proves traditional advice may have been inaccurate. The work of linguists is essential for making such calls on the best evidence available. So, we have, at times, noted in this book old rules we think need to be updated.

Grammar and Confidence

Even professional writers often lack confidence in their grammar skills. Many people discover that studying practical grammar not only directly improves their ability to express themselves but also gives them greater confidence in their work, freeing them to concentrate on what's more important—the content and vision of their writing.

Communicating Well

Grammar is most useful, though, when it's not just helping you conform to conventions or feel confident that you know what you're doing—as important as those things are—but rather when it helps you get your message across better. Some sentences can be so ungrammatical and confusing, it's impossible to understand what the writer is trying to say.

Other times, the mistakes are unintentionally funny or totally misleading.

> CONFUSING   As one of the worst examples of a convicted sexual harasser in many years, she said she was shocked at his behavior.

Who is the sexual harasser: the man, or the woman who was shocked at his behavior? Here, we have not only confusion but also a possible lawsuit. If the writer had learned the rule to place modifiers next to what they describe, he or she could have avoided that problem.

> RIGHT   She said she was shocked at the behavior of the man, whom she called one of the worst examples of a convicted sexual harasser in many years.

Talking Shop

Grammar terms are part of the "shop talk" of people who work with words. Just as sports have terms for what happens on the court or playing field, so speaking and writing have terms to describe what goes on in an utterance.

Writers and editors often use these grammar terms to communicate with one another about writing.

But grammar terminology is confusing to many people. It's usually something studied too long ago to be remembered clearly. Most people, however, at least vaguely recall learning the eight *parts of speech*:

nouns and *pronouns* (sometimes called *substantives*)

verbs

adjectives, *adverbs* and *interjections* (also called *modifiers*)

prepositions and *conjunctions* (also called *connecting words, connectives* or *connectors*)

You probably also learned at least some of another set of terms called the *parts of a sentence*:

appositives

direct objects

indirect objects

nouns of direct address

predicate complements (*predicate nominatives* and *predicate adjectives*)

predicates

prepositional phrases

sentence adverbs

subjects

subjects of an infinitive

And so on. It's usually said that the parts of speech refer to what words *are*, the parts of a sentence to what words *do*—that is, how they are used in a sentence.

Then there are the *verbals*, which don't fit well in either category: *infinitives*, *gerunds* and *participles*. And, of course, there are the terms for groups of words: *phrases*, *clauses* and *sentences*.

Separating grammatical terms into these categories helps, but don't feel bad if the groupings don't always make sense to you. For example, if you look closely at the definitions in this book, which are fairly standard ones, you'll see that some of the parts of speech are defined by what they *are* but others are defined by what they *do*—just as we define parts of a sentence.

Also, if you look in a dictionary, you'll find that many words can be more than one part of speech, depending on how they're used. For example, in the sentence *The mayor likes jogging*, the word *jogging* is a noun. But in the sentence *The mayor was jogging down the road*, the word *jogging* is a verb. And in the sentence *The jogging man crossed the park and headed north*, the word *jogging* is an adjective.

Confused? When English grammarians began in the 18th century to write books about the language, they based them on Latin and Greek grammar books. "Parts of speech" is really a mistranslation of "parts of a sentence." So, the two categories are not really logically separate. But sometimes, it seems more useful to speak of a word in a sentence as a noun and at other times as a subject or direct object, so you need to know both sets of terms.

Rather than define right now all the parts of speech, parts of a sentence, verbals and kinds of word groupings, we'll introduce the terms as they arise in the following chapters. That way, you will have to take in only as much terminology at a time as necessary. Meanwhile, consult the index at the back of the book if you need to track down a definition.

Key Principles of Grammar

There seem to be so many grammar rules that learning them can be intimidating at first. It gets easier, though, once you realize that the most commonly violated rules boil down to just five basic ideas:

1. Make sure your words agree and go together.
2. Make sure your words are in the right order.
3. Use the right form of the word.
4. Use the right word.
5. Punctuate according to sentence grammar.

Let's look at these one at a time and expand on them. We'll also give you cross-references to more detailed explanations.

1. Make sure your words agree and go together.

A verb must agree with its subject that's doing or acting, and a pronoun must agree with its *antecedent*—the noun to which it refers. Similar items and ideas need to be expressed in similar ways in parallel structure. And certain words belong together—when you use one, you also use the other.

○ **Make subjects and verbs agree.**

A subject should agree with its verb in number. Singular subjects take singular *predicates* (verbs), and plural subjects take plural predicates. That's called *subject-predicate*, or *subject-verb*, *agreement*. (For a detailed explanation, see Chapter 5.)

One of the prisoners *are* missing.
                   is

[*One* is the subject of the sentence. Because it is singular, it should take a singular verb. *Prisoners* is the object of the preposition *of*, so the verb does not agree in number with it. Beware of words coming between the subject and predicate that might confuse you as to the real subject.]

has
None ~~have~~ confessed.

[The indefinite pronoun *none* is singular when it means *no one* or *not one*, as it most often does and as it does here. Thus, in this example, *none* should take a singular verb.]

Make nouns and pronouns agree.

Pronoun-antecedent agreement makes pronouns agree with the nouns they refer to in *number* (singular or plural), *gender* (feminine, masculine or neuter) and *person* (first, second or third). (For a variety of situations where this may not be obvious, see Chapter 5.)

WRONG	A teacher should do *their* best. [Don't use the plural pronoun *their* in place of *his* or *her* when the context means either an individual woman's or an individual man's. *Their* is a good choice from both a grammatical and nonsexist perspective, however, when there does not need to be an emphasis on individuality and the entire sentence can be recast in the plural. (See the section on pronoun-antecedent agreement on Pages 92–93.)]
SEXIST	A teacher should do *his* best. [The problem is, not all teachers are male. So gender-neutral wording is preferred unless the context indicates male or female.]
AWKWARD	A teacher should do *his or her* best.
RIGHT	Teachers should do *their* best.
WRONG	The committee decided *they* would meet again next Monday. [*Committee* is singular—the plural would be *committees*. So a pronoun referring to the singular committee must be singular, also.]
RIGHT	The committee decided *it* would meet again next Monday.

Make sure parallel items in a sentence are worded in similar ways.

If you have more than one of anything in a sentence—subjects, verbs, objects and so on—they all usually need to be said in a similar way. (See Chapter 5.)

writing
He liked *gathering* information and then ~~to write~~ about it.

[gerund and infinitive not balanced]

Make sure words that belong together are both there.

With some words, it's important to have the right companion words accompanying them. Following is an abbreviated list. More of these can be found in the list of misused words and mistaken phrases in Chapter 8.

centers around   Change to *centers on* or *revolves around* because the center is in the middle.

convince that, convince of, persuade to   You're *convinced that* or *convinced of* something, but you're *persuaded to* do something.

different than   Change to *different from*.

forbid to, prohibit from   You *forbid to* or *prohibit from*. Don't mix these verbs and prepositions.

not only . . . but also   *Not only* must always be followed by *but also* later in the sentence.

2. Make sure your words are in the right order.

It can be hard to understand a sentence if the words are out of their proper order. This is especially true of misplaced modifiers. Prepositions at the end of sentences and split infinitives are not really confusing, but they are often frowned on in media writing. (See Chapter 7.)

○ **Put modifiers next to what they modify.**

To avoid confusion, place modifiers as close as possible to what they modify. (See Pages 111–14.)

WRONG   *Standing on her head, he* watched the yoga teacher.
[*Standing on her head* appears to modify *he*, the word that the phrase is next to, so it sounds as if he's standing on her head. This is an example of a *dangling participle* because the participial phrase *standing on her head* dangles at the start of the sentence instead of being next to the word it should modify.]

RIGHT   He watched the yoga *teacher standing on her head*.

WRONG   The mayor *said Friday* she would resign.
[*Said Friday* acts as a *squinting modifier*, confusing us as to whether it says when she made the statement or when she would resign.]

RIGHT   The mayor said that she would *resign Friday*.

RIGHT   The mayor *said Friday that* she would resign.

○ **Move prepositions away from the end of a sentence.**

Most editors prefer that you not end a sentence with a preposition, unless it's impossible to rewrite the sentence to avoid doing this and still be conversational. (See Pages 114–15.)

WRONG   The president's economic policy is one thing he disagrees *with*.

RIGHT   The president's economic policy is one thing *with which* he disagrees.

RIGHT   He disagrees with the president's economic policy.

○ Keep the *to* next to the verb in an infinitive.

Most editors prefer that you not split the *to* from the verb in an infinitive. (See Pages 114–15.)

WRONG	*to boldly go* where no one has gone before
RIGHT	*to go boldly* where no one has gone before [unless you're quoting Captain Kirk]

3. Use the right form of the word.

Five of the eight parts of speech—nouns, pronouns, verbs, adjectives and adverbs—are shape shifters. That is, they change their form depending on how they're used in a sentence and the number of items to which they refer.

○ Use the right noun form.

To use the right form of a noun, you have to determine whether it's singular or plural and then whether it's possessive. (See Pages 44–47.)

WRONG	The *Finnegan's* live in Portland, Ore. [The meaning of the sentence calls for the plural and nonpossessive form of *Finnegan*, but *Finnegan's* is singular and possessive.]
RIGHT	The *Finnegans* live in Portland, Ore.

○ Use the right pronoun form.

Pronouns are like nouns in that to pick the right form, you have to determine whether they're singular or plural (*I* or *we*) and whether they're possessive (*your* or *you*). In addition, you have to determine whether they're used in the sentence as a subject or an object (*he* or *him*). (See Pages 47–51.)

The following list includes words—some are pronouns, some not— and situations that often confuse writers when it comes to choosing the correct pronoun form.

as / like *As* is a conjunction and should be used to introduce a clause, implied or present, with a noun or *nominative-case* (subject) pronoun. *Like* is a preposition and should be used to introduce just a word or phrase with a noun or an *objective-case* (object) pronoun.

RIGHT	He did it the same as *she* [*did it*]. [*As* introduces an implied clause, so the pronoun should be in nominative case as the subject of the implied clause.]
RIGHT	It was just like *him*. [*Like* introduces a single word, with no implied clause, so the pronoun should be in objective case as the object of the preposition *like*.]

as / than   When either of these words is followed by a pronoun at the end of a sentence, the pronoun should be in nominative case because it is the subject of a clause in which the verb may be implied.

> **WRONG**   She's faster than *him*.
>
> **RIGHT**   She's faster than *he* [*is*].

pronouns   When nouns or pronouns appear together as compound subjects or compound objects, use the form of each pronoun that would be used in the sentence if it were the only pronoun. If one of the pronouns refers to you yourself, put it last.

> **WRONG**   Give the report to the committee and *I*.
> [Give the report to *I*? No.]
>
> **RIGHT**   Give the report to the committee and *me*.
> [Give it to *me*? Yes.]

myself   Use only in a sentence in which *I* has been used earlier.

> **WRONG**   You can give it *to myself or Christine*.
> [no *I* earlier in the sentence]
>
> **RIGHT**   You can give it *to Christine or me*.
> [Notice, also, that for politeness, the *me* follows the other person.]
>
> **RIGHT**   *I* hurt *myself*.
> [used to show *I* acted on *myself*]
>
> **RIGHT**   *I, myself,* believe otherwise.
> [used for emphasis after *I*]

pronoun in front of a noun or gerund   Only possessive pronouns can act as adjectives in front of a noun or *gerund*. Gerunds are *ing* forms of a verb used in place of a noun. If a pronoun directly precedes a noun or gerund, the pronoun should be possessive. (See Page 51.)

> **WRONG**   They appreciated *us* staying to help.
>
> **RIGHT**   They appreciated *our* staying to help.

that / which   Use *that* to introduce *restrictive (essential) clauses* that do not require commas. Use *which* to introduce *parenthetical (nonrestrictive or nonessential) clauses* that do require commas. (See Page 52.)

that / who   Use *that* for inanimate objects and animals without names. Use *who* for people and animals with names.

who / whom, whoever / whomever   *Who* and *whoever* are used as subjects of clauses. *Whom* and *whomever* are used as objects. A handy way to make sure you use each pair correctly is to begin reading a sentence after the choice between *who / whom* or *whoever / whomever*, adding either *he* or *him* to complete the thought. If *he* works better, use *who* or *whoever*. If *him* works better, use *whom* or *whomever*. (See Pages 53–54.)

○ **Use the right verb form.**

Verbs change form according to *tense* (time), *mood* (how the speaker feels about the truth of the statement) and *voice* (whether the verb shows the subject as being active or being passively acted upon).

- **Verb tense:** The main problems with verb tense involve using the wrong principal part of irregular verbs (see Pages 64–67), the wrong verb in a changing time sequence (see Pages 70–71) or an incorrect verb tense in an unchanging time sequence (see Pages 67–70). Here are a couple of examples of verbs that pose common problems:

  lead / led   *Lead* is the main present-tense form of the verb *to lead*. It is also a noun that names an element that used to be put in paint and gasoline, or the graphite in a pencil. The past tense of the verb *lead* is *led*.

  supposed to, used to   These verbs need to be in past tense when followed by *to*.

- **Passive voice:** In a passive-voice sentence, the subject is being passively acted on by someone or something—as the word *subject* is earlier in this sentence. Active voice is when the subject acts rather than is acted upon. Technically, passive voice is not a grammatical error, but it becomes a problem when writers use it for no apparent reason. (See Pages 71–76.)

  PASSIVE   The complaints *were read by the manager*, and then action *was taken by him*.

  ACTIVE   *The manager read* the complaints and then *took action*.

- **Verb mood:** The main problem with verb mood is determining when to use the conditional- or the subjunctive-mood forms. Here are a couple of the most common problems. (See Pages 76–81.)

  can / could, may / might, shall / should, will / would   The second word in each of these pairs is the *conditional-mood* form. With something that is not now true but could be true under the right conditions, use the conditional-mood form. This distinction comes up often in stories about government considering ordinances or bills.

  WRONG   The bill *will* make gun owners register their automatic rifles.

  RIGHT   The bill *would* make gun owners register their automatic rifles [*if passed into law*].
  [*Could, might, should* and *would* are also used for past tense.]

  If I were (rich, you, etc.) . . .   This is probably the most common phrase in English requiring the *subjunctive mood*—in this case, *I were* instead of the usual *I was*. The subjunctive mood is used with wishes, doubts, prayers, conditions contrary to fact and with most verbs that are followed by the word *that*. (See Pages 78–81.)

○ Use the right adjective or adverb form.

Adjectives and *adverbs* have three different forms apiece, depending on whether they're describing one thing, comparing two things or comparing more than two things. (See Pages 98–99.)

> WRONG   He was the *oldest of two* brothers.
> [*Oldest* is for comparing three or more.]

> WRONG   He was the *older of three* brothers.
> [*Older* is for comparing two.]

In addition to confusing which of the three forms to use, people also commonly cross categories and use an adjective form when an adverb is needed. Remember, adjectives modify nouns or pronouns, and adverbs modify verbs, adjectives or other adverbs. (See Pages 99–100.)

> WRONG   The vote *was taken quick* despite the shouts of dissenters.
> [*Quick* is an adjective, but an adverb is needed instead to modify the verb *was taken* and tell us the manner in which the action happened.]

> RIGHT   The vote *was taken quickly* despite the shouts of dissenters.

Also, some people have trouble deciding when to use the *articles* (a kind of adjective) *a* and *an*. Use *a* before a word that begins with a consonant sound and *an* before a word that begins with a vowel sound. If the word after *a* or *an* is an abbreviation, remember that the choice is determined by the initial *sound* of the following word, not by the letter itself:

> *an* [not *a*] *FBI inquiry* [because the initial sound is "eff"]

Many people also get confused by an *h* at the beginning of a word:

> *a* [not *an*] *historical event* [because the initial sound is "hih"]

4. Use the right word.

We hear some words so often we think we know what they mean when we really don't. Then, when we write, we find ourselves using the wrong word for what we intend to say. Chapter 8 covers many such words, but here are some of the most common.

○ Know the meaning of words often confused.

adopt / pass   You *adopt* a resolution, but you *pass* an ordinance.
affect / effect   *Affect* is a verb meaning "to influence." *Effect* is a noun meaning "result" and a verb meaning "to cause."
among / between   Use *between* for two items, *among* for three or more.
burglary / robbery   For a crime to be a *robbery*, violence or the threat of violence must be involved. Someone who *burglarized* a house while its occupants were away did not *rob* the house. Instead, the crime should be called a *burglary* or *theft*.

Grammar Basics

compose / comprise / constitute   The whole *is composed of* the parts or *comprises* the parts. But the parts *constitute* the whole. Never use *comprise* with *of*—that should be *composed of*. Also don't use *comprise* to mean "make up"—that should be *constitute*.

farther / further   *Farther* is used for literal distance, such as *farther down a road*. *Further* is used for figurative distance, such as *further into a subject*.

fewer / less   Use *less* to modify singular words, *fewer* to modify plural words. Remember that a word that is plural in form is sometimes singular in concept, as when *dollars* or *pounds* refers to a set amount as opposed to individual units. Use *fewer* with items that would take *many* and *less* with items that would take *much*: He weighs *less than 200 pounds* because *200 pounds* is how *much* he weighs, not how *many*.

hanged / hung   A condemned man was *hanged* by a rope. A picture was *hung* on the wall.

homicide / murder   A *homicide* is not a *murder* until someone is convicted of the charge of murder—after all, it may prove to be a case of *manslaughter* or even a killing in self-defense.

if / whether   *If* is used for conditions, as in *If a, then b*. *Whether* is used to introduce a choice, as in *I don't know whether to go*. (Notice that the *or not* that some people add is redundant.) Because many people misuse *if* when they mean *whether* but never the other way around, a handy test is to say the sentence with *whether*. If *whether* will work, it's the right word. If not, use *if*.

imply / infer   A speaker or writer *implies*. A listener or reader *infers*.

its / it's   *Its* is the possessive pronoun. *It's* is the contraction for *it is* (or *it has* when *has* is a helping verb, as in *it's been a cold summer*).

lay / lie   *Lay* is a transitive verb (takes a direct object) meaning "to set something down." *Lie* is an intransitive verb (does not take a direct object) meaning "to rest."

presently   This word's standard meaning is "soon," not "now." Change to *at present, currently* or *now*, or simply use the present tense of the verb.

raise / rise   *Raise* is a transitive verb meaning "to lift" something. *Rise* is an intransitive verb meaning "to get up."

set / sit   *Set* is a transitive verb meaning "to put something." *Sit* is an intransitive verb meaning "to take a seat."

their / there / they're   *Their* means something belongs to them. *There* points to something, as in *It's over there*. *They're* is the contraction for *they are*.

to / too / two   *To* is a preposition, as in *She went to the store*, or part of the infinitive, as in *He likes to sleep*. *Too* means "also" or as a modifier can mean "excessive," as in "too much." *Two* is the number.

while   For clarity, use only to mean "simultaneously." If contrast is meant, change to *although* at the beginning of a clause. *Though* is used for contrast in the middle of a clause.

◯ Know which nouns *not* to use as verbs.

Some verbs work fine as nouns, but many don't, and certain nouns should only be used as nouns and not as verbs. (See Pages 81–82.) Here are a few of the most common nouns to avoid using as verbs:

author   Use only as a noun, not as a verb. Change to *write*.

contact   An "Ask the Editor" at www.apstylebook.com now accepts *contact* as a verb. But we suggest it's best to avoid such a usage because it's clearer to change the word to *call, write, email* or *visit*, depending on whether a street address, email address or phone number follows.

dialogue   Use only as a noun, not as a verb.

debut   Use only as a noun, not as a verb. Don't write that a movie *will debut* but that it *will have its debut.*

host   Use only as a noun, not as a verb. Don't write that someone *will host* a party but that someone *will hold* a party or *be host at* a party.

premiere   Use only as a noun, not as a verb. Don't write that a play *will premiere* but that it *will have its premiere.*

5. Punctuate according to sentence grammar.

Punctuation rules are generally considered style matters, and we've listed them in Chapter 9, in the part of the book dealing with mechanics. But punctuation can be most easily learned and consistently applied if you keep in mind that it's determined by grammar. For example, the placement of commas is determined by grammar and not just voice pauses.

◯ A fragment is not a sentence.

A period, a question mark or an exclamation point at the end of a group of words suggests to the reader that's the end of a sentence. But to be a sentence, a group of words has to have a subject and predicate and express a complete thought. If it doesn't, it's a *fragment*, and to fix the problem, you need to add other words to complete the thought. (See Page 35.)

WRONG   When the ice they were fishing from broke.
[This is a fragment because it isn't a complete thought. What happened when the ice broke?]

RIGHT   Thirty people on Lake Erie were rescued Thursday when the ice they were fishing from broke.

◯ Use a comma and a coordinating conjunction between two or more complete thoughts.

When writers want to join two or more complete sentences, they should put a comma and a *coordinating conjunction* like *and* or *but* between them.

Grammar Basics

WRONG   The police funding was increased 5 percent for the year the Fire Department funding was increased 3 percent.
[This is a *fused-sentence* error.]

WRONG   The police funding was increased 5 percent for the year, the Fire Department funding was increased 3 percent.
[This is a *comma-splice* sentence error.]

RIGHT   The police funding was increased 5 percent for the year, and the Fire Department funding was increased 3 percent.

⬤ **Put a comma after an introductory word, phrase or clause.**

Put a comma after an introductory word, phrase or clause at the beginning of a sentence. If two or more prepositional phrases come in a row at the beginning of a sentence, put a comma only after the final one.

WRONG   Because it was raining she took her umbrella.

RIGHT   Because it was raining, she took her umbrella.

WRONG   In the summer, of 2011, he went to Europe to bum around by foot.

RIGHT   In the summer of 2011, he went to Europe to bum around by foot.

⬤ **Put a comma before a coordinating conjunction introducing a clause that could stand alone.**

Put a comma before a conjunction such as *and* or *but* only if the conjunction and what follows could stand alone as a complete sentence.

WRONG   First, he'd make the phone calls, and then would write the story.
[There's no subject after the *and,* so *and then would write the story* could not be a complete sentence.]

RIGHT   First, he'd make the phone calls and then would write the story.

RIGHT   First, he'd make the phone calls, and then he would write the story.

But if what follows the *and* is part of two or more things someone is being paraphrased as having said, leave out the comma so that it's clear the person said both things.

RIGHT   He said that first he'd make the phone calls and then he would write the story.

⬤ **Put a comma before *and* in a series only if the *and* could be confusingly read as linking the last two items as one rather than leaving them separate.**

WRONG	corn, squash, and beans
RIGHT	corn, squash and beans
RIGHT	corn, pork, and beans

        [Without the comma, the series could possibly mean pork and beans as one selection, although that would be more likely if there were also an *and* before *pork*.]

Change the commas in a series to semicolons if even one of the items in the series has a comma in it already.

WRONG	Plymouth, Mich., Paris, Tenn., and Chicago
RIGHT	Plymouth, Mich.; Paris, Tenn.; and Chicago

○ Use commas to separate parenthetical items.

Words, phrases or clauses that modify something they follow are set off by commas if they are a parenthetical afterthought. But if they restrict (are essential to) the meaning of the sentence, they are not set off by commas. Note that if the parenthetical element comes in the middle of the sentence, there should be commas on each side of it. If it comes at the end of the sentence, however, there should just be a comma in front of it. (See Pages 31–32.)

WRONG	The director of "Chloe in the Afternoon" Eric Rohmer also made the film "Claire's Knee."

        [*Eric Rohmer* should be set off by commas as a parenthetical afterthought because the sentence means the same without this detail.]

RIGHT	The director of "Chloe in the Afternoon," Eric Rohmer, also made the film "Claire's Knee."

○ Use dashes to set off parenthetical items containing a comma.

When a parenthetical element has at least one comma inside it, set off the parenthetical element with dashes instead of commas.

WRONG	One of the students, Heather Terry, a sophomore, won an award for feature writing.
RIGHT	One of the students—Heather Terry, a sophomore—won an award for feature writing.

○ Use apostrophes for contractions and possessives, not merely plurals.

Apostrophes should never be used to make possessive forms of any pronouns, except for pronouns that end with *one* or *body*.

WRONG	Who's book is this?

        [*Who's* is a contraction for *who is* (or *who has* when *has* is a helping verb as in *Who's been attending the meetings?*).]

Grammar Basics

RIGHT	Whose book is this?
WRONG	Terrorism is everyones concern.
RIGHT	Terrorism is everyone's concern.

Apostrophes should not be used to make nonpossessive plural forms of nouns. (See Pages 45–47.)

WRONG	The Fillmores' founded Unity in the late 19th century.
RIGHT	The Fillmores founded Unity in the late 19th century.

◯ **Know when to use a comma, a hyphen or nothing between multiple modifiers.**

If two modifiers in a row can be reversed and the word *and* put between them, then normally you should use a comma to separate them—but there are exceptions. (See Pages 100–101.)

WRONG	tall tan speaker
RIGHT	tall, tan speaker
	[Use a comma because you could say *tall and tan speaker*.]

If two modifiers in a row fail the previous test for a comma, see whether the first modifies the second. If so, put a hyphen between them. Again, there are exceptions. (See Pages 101–3.)

WRONG	well respected speaker
RIGHT	well-respected speaker

If two modifiers in a row fail both of the previous tests (or qualify as exceptions), put no punctuation between them.

WRONG	red, brick building
WRONG	red-brick building
RIGHT	red brick building

◯ **Capitalize after a colon only if what follows is a sentence.**

Capitalize the first word after a colon if what follows is a complete sentence. Otherwise, the word after a colon is lowercased. (See Pages 191–93.)

◯ **Know how to punctuate quotations.**

At the end of a quotation, periods and commas always go inside quotation marks; colons and semicolons always go outside; and question marks and exclamation points go inside if they're part of the quotation, outside if they're not. In front of a quotation, after a verb such as *said* attributing the quotation, use a colon to introduce a quotation of more than one sentence, a comma for a quotation of one sentence and no punctuation for a partial quotation (less than a sentence) or a paraphrase. (See Pages 183–91.)

○ Use semicolons between items in a series only when at least one of the items has a comma inside it.

The main use of semicolons in journalism is to connect items in a series that may not be complete sentences but have commas inside the items. In such a case, the word *and* at the end of the series should be preceded by a semicolon. (See Page 25.) Journalists normally avoid using a semicolon in place of a comma and a conjunction to connect clauses that could stand alone as complete sentences.

Web Resources

GRAMMAR HELP

Many websites provide answers to questions about grammar. Here are some of the better ones.

○ Good Grammar, Good Style Pages
   www.protrainco.com/info/grammar.htm

○ Grammar Girl
   http://grammar.quickanddirtytips.com

○ Grammar Now
   www.grammarnow.com

○ Guide to Grammar and Writing
   http://grammar.ccc.commnet.edu/grammar/

○ The Linguist List
   www.linguistlist.org

CHAPTER 2

Phrases, Clauses and Sentences

A good sentence has a kind of rightness to it—a clear, exact way of saying something. And when a sentence works well, it has a certain lightness to it—a conciseness and charm that let it soar. As philosopher Eric Hoffer writes, "There are few things so subtle and beautiful as a good sentence."

We'll start our look at grammar with the big picture before focusing on the finer details. This chapter examines the groups of words that make up a sentence—phrases and clauses—and how they determine whether a sentence works well.

Let's begin with a few definitions and examples. Then, we'll look more thoroughly at what's useful to know about each of these terms.

○ *Phrases* are groups of related words that lack either a *subject* (a doer) or a *verb* (an action or a state of being) or both:

> to the restaurant
>
> walking along the beach
>
> as long as his arm

Phrases serve many roles in a sentence, replacing parts of sentences such as subjects and objects.

○ *Clauses* are groups of related words that have both a subject and a verb:

> He wants it all.
> [*independent clause*—forms a complete thought independently]
>
> because he wants it all [*dependent clause*—not a complete thought but depends on something else for it to make a statement]

○ *Sentences*, like clauses, are groups of related words with a subject and verb, but, in addition, sentences *must* make a complete statement. Sentences have at least one independent clause and may have any number of dependent clauses:

He loves to watch television to relax. [one independent clause]

She spends most of her time studying, but she sometimes regrets doing that. [two independent clauses joined by a comma plus *but*]

Jimmy Kimmel's show proved popular *even though it was scheduled late at night*. [one independent and one dependent clause (italicized here)]

Phrases

Single words can be *subjects* (people or things doing or being), *objects* (people or things on the receiving end of actions), *verbs* (actions or states of being), *modifiers* (descriptions) or *connecting words* (sentence glue). So can phrases. Using phrases in different ways can be especially effective in bringing variety to your sentences.

After each of the following examples, grammatical terms explain the italicized phrases. If you're unfamiliar with some of the vocabulary, don't worry. You can look up the terms in the index if you like, but feel free to skip them for now if you prefer. By the time you finish this book, they'll be familiar to you, and when you look back on this later as a reference, the descriptions will prove additionally helpful.

Phrases as Subjects, Objects and Predicate Nominatives

Playing the mandolin is like *plucking a violin*.
[two *gerund phrases*, the first used as the subject of the sentence, the second as the object of the preposition *like*]

To try is *to succeed*.
[two *infinitive phrases*, the first the subject of the sentence, the second the *predicate nominative*]

Over there is where police found the body.
[*prepositional phrase* used as the subject of the sentence]

Phrases as Verbs

Wagner *had been going* to college for three years at the time.
[main verb *going* with two helping verbs]

You *shouldn't drink* the water.
[main verb *drink* with helping verb *should* and adverb *not*]

Phrases as Modifiers

Looking through the book, Chou decided to buy it.
[*participial phrase* used as an adjective modifying *Chou*]

Benitez had been visiting *with his sister* when the accident occurred.
[prepositional phrase used as an adverb modifying the verb *had been visiting*]

Phrases as Connecting Words

In spite of that, the commission turned down the request.
[*In spite of* is a phrase taking the place of a single preposition such as *despite*.]

The programs are *similar to* each other.
[phrase taking the place of a single preposition such as *like*]

Clauses

Clauses come in two principal kinds—independent and dependent—although the second can be further divided into two types. When we look at sentences, we'll see how these kinds of clauses are a useful way to vary your writing.

Independent Clauses

○ An *independent* (or *main*) *clause* is one that can stand alone as a complete sentence.

You could think of an independent clause as a sentence within a sentence because other clauses are often attached to it to make a longer sentence. In a sentence with more than one independent clause, one of the clauses may start with a *coordinating conjunction* or a *conjunctive adverb*:

The City Council approved a budget for next year.

The City Council approved a budget for next year, *but* it stuck to its promise of keeping increases to 4 percent.
[The second clause starts with the coordinating conjunction *but*.]

The City Council approved a budget for next year; *however*, it stuck to its promise of keeping increases to 4 percent.
[The second clause starts with the conjunctive adverb *however*, although both the semicolon and the word *however* are rare occurrences in journalism.]

Dependent Clauses

○ A *dependent clause* is one that cannot stand alone as a complete sentence—it works as a noun, an adjective or an adverb rather than as a complete statement—and must be joined to an independent clause.

The two kinds of dependent clauses are *subordinate clauses* and *relative clauses*.

○ *Subordinate clauses* begin with a *subordinating conjunction*:

The County Commission rejected the idea *because no one really pushed for it.* [subordinate clause acting as an adverb modifying *rejected*]

(For more on subordinating conjunctions, see Pages 109–10.)

○ *Relative clauses* begin with a *relative pronoun*:

> *Whoever made that rule* no longer works there.
> [relative clause acting in place of a noun as the subject]

> He never did figure out *who had been at the door.*
> [relative clause acting in place of a noun as the direct object]

> The person *who had been there* was long gone.
> [relative clause acting as an adjective modifying *person*]

(For more on relative clauses, see Pages 51–54.)

Restrictive Versus Nonrestrictive

Phrases and clauses (and even single words) can be classified as either *restrictive* or *nonrestrictive* (also called *essential* or *nonessential*). Knowing the difference helps you punctuate properly. Understanding about restrictiveness versus nonrestrictiveness can also help you know whether to use the word *that* or *which* in a sentence. (See Page 52.)

A *restrictive* word, phrase or clause is essential to a sentence's meaning and is not set off by commas. A *nonrestrictive* word, phrase or clause is not essential to a sentence's meaning and is set off by commas, dashes or parentheses. Nonrestrictive items are always parenthetical.

○ **To distinguish a restrictive from a nonrestrictive element, ask yourself whether the element could be set off by parentheses. If it could, it's nonrestrictive, so set it off with commas because journalism style tries to avoid parentheses.**

Here are some examples of words, phrases and clauses that are *nonrestrictive* (*nonessential* or *parenthetical*) and therefore should be set off by commas or dashes:

> "Yes, *Mena*, I'm over here."
> [*Mena* is a noun of direct address and is nonessential—the sentence carries the same meaning without it.]

> Kansas City's Dwight Frizzell, *an eclectic avant-garde composer*, released an album titled "Bullfrog Devildog President."
> [The phrase *an eclectic avant-garde composer* is acting as an *appositive* and is nonessential.]

> That actor—*who had never played professionally before*—won the part.
> [The relative clause *who had never played professionally before* works as an adjective modifying *actor* and is nonessential.]

Punctuating restrictive and nonrestrictive elements correctly clarifies what a sentence means. Look at this sentence, for example: *Their daughter Dawn arrived with her husband, Kirk.* The absence of commas around *Dawn* indicates that they have more than one daughter, so the name is

---

Journalism Tip

Punctuating Nonrestrictive Phrases and Clauses

Journalists usually avoid parentheses and set off nonrestrictive elements with commas. They use dashes instead of commas, though, when the parenthetical element has commas inside it or if they want a longer pause:

WRONG	Kei Kamara (*the Sierra Leone forward*) ran up the left side to receive the pass.
RIGHT	Kei Kamara, *the Sierra Leone forward*, ran up the left side to receive the pass.
WRONG	The whole package (*two tickets, two soft drinks and two hot dogs*) cost $60.
WRONG	The whole package, *two tickets, two soft drinks and two hot dogs*, cost $60.
RIGHT	The whole package — *two tickets, two soft drinks and two hot dogs* — cost $60.

---

essential to the meaning of the sentence. *Kirk,* however, is set off by a comma, which indicates that Dawn has only one husband, so his name is not essential to the meaning of the sentence.

Compare these nonrestrictive and restrictive versions of similar sentences:

> When he was a child, he said, other boys made fun of him. [The commas around *he said* indicate that those words are not essential and that a statement was made later in life about incidents that happened during childhood.]

> When he was a child, he said other boys made fun of him. [Here, a comma sets off only the introductory clause. The absence of a comma after *he said* indicates that those two words are essential to the independent clause. In other words, he made the statement when he was a child rather than later in life.]

ONLINE GRAMMAR HELP
bedfordstmartins.com/newscentral

For practice using commas in nonrestrictive elements, log on to *Exercise Central for AP Style* (see inside front cover for instructions on how to use the website) and go to **No. 4. Missing comma(s) with a nonrestrictive element**.

Sentences

On the simplest level, a sentence consists of a subject and a verb — that is, someone or something doing or being: "Existence exists," says novelist Ayn Rand in a grammatically simple but philosophically complex sentence. In some sentences, the subject is understood, as in a command: *Run!* Sometimes, the sentence contains a direct object and sometimes an indirect object: *Congress sent the president the bill* (indirect object: *Congress*; direct object: *bill*). Sometimes, the sentence contains a predicate complement: *"This looks like the big one," the general said* (predicate complement: *the big one*). Sentences also may contain modifiers and additional phrases and clauses.

Mastering the following forms of sentences gives your writing variety.

○ A *simple sentence* has one independent clause:

> The team is in a slump.

Note that a sentence may have more than one subject and verb and still be a simple sentence because it has just one independent clause:

> The team and the coach are hoping and praying.
> [This sentence has a compound subject (*The team and the coach*) and compound predicate (*are hoping and praying*) but only one clause.]

○ A *compound sentence* has two or more independent clauses, each expressing a complete thought.

Compound sentences are used to show that thoughts are related and equal. They can be constructed in three ways:

- Independent clauses may be connected by a comma and a *coordinating conjunction* (*and, but, for, nor, or, so, yet*):

> The team is in a slump, *but* the coach is unconcerned.

- Independent clauses may be connected by a semicolon:

> The team is in a slump; the coach is unconcerned.
> [Grammatically correct, but journalists would avoid this.]

- Independent clauses may be connected by a *conjunctive adverb* with a semicolon in front of it and usually a comma following it:

> The team is in a slump; *however*, the coach is unconcerned.
> [This, also, is usually avoided in journalism.]

Conjunctive Adverbs

accordingly	besides	nevertheless	then
also	consequently	otherwise	therefore
anyhow	moreover	still	thus

○ A *complex sentence* contains one independent clause and one or more dependent clauses:

> The team was in a slump already [independent clause] when its best pitcher broke his arm [dependent clause].

Dependent clauses are subordinated to the independent clause by *subordinating conjunctions* or *relative pronouns*. If you see a subordinating conjunction or relative pronoun, what follows is probably a dependent clause.

Subordinating Conjunctions

although	as though	if	till	when
as	because	since	unless	where
as if	before	that	until	whether

Journalism Tip

Using Different Types of Sentences

Media writers should remember the following points about sentences:

○ *Simple sentences* are the easiest to understand and make a great way to stress a point clearly. But too many of them in a row sound choppy and distracting.

○ *Compound sentences*, *complex sentences* and *compound-complex sentences* should be used only when the writer wants to stress that two ideas or more are closely related. Otherwise, the writing can become illogical or confusing:

WEAK   The Ann Arbor Art Fairs attract about 700,000 visitors, and Ypsilanti used to attract visitors with its annual Frog Island Jazz Festival. [What is the connection between these events? This compound sentence implies there is one but doesn't actually state it.]

BETTER   The Ann Arbor Art Fairs attract about 700,000 visitors annually. Next door, the town of Ypsilanti used to attract visitors with its annual Frog Island Jazz Festival.

WEAK   Palmer, who also has a master's degree in philosophy, is socially adept when it comes to interacting with her patients.
[What is the logical connection between her master's degree and her social skills? The sentence implies one, intentionally or not.]

BETTER   Palmer is socially adept when it comes to interacting with patients. But there's a more solitary, intellectual side of her, as well, as evidenced by her master's degree in philosophy.

○ With *complex sentences*, it's usually clearer not to separate the subject and verb of an independent clause with a dependent clause:

WEAK   The president, although the Cabinet advised against doing so, vetoed the measure.

BETTER   The president vetoed the measure, although the Cabinet advised against doing so.

○ *Compound-complex sentences* usually are too long to make good leads for articles, so if you've led with one, consider breaking it down.

Relative Pronouns

that	what	which	who	whoever
		whichever	whom	whomever
			whose	whosoever

Phrases, Clauses and Sentences

○ A *compound-complex sentence* contains two or more independent clauses and one or more dependent clauses:

> The cat was on the mat [independent clause], and the dog was eyeing him [independent clause] when Mandeville came home [dependent clause].

Sentence Errors

Common problems with sentences include fragments, fused sentences, comma-splice sentences and run-on sentences. (Some books and instructors identify fused sentences as run-ons or group fragments, or they classify fused sentences and comma-splice sentences together under the term *run-ons*.)

Fragments

○ A *fragment* is a word or group of words that isn't a complete sentence. Either it lacks a subject or verb, or it's a dependent clause:

> A team for all seasons.

> Takes the guesswork out of the game.

> Because he was sick.

The use of fragments is becoming acceptable to more editors these days, but you shouldn't use fragments unless you have a specific reason. For example, fiction writers use them to capture the way people speak. Ad writers use them to stress a product name: *Joe's Shoes. For people who love their feet.*

Also, some editors consider an answer to a question a sentence even though it may be incomplete by itself. They consider the other elements implied: *Why didn't he come? Because he was sick.* Some are also willing to accept a brief transition or a short question as a sentence:

> And now the news.

> Why?

> What more could I do? Sing? Dance?

> **ONLINE GRAMMAR HELP**
> bedfordstmartins.com/newscentral
>
> For practice avoiding fragments, log on to *Exercise Central for AP Style* and go to **No. 3. Sentence fragments**.

Fused Sentences

A *fused sentence* unacceptably combines two or more independent clauses without putting punctuation between them.

WRONG   The mayor left town the auditor did, too.

RIGHT   The mayor left town, and the auditor did, too.

RIGHT   The mayor left town. The auditor did, too.

RIGHT   The mayor left town; the auditor did, too.
[Journalists usually avoid this approach and either use a comma and conjunction to make a compound sentence or break it into two simple sentences.]

Comma-Splice Sentences

A *comma-splice sentence* unacceptably connects two or more independent clauses with only a comma:

WRONG   The officers were fired, the police chief was, too.

RIGHT   The officers were fired, and the police chief was, too.

RIGHT   The officers were fired. The police chief was, too.

RIGHT   The officers were fired—the police chief was, too.

RIGHT   The officers were fired; the police chief was, too.
[Again, journalists would usually choose one of the previous correct versions rather than use a semicolon.]

Journalists should avoid comma-splice sentences, but some fiction writers use comma splices occasionally to imitate a rapid speaker. Also, many grammarians now say that a series of three or more short sentences may be connected with commas, if you like, as in Caesar's famous "I came, I saw, I conquered." These could also be written with semicolons or, as we'd suggest, periods.

ONLINE GRAMMAR HELP
bedfordstmartins.com/newscentral

For practice correcting comma-splice sentences, log on to *Exercise Central for AP Style* and go to **No. 2. Comma splice**.

Run-on Sentences

A *run-on sentence* may or may not be grammatical, but it usually doesn't work well because unrelated items, unimportant details or extra clauses are added as though the writer didn't know when to stop.

The novelist Ernest Hemingway, however, sometimes used this device to cover ground quickly and let the gaps imply details he didn't want to spell out. The following run-on sentence, although not from Hemingway, is either acceptable or not, depending on how effective you judge it to be:

The blind man's Seeing Eye dog died, and it was a sad occasion, and all the man's friends went to the funeral then went to the bar and drank to his health and said how unfair it was.

Such a sentence might work in fiction, but few magazine or newspaper editors are likely to approve it. The novels of William Faulkner notwithstanding, the best sentences rarely are longer than 2½ typed lines. Sentences containing much technical information shouldn't average more than about 20 words.

CHAPTER 3

Subjects and Objects

Subjects and objects are sometimes called *substantives* and are the only words in a sentence that can name something that has substance—people, places and things. They also name ideas or qualities. The *subject* is the part of a clause or sentence that's doing something or being something, and *objects* are, among other things, receivers of the actions.

Before we look at the various kinds of subjects and objects, let's review what words can be subjects or objects.

- A *noun* names a person, place or thing, or an idea or quality. It can be a subject or an object:

    Marcela, Michigan, book, freedom, intelligence

Sometimes other words, such as pronouns, gerunds and infinitives, act as nouns.

- A *pronoun* is a word that takes the place of a noun. It can be a subject or an object:

    I, you, him, our, its, theirs, one, someone, everybody

- A gerund or an infinitive can also take the place of a noun and be a subject or an object. A *gerund* is a form of the verb, usually ending in *ing*, *ed*, *t* or *en*, that is used as a noun. An *infinitive* is a form of the verb starting with *to*:

    His cousin was a state champion in *swimming*. [gerund as the object of a preposition (*in*)]

    The whole family enjoys *traveling the country*. [gerund phrase acting as a direct object of a verb (*enjoys*)]

    Mekie loves *to edit*. [infinitive acting as a direct object of a verb (*loves*)]

- Often, an entire phrase or clause acts as a single noun and thus can be a subject or an object:

    Johnston said *police have obtained a search warrant to search the suspect's home*. [clause acting as the direct object of a verb (*said*)]

Running a marathon takes stamina.
[phrase acting as the subject of a sentence]

To tell whether such a phrase is acting as a noun, try substituting a pronoun for it. If the pronoun makes sense, the phrase is acting as a noun:

Johnston said *it*.

It takes stamina.

Kinds of Subjects

Subjects and objects are divided into a variety of kinds.

○ A *subject* is the noun or pronoun that is doing the acting or being in a sentence. To find the subject, ask "Who?" or "What?" before the verb:

The Nebraska *Cornhuskers* won the game.
[Who won the game? The Nebraska *Cornhuskers*.]

The *fee* for graduate students is more this year.
[What is more this year? The *fee*.]

Sometimes, the subject is also called the *simple subject* to distinguish it from the *complete subject,* which is the subject and its modifiers. In the preceding examples, *The Nebraska Cornhuskers* is the complete subject of the first sentence and *The fee for graduate students* is the complete subject of the second.

○ A *predicate nominative* is a noun or its substitute that follows a linking verb (see Page 59) and restates the subject. Although the predicate nominative is not actually the subject, it helps to think of it as the subject because if it is a pronoun, it should take the same form it would as a subject:

The change in party control of the Senate became *a problem for the president's agenda.* [linking verb: *became*]

That is *she.* [linking verb: *is*]

○ A *subject of an infinitive* is a noun (or its substitute) that comes between the verb and the infinitive. Oddly, if the subject of an infinitive is a pronoun, it takes the same form it would if it were an object of some kind:

The police took *her* to be a modern Dillinger.
[verb: *took*; infinitive: *to be*]

He encouraged *his children* to play sports.
[verb: *encouraged*; infinitive: *to play*]

Subjects and Objects

Kinds of Objects

○ A *direct object* is the direct receiver of the action in a sentence. To find the direct object, ask "Whom?" or "What?" after the verb:

> The board thanked *him* for his 20 years of service.
> [Thanked whom? *Him*.]

> The company installed additional *servers* to handle the increased demands.
> [Installed what? *Servers*. The word *additional* is an adjective describing *servers*.]

○ A *predicate objective* (or *objective complement*) sometimes follows a direct object and restates it:

> The American public elected him *president*. [direct object: *him*]

> The proud parents named their new son *Taylor*. [direct object: *son*]

○ An *indirect object* is the person or thing to whom or to which, or for whom or for which, an action is done. To tell the difference between an indirect object and a direct object in front of a predicate objective, remember that you can put *to* or *for* in front of an indirect object:

> He gave the *Detroit Free Press* an exclusive.
> [He gave an exclusive to whom? The *Detroit Free Press*.]

> She gave *them* the report this morning.
> [She gave the report to whom? *Them*.]

○ An *object of a preposition* is a noun or its substitute following a preposition:

> In the *movie*, apes rule the planet. [preposition: *in*]

> The skid marks began near this *driveway*. [preposition: *near*]

If the object of the preposition is also acting as the indirect object of the sentence, by convention its role as indirect object takes precedence in labeling it. This is because usually a prepositional phrase acts as an adjective or adverb, not as a noun or pronoun, except when the object of the preposition is the indirect object:

> Rogelio recalled for his *parents* the events of that day.
> [*Parents* is the object of the preposition *for* but should more precisely be called the indirect object of the sentence.]

> The editor gave the assignment to *her*.
> [*Her* is the object of the preposition *to* but should be called the indirect object of the sentence because the sentence could be rewritten as *The editor gave her the assignment*.]

Subjects and Objects

○ An *object of a participle* is a noun or its substitute following a participle:

> The company will take an expected $200 million loss, including a probable *decline* in investments. [participle: *including*]

> A blond-haired man was spotted carrying a *gun*. [participle: *carrying*]

○ An *object of a gerund* is a noun or its substitute following a gerund:

> Playing *poker* with them left him poorer. [gerund: *playing*]

> The witness said he didn't believe in naming *names*. [gerund: *naming*]

○ An *object of an infinitive* (or *infinitive complement*) answers "What?" "Whom?" or "Where?" after an infinitive:

> The police want him to answer some *questions*.
> [What do they want him to answer? *Questions*.]

> They thought Sumey to be *her*.
> [Whom did they think Sumey to be? *Her*. Notice that if the linking verb *was* replaced *to be*, the pronoun would change to the *nominative case* form of *she*. But as the sentence is written, *her* is in *objective case* as the object of the infinitive. See Pages 50–51.]

> They said they intend to return to *Oregon*.
> [Where do they intend to return? *Oregon*.]

Common Nouns Versus Proper Nouns

In centuries past, people capitalized many nouns we wouldn't today. Now, we capitalize just proper nouns (such as *Andrew*, *Colorado* or *January*) and lowercase common nouns (generic nouns, such as *truck* or *toothpaste*). But two main problems complicate this: trademarks and names of animals, plants and foods.

○ Don't confuse trademark terms with generic ones. Generic terms should always be used unless the specific brand name is being singled out.

Here's a list of some trade names that are often used incorrectly when the generic term is meant.

BRAND NAME	GENERIC
Aqua-Lung	underwater breathing apparatus
AstroTurf	artificial surface
Bake-off	baking contest
Band-Aid	adhesive bandage

Subjects and Objects

Bubble Wrap	packaging material
ChapStick	lip balm
Coke	cola
Crayola	crayons
Crisco	vegetable shortening
Crock-Pot	slow cooker
DayGlo	fluorescent colors
Deepfreeze	freezer
Disposall	garbage disposer
Dumpster	trash bin
Fiberglas	fiberglass
Formica	plastic laminate
Freon	refrigerant
Frisbee	flying disk
Fudgsicle	fudge ice-cream bar
Google	search the Web
Hi-Liter	highlighting marker
iPad	tablet computer
iPhone	smartphone
iPod	digital music player *or* MP3 player
Jacuzzi	whirlpool bath
Jeep	*jeep* for military vehicle; otherwise, four-wheel-drive vehicle
Jell-O	gelatin
Jockey shorts	underwear
Kitty Litter	cat-box filler
Kleenex	tissue
Kool-Aid	soft-drink mix
Krazy Glue	super adhesive
Land Rover	all-terrain vehicle
Laundromat	coin-operated laundry
Levi's	jeans
Little League Baseball	youth baseball
Lucite	acrylic plastic
Mace (short for *Chemical Mace*)	tear-gas spray
Magic Marker	felt-tip marking pen
Moon Pie	marshmallow sandwich
Nerf	foam toy
Novocain	procaine hydrochloride
Oreo	cookie

Ouija	fortunetelling board game
Pablum	baby food
Photostat	photocopy
Ping-Pong	table tennis
Popsicle	flavored ice on a stick
Post-it	self-stick note
PowerPoint	slide presentation
Pyrex	oven glassware
Quaalude	methaqualone
Q-tips	cotton swabs
Realtor	real estate agent
Rollerblade	in-line skate
Rolodex	address-card file
Scotch tape	transparent tape
Seeing Eye dog	guide dog
Sheetrock	gypsum wallboard
Slim-Fast	diet shake
Spam	luncheon meat or unsolicited commercial email
Styrofoam	plastic foam
Tabasco	hot-pepper sauce
TiVo	digital TV recorder
Vaseline	petroleum jelly
Velcro	fabric fastener
Windbreaker	lightweight jacket
Windex	glass cleaner
Xerox	photocopy
Ziploc	zippered plastic bag

Subjects and Objects

Journalism Tip
Using Trademarks

When a trademark has become so well-known that people start using it generically, the company might lose its exclusive use of the brand name. *Adrenalin, aspirin, heroin, pacemaker, thermos* and *yo-yo* were formerly trademarks but have since become acceptable as generic terms in the U.S.

To protect their trademarks, companies often try to enforce their legal claims to brand names by threatening publications with legal action when the terms are used generically. This typically means that a company will send a letter to an offending publication to inform the editors of the trademark violation and threaten legal action if it happens again.

○ With animals, foods and plants, capitalize only the parts of a compound name that would be capitalized by themselves:

> German shepherd, basset hound
>
> Boston cream pie, chocolate fudge sundae
>
> Virginia pine, lily of the valley

Wire-service exceptions include *french fries*, *graham crackers* and *Manhattan cocktails*, as well as *Black Angus beef* and *bloody mary*. Check the latest edition of the AP Stylebook for more terms.

The Forms Nouns Take

Nouns in English change their spellings for singular versus plural (*number*) and possessive or not (*case*).

A few nouns also change their spellings for *gender*, but these are mostly disappearing. For example, a woman who writes poetry used to be called a *poetess*, but that is seen as a demeaning term today, and the preferred word is *poet* for both men and women. Some words have kept the distinction, but even *actress* and *hostess* are being replaced by *actor* and *host*. (See Page 301 in Chapter 13.)

Forming Singulars and Plurals of Nouns

○ The rule for making an English noun plural is, in most instances, to add *s* to the singular form if it does not end in *s*, or *es* if it does.

○ The plural of common nouns ending in *ch*, *s*, *sh*, *ss*, *tch*, *x*, and some ending in *z* or *zz* is usually formed by adding *es*: *churches*, *buses*, *washes*, *glasses*, *ditches*, *foxes*, *waltzes*, *buzzes*. But some nouns ending in *z* double the *z* before adding *es* to make the plural: *quizzes*, *whizzes*.

○ The plural of common nouns ending with a consonant followed by *y* is generally formed by changing the *y* to *i* and adding *es*: *try*, *tries*. The plural of proper nouns ending in a consonant followed by *y* is formed by adding *s*: *Holly*, *Hollys*.

○ If the noun ends with a vowel followed by *y*, generally the *y* stays the same and *s* is added: *day*, *days*.

○ The plural of nouns ending in *fe* or *lf* is often formed by changing the ending to *ve* and adding *s*: *knife*, *knives*; *self*, *selves*; *wife*, *wives*; *wolf*, *wolves*. The plural of some nouns ending in *f*, however, requires adding only *s*: *roof*, *roofs*; *proof*, *proofs*.

○ The plural of nouns ending in *o* is often formed simply by adding *s*: *duos*, *ghettos*, *pianos*, *radios*, *solos*, *trios*, *zeros*.

The plural of many such nouns, however, requires *es*: *heroes, potatoes, tomatoes, tornadoes, volcanoes*.

○ The plural of most proper nouns ending in *es*, *s* or *z* is formed by adding *es*. The plural of most other proper nouns is formed by adding *s*: *Cortes, Corteses; Schwartz, Schwartzes; BlackBerry, BlackBerrys; Pacino, Pacinos*.

○ The plural of a few words is formed using *en*: *child, children; ox, oxen; woman, women*. This is a leftover from Old English (450 to 1066).

○ Some singular words from foreign languages maintain the foreign plural: *Bacterium* (singular) becomes *bacteria*, *criterion* (AP doesn't like *criterium*) becomes *criteria*, *datum* becomes *data*, *graffito* becomes *graffiti*, *medium* becomes *media*, *phenomenon* becomes *phenomena*, and *stratum* becomes *strata*. Notice that many people misuse the plural form of some of these for the singular. Two that don't follow this rule in AP are *cactus*, which becomes *cactuses*, and *memorandum*, which becomes *memorandums*. Note that similarly, *alumnus* (male singular) becomes *alumni* (male plural or the plural when both men and women are meant), and *alumna* (female singular) becomes *alumnae* (female plural for when only women are included).

○ Some words have the same form in the plural as in the singular: *deer, sheep*.

○ The plural of compound words where the main sense is carried by the first word in the compound is formed by adding *s* to the end of the first word: *attorneys general, mothers-in-law*.

○ The plural of a single letter is formed by adding *'s*: *A's*. The plural of a multiletter word or abbreviation, or of a single-digit or multidigit number, is formed without the apostrophe: *ABCs, 1s, 2010s*.

Forming Possessives of Nouns

Unlike in some languages, English nouns are spelled the same whether they're used in a sentence as a subject or as an object. (That is not true of pronouns, as we'll see later in this chapter.) But the spelling of a noun does change if the noun owns something (*the girl's doll*) or has an attribute that's being discussed (*the computer's power*). When we add an apostrophe or *'s* to the end of a noun, we say that noun is in *possessive case*.

○ The rule for forming the possessive case of a noun is to add *'s* to the end of a noun not ending in *s* and just an apostrophe to the end of a noun ending in *s*: *a boy's goal, the boys' goals. Smith's house, the Smiths' house, Jones' car,* the *Jones's car.* But there are numerous exceptions, as the rest of this list shows.

○ Singular *common nouns* (generic names such as *witness, goodness, appearance*) that end in *s* or an *s* sound normally add *'s*: *a witness's testimony.* But if the next word starts with *s* or an *s* sound, the possessive common noun takes only an apostrophe: *witness' story, for goodness' sake, for appearance' sake.*

○ *Compound words* add the apostrophe or *'s* to the word nearest the object possessed: *attorney general's* (singular, possessive) *opinion, mothers-in-law's* (plural, possessive) *affection.*

○ In case of ownership by two people, either one or two possessives may be used, depending on the sense: *Mary and Bill's cars* (they own them together, so use just one *'s* for the two), but *Mary's and Bill's cars* (they own them separately, so each takes *'s*).

○ If you can turn the phrase around and insert *for* between the words, it's a descriptive phrase rather than truly possessive and does not need the apostrophe or *'s*: *citizens band radio* (radio band for citizens), *teachers college* (college for teachers, not one they own), *writers guide* (a guide for writers).

Sometimes, despite this rule, you have to use *'s* with descriptive phrases because the plural form doesn't end in *s*: *children's play, women's college.* Sometimes, too, a phrase can be turned around and *for* inserted, but *of* would work just as well: *teachers salaries.* Does this mean "salaries for teachers" or "salaries of teachers"? When it could go either way, the plural often substitutes for the possessive. In this particular example, however, you could drop the *s* and avoid the problem: *teacher salaries.*

Other exceptions include *baker's dozen, confectioners' sugar, nurse's aide* and *tinker's damn.* If the descriptive phrase is used in the name of an organization, use the apostrophe or not according to the organization's preference: *Actors' Equity, Ladies' Home Journal, Professional Golfers' Association of America.*

○ Some phrases that are merely descriptive rather than possessive are better hyphenated instead:

> **NOT TRULY POSSESSIVE**   three weeks' vacation
>
> **BETTER**   three-week vacation

○ Some editors insist that inanimate objects that could not really own something should not be made possessive. They would have you write *the power of the computer* rather than *the computer's power*, for example. But such a rule can cause problems with some idioms, such as *a week's pay*. Would anyone really write *the pay of a week*?

○ Double possessives, such as *a brother of Bill's*, occur only when two conditions are met: The word before *of* must involve only some of the possessions—in this case, one brother, not all of them—and the word after *of* cannot be an inanimate object. So, for example, write *a friend of the company*, not *a friend of the company's*, because a company is an inanimate object.

Pronoun Person, Number and Gender

○ A pronoun must agree with its *antecedent* (the noun or pronoun to which it refers) in *person* (first, second or third), *number* (singular or plural) and *gender* (masculine, feminine or neuter). (See also Pages 92–93.)

○ The term *person* is easier to understand by example than by explanation. It refers to who or what is speaking, is spoken to or is spoken about. There are three persons, each of which has particular pronoun forms:

FIRST PERSON | I, we
[for when I am speaking for myself or my group]

SECOND PERSON | you, you
[for when a person or group is being spoken to]

THIRD PERSON | he, she, it, one, they
[for when a person, thing or group is being spoken about]

○ A pronoun can be singular or plural. Some *singular pronouns* include *I*, *he*, *she*, *it* and *one*. Some *plural pronouns* include *we* and *they*. *You* can be either singular or plural, depending on the meaning. The singular pronouns *thou* and *thee*, found in the King James Bible, Shakespeare and other early sources, have disappeared from modern usage except in religious contexts.

> **ONLINE GRAMMAR HELP**
> bedfordstmartins.com/newscentral
>
> For practice using pronoun agreement, log on to *Exercise Central for AP Style* and go to **No. 14. Lack of agreement between pronoun and antecedent**.

○ Most English pronouns are neuter in gender, but the exceptions—some of those in third-person singular, which are masculine or feminine—include:

MASCULINE   he, him, his, himself

FEMININE   she, her, hers, herself

Subjects and Objects

Pronoun Cases

Cases are the forms pronouns take, depending on how they are used in a sentence.

- The *nominative case* is used when the pronoun is the subject, predicate nominative or noun of direct address.

- The *objective case* is used when the pronoun is the direct object; the indirect object; the object of a preposition, participle, gerund or infinitive; or the subject of an infinitive.

- The *possessive case* is used to show possession or attribute.

When writing or speaking, use the correct form of the pronouns, as shown in the following list, according to the preceding rules about their functions in a sentence.

Pronoun-Case Forms

NOMINATIVE	OBJECTIVE	POSSESSIVE
I	me	my, mine
you	you	your, yours
he	him	his
she	her	her, hers
it	it	its
we	us	our, ours
they	them	their, theirs
one	one	one's
who	whom	whose

Two points about this list are worth adding.

- Unlike nouns, pronouns don't normally add *'s* to show possession. The only pronouns that show possession with *'s* end with *one* or *body*: *anyone's, everyone's, anybody's, everybody's*.

This is a handy rule to remember to separate *its* (possessive) from *it's* (*it is* or *it has*), or *whose* (possessive) from *who's* (*who is* or *who has*) and to spell *hers, ours, yours* and *theirs*.

- When a pronoun has two possessive forms, the first one in the list of pronoun-case forms is used before a noun, the second one after it:

> She said that was *her* idea originally. [*Her* precedes the noun *idea*.]
>
> She said that idea was originally *hers*. [*Hers* follows the noun *idea*.]

Nominative Case With Pronouns

○ If a pronoun is the subject or *predicate nominative* (a noun following a linking verb such as *is*), it must be in the nominative case:

> She is the top *singer* on the charts in Britain.
> [Nouns have only one form for both nominative and objective case.]
>
> It's *she*. [Not *It's her.*]

○ Compound subjects are all in the nominative case:

> **WRONG**   *Me and him* are covering the game.
>
> **WRONG**   *He and myself* are covering the game.
>
> **RIGHT**   *He and I* are covering the game.

○ A pronoun in the complete subject introduced by *as well as* is in the nominative case, even though it does not influence the number of the verb:

> That photographer, as well as *we* two reporters, was in France to cover the summit.

○ A pronoun following *as* or *than* at the end of a sentence is usually in the nominative case, although many people mistake a pronoun in such a position for the object of a preposition. Actually, *as* and *than* are conjunctions, and a pronoun following a conjunction is typically the subject of a clause for which the predicate may be implied:

> He finished the test as quickly *as she* (did).
>
> The Rolling Stones were a more popular band in the '60s than *they* (were).

Journalism Tip

Predicate Nominatives in Formal Writing Versus Broadcast

It's she may sound either odd or pretentious to you, but that's because in daily conversation, nominative-case pronouns are reserved mainly for subjects only, not for predicate nominatives. In formal writing, however, *It's she* is preferred over the more conversational *It's her*.

Broadcasters or people writing personal columns may prefer the more conversational use of objective-case pronouns in predicate nominatives.

Subjects and Objects

Objective Case With Pronouns

○ If a pronoun is the direct object; indirect object; object of a preposition, participle, gerund or infinitive; or subject of an infinitive, it must be in the objective case:

Rescuers couldn't reach *them* in time. [*Them* is the direct object.]

David Beckham kicked *him* the ball. [*Him* is the indirect object.]

His brother borrowed the bike from *him*.
[*Him* is the object of the preposition *from*.]

Missing *him*, she wrote a letter.
[*Him* is the object of the participle *missing*.]

Cleaning *it* proved difficult. [*It* is the object of the gerund *cleaning*.]

They took *him* to be *me*.
[*Him* is the subject of the infinitive *to be*. The object of the infinitive is *me*.]

○ A pronoun used in a compound object should be in the objective case:

WRONG   *Between you and myself . . .*

RIGHT   Between you and *me* . . .
[The pronouns form a compound object of the preposition. Substitute another preposition for *between*, and you wouldn't say, for example, "for I."]

WRONG   They invited a friend and *he*.

RIGHT   They invited a friend and *him*.
[*Friend* and *him* are compound direct objects. You wouldn't say "They invited he."]

○ If you have a noun or its substitute between a verb and the infinitive *to be*, use the objective case after the infinitive. If not, use the nominative case:

Police took Talbot to be *her*.
[*Talbot* is between the verb *took* and the infinitive *to be*.]

Palmer was thought to be *she*.
[There is no noun or pronoun between the verb *thought* and the infinitive *to be*.]

ESL Tip

After verbs, pronouns are the most difficult grammatical element to master in most languages. Paying close attention to American conversation helps make the proper use of pronouns nearly automatic, but be aware that conversation often differs from what is considered correct in writing, as shown by examples in this chapter.

Subjects and Objects

The second example at first seems to be an exception to the rule that the object of an infinitive—like any other object—must be in the objective case. But actually, *was thought to be* is functioning here as a linking verb, making the following pronoun a predicate nominative.

Possessive Case With Pronouns

○ Use the possessive case if the pronoun owns something or shows attribution:

> The president continued *his* address without missing a beat, even when the teleprompter failed.

○ Use the possessive case when the pronoun is followed by a gerund:

> A producer from Motown Records was there to hear *his* [not *him*] singing that night.

ONLINE GRAMMAR HELP
bedfordstmartins.com/newscentral

For practice using pronoun case, log on to *Exercise Central for AP Style* and go to **No. 13. Incorrect pronoun case**.

Relative Pronouns

Relative pronouns (*who, whom, whoever, whomever, whose, which, that* and sometimes *what*) are pronouns that introduce a dependent clause closely connected with the relative pronoun's *antecedent*, the noun to which it refers. Such dependent clauses are called *relative clauses*. While working as connectives, relative pronouns also serve as the subject or object of the clause in which they occur. The choice of the correct relative pronoun depends on three things: *antecedent, restrictiveness* and *case*.

If all that sounds complicated, that helps explain why speakers and writers often misuse relative pronouns. But we have a relatively simple solution—simpler when you try it than it first looks. Whenever any of these words appears in a sentence, run through the following three-step procedure:

Step 1: Decide Between the **That** and **Who** Families

○ When the word refers to a *collective noun* (such as the name of an association, a business or a governing body), a thing (an inanimate object, abstraction and so on) or an animal without a proper name, the relative pronoun should be from the *that* family (*that* or *which*). When the word refers to a person or to an animal with a proper name, the correct relative pronoun should be from the *who* family (*who, whom, whoever, whomever, whose* or *who's*):

> Mobil is the oil company *that* [not *who*, despite the ads] wants to invite you to support public television.
> [The antecedent, *company*, refers to a business.]

Subjects and Objects

The dog *that* bit the child has not been found.
[The antecedent, *dog*, refers to an animal without a name.]

Who is this playwright David Henry Hwang *whom* everyone
is discussing?
[The antecedent, *David Henry Hwang*, refers to a person.]

Their cat Fluffy, *who* just had kittens, wasn't straying far from
the closet.
[The antecedent, *Fluffy*, refers to an animal with a name.]

Step 2: Decide Between **That** *and* **Which** *(or Possibly,* **What***)*

◯ Choose *which* to set off something *nonrestrictive* (nonessential to the meaning of the sentence)—or, as we say,
parenthetical. Choose *that* to set off something *restrictive*
(essential)—something you wouldn't put in parentheses:

NONRESTRICTIVE   The Nile, *which flows into the Mediterranean*, gives
                  Egypt life.

RESTRICTIVE   The Nile is the river *that gives Egypt life.*

◯ If you think of a nonessential clause as something
parenthetical—an aside—you can remember that *which*
introduces a clause set off by parentheses, dashes or commas.
That introduces a clause *not* set off by parentheses, dashes or
commas:

RESTRICTIVE   The policy *that critics charged was flawed from the
                  beginning* was amended.
                  [The clause tells what policy of several.]

NONRESTRICTIVE   The policy, *which critics charged was flawed from the
                  beginning,* was amended. [The clause merely adds a
                  fact parenthetically about the policy under discussion.]

RESTRICTIVE   The house *that had a brick front* was theirs.
                  [The clause tells what house.]

NONRESTRICTIVE   The corner house, *which had a brick front*, was
                  theirs. [The clause merely adds a fact parenthetically
                  about the house.]

◯ Use *what* rather than *that* or *which*
mainly in questions and in place of the
phrase *that which* or *those which*:

What book has Democrats seeing red
these days? [question]

Pundits say he stands a good chance to
get *what* he wants. [meaning *that which*]

ONLINE GRAMMAR HELP
bedfordstmartins.com/newscentral

For practice deciding between
that and *which*, log on to *Exercise
Central for AP Style* and go to **No. 5.
Confusion of *that* and *which*.**

***Step 3: Decide Between* Who *and* Whom, *or* Whoever *and* Whomever**

The problem here is that *whom* and *whomever* seem to be on the way out in spoken English. For broadcast or more conversational writing, you might do what most people do in conversation and use *whom* or *whomever* only after a preposition. Even less formally, some people get rid of *whom* and *whomever* altogether. But the distinction traditionally drawn, and that most editors still follow, especially in print and online, is this:

○ Use *who* or *whoever* when the clause calls for the nominative case and *whom* or *whomever* when the clause calls for the objective case. (See Pages 48–51.)

The hard part, often, is determining which case to use, especially when the sentence has more than one clause, because the correct case must reflect the way the pronoun is used in the clause of which it's a part. Look at this sentence:

> Word got out that disgruntled employees were giving free meals to *whoever* asked for one.

Here the preposition *to* can mislead many people into saying or writing *giving free meals to whomever*. Actually, though, the pronoun here is the subject of the clause *whoever asked for one*. This entire dependent clause takes the place of a single noun and acts as the object of the preposition *to*.

Here's another tricky one:

> The police officer asked the witness to point out *whomever* he saw at the scene of the crime.

This time, *whomever* is correct because it's the direct object of the verb *saw*.

If determining the correct case in those last two examples left you scratching your head, help is on the way. It is possible to get *who* versus *whom* right every time without doing any extensive grammatical analysis. Here's how:

○ Begin reading the sentence immediately after the point at which you have a choice between *who* or *whom, whoever* or *whomever*. (If the sentence has more than one clause, this will ensure that you are looking at the correct one.) Then, insert *he* or *him, she* or *her*, or *they* or *them* wherever it makes sense. If *he, she* or *they* works best, use *who* or *whoever*. If *him, her* or *them* works best, use *whom* or *whomever*:

> *Who* did you say wrote the Miss Minimalist blog?
> [subject of clause, so nominative case: *Did you say she wrote the Miss Minimalist blog?*]

> *Whoever* is going had better get ready.
> [subject of clause, so nominative case: *He is going.*]

Subjects and Objects

To *whom* are you speaking?
[object of preposition, so objective case: *Are you speaking to them?*]

Talk with *whomever* you like, and you'll get the same answer.
[object of preposition, so objective case: *You like her.*]

○ To decide when *who* or *whom* needs *ever* at the end, remember that *whoever* is used in place of *anyone* or *anyone who* and *whomever* is used in place of *anyone whom*:

Whoever [*Anyone who*] was interested could pick up a brochure at the fair.

Whomever [*Anyone whom*] you want to invite may come.

Whose Versus *Who's*

○ Don't confuse the relative pronoun *whose* (the possessive form of *who*) with the contraction *who's*, meaning "who is" or "who has." Here, the test is, "Could I substitute *who is* or *who has*?" If yes, the correct word is *who's*. If no, the correct word is *whose*:

Who's⟩
~~Whose~~ going to see the new Will Ferrell movie?

                              whose⟩
She said she didn't care ~~who's~~ feelings were hurt.

Pronouns Ending in *Self* or *Selves*

Reflexive and *intensive pronouns* (*myself, yourself, himself, herself, itself, ourselves, yourselves, themselves*) should be used only when the corresponding pronouns or nouns to which they refer have been used earlier in a sentence.

A pronoun is used *reflexively* when something acts on itself: *I hurt myself.* A pronoun is used *intensively* when drawing attention to the noun or pronoun to which it refers: *I, myself, will do it.*

○ The first- and second-person forms of these pronouns come from the possessive case (*my, our, your*), but the third-person forms come from the objective case (*him, her, it, them*). Never say or write *hisself, theirselves* or *theyselves*—or for that matter, *ourself* rather than *ourselves*.

○ Don't confuse pronouns ending in *self* or *selves* with the properly required pronoun case in a sentence. *Myself* is the biggest offender, especially in a compound subject or object:

me

From JeanAnn and ~~myself~~, good night.

[objective-case pronoun needed for object of preposition]

I

Bill and ~~myself~~ are making a list of people who will attend.

[nominative-case pronoun needed for subject]

Sportswriter Red Smith said that *myself* is the refuge of idiots taught early that *me* is a dirty word.

Verbal Nouns: Gerunds and Infinitives

○ A *verbal noun* is a noun made from a verb. The two kinds are *gerunds* and *infinitives*. We discuss gerunds here but will discuss infinitives in Chapter 4.

○ A *gerund* is a verb form ending in the present-participle form (*ing*) or sometimes in the past-participle form (*ed*, *t* and so on) that is used in place of a noun:

> *Fishing* is a relaxing way to spend a morning.
>
> She was one of the *neglected*.
>
> He was a *drunk*.

○ If a *gerund* is directly preceded by a pronoun or noun, the pronoun or noun must be in the possessive case:

> He's sorry about his *friends'* bickering.

○ But don't confuse a gerund with a participle. Whereas a pronoun before a gerund should be in the possessive case, one before a participle should be in the objective case:

> Can you imagine (*him*, *his*) singing?

The correct pronoun in that sentence could be either *him* or *his*, depending on what is meant. If the writer is interested in the singing, then *singing* is a gerund and takes *his*. If the writer is more interested in this particular person's abilities, then *singing* is a participle acting as an adjective and takes *him*. Say these sentences aloud, stressing the italicized word, and notice the shift in meaning:

> Can you imagine his *singing*?
>
> Can you imagine *him* singing?

How can *singing* be an adjective? Substitute another adjective, and the grammar becomes clearer:

> Can you imagine him *fat*?

CHAPTER 4

Verbs

Verbs are the most important part of speech to master in speaking and writing. Look at any piece of good writing, and you'll see that verbs give a sentence life.

○ A *verb* expresses action or state of being and tells what a noun or its substitute is doing or being: *runs, writes, is, seems*. It can sometimes stand alone as a complete sentence: *Go!*

○ A *predicate* is a verb used as a part of a sentence. Sometimes, it is called the *simple predicate* to distinguish it from the *complete predicate*, which is the verb and its associated words, such as modifiers, objects or complements:

> Two of the candidates *have dropped* from the race. [simple predicate: *have dropped*; complete predicate: *have dropped from the race*]

> Lathrop *is* the Republican expected to run in the next election. [simple predicate: *is*; complete predicate: *is the Republican expected to run in the next election*]

All verbs can be classified as either *helping verbs* or *main verbs* and *transitive* or *intransitive*. Verbs also have a *tense, voice* and *mood*, as well as *person* and *number*. Let's discuss these terms and their practical uses.

Helping Verbs Versus Main Verbs

Verbs are either *main verbs* or *helping verbs*.

○ A *main verb* may stand alone, or it may have helping verbs accompanying it:

> The mayor *loves* her job. [*Loves* is the main verb.]

> She *has loved* working as mayor.
> [*Loved* is the main verb, *has* the helping verb.]

56

○ *Helping verbs* are primarily used to make some verb forms, such as the *simple future tense*, *perfect tenses*, *progressive tenses* and *conditional mood*. These verbs will be discussed later in this chapter.

Common Helping Verbs

am	could	have	shall
are	did	is	should
be	do	may	was
been	does	might	were
being	had	must	will
can	has	ought	would

Helping verbs that show *mood* (see Pages 76–81) are called *modal verbs* and include *can, could, may, might, shall, should, will, would* and *must*. Other words or phrases act like modals in some ways but like main verbs in others. They're called *semimodal verbs* and include *be able to, dare to, have to, have got to, like to, need to, ought to, used to* and *want to*.

Helping verbs are also sometimes used to help show emphasis. For example, we may use a form of the verb *to do* as a helping verb to show emphasis. Often, we underline or italicize the helping verb for emphasis. Less often, we change the helping verb *shall* to *will* or *will* to *shall* to show emphasis. (See Page 64.) Sometimes, we combine a couple of these techniques, although it's important to be consistent about using either an underline or italics for emphasis in one work. (Bold is not used for emphasis.) Here are a few examples:

TO DO	I do edit, he did edit
UNDERLINE OR ITALICS	I <u>have</u> edited, he *has* edited
REVERSAL OF *WILL* AND *SHALL*	I will edit, you shall edit

Helping verbs are often misused in several ways.

○ Don't confuse the preposition *of* with the verb *have*:

WRONG	RIGHT
could of	could have
might of	might have
must of	must have
should of	should have
will of	will have
would of	would have

○ Don't use *can, may, shall* or *will* in tenses further in the past than the simple present. Instead, use their past-tense forms—*could, might, should* and *would*—which are the same as their conditional-mood forms:

couldn't,
He can't have gone far.

might,
She said she may have done it differently.

○ Don't use a form of *have* in situations where it might imply volition when none is intended:

WRONG   He *had* his arm broken.
         [implies the subject hired someone to break his arm]

RIGHT   He *broke* his arm.

○ Don't use *would have* with *could have*:

had,
If he would not have had an operation the week before, he *could have* finished the race.

○ Don't use helping verbs such as *had* or *should* with *ought*:

The settlers had ought to leave.

○ Don't use *might* as a helping verb to *could*:

be able to,
He said he might could help.

We don't insist, as some editors do, that the helping verb be kept next to the main verb in *compound tenses* (tenses that require a helping verb in their formation). For example, some editors would rewrite *She would absolutely like to excel* to keep the adverb *absolutely* from interrupting the parts of the verb: *She absolutely would like to excel.*

But we have been unable to find any grammar book that agrees with insisting on always keeping helping verbs next to main verbs. In fact, Wilson Follett's influential book "Modern American Usage" says of this approach, "The results are uniformly bad." We discourage the practice for several reasons, including that it makes for sentences written in a nonconversational order, that the adverb *not* must be placed between the parts of the verb regardless and that changing the order may change the meaning of the sentence. See the discussion of adverb order on Pages 113–14.

Transitive Verbs Versus Intransitive Verbs

All verbs are either *transitive* or *intransitive* in any given sentence. Some are transitive in one sentence but intransitive in another.

● *Transitive verbs* have a *direct object* (a receiver of the action) that tells to what or to whom the action was done:

> The legislature *passed* the bill.
> [Passed what? Passed *the bill*, the direct object.]
>
> Police *arrested* Fred Wilson.
> [Arrested whom? Arrested *Fred Wilson*, the direct object.]

● *Intransitive verbs* do not take a direct object. The two kinds of intransitive verbs are *linking* (or *copulative*) *verbs* and *complete verbs*.

● *Linking verbs* take a *predicate complement*—either a *predicate nominative* (noun or pronoun following the linking verb) or a *predicate adjective* (adjective following the linking verb):

> That is *she*. [predicate nominative]
>
> He is *impressed*. [predicate adjective]

A linking verb can be thought of as an equals sign indicating an equation between the subject and the predicate complement.

A predicate adjective may be modified by an adverb:

> He said he *was excrutiatingly* hungry. [*Was* is a linking verb, *hungry* a predicate adjective and *excrutiatingly* an adverb modifying *hungry*.]

Linking Verbs

TO BE VERBS

am	was	have been	will be
is	were	had been	
are	has been	shall be	

VERBS USED FOR THE FIVE SENSES

appear	look	sound
feel	smell	taste

OTHER LINKING VERBS

act	grow	stay
become	remain	turn
continue	seem	wax

Knowing when a verb is a linking verb helps you deal with troublesome choices between adjectives and adverbs, such as whether a person feels *good* or feels *well*. (See Pages 99–100.)

● *Complete verbs* take neither a direct object nor a predicate complement:

> The woman *hesitated*.

Verbs

Transitiveness or intransitiveness can be a useful distinction to keep in mind when you are trying to decide among three of the most commonly confused pairs of verbs: *sit* versus *set, rise* versus *raise,* and *lie* versus *lay.* The first verb of each of those pairs—*sit, rise* and *lie*—is intransitive. You don't *sit something down, rise something up* or *lie something down.* The second of each pair—*set, raise* and *lay*—is transitive. You do *set something down, raise something up* or *lay something down.* For the *principal parts* (main forms) of these verbs, see the list beginning on Page 65.

But note these idiomatic exceptions: The sun, a hen or concrete sets, as could glue or a food dish, such as a pie.

Tenses

○ *Verb tense* refers mainly to time—when the action or state of being that the verb represents takes place.

Grammar books disagree on the number of tenses in English, depending on how the term *verb tense* is defined. Essentially, although we speak in English of *three broad time frames*—past, present and future—we have a number of ways to express those time frames with different nuances in meaning.

We believe it makes most sense to think of six basic verb tenses: *past perfect, past, present perfect, present, future perfect* and *future,* in that order from furthest in the past to furthest in the future with six additional *progressive verb tenses* for the same time periods.

ESL Tip

Speakers of other languages may note how much easier English verbs are to learn than those in most languages when it comes to the relative scarcity of *inflections*—changes in verb endings for different tenses and persons. But English verb forms may still be difficult to master because of the numerous specialized rules for their use.

Using the Simple Tenses

Each of the three broad time frames has a form we'll call a *simple tense.* These are usually just called the past, present and future tenses. To demonstrate them, we'll show the *conjugations* (various forms) of a typical verb—*to edit*—for each of these tenses.

In the following list, the two columns represent the *number* of the verb, with *singular* on the left and *plural* on the right. The three lines for each tense represent the *person* of the verb, in descending order: *first person, second person* and *third person.*

Another way to think of the number and person of a verb is as the form the verb takes with different pronouns. All nouns, except *nouns of direct address*, are considered to be in third person—singular or plural, depending on the ending—and require a verb of the same person and number.

Simple Tenses

PAST

I edited	we edited
you edited	you edited
he, she, it, one edited	they edited

PRESENT

I edit	we edit
you edit	you edit
he, she, it, one edits	they edit

FUTURE

I will/shall edit	we will/shall edit
you will edit	you will edit
he, she, it, one will edit	they will edit

○ Use one of these simple tenses to identify a specific point of time. Some words that commonly suggest that a simple tense should be used include *ago, at, at that time, in* [*2011* or some other year], *last* [*week, month, year, century*], *on, then* and *when* (as a question).

> ### ESL Tip
>
> Notice that in English, the verb's conjugations are often the same as the infinitive minus the *to*. For example, in the present tense, the only exception for most verbs other than *to be* is that the third-person singular of almost all English verbs in the present tense ends with s. Verbs that don't end in s in the third-person singular are the modal verbs, such as *can, may, must, shall* and *will*. The perfect tenses use the past-participal form in place of the infinitive form and add one or more helping verbs.

Using the Perfect Tenses

In addition to the simple past, present and future, each of those time periods has a second form of expression called the *perfect tenses*, or *perfects*. They refer to completed (perfected) events taking place previous to other events in the same general block of time. In other words, they offer ways to form a verb indicating these possibilities:

Verbs

- Something took place before another event in the past:

    She *had edited* that story before she *edited* the next one.

- Something in the present started and finished before right now:

    They *have edited* three stories and *are editing* another one apiece now.

- Something will already have happened when another event in the future takes place:

    You *will have edited* about 30 stories by the time your shift *is* over.

Perfect Tenses

PAST PERFECT

I had edited	we had edited
you had edited	you had edited
he, she, it, one had edited	they had edited

PRESENT PERFECT

I have edited	we have edited
you have edited	you have edited
he, she, it, one has edited	they have edited

FUTURE PERFECT

I will/shall have edited	we will/shall have edited
you will have edited	you will have edited
he, she, it, one will have edited	they will have edited

The perfects sometimes also suggest implications other than that the actions merely occurred earlier. For example, look at the following sentences:

RIGHT   Koch *has spent* time in Paris living among the artists.
[present perfect]

RIGHT   Koch *spent* time in Paris living among the artists.
[simple past]

Either sentence is correct if Koch is still alive. Often, simple past and present perfect are interchangeable in everyday use.

But what if the sentence is about someone who has died?

WRONG   George Washington *has slept* here. [present perfect]

RIGHT   George Washington *slept* here. [simple past]

If you were writing a story about a modern-day inn in New Jersey with a historic past, you wouldn't write the first sentence because it implies that George Washington is still alive. Clearly, you'd write the second sentence, in the simple past.

A useful guideline for deciding between using a simple tense and a perfect is to ask yourself whether the larger time frame referred to is completed by the action in the statement or whether it continues beyond that action. Words that commonly suggest that a larger time frame is continuing, thus calling for a perfect, include *already, during, for, how long, not anymore, not yet, since, still, this* [*week, month, year, decade*], *today, until* and *up to now.*

ESL Tip

The use of the perfect tenses in English can be troublesome for speakers of English as a second language because the perfects force distinctions many students may not be used to making in their own languages. For example, the perfects are dying in many European languages, such as German and French.

Using the Progressive Tenses

The third way of writing about the past, present or future uses the *progressive tenses*, or *progressive aspects*.

There are two progressive forms for each broad time frame—one corresponding to the simple tense and one to the perfect. The progressives are formed using some form of *to be* as a helping verb and the *progressive* (*ing*, or *present-participle*, form) of the main verb. We'll give examples of just the first- and third-person singular for each:

Progressive Tenses

PAST-PERFECT PROGRESSIVE	I had been editing he, she, it, one had been editing
PAST PROGRESSIVE	I was editing he, she, it, one was editing
PRESENT-PERFECT PROGRESSIVE	I have been editing he, she, it, one has been editing
PRESENT PROGRESSIVE	I am editing he, she, it, one is editing
FUTURE-PERFECT PROGRESSIVE	I will/shall have been editing he, she, it, one will have been editing
FUTURE PROGRESSIVE	I will/shall be editing he, she, it, one will be editing

○ *Progressives* stress the ongoing nature of an activity of limited duration. But they can be more complicated:

PRESENT	She *is sleeping.* [She started earlier and is still asleep now.]
SIMPLE PRESENT	She *sleeps.* [Possibly suggests this is something she does occasionally.]

Verbs

PRESENT PROGRESSIVE	The town *is bordering* on the Mississippi River.
SIMPLE PRESENT	The town *borders* on the Mississippi River. [This seems to convey the sense of continuation from the past better than does the progressive.]

Shall Versus *Will*

You might have noted on Pages 61–63 the choice between *will* and *shall* in first-person singular in the future tenses (simple future, future perfect, future progressive and future-perfect progressive). *Will* is more common in conversation, but the strictest traditional grammarians insist on *shall* rather than *will* for first-person verbs. We think *shall* sounds too pretentious and old-fashioned to most Americans, and we don't insist on it, particularly in broadcast. *Shall* is used more often in Britain than in the United States, but it's losing ground there, as well.

ESL Tip

Speakers of English as a second language should avoid the mistake of forgetting either the *to be* verb or the *ing* ending in progressives:

WRONG	We *learning* grammar. [But you sometimes hear this done in broadcast news as a kind of approximation of a headline, as in "Congress *going* home this weekend without a vote on the budget."]
WRONG	We *are learn* grammar.
RIGHT	We *are learning* grammar.

If you do decide to use *shall* in the first person, you should know that the same people who insist on *shall* also usually teach that, for emphasis, you should use *shall* where you would normally use *will* and vice versa:

NORMAL	EMPHATIC
I *shall* sing.	I *will* sing!
You *will* leave tomorrow.	You *shall* leave tomorrow!

It seems to us, though, that *will* and *shall* can be equally emphatic in the same places. Gen. Douglas MacArthur, for example, said, when leaving the Philippines in World War II, "I *shall* return!" not "I *will* return!" Likewise, in the 1960s, the civil rights marchers sang "We *shall* overcome," not "We *will* overcome." In common usage, in fact, it seems more likely that *shall* will be used to show emphasis, and that's the main time you hear *shall* used.

Regular Verbs Versus Irregular Verbs

Most, but not all, verbs form their conjugations as the verb *to edit* does. *Regular verbs* distinguish the past from the present by adding *ed* or *t*: *edit*, *edited*; *leap*, *leaped* (or *leapt*). (Sometimes a final *y* becomes *i* before the ending: *rely*, *relied*, *relied*.)

But in English, as in all languages, many of the most commonly used verbs are irregular. *Irregular verbs* in English distinguish the past from the present by changing the middle of the verb, by having a different past-participle form (for use with the perfects) from the simple-past form or by not changing from present to past to past participle at all:

sing, sang, sung [change in middle]

fall, fell, fallen [change in middle and different past participle]

broadcast, broadcast, broadcast [no change]

A common mistake with irregular verbs is to use an incorrect past participle. Because the past and past-participle forms are the same with regular verbs, mistaking the two forms is a problem only with irregular verbs, where the two may differ.

He had already ~~went~~ gone home by the time his date arrived late.

Here is a list of irregular, and some regular, verbs that cause the most trouble. We have listed the *principal parts* (the most common verb forms) of each: the present, past, past-participle and present-participle forms.

Principal Parts of Common Irregular and Other Confusing Verbs

PRESENT	PAST	PAST PARTICIPLE	PRESENT PARTICIPLE
awake	awoke *or* awaked	awaked *or* awakened	awaking *or* awakening
be	was	been	being
bear	bore	borne	bearing
bid (*offer*)	bid	bid	bidding
bid (*command*)	bade	bidden (not *bidded*)	bidding
bring	brought	brought	bringing
broadcast	broadcast	broadcast	broadcasting
burst	burst	burst	bursting
cling	clung	clung	clinging
come	came	come	coming
dive	dived	dived (AP)	diving
do	did	done	doing
drink	drank	drunk	drinking
drive	drove	driven	driving
drown	drowned	drowned	drowning

(Don't say a victim *was drowned* unless an assailant held the person's head under the water.)

| eat | ate | eaten | eating |

Verbs

fall	fell	fallen	falling
flow	flowed	flowed	flowing
fly (*soar*)	flew	flown	flying
fly (*hit a baseball high*)	flied	flied	flying
forbid	forbade	forbidden	forbidding
forsake	forsook	forsaken	forsaking
get	got	got *or* gotten	getting
go	went	gone	going
hang (*suspend*)	hung	hung	hanging
hang (*execute*)	hanged	hanged	hanging
have	had	had	having
hide	hid	hidden	hiding
keep	kept	kept	keeping
kneel	knelt *or* kneeled	knelt *or* kneeled	kneeling
lay (*set down*)	laid	laid	laying
lead	led	led	leading
lie (*recline*)	lay	lain	lying
make	made	made	making
pay	paid	paid	paying
plead	pleaded (AP: not *pled*)	pleaded	pleading
prove	proved	proved (*proven* is an adjective)	proving
put	put	put	putting
raise	raised	raised	raising
ring	rang	rung	ringing
rise	rose	risen	rising
see	saw	seen	seeing
set	set	set	setting

(*place down*; also, *hens set, cement sets* and *the sun sets*)

shake	shook	shaken	shaking
shine	shone	shone	shining
show	showed	showed *or* shown	showing
shrink	shrank	shrunk	shrinking
sit (*seat oneself*)	sat	sat	sitting
slay	slew	slain	slaying
sleep	slept	slept	sleeping
spring	sprang	sprung	springing
steal	stole	stolen	stealing

strive	strove	striven	striving
swear	swore	sworn	swearing
swim	swam	swum	swimming
swing	swung	swung	swinging
tread	trod	trodden *or* trod	treading
wake	woke	waked	waking
weave	wove	woven	weaving
wring	wrung	wrung	wringing

Sequence of Tenses

To use the right verb for what you're trying to say, you need to understand two especially important things:

1. *The time order of the forms from furthest in the past to furthest in the future.* That order, called the *sequence of tenses*, is as follows: *past perfect, past, present perfect, present, future perfect, future.* Remember, for each tense, the perfect form precedes the simple form.
2. *Special rules regarding the use of each form.* Following are some of the most important guidelines for using verbs in the three broad time frames in English.

Past Tenses

Past Perfect.   Use past perfect for events that occurred before those described in the past tense and are now concluded. It's often used with *after, before, by, by the time, until* or *when* to show that one event occurred before another:

> *Until* he turned 50, he *had* never *tried* his hand at writing poetry.

Past-Perfect Progressive.   Use past-perfect progressive for actions continuing from one point in the past to another one closer to the present before concluding:

> The killing in Bosnia *had been going* unchecked until NATO intervened.

Past.   Use past for events that occurred in the past and are now concluded. Use if the sentence answers the question "How long ago?" or, often, if you can use *in* or *on* to express a time element:

> He first *exhibited* the signs of Parkinson's disease in 2011.

Present for Past.   Journalists usually use the simple present to express the past in a headline:

> Governor *Signs* Death Penalty Into Law

In addition, in daily conversation, people often use the simple present to express the past:

"So, then I *say* to him, 'What are you trying to pull?'"

Past Progressive.   Use past progressive for something that was happening in the past but has since ended:

The band *was playing* to packed stadiums in 2007.

Present Tenses

Present Perfect.   Use present perfect for events that started in the past and have continued into the present or have some connection with the present. Usually, but not always, it's used when *already*, *ever*, *for*, *never*, *not yet* or *since* is used to express a time element:

If you *have ever wondered* what makes fast-food french fries taste so good, the answer is a sugar coating.

Present-Perfect Progressive.   Use present-perfect progressive for actions that began in the past and are still continuing in the present. Use if the statement answers the question "How long has this been happening?" A sentence in the present-perfect progressive often uses the word *for* or *since*:

The Seattle Sounders *have been playing* well *since* opening day.

Journalism Tip

Journalism and Sequence of Tenses

○ Many editors insist on using a special rule governing the sequence of tenses in *reported speech*. Under this rule, when one is paraphrasing (not directly quoting) what someone has said, simple present becomes simple past (for example, *edit* becomes *edited*, *can* becomes *could*, and *may* becomes *might*), simple past becomes past perfect (*edited* becomes *had edited*), and *shall* or *will* in the simple future or future perfect becomes *should* or *would* (although *should* is almost never used this way in conversation or in print, *would* being substituted):

QUOTE   "I am young, but I am wise."

REPORTED SPEECH   She said she was young but she was wise.

The New York Times Manual of Style and Usage is one place where the reported-speech rule is spelled out and urged. But the manual allows for three exceptions:

1. When an eternal truth is expressed:

ACCEPTABLE   The rabbi said God *loves* [not *loved*] us.

2. When a time element is specified:

ACCEPTABLE   He said he *was* [not *had been*] depressed Monday when he heard of the trade.

3. When the attribution is in the middle or at the end of the sentence rather than at the beginning:

RIGHT   Halperin said she *would* [not *will*] vote for the amendment.

RIGHT   She *will* vote for the amendment, Halperin said, as long as it's not changed.

RIGHT   She *will* vote for the amendment, Halperin said.

The Reuters Handbook for Journalists allows only the third exception, and then only when the attribution is at the end of the sentence. The Los Angeles Times Stylebook allows for exceptions whenever the action expressed is habitual, customary, characteristic, a general truth or continuing. As it notes, "There are major exceptions to this rule, and a great deal of newspaper writing is in the realm of exceptions."

Indeed, the rule, if followed, applies only to hard-news stories, not features or any other writing in the present tense, where *says* is used in place of *said*.

We are skeptical about using the rule at all, for these reasons:

1. It seems to be potentially confusing:

She said she *was* in favor of the plan. [But is she still?]

She said she *would* speak to the class. [But is that based on some condition?]

Common usage here — *She said she is in favor of the plan* and *She said she will speak to the class* — is capable of more nuances of meaning.

2. Contrary to what its supporters — who often call this *the* sequence-of-tense rule — believe, it really is not a typical sequence-of-tense issue, and even if it were, it would certainly not be the only issue.

Sequence of tense involves making the verbs in a sentence clear as to the time relationship between the events they describe. But with the reported-speech rule, the verb tense is changed in relation to what was originally said, not in relation to the attribution verb *said*. If the latter were the case, then all the verbs in the sentence would have to be previous to the simple past of *said*. Instead, the rule specifies that something someone said in simple present should become simple past.

ORIGINAL STATEMENT   The issue *is* controversial.

REPORTED SPEECH   She said the issue *was* controversial. [But if this were a true sequence-of-tense issue, *was* would have to become *has been* or *had been*.]

3. The reported-speech rule is not as universally urged in style and grammar books as its supporters imply. Not only do the stylebooks mentioned have different versions of the rule, but also the AP Stylebook and the UPI Stylebook and Guide to Newswriting, for example, don't have an entry for it at all. If your stylebook requires it, use it. If it doesn't, we suggest being flexible.

Verbs

Present.   Use present for something happening now:

> Her book *sits* prominently on the coffee table.

Present Progressive.   Use present progressive in place of the simple present for many situations in which something is happening right now:

> The president *is meeting* with his advisers at this moment.

Future Tenses

Present for Future.   English often permits the use of the simple present with an adverb of time to convey future action:

> She *leaves tomorrow.*

Future Perfect.   Use future perfect for events that will have been completed in the future before something else happens. Future perfect is usually used with *by*, *by the time* or *when*:

> *By the time* you read this column, the World Series *will have been decided.*

Future-Perfect Progressive.   Use future-perfect progressive for actions continuing from now into the future when the focus is on what will have been happening to that point. Future-perfect progressive, then, projects into the future and looks back:

> This Monday, Tom Williams *will have been coaching* 30 years at Central.

Future.   Use future for events that will definitely occur in the future:

> The statewide referendum *will decide* the issue this November.

Future Progressive.   Use future progressive for events continuing in the future with no end in sight:

> A hundred years from now, parents *will* still *be shaking* their heads at their teenagers' taste in music.

Keeping Verb Tenses Consistent

○ **Once you've selected the proper verb tense, for the most part you'll want to keep the tense consistent.**

For example, don't start out using *said* to attribute every quotation and then switch later to *says*. Pick one or the other (generally, use *says* for a feature story only) and stick to it.

○ You can, however, switch tenses for a reason—such as to go into a flashback or to mention an event that occurred at an earlier time or will occur in the future.

If switching tenses becomes necessary, it is important to follow the correct sequence of tenses, using an earlier tense for an event that occurred earlier, a later one for something later. For example, if you've been writing in present tense and now write about something that took place earlier, you would switch to the present perfect, past or past perfect.

Or, if you want to express that something was already taking place when another action occurred, use the past progressive in one clause and the simple past in another:

He *was speaking* [past progressive] when the alarm *rang* [past].

If we tried to use the past perfect with the past in that example, the meaning would be different:

He *had spoken* [past perfect] when the alarm *rang* [past].

> **ONLINE GRAMMAR HELP**
> bedfordstmartins.com/newscentral
>
> For practice using verb forms, log on to *Exercise Central for AP Style* and go to **No. 20. Incorrect verb form.**

This second sentence implies that he had already finished speaking before the alarm rang.

Active Voice Versus Passive Voice

All verbs are in either the active voice or the passive voice, but it may be easier to think of all *sentences* as being either active or passive.

○ *Active-voice sentences* stress the doer of an action by making the doer the subject:

ACTIVE VOICE,   The printer *publishes* the magazine.
PRESENT TENSE

ACTIVE VOICE,   The printer *published* the magazine.
PAST TENSE

○ *Passive-voice sentences* stress the receiver of an action by making the receiver the subject of the sentence and having the subject acted upon:

PASSIVE VOICE,   The magazine *is published* by the printer.
PRESENT TENSE

PASSIVE VOICE,   The magazine *was published* by the printer.
PAST TENSE

Verbs

Note that the passive voice always contains a form of the verb *to be* as a helping verb in addition to the past participle of the main verb (in these examples: *is published* and *was published*). The active voice (*published*) does not have a form of *to be* as a helping verb but may have a form of *to have*. In the passive voice, there is also always a phrase starting with *by* or *for* either expressed or implied:

> **PASSIVE VOICE, EXPRESSED**   The magazine was published *by the printer*.

> **PASSIVE VOICE, IMPLIED**   The magazine was published.
> [Grammarian Richard Mitchell calls sentences like this, in which the doer has been left out, the "divine passive" because only God knows who did it. From now on, we'll use that term, also.]

Many students have been taught—incorrectly—always to avoid passive voice. The fact is, it should *usually* be avoided, but there are times when it's perfectly fine. Also, few students know how to recognize passive voice when they see it and so don't know when to rewrite a sentence because of it. To help overcome these problems, let's start with why we normally avoid passive voice, then look more closely at what it is, what it's confused with and when it makes sense to use it.

◯ Normally, avoid passive voice.

Grammatically speaking, there's nothing wrong with writing sentences in passive voice, but from a literary standpoint, passive voice lacks the appeal of active voice. Passive-voice sentences are wordier, more awkward sounding, less interesting, more stilted or formal, and often vaguer. Which of the following sounds best to you?

> **PASSIVE VOICE**   A contract proposal *has been rejected* by area teachers.

> **(DIVINE) PASSIVE VOICE**   A contract proposal *has been rejected*.

> **ACTIVE VOICE**   Area teachers *have rejected* a contract proposal.

The active-voice sentence is shorter than the first and more specific than the second, while sounding less stilted and more to the point than the other two.

What we might call *extreme passive-voice sentences* can also turn powerful verbs into weak nouns:

> **ACTIVE VOICE**   The military *interrogated* the prisoners.

> **PASSIVE VOICE**   The prisoners *were interrogated* by the military.

> **(DIVINE) PASSIVE VOICE**   The prisoners *were interrogated*.

(EXTREME) PASSIVE VOICE	Interrogations of prisoners *were made* by the military. [Here, the subject is *interrogations*, a thing, rather than *military*, a doer.]
(DIVINE AND EXTREME) PASSIVE VOICE	Interrogations of prisoners *were made*.

○ Learn how to spot passive voice using the following guidelines:

• The subject is acted upon rather than doing or being anything itself.

ACTIVE VOICE	The City Council *voted* to censure the mayor. [The City Council took action.]
PASSIVE VOICE	The mayor *was censured* by the City Council. [The mayor was acted upon by the City Council.]
(DIVINE) PASSIVE VOICE	The mayor *was censured*. [The mayor was acted upon by someone or something else.]
(EXTREME) PASSIVE VOICE	Censure *was effectuated* by the City Council. [The subject has been turned into a thing being acted upon.]

• Passive voice uses some form of the verb *to be* as a helping verb.

ACTIVE VOICE	Police *arrested* a suspect this morning. [no *to be* helping verb]
PASSIVE VOICE	A suspect *was* [*to be* helping verb] *arrested* this morning by police.

• Passive voice uses the past participle of the main verb. (For regular verbs, this is the form ending in *ed*. For irregular verbs, see the list of principal parts on Pages 65–67 or in a dictionary.)

• In a passive-voice sentence, the word *by* or *for* is either present or implied. Passive voice is shorter than active voice only when a phrase introduced by *by* or *for* is missing, but that, of course, leads to a lack of clarity about who is doing the acting.

• Only transitive verbs have a passive-voice form. The active-voice subject becomes the word after *by* or *for* in the passive-voice sentence.

○ Don't confuse passive voice with other verb forms.

The verb conjugations listed earlier in this chapter were all in the active voice. To help you recognize the difference between active and passive voice, here are sample sentences showing the passive voice beside the same sentence in active voice for the six basic verb tenses.

Verbs

Passive and Active Forms for Simple and Perfect Tenses

	PASSIVE VOICE	ACTIVE VOICE
PAST PERFECT	It *had been edited* by me.	I *had edited* it.
PAST	It *was edited* by me.	I *edited* it.
PRESENT PERFECT	It *has been edited* by me.	I *have edited* it.
PRESENT	It *is edited* by me.	I *edit* it.
FUTURE PERFECT	It *will have been edited* by me.	I *will have edited* it.
FUTURE	It *will be edited* by me.	I *will edit* it.

Notice in the sentences in this list that only the passive-voice sentences use some form of the verb *to be* as a helping verb. Passive voice should not be confused with the progressive tenses, however, which also use *to be* as a helping verb.

Look at the differences between passive-voice forms and active-voice progressive forms in the following list. Notice the passive voice always uses the past participle of the main verb, the *ed* form, never only the present participle, the *ing* form, used by the active progressive tenses. (Following this list are examples of the use of the *ing* form of *to be* as a helping verb, not the main verb, in passive progressive constructions.) Also, active voice in the progressive does not have or imply *by* or *for* and the subject always is doing something rather than being acted upon.

	PASSIVE VOICE	ACTIVE VOICE
PAST PERFECT	It *had been edited* by me.	I *had been editing* it.
PAST	It *was edited* by me.	I *was editing* it.
PRESENT PERFECT	It *has been edited* by me.	I *have been editing* it.
PRESENT	It *is edited* by me.	I *am editing* it.
FUTURE PERFECT	It *will have been edited* by me.	I *will have been editing* it.
FUTURE	It *will be edited* by me.	I *will be editing* it.

There are only these two passive progressive tenses:

PASSIVE PRESENT PROGRESSIVE	It *is being edited* by me.
PASSIVE PAST PROGRESSIVE	It *was being edited* by me.

Another culprit that confuses some writers into needless changes is a sentence with a linking verb followed by an adjective or by a participle used as an adjective:

ACTIVE VOICE	The bagel was *burnt*. [participle used as an adjective]
ACTIVE VOICE	The bills were long past *due*. [adjective]

At first, these sentences might seem to be in passive voice. In the first one, you can even imagine an implied *by*. But in these examples, what might look like a past participle is an adjective, not a part of the verb, and so the sentences are in active voice. How can you tell?

Journalism Tip

When Not to Change Passive Voice to Active

Good writers rewrite passive-voice sentences in active voice unless they have a specific reason not to do so.

○ Journalists may choose the passive voice in the following instances:

· When the person being acted upon is more important than the person doing the acting, such as is often the case in a crime or an accident story.

The nation's prime minister *was shot* and *killed* by an assassin today.

· When the person doing the acting is unknown.

A one-arm man *is being sought* in connection with the death of a woman in Chicago.

· When reporters seek to preserve the confidentiality of their sources.

It *is reported* that . . .

○ Occasionally, but rarely, a sentence may imply the past participle of the main verb:

There will be no presentation by the candidate.

Is that sentence in passive voice? We think that in this sentence, there's actually an implied past participle *made*:

PASSIVE   There will be no presentation *made* by the candidate.

But passive voice or not, the sentence would be better rewritten:

ACTIVE   The candidate will make no presentation.

○ Some verbs should be used in passive voice. The verb *divorce* must always be passive voice or transitive:

WRONG   They married then divorced. [active]

RIGHT   They were divorced. [passive]

RIGHT   He divorced her. [transitive]

Many purists also insist that the verb *graduate* should be used in the passive voice, as in *She was graduated from the University of Arizona*. The AP Stylebook, however, says that the active voice, *She graduated from the University of Arizona*, is preferred although both are correct. Either way, don't forget the *from*.

○ Don't shift between active and passive voice in the same sentence. (See Page 95.)

Verbs

◯ If you can put the word *very* in front of what you think is the past participle, the word is an adjective, not a verb:

The bagel was *very* burnt.

The bills were *very* long past due.

Mood

Verb mood is hard to define but has to do with how the speaker or writer regards the statement being made. There are four moods: *indicative*, *imperative*, *conditional* and *subjunctive*. It's easier to understand them when we see how each is used.

Indicative Mood

We would guess 90 percent of English sentences are in the *indicative mood*, meaning that the sentence in which the verb appears either states a fact or asks a question about a fact. All of the verb conjugations we've listed so far are in the indicative mood. Assume a verb is in indicative mood unless the situation clearly calls for one of the other three moods.

Imperative Mood

Some verbs are in the *imperative mood*, meaning that the sentence makes a command, issues instructions or entreats:

Add 1 cup of flour.

Please *be* careful as you pour in the boiling water.

Conjugating imperative-mood verbs is easy because there is only one verb tense (present) with only two conjugations:

Edit! [second-person singular or plural]

Let's [Let us] edit! [first-person plural]

Note that the imperative mood leaves out the subject of the clause, instead implying it.

Conditional Mood

Some sentences use the *conditional mood*, which, as the name implies, expresses a condition. The conditional mood in English is usually represented by one of four helping verbs, although it can use the other modal verb *must*, as well as the *semimodal verbs*. (See Page 57.) In the conditional:

can becomes *could*

may becomes *might*

shall becomes *should*

will becomes *would*

The conditional mood has forms for many but not all of the indicative simple tenses, perfects and progressives, as these examples show.

Conditional Mood

PAST PERFECT	None
PAST-PERFECT PROGRESSIVE	None
PAST	I *could/might/should/would* edit.
PAST PROGRESSIVE	I *could/might/should/would* have been editing.
PRESENT PERFECT	I *could/might/should/would* have edited.
PRESENT-PERFECT PROGRESSIVE	I *could/might/should/would* have been editing. [same as past progressive]
PRESENT	I *could/might/should/would* edit. [same as past]
PRESENT PROGRESSIVE	I *could/might/should/would* be editing.
FUTURE PERFECT	I *could/might/should/would* have edited. [same as present perfect]
FUTURE-PERFECT PROGRESSIVE	I *could/might/should/would* have been editing. [same as past progressive]
FUTURE	I *could/might/should/would* edit. [same as past]
FUTURE PROGRESSIVE	I *could/might/should/would* be editing. [same as present progressive]

○ Use *can* and *will* to express certainty, *could* and *would* when a condition is mentioned or implied:

> I *can* go. [definite]
>
> I *could* go if I finished work early. [conditional]
>
> The law *will* close tax loopholes. [definite]
>
> The bill *would* close tax loopholes.
> [This sentence requires the conditional form because the bill is not yet a law—it would close tax loopholes if it were passed into law.]

The idea of the indicative form as being more certain than the conditional form is not as apparent with *may* and *might* and with *shall* and *should* because neither pair is used in everyday conversation the way traditional grammar asks us to use it in formal written language.

○ We suggest that when either *may* or *might* is needed, you use *may* in the present tense and *might* in the past and not bother with trying to figure out whether the situation is conditional because the meanings are too close to make much difference.

○ We suggest *would* as a more conversational alternative to the conditional *should*, especially in broadcast.

Because few people use the formal *shall* in conversation, instead using *will*, they're more likely to use *would* for the conditional form.

In conversation, *should* is usually used only to mean "ought to." This is simply a case where the language has changed except in a few phrases that have persisted, such as *I should think not!*

Subjunctive Mood

The *subjunctive mood* should be used to talk about any condition contrary to fact, or to express a wish, doubt, prayer, desire, request, hypothetical situation or hope.

Consider the following sentence:

The bill would close tax loopholes if it *were* [not *was*] passed into law.

The *were* is in the subjunctive mood because it's proposing a hypothetical situation. In other words, although it may be a fact that I wish something, what I wish for has not yet come true, or I wouldn't be wishing for it.

By the way, the subjunctive is often used after *if* in sentences in which the verb in the main clause is in the conditional. But the subjunctive mood doesn't have to follow *if*.

Few people have trouble with the indicative and imperative moods, or with half of the conditional forms (although *may* and *might, shall* and *should* can cause problems). The subjunctive, however, is not used nearly so often in English, and few people know how to use it correctly.

Here are some examples of the subjunctive:

If I *were* you [*but I'm not*], I'd quit.

I wish I *were* a cowboy [*but I'm not*].

The hijackers demanded that 17 terrorists *be* set free [*they have not yet been freed*].

The first two sentences may sound odd because many people use *I was*, the indicative-mood form, even when the subjunctive form is needed. You can tell that *was* is incorrect, however, because it is a past-tense verb, but the action of each sentence does not happen in the past.

Journalism Tip

Verb Moods

Journalists do most of their writing in the indicative mood, except for pieces that tell people how to do things, such as cooking or crafts articles. Such articles use the imperative mood in their instructions. But the conditional mood should be used whenever an article discusses what bills or other proposals would do if they were made into law. Editors should check for the subjunctive mood in sentences in which one of the clauses is in the conditional, as in the previous one.

As for the third example, most people would probably correctly use *be* because it sounds right, even though they would not even realize that they were using the subjunctive.

First, let's learn the conjugations in the subjunctive. Then, we'll look more closely at how this mood is used.

The most distinctive subjunctive forms occur for the verb *to be*.

Subjunctive Forms of **To Be**

PRESENT TENSE

I be	we be
you be	you be
he, she, it, one be	they be

PAST TENSE

I were	we were
you were	you were
he, she, it, one were	they were

It's important to remember the past-tense forms because some of the most common mistakes using (or not using) the subjunctive involve the verb *to be*. Notice that in the indicative mood, the first- and third-person singular forms use *was* but the subjunctive calls for *were*: *if I were you*; *if she were taller.*

For all verbs other than *to be*, the *present tense of the subjunctive mood* is the infinitive minus the *to*. This form differs from the present tense of the indicative mood only in the third-person singular: *He asked that the editor edit* [not *edits*] *his story carefully for potential libel.*

PRESENT TENSE OF THE SUBJUNCTIVE MOOD

I edit	we edit
you edit	you edit
he, she, it, one edit	they edit

The *past tense of the subjunctive mood* for all verbs other than *to be* is the same as the past tense of the indicative mood (*I edited*, etc.).

Because all the other tenses are the same in the subjunctive as in the indicative, we often use the subjunctive without realizing it.

Following are some specific situations in which to use the subjunctive.

○ **Use the subjunctive in most dependent clauses beginning with *if*.**

If usually introduces a condition contrary to fact, so the subjunctive is needed. Occasionally, the condition is not contrary to fact: If the condition is either true or noncommittal (as in this sentence), the indicative is required. Recognizing the difference can sometimes be tricky.

Here are some sentences that use the subjunctive because they contain an *if* that introduces a condition contrary to fact:

If she *were* rich [*but she's not*], she would quit her job.

If compassion *be* a crime, then judge me guilty.
[The speaker does not really believe compassion should be considered a crime.]

By contrast, here are some sentences that use the indicative because they contain an *if* that introduces a condition that is true or about which the speaker is noncommittal as to truth or falsity:

If this experiment *works*, I will be famous.
[It may or may not work—it is not clearly false.]

He must have found a ride home if he *is* not in his office.
[He probably found a ride home if he's not in his office.]

○ If the verb in the independent clause is in the indicative mood, the verb in the dependent clause is also usually in the indicative. But if the verb in the independent clause is in the conditional mood, the verb in the dependent clause is usually in the subjunctive:

I *can* do it if I *have* the proper tools. [*Can* and *have* are both indicative.]

I *could* do it *were* I *given* the proper tools.
[*Could* is conditional; *were given* is a passive-voice form of the subjunctive.]

Note, however, that although linguists consider *must* and the semi-modal verbs as conditional, those verbs—unlike *could, might, should* and *would*—do not take the subjunctive mood in an accompanying clause. Rather, they take the indicative:

The president must take action quickly if he *wants* (not *want*) to avert a disaster.

Likewise, when *should* is used in its normal conversational meaning of "ought to," it doesn't take the subjunctive in another clause:

The president should take action quickly if he *wants* (not *want*) to avert a disaster.

○ Use the subjunctive in dependent clauses after verbs requiring *that* when the suggestion following is contrary to fact at present: *advise that, anxious that, ask that, demand that, doubt that, eager that, forbid that, hope that, insist that, move that, pray that, prefer that, propose that, recommend that, request that, require that, rule that, suggest that* and *urge that.*

The terrorists *demand that* $1 million *be* paid for the hostages' release.

They *insist that* the police negotiator *come* unarmed.

The contract requires that new hires *be* enrolled in the existing pension fund. [correct, but many editors would probably prefer *The contract requires new hires to be enrolled . . .*]

⬤ Verbs requiring *that* but not implying a condition contrary to present reality do not need the subjunctive: *believe that, conclude that, guess that, imply that, infer that, know that, notice that, say that, suppose that, think that* and *wonder that.*

> I *believe that* this *is* true.

> I *suppose that* he *is* tired.

⬤ Use the subjunctive after *as if*:

> He sings *as if* he *were* a professional.

⬤ Use the subjunctive in these idioms: *be it said, be that as it may* (but note the indicative *may* instead of the conditional in this expression even though used with the subjunctive), *come Monday, come what may, far be it (for, from) me, God be with you, God bless, God forbid, lest we forget, long live the king, so be it, suffice it to say* and *would that I were.*

> *Suffice it to say* she was mad.

> *God bless* America!

⬤ People sometimes use the subjunctive with some constructions that do not really require it:

> *are*
> If there ~~be~~ . . .

> *are*
> . . . whether you ~~be~~ . . .

> **ONLINE GRAMMAR HELP**
> bedfordstmartins.com/newscentral
>
> For practice using subjunctive mood, log on to *Exercise Central for AP Style* and go to **No. 18. Incorrect use of subjunctive mood**.

Nouns Used as Verbs

Although many nouns are also used as verbs in English, many editors object to using the following ones as verbs.

Nouns to Avoid Using as Verbs

NOUN	CHANGE TO
author	write
contact	call, write, visit, email
debut	have its debut
effort	try
gift	give
is headquartered	has headquarters in
host	hold
impact	affect

Verbs

ink	sign
jet	fly
journal	write a journal
language	express, say, write
parent	rear
partner, partnership	to form a partnership with
pastor	lead a congregation
pen	write, sign
premiere	have its premiere
script	write
summer	to spend the summer
target	aim at

In addition, you should avoid using these verbs as nouns:

VERB	CHANGE TO
disconnect	disconnection
win	victory

But check the dictionary or AP Stylebook for recent changes in the language, especially from technology. For example, *friend* and *like* are OK as verbs in stories about Facebook, according to AP Online.

Verbals

Sometimes, a form of a verb is used as a part of speech other than a verb. A verb form used as something other than a verb is called a *verbal*, and the three kinds are *gerunds*, *participles* and *infinitives*.

Gerunds

○ A *gerund* is the present- or past-participle form of a verb used as a noun. (See Page 55.)

Participles

○ A *participle* is the present- or past-participle form of a verb used as an adjective. (See Pages 97, 105 and 112.)

Infinitives

○ An *infinitive* is the form of a verb that normally has *to* in front of it, although sometimes *to* can be omitted:

May I help *cook*?

To is usually considered a preposition, but it isn't when the word is part of an infinitive. When *to* is followed by a verb, the construction is an infinitive, not a prepositional phrase.

○ **Don't confuse the conjunction *and* with the word *to* in an infinitive in American English.**

Many people substitute *and* for *to* in an infinitive preceded by *try* or *come*. For example, they might write, *I'll try and do it* or *He'll come and work*. Although the English poet John Milton used the idiom *try and* in the 17th century, most editors incorrectly think the phrase a modern illiteracy and insist you write *try to*. *Try and* is the way it's said still today in England, but you should avoid it in American media writing.

○ **Infinitives may be used as nouns (*To eat* is *to live*), adjectives (*The issue to be argued is a complex one*) or adverbs (*He went to visit his mother*).**

Although an infinitive is never used in a sentence as a verb by itself, it can be part of a verb phrase, with or without the *to*: *He was supposed to leave today. I may leave, also.*

○ **When the infinitive *to be* is part of a linking verb, as in *believed to be* or *thought to be*, a pronoun following it should be in the nominative case, although this construction is rare in conversation:**

The benefactor *was believed to be* she.

○ **It's still generally considered bad grammar to split an infinitive—to put another word between the *to* and the verb—except where not doing so would sound too awkward. (See Pages 114–15.) But there is no problem with a helping verb between the *to* and the main verb of the past-tense infinitive:**

to *be* completed

to *have* read

to *have* loved

CHAPTER 5

Making the Parts Agree

For sentences to be grammatical and clear, it's important the words agree with each other. These are the three main ways they must do this:

- Each subject and its verb must agree in *number* (singular or plural).

- Each pronoun must agree with its *antecedent*—the noun it replaces—in number, gender (male, female or neuter) and person (first, second or third).

- Each word, phrase or clause in a series must be stated in *parallel*—similar—wording.

SUBJECT-VERB AGREEMENT

Subject-verb agreement problems are some of the most common ways sentences go wrong. A singular subject needs a singular verb, and a plural subject needs a plural verb. Although that sounds easy enough, some situations can be tricky. Here are some likely sources of trouble.

Conjunctions

A *conjunction* connects words, phrases or clauses. We will discuss conjunctions in greater detail in Chapter 6.

- *And* connecting two or more items in a subject usually makes the verb plural. The exception is when the words connected by *and* are part of a single thing:

    Larson and Shichtman *oppose* the bill.
    [plural subject (*Larson and Shichtman*), plural verb]

    Pork and beans *is* not exactly the chef's favorite dish.
    [The subject *Pork and beans* refers to a single dish, so the verb is singular.]

- *Or* used alone to connect two or more items in a subject makes the verb singular unless one of the items is plural. Then, the verb agrees with the nearest noun or pronoun:

    Mary Teagate or *Phil Anderson is* answering calls today.

    Mary Teagate or *her colleagues are* answering calls today.

- The number of the subject is not affected by parenthetical words, phrases or clauses that are set off by commas—such as those starting with *along with, as well as, in addition to, including, such as* or *together with*:

    Blaylock, as well as they, *is* voting in favor of annexation.

- When the correlative conjunctions *not only . . . but also* are used, the following verb should agree with the nearer subject, and there should not be a comma before the *but also*:

    Not only Mark but also his sister *has* won a scholarship.
    [There is only one clause here, so there's no comma before *but also* and the verb is singular.]

    But if *not only . . . but also* connect a dependent and an independent clause, the verb following *but also* should agree with the subject of the independent clause:

    Not only has Mark won a scholarship, but also so *has* his sister.
    [There are two clauses here, a dependent one introduced by *Not only* and an independent one introduced by *but also*. So, there is a comma before *but also*, and the verb following it agrees with the singular subject of the independent clause, *sister*.]

Collective and Uncountable Nouns

Collective nouns are singular in form but plural in meaning. When it comes to verb agreement, form trumps meaning, and collective nouns generally take singular verbs in American English.

Collective nouns include *army, assembly, audience, board, breed, cast, choir, class, club, commission, committee, community, company, corporation, council, couple, covey, crew, crowd, department, faculty, family, firm, flock, furniture, gang, group, herd, jury, mob, orchestra, panel, press, public, remainder, staff, team, union* and *U.S.* The names of associations, boards, companies and so on are also considered collective nouns.

- Use a singular verb when the collective noun is being used in the sense of a single group operating together in agreement. Use a plural verb if the noun is used to name a group operating as individuals or in disagreement:

The jury *was* seated. [acting as a unit]

The jury *were* split.

[Sounds odd, but you can't always trust your ear when it comes to traditional grammar. To avoid the obvious ugliness—to American ears, at least—of this sentence, add the word *members* after *jury*, or, better yet, substitute the word *jurors*. But don't add *members* or change *jury* to *jurors* if they're acting in agreement.]

○ **The word *couple*, in particular, is often plural rather than singular.**

Couple is singular when it refers to a unit and plural when it refers to two individual people, as in the rule for other collective nouns.

SINGULAR	A married couple often *pays* more under U.S. tax law than two people living together but filing separately. [The *couple* here is two people acting as a unit, filing jointly.]
PLURAL	A couple *were* holding hands in the park. [The *couple* here refers to two people acting as individuals, holding each other's hands.]

But be careful when deciding whether the two are acting as a unit or separately. As that great copy-editing teacher John Bremner used to point out, if you write that *a couple was married,* then for pronoun consistency, you'd also have to write that *it went on a honeymoon but had a falling out, and it later divorced.* It would have been better originally to treat the couple getting married as two separate people rather than as a unit acting together.

○ *Uncountable* (also called *noncountable*) *nouns* are nouns that have no plural, although many of them look plural already. They are not so consistent as collective nouns in that some take a singular verb, some a plural.

Journalism Tip
Groups of People in the News

Many news stories focus on meetings of and actions by groups of people—boards, commissions, committees, councils and juries, for example. Remember, although each of these collective nouns names a number of people, the noun itself is considered singular for both verb and pronoun agreement:

WRONG	The City Council *are* holding *their* next meeting at a working retreat.
RIGHT	The City Council *is* holding *its* next meeting at a working retreat.

> ## ESL Tip
>
> In British English, collective nouns are typically plural, even when American English treats them as singular:
>
> **BRITISH**   The government *have* cracked down on terrorists.
>
> **AMERICAN**   The government *has* cracked down on terrorists.
>
> If you're writing for American media but are used to the British approach, you'll need to adjust your usage.

○ These uncountable nouns take a singular verb: *advice, apparatus, athletics, civics, courage, economics, fun, health, information, jazz, kudos, linguistics, mathematics, measles, mumps, news, remainder, shambles, summons* and *whereabouts.*

○ These uncountable nouns take a plural verb: *assets, barracks, earnings, goods, odds, pants, pliers, proceeds, remains, riches, scissors, shears, tactics, thanks, tongs* and *wages.*

○ These uncountable nouns may take a singular or plural verb depending on the context: *ethics, gross, headquarters, mechanics, politics, savings, series, species* and *statistics.* Often, why one of these words is singular in one place, plural in another cannot be easily explained other than as idiomatic use:

    Politics *is* her favorite subject.

    Her politics *are* socialistic.

Names of Teams and Musical Groups

We think names of teams and musical groups should logically be treated as singular if the name is singular, plural if the name is plural:

    The Kansas City Royals *are* playing the Detroit Tigers on Friday.

    Manchester United *is* playing Barcelona for the cup.

    The Beatles *were* his biggest influence.

    ZZ Top *was* his favorite Southern rock band.

But the AP Stylebook has a different idea in its sports section's entry on collective nouns. It says singular team names, such as the Jazz, the Magic and the Avalanche, should take plural verbs. It's silent on the issue of musical groups. If your paper uses the AP Stylebook, as most American publications do, we suggest following its advice for teams, ours for bands unless your publication has its own rule for them. (For example, note that Rolling Stone magazine uses plural verbs with singular band names: "The Clash *were* very much dependent on the band chemistry. . . ." [italics added].)

Other Confusing Nouns

○ Don't mistake plural nouns ending in *a* with their singular forms ending in *on* or *um*. *Criteria*, *data* and *media* are plural, not singular. (For examples, see Pages 44–45.)

○ Units of measurement, such as distances, money, time and weight, take a singular verb even though they are plural in form when referring to a single amount rather than the units of measurement individually:

> Five dollars *is* not too much to ask of a friend.

○ In American usage, *number* and *total* are usually singular if preceded by *the*, plural if preceded by *a*:

> *The number* of people expected *is* small.
>
> *A total* of 50 people *are* expected to attend.

○ According to the entry for *majority* in the AP Stylebook, *majority* and *plurality* are singular by themselves but may be either singular or plural when followed by *of*, depending on the sense of the sentence:

> SINGULAR   "A majority of two votes is not adequate to control the committee."
>
> PLURAL   "The majority of the houses on the block were destroyed."

○ We would suggest the same rule should apply for nouns like *abundance*, *array*, *cornucopia*, *myriad* and *variety*, which are normally not considered collective nouns but which are also singular in form, although they describe a plural number:

> SINGULAR   A variety *is* available.
>
> SINGULAR   A variety of choices *is* not possible under these conditions.
>
> PLURAL   A variety of choices *are* available.

○ Fractions and percentages are singular or plural, depending on the noun or pronoun following them:

> One-third of the *book is* a flashback.
>
> One-third of the *customers are* regulars.

Fifty percent of the *budget is* for debt retirement.

Fifty percent of the *cases are* cured.

This is not an exception to the rule that a verb agrees in number with its subject rather than agreeing with something that comes between them like a prepositional phrase (see Pages 90–91). Instead, as with the examples on Page 88 on the correct use of *majority*, fractions and percentages can be either singular or plural depending on the sense of the sentence. But whereas the number of an object of a preposition after *majority* or *plurality* is not a reliable indicator in itself of the sense, the number of the object of a preposition after a fraction or percentage is.

Indefinite Pronouns

○ *Both*, *few*, *many*, *others* and *several* are plural:

Many *were* inspired by the candidacy of Barack Obama in 2008.

○ *Another*, *anybody*, *anyone*, *anything*, *each one*, *either*, *everybody*, *everyone*, *everything*, *little*, *many a*, *more than one*, *much*, *neither*, *nobody*, *no one*, *nothing*, *other*, *somebody*, *someone* and *something* are singular, even though some of those words seem to refer to more than one:

More than one *has* deplored the situation.

○ *All*, *any*, *each*, *more*, *most*, *none*, *plenty*, *some* and *such* can be either singular or plural depending on the context:

All *are* here.

All *is* lost.

Some *are* coming.

Some *is* left.

○ Make *none* singular if it means "no one" or "not one" (which it means most of the time), plural if the sense is "no two" or "no amount":

None of the people invited *has* arrived. [not one]

None of the experts *agree*. [no two]

This is the rule the AP Stylebook follows, despite common usage of most Americans to make *none* always plural and despite the pleas of many authorities—including Theodore Bernstein, Bergen Evans, and William and Mary Morris—that *none* is more often plural than singular.

The UPI Stylebook, though, says that *none* can be either singular or plural provided any related pronoun agrees, as in these two examples it cites:

RIGHT   "None *are* so blind as *those* who will not see."

RIGHT   "None *is* so blind as *he* who will not see."

○ *Each* is singular:

Each is going by car.

They *are each* going by car.
[Here the real subject is *They*, not *each*. Don't write "They *each are* going by car."]

○ *Either* and *neither* used by themselves are singular pronouns:

Neither of them ~~have~~ *has* been found.

Either of the two ~~offer~~ *offers* law-enforcement experience.

○ In the constructions *either . . . or* and *neither . . . nor*, the words are used as conjunctions, not pronouns. The verb following them is singular or plural, depending on whether the noun or pronoun following the *or* or *nor* is singular or plural:

Neither his parents nor *John is* sure what happened next.

Neither John nor his *parents are* sure what happened next.

Intervening Nouns and Pronouns

○ If a noun or pronoun comes between the subject and the verb, the verb still agrees with the subject, not with the intervening noun or pronoun:

Wednesday's *newspaper*, along with its supplements, *is* our biggest edition ever.
[The subject is the singular noun *newspaper*. The phrase *along with its supplements* is a parenthetical modifier, so the plural noun *supplements* does not influence the number of the verb.]

Prepositional Phrases

○ If a subject contains a prepositional phrase, the noun or pronoun following the preposition is almost never the actual subject, so the verb instead agrees with the noun or pronoun before the preposition:

Three *trees* in the garden *were* blown over.

● But if a phrase beginning with *one of the*, *one of these* or *one of those* is followed by a relative clause, the relative pronoun (*who*, *which* or *that*) that is the subject of the dependent clause takes as its antecedent the noun or pronoun following *of*:

> She is one of those *people* who *are* always on time.
> [Because the plural *people* is the antecedent of *who*, *who* is also plural: Of the people who are always on time, she is one.]
>
> One of those *solutions* that *are* cheap looks good.
> [Because the plural *solutions* is the antecedent of *that*, *that* is also plural: Of those solutions that are cheap, one looks good.]

● If the *one* in such a construction is preceded by *only*, *one* is usually the antecedent, and the construction becomes singular again:

> She is the *only one* of those people who *is* always on time.
> [She's the only one who is on time.]

But there is an exception to this rule:

> *Only one* of those solutions that *are* cheap *looks* good.
> [*One* is the subject here of *looks*, so *one . . . looks good*. But the antecedent of the relative pronoun *that* is solutions, so *solutions that are cheap*.]

Subject and Predicate Nominative in Disagreement

When the subject is plural and the predicate nominative is singular, or vice versa, many people are unsure what the number of the verb should be.

● The number of the verb should always agree with the number of the subject. Both of the following sentences, therefore, are correct:

> The committee *is* Ernie Havens, Ruth Brent and Bree Oliver.
>
> Ernie Havens, Ruth Brent and Bree Oliver *are* the committee.

Inverted Order

Although the subject precedes the verb in most sentences, the subject in some sentences follows the verb. This inverted order occurs most often in questions and causes little confusion. But here are a couple of other situations in which subject-verb agreement problems arise as a result of subjects following verbs.

Making the Parts Agree

○ In a sentence beginning with *here* or *there*, the verb agrees with the number of the subject, which follows the verb:

> *are*
> Here ⟨is⟩ the *answers* to Sunday's crossword.

> *are*
> There ⟨is⟩ no two *ways* about it.

○ Don't write stilted sentences with inverted word order. They sound awkward and can sometimes result in confusion about subject-verb agreement:

WRONG	From the mouths of fools sometimes *come* wisdom.
STILTED	From the mouths of fools sometimes *comes* wisdom.
BETTER	Wisdom sometimes *comes* from the mouths of fools.

> **ONLINE GRAMMAR HELP**
> bedfordstmartins.com/newscentral
>
> For practice using agreement between subjects and verbs, log on to *Exercise Central for AP Style* and go to **No. 16. Lack of agreement between subject and verb**.

MAKING PRONOUNS AND ANTECEDENTS AGREE

Just as verbs have to agree with their subject, pronouns have to agree with the noun to which they refer—their *antecedents*—in number, gender and person.

Some of the same issues that cause difficulty in knowing whether a subject is singular or plural can occur when you are choosing the right number for a pronoun: Collective nouns, uncountable nouns and indefinite pronouns are often the culprits. So, to make pronouns and antecedents agree, it's important to master subject-verb agreement, as well.

Pronoun-Antecedent Agreement

Here are a few of the most common problems with pronoun-antecedent agreement:

○ Don't refer to a collective noun that represents a business, a government, an association or other group as *they*, *their* or *theirs* but rather as *it* or *its*:

> *its*
> The City Council gave ⟨their⟩ approval.

○ Despite common spoken American English, do not use *they*, *their* or *theirs* to refer to a singular antecedent that could be either male or female:

WRONG	*A reporter* should check *their* facts.
RIGHT BUT SEXIST	*A reporter* should check *his* facts.
RIGHT BUT WORDY	*A reporter* should check *his or her* [or worse, *his/her*] facts.
RIGHT	*Reporters* should check *their* facts. [Make the whole thing plural.]

For more on gender bias in language, see Chapter 13.

○ When *one* is the antecedent, the pronoun following should be *one* again, not *he* or *you* unless both are changed to agree:

One does what you have to do. [*one has*]

One should be prepared because *you* never know who might call. [*You*]

[person of subjects not balanced]

○ After *neither . . . nor*, the pronoun must agree with the number—and we would suggest also the gender to be logical and nonsexist—of the noun that follows *nor*:

> ONLINE GRAMMAR HELP
> bedfordstmartins.com/newscentral
> For practice using pronoun agreement, log on to *Exercise Central for AP Style* and go to **No. 14. Lack of agreement between pronoun and antecedent**.

Neither Frank nor Jennifer would do *her* [not *his* or *their*] part.

Better yet, rewrite the sentence to avoid this awkward construction.

Clear Pronoun Reference

○ Make sure it's clear to which noun a pronoun refers. Try repeating the antecedent or otherwise rewriting the sentence:

CONFUSING The man spoke loudly because he was hard of hearing—which practically drove his wife crazy.
[What drove the woman crazy? Her husband's loud speaking or his hearing problem? The antecedent of *which* is unclear.]

CLEAR The man spoke loudly because he was hard of hearing, but the noise practically drove his wife crazy.

CONFUSING Juanita's mother died when she was 30.
[Who was 30? Juanita or her mother?]

CLEAR When Juanita was 30, her mother died.

CLEAR Juanita's mother died at 30.

POSSIBLY CONFUSING   The Senate passed the bill when it voted on it. [Readers would probably understand that sentence, but why make them work at it?]

CLEAR   The Senate passed the bill.

In his book "Less Than Words Can Say," Richard Mitchell cites this sentence from a Department of Transportation manual: "If a guest becomes intoxicated, take his or her keys and send them home in a taxi." Are we to call a cab for the keys or the guest? Because *guest* is singular and *keys* plural, *them* must grammatically refer to *keys*. But many people incorrectly use *them* in a situation referring to a man or a woman.

How about this instead? *If a guest becomes intoxicated, take the car keys and send the person home in a taxi.* We added the word *car* in front of *keys* because how would the person get in the door if you took the house key, too?

⬤ It's usually best not to use a pronoun before you introduce the noun to which it refers:

POSSIBLY CONFUSING   If he loses the race, Paul Bennett says, he won't return to his district.

BETTER   Paul Bennett says that if he loses the race, he won't return to his district.

MAKING SENTENCES PARALLEL

When parallel ideas are not expressed in a parallel manner, the rhythm of the sentence is thrown off, and the logical relationships are muddied.

Make Items in a Series Parallel

⬤ To make ideas parallel, similar items should be written in similar ways. For example, the items in a series should be alike, whether all nouns, all gerunds, all infinitives, all phrases or all clauses. A series of verbs should all be in the same tense, voice and mood, except in instances such as flashbacks or flash-forwards, in which a change in time is clearly intended:

WRONG   He admires Kathy for her intelligence, energy and because she is a good leader.
[The nouns *intelligence* and *energy* are out of balance with the clause *because she is a good leader.*]

RIGHT   He admires Kathy for her intelligence, energy and leadership.

WRONG   The fishing equipment cost as much or more than a bicycle. [The conjunctions are not balanced because part of one is missing.]

RIGHT   The fishing equipment cost as much *as* or more than a bicycle.

Make Verbs Parallel

○ Verbs in a sentence or longer piece of writing should agree with each other in tense unless you have a reason to shift to a different time period:

WRONG   First, he walked in, then he smiled, and then he *says,* "Hello." [Past and present tenses of the verbs are mixed.]

RIGHT   First, he walked in, then he smiled, and then he *said,* "Hello."

RIGHT   I work in Detroit now, but last year I worked in Chicago. [The verb tenses change because they describe different times.]

○ Verbs should agree with each other in voice and not needlessly shift from active to passive:

WRONG   She *was presented* [passive voice] the award and then *left* [active voice].

RIGHT   She accepted the award and then left.

○ The mood of the verbs should be as consistent as possible.

WRONG   Read the book, and then you should complete the exercises. [The first clause is in the imperative mood, the second in the conditional.]

RIGHT   Read the book, then complete the exercises.

RIGHT   You should read the book, and then you should complete the exercises.

Of course, it's normal for the conditional to accompany the subjunctive in multiclause sentences. (See Pages 79–81.)

CHAPTER 6

Modifiers and Connecting Words

Five of the eight traditional parts of speech fall into two categories: modifiers and connecting words. Adjectives, adverbs and interjections are *modifiers*, and prepositions and conjunctions are *connecting words*. And yet, there's not nearly so much to learn about these as about nouns, pronouns and verbs.

○ *Modifiers* are words that describe or limit subjects, objects or verbs. They provide details.

○ *Connecting words* join together parts of a sentence.

MODIFIERS

○ An *adjective* modifies a noun or its substitute by telling how many, what kind, which or whose:

    red balloon, *short* dog, *superior* medicine, *good* job

○ An *adverb* typically modifies a verb, an adjective or another adverb, generally by telling how, when, where, to what degree or extent, or how much:

    turning *slowly*, *extremely* stupid, *rarely* seen

In addition to these main uses, an adverb may sometimes modify a verbal (participle, gerund or infinitive), preposition, conjunction or clause:

    completely drunken sailor [modifying participle *drunken*]

    boldly go [modifying infinitive *go*]

    Frankly, I don't care. [modifying the clause]

○ An *interjection* expresses an emotional outburst. It may stand alone, modifying an implied sentence, or it may appear at the beginning of a sentence it modifies. The interjection is punctuated with an exclamation point when it stands alone, or with a comma when followed by the sentence it modifies:

Ouch!

Ouch! That hurts!

Ouch, that hurts!

○ A *participle* is a form of a verb, usually ending in *ing, ed, t* or *en,* that is used as an adjective:

Add one *beaten* egg. [adjective modifying *egg*]

Finishing a doctoral degree, she found she had little time for her personal life. [participial phrase acting as an adjective modifying *she*]

Participles also are used in making verb tenses and progressive forms of the verb. In this case, they function as part of the verb itself:

The president *is considering* a veto of the bill.

○ An *infinitive* is a form of a verb preceded by *to.* It may be used in place of a noun, an adjective or an adverb:

To win would be a long shot. [infinitive acting as a noun]

It was a good day *to run.* [adjective modifying the noun *day*]

That's unlikely *to happen,* she said. [adverb modifying adjective *unlikely*]

○ A *predicate adjective* is an adjective that follows a linking verb and describes the subject:

The bridge seems *unsafe.* [linking verb: *seems*]

He felt *small,* he said, in the presence of the basketball stars. [linking verb: *felt*]

○ A *noun of direct address* modifies the sentence by naming the person to whom a statement is addressed:

Tom, can you hear me?

Here it is, *Shirley.*

○ An *appositive* is a word or phrase that follows a noun or one of its substitutes and modifies it by renaming it. Although appositives act as adjectives, an appositive could replace the noun it modifies:

The runner, *Gustav,* sat on the ground doing yoga stretches to warm up.

His house—*the one without a roof*—is for sale.

Forms of Adjectives and Adverbs

Most adjectives and adverbs have three forms that show comparison: the *positive*, the basic form of an adjective or adverb that implies no comparison; the *comparative*, the form used in comparisons of two items or groups; and the *superlative*, the form used in comparisons involving more than two items or groups. Some adverbs have only the positive form.

○ For most short adjectives, to make the comparative form, add *er* to the end of the positive form or *less* as a separate word in front of the positive form. To make the superlative form, add *est* to the end of the positive form or *least* as a separate word in front of the positive form:

> tall [positive]
>
> taller *or* less tall [comparative]
>
> tallest *or* least tall [superlative]

○ For most longer adjectives, add the word *more* or *less* in front of the positive form to make the comparative and *most* or *least* in front of the positive to make the superlative:

> beautiful [positive]
>
> more beautiful *or* less beautiful [comparative]
>
> most beautiful *or* least beautiful [superlative]

Two main exceptions are *good, better* and *best,* and *bad, worse* and *worst.*

○ To form most adverbs, add *ly* to the end of the positive form of an adjective. This *ly* form is then the positive form of the adverb. Form the comparative by putting the word *more* or *less* in front of the positive form, and the superlative by putting the word *most* or *least* in front of the positive form:

> quick [adjective]
>
> quickly [positive form of the adverb]
>
> more quickly *or* less quickly [comparative form of the adverb]
>
> most quickly *or* least quickly [superlative form of the adverb]

○ **Don't confuse the comparative and superlative forms.**

Don't say someone is "the *oldest* of the two brothers." If there are only two, he's the *older.*

Also, sometimes writers list several items and then refer to *the latter one.* But *latter,* like *former,* should be used only when two items have been listed. That's because they are comparative, not superlative, forms. *Last* and *first* are called for, instead, in such cases.

⬤ Don't include more items than intended in a comparison by leaving out the word *else* when it's needed:

> *else*
> The new reporter is *faster than anyone on the staff.*
>
> [Assuming the new reporter is also on the staff, he or she cannot be "faster than anyone on the staff" because the staff includes this reporter.]

⬤ Don't use comparative or superlative forms with modifiers referring to something absolute.

Something cannot be *more unique* than something else because *unique* means "one of a kind." Something is either one of a kind or it isn't. Likewise, something cannot be *most unique, rather unique, somewhat unique* or *very unique.* Another word that should not be used with comparatives is *perfect,* contrary to the famous phrase in the Preamble to the Constitution "in Order to form a more perfect Union." Still others include *complete, limitless* and *square.*

Adjectives Versus Adverbs

⬤ Use adjectives to modify nouns or pronouns. Use adverbs to modify verbs, adjectives or other adverbs.

⬤ Don't mistakenly use an adjective when an adverb is required to describe the manner in which something happens:

> *smoothly*
> The microbrew is noted for going down ~~smooth.~~
>
> *more quickly*
> The sports car brakes ~~quicker~~ than the sedan.

⬤ Don't confuse a predicate adjective with an adverb. Linking verbs—such as *appear, be, become, feel, grow, look, seem, smell, sound, taste* and *wax*—take a predicate adjective rather than an adverb as a modifier. The predicate adjective follows the linking verb and refers back to the subject:

> *poetic*
> He waxed ~~poetically.~~

⬤ Some intransitive verbs in some uses may be *linking verbs* and take a predicate adjective, but in other uses they may be

> ## ESL Tip
>
> Speakers of English as a second language should note that English modifiers other than predicate adjectives and appositives usually come *before* the word modified, contrary to the usage in a number of other languages. There are also sentences in English where the modifier may follow what it describes, but when in doubt, try putting the modifier before the word modified.

complete verbs or *transitive verbs* (see Pages 58–60) and be followed by an adverb:

> He says it feels *good* to be alive.
> [*Feels* is a linking verb here and is followed by the predicate adjective *good*, which modifies the subject *it*. The word *good* is an adjective, so you use it after a linking verb.]

> The sculptor said her hands cannot feel the clay *well* with heavy gloves on.
> [*Well* is an adverb modifying the transitive verb *feel*. If you want to describe the action of touching rather than the clay, you should use the adverb *well*.]

> The patient feels *well* enough to be discharged.
> [*Feels* here is a linking verb, and the predicate adjective *well* modifies the subject *patient*. When *well* describes someone's health, it's an adjective.]

Consider this sentence: *The thunder sounded* [*loud* or *loudly*]. To choose between an adjective and an adverb, decide whether the subject is acting. If the sentence means the thunder *clapped* (acted), then it sounded *loudly* (adverb). If it means the thunder *was* (being) loud, then it sounded *loud* (adjective).

So, a flower smells *sweet*, not *sweetly*, because the flower is not acting, just being—it has no nose with which to smell. Likewise, you wax (linking verb) *poetic*, but you wax (transitive verb) *carefully* your car.

> **ONLINE GRAMMAR HELP**
> bedfordstmartins.com/newscentral
>
> For practice deciding between adverbs and adjectives, log on to *Exercise Central for AP Style* and go to **No. 17. Incorrect complement with linking verb**.

Coordinate Adjectives Versus Compound Modifiers

Many times, a pair of modifiers precedes a noun or pronoun. Such modifiers usually work either as *coordinate adjectives* or as *compound modifiers*.

○ *Coordinate adjectives* are adjectives equal in importance. You can recognize them by this test: If you reverse their order, they still sound right.

The *long, narrow* passage was hard to navigate.

[*Long* and *narrow* are coordinate adjectives because you could write them as *narrow, long.*]

ONLINE GRAMMAR HELP
bedfordstmartins.com/newscentral

For practice placing commas between coordinate adjectives, log on to *Exercise Central for AP Style* and go to **No. 7. Missing comma(s) between coordinate adjectives**.

Notice that coordinate adjectives are punctuated with a comma unless there is an *and* between them.

◯ We suggest systematically *not* placing a comma between adjectives when one or more of them refers to number, color, age, material, ethnicity, nationality or race:

> *three pink* flamingos [number and color]
>
> *old silk* dress [age and material]
>
> *tall Hispanic* male [ethnicity]
>
> *healthy Italian* man [nationality]
>
> *intelligent African-American* woman [race]

These exceptions are based on three problems:

- In the case of number, reversing the two adjectives won't work grammatically.

- In the cases of ethnicity, nationality and race, common professional usage follows the practice of positioning these adjectives right before the noun.

- In the cases of color, age and material, we suggest these exceptions because people tend to disagree about the results of the coordinate adjective reversal test when one of these is in the phrase. It's better just to agree not to put the comma there than to argue about it.

Also, note that although these categories are exceptions to putting a comma between modifiers, they do not necessarily imply that no hyphen might be required:

> *light-blue* sky
>
> *Polish-American* hero

◯ *Compound modifiers* are pairs of words in which the first word, no matter what part of speech it normally is, modifies the second word. Together, the two then modify the noun or pronoun that follows:

> *well-intentioned* friend
>
> *oil-depletion* allowance

◯ Use a hyphen between compound modifiers that precede the word they modify:

> Price is an *out-of-state* athlete.

Remember that this rule applies only to modifiers that precede the word modified. Compare:

> She was a *part-time* worker.
> [*Part-time* precedes the word it modifies, the noun *worker*.]
>
> She worked *part time*.
> [*Part time* follows the word it modifies, the verb *worked*.]

ONLINE GRAMMAR HELP
bedfordstmartins.com/newscentral

For practice using hyphens between compound modifiers, log on to *Exercise Central for AP Style* and go to **No. 11. Missing or misused hyphen(s) in a compound modifier.**

◯ The hyphen is usually retained, however, in a compound adjective that follows a linking verb — in other words, if the compound is a predicate adjective:

> The work was *part-time*.
>
> The object floating in the sky appeared *saucer-shaped*.

◯ Sometimes, however, the hyphen will be dropped, especially if the sentence continues past the predicate adjective. Compare:

> The *better-qualified* candidate was Sally.
> [The compound adjective needs the hyphen.]
>
> Sally was *better-qualified*.
> [Some would drop the hyphen here, but we suggest retaining it to minimize confusion.]
>
> Sally was *better qualified* than the other applicant.
> [This sentence is clear without the hyphen.]

◯ Do not use a hyphen after *less, least, many, most, very* or an adverb ending in *ly*:

> They had a *very enjoyable* trip.
>
> This is an *easily remembered* rule.

◯ Use a hyphen in a compound modifier after any word ending in *ly* other than an adverb, such as the adjectives *friendly, likely, seemly, surly, timely* and *ugly* or the noun *family*:

> He described it as a *"friendly-service"* company.
>
> Doctorian's is a *family-owned* business.

◯ Ages are not hyphenated in a predicate adjective:

> He is *4 years old*.
> [The AP Stylebook does not hyphenate an age when it's a predicate adjective despite the fact that other compound predicate adjectives normally *are* hyphenated.]

Journalism Tip
Compound Modifiers Without Hyphens

Despite these rules, some phrases are not hyphenated because of either the rules in the AP Stylebook or common professional practice.

○ According to AP style, the following modifying phrases should not be hyphenated:

administrative law judge	*search engine* optimization
air force base	*social media* optimization
birth control pill	*standing room* only
blue chip stock	*stock index* futures
data processing entry	*stock market* prices
full faith and credit bond	*wholesale price* index
general obligation bond	*winter storm* warning
health care center	*winter storm* watch
moral obligation bond	*word processing* program
savings and loan associations	

○ The following modifying phrases are not listed in stylebooks or dictionaries, but it is common professional practice to use them without a hyphen:

gasoline [or *income*] *tax* increase
high school cheerleader [but *middle-school* teacher]

He is a *4-year-old boy*.
[The compound adjective *4-year-old* modifies the predicate nominative, *boy*. Therefore, *4-year-old boy* is hyphenated.]

○ The AP Stylebook and Webster's New World College Dictionary say some words are always hyphenated as compound modifiers, such as *old-fashioned* and words beginning with *well*:

He took pride in being *old-fashioned*.

Henry, *well-dressed* as always, caught everyone's attention.

Articles

○ *Articles* are the adjectives *the*, *a* and *an*. *The* is called the *definite article* and indicates a particular, unique item. *A* and *an* are called *indefinite articles* and indicate a particular item from a number of similar items. *A* is used before a word that begins with a consonant sound. *An* is used before a word that begins with a vowel sound.

a history book

a
~~*an*~~ historical event

an owl

an hour

If an indefinite article precedes an abbreviation, remember to choose between *a* and *an* by the first sound of the abbreviation, not the letter itself: *a UFO*, not *an UFO*, because the first sound is of a consonant: *yoo-eff-oh*.

The articles do not have comparative forms, and, for that reason, some grammarians treat them as a separate part of speech rather than as adjectives.

Sentence Adverbs

○ *Sentence adverbs (frankly, hopefully, personally, regrettably, sincerely, strictly speaking, to be honest)* modify the whole sentence of which they are a part rather than a particular word.

The most controversial sentence adverb is *hopefully*. Although many experts think it is ungrammatical to begin a sentence with *hopefully*, others have defended the word as a sentence adverb no better or worse than any other.

One common objection to the use of the word is that it is not clear who is doing the hoping in a sentence such as "*Hopefully*, it won't snow today." But nobody seems to be bothered by that with any sentence adverb other than *hopefully*: "*Strictly speaking*, you shouldn't misuse *hopefully*."

Perhaps a better argument against *hopefully* used in this way is that the word means "in a hopeful manner." But a sentence such as *Hopefully, it won't snow today* doesn't mean *It won't snow today in a hopeful manner* but rather *I hope it won't snow today*. So, using *hopefully* in this way isn't true to what the word means and in journalism would seem to imply an opinion by the reporter who otherwise may not be in the story.

But language changes, and as words are used more often in certain ways, their use in those ways becomes more acceptable to language experts, who at some point decide they're fighting a losing battle. This has happened with *hopefully* now for both the American Heritage Dicionary's usage panel and more recently AP.

○ Despite those who have said never to use *hopefully* at all, it should always have been acceptable in place of "in a hopeful manner." And although you may still find resistance to its use in place of "I hope" or "it is hoped," you now have AP's OK to use it that way, too.

Participles

We've already seen how *participles* (a verb form usually ending in *ing*, *ed*, *t* or *en*) are used in making verb tenses and progressive forms. (See Pages 60–63.)

○ The other major use for participles is as adjectives:

Talking, they reached an agreement. [*Talking* describes *they*.]

The *frightened* victim was *hurt*. [*Frightened* and *hurt* describe *victim*.]

Lawyers gathered *written* statements from the witnesses. [*Written* describes *statements*.]

○ Participles are also used occasionally as prepositions or conjunctions, as in the case of *excepting*, *including* and *regarding*:

All were right, *excepting* the last one. [as conjunction]

Regarding that, we'll have to wait. [as preposition]

Double Negatives

○ Avoid double negatives such as *not never*, *not no*, *not none* and *not nothing*.

○ The adverbs *hardly*, *rarely* and *scarcely* are also considered negative and do not take a *not*:

He ~~can't~~ hardly write. [*can* inserted above]

○ The word *but*, which is normally a conjunction, is sometimes used as an adverb, and it, too, is considered negative and doesn't take a *not*:

She ~~doesn't have~~ but one friend, she said. [*has* inserted above]

○ The prefixes *im*, *in*, *ir*, *non* and *un* make adjectives negative. Negative adjectives may be used with negative adverbs, but it is often clearer to rewrite them more positively:

ACCEPTABLE   It is *not improbable* that Margaret Thatcher will go down in history as one of the greatest British prime ministers.

CLEARER   Margaret Thatcher may go down in history as one of the greatest British prime ministers.

Modifiers and Connecting Words

Interjections

○ An *interjection* is an exclamation expressing strong emotion: *Ah! Ouch!* Interjections can stand alone or be used to modify entire sentences: *Ouch, that hurts!*

Not all grammarians consider interjections to be modifiers. In fact, many books say interjections don't have a grammatical connection to other words in a sentence. We disagree.

Although often used alone or set off from the rest of the sentence it modifies by an exclamation point, an interjection also may be connected to the beginning of the sentence by a comma. Written this way—which is common because journalists don't like to use exclamation points—interjections work like sentence adverbs, modifying the entire sentence.

Grammarians who consider them adverbs reason that interjections don't have the comparative forms of other adverbs, but then neither do the adverbs *no* or *yes*.

Note that other parts of speech, such as the verb *Damn!* or phrases like *For heaven's sake!* or even whole sentences such as *Damn it all!* can be used as interjections.

In general, the interjection is the part of speech that gives us the least trouble. But a couple of rules are worth noting:

○ Never use more than one exclamation point with an interjection (or anywhere else for that matter).

○ Avoid interjections that use profanity or off-color slang in family publications such as newspapers, unless, as the AP Stylebook says, the words "are part of direct quotations and there is a compelling reason for them."

CONNECTING WORDS

Prepositions, conjunctions and *conjunctive adverbs* are the glue that holds sentences together and makes transitions between ideas possible.

Prepositions

○ A *prepositional phrase* consists of a preposition and the noun or noun substitute that follows it (the *object of the preposition*):

to school, *after* the fall, *toward* the future, *in spite of* it all

○ The preposition shows the relationship between its object and something else in the sentence. Usually, the prepositional phrase acts as either an adjective or adverb:

The computer *with a Blu-ray burner* is more expensive.
[acts as an adjective modifying *computer*]

The suspect was seen running *from the scene* of the crime.
[acts as an adverb modifying *running*]

Prepositions usually indicate direction (*to, toward, over, under, from*) or location (*on, at, beside, near*). To spot most of these types of prepositions, imagine a bird and some trees. Prepositions are those words that describe the relationship the bird could have with the trees as it flies. It could fly *between* the trees, *toward* the trees, *in* the trees, *at* the trees, *from* the trees, *under* the trees, *over* the trees and so on.

Other prepositions show time (*in, at, during, until*), indicate possession (*of, with*), show responsibility (*for*) or agency (*by*), exclude (*except, without*), or show similarity (*like*).

In form, prepositions may be single words (*at, to, from*), compound words (*into, upon*) or phrases (*according to, because of, in accordance with, in spite of, on top of*). Sometimes, as we've seen, participles are also used as conjunctions or prepositions (*excepting, regarding*). (See Page 105.)

○ **Repeat the preposition in parallel prepositional phrases if that helps avoid confusion.**

Some editors insist that parallel prepositional phrases should always be used to repeat the preposition. For example: *The protesters said they were concerned about pollution and about road congestion.* We, however, wouldn't insist on the second *about* in this example because the sentence is clear without it.

Sometimes, though, parallel prepositions help avoid confusion. Notice the lack of parallel prepositions in this sentence: *Obscurantism means opposition to progress or enlightenment.* Does this mean *obscurantism* is enlightenment or opposition to it? If the former, reverse the sentence order: *Obscurantism means enlightenment or opposition to progress.* If it's the latter, add *to* before *enlightenment*: *Obscurantism means opposition to progress or to enlightenment.* (By the way, it's the latter.)

○ **Use prepositions to separate items that might otherwise run together confusingly.**

Usually, this involves proper nouns appearing next to each other: *Ted Winston Sunday said*. . . . In such cases, either put *on* between *Winston* and *Sunday* or rewrite: *Ted Winston said Sunday*. . . .

○ **Try not to end a sentence with a preposition because many editors still object to the practice. But if rewriting the sentence would make it sound awkward or overly formal, we'd say it's better to go ahead and leave the preposition at the end. (See Page 114.)**

Modifiers and Connecting Words

◯ Avoid using *up* as a verb by itself or with a verb when it is not needed for the meaning of the verb itself:

The candidate said she would ~~up~~ the spending on social services. [*increase*]

The EPA spokesman said workers would hurry ~~up~~ the project.

Don't forget to look up any words you're not sure how to spell. [Here, the *up* is necessary because *to look* is to see but *to look up* means to check in a reference.]

Conjunctions

◯ A *conjunction* connects words, phrases or clauses:

this *and* that

Either the city cleans the lake *or* the state will intervene.

It's been two years *since* the war in the region ended.

That was then. *But* today, he had a different story.

Coordinating Conjunctions

◯ *Coordinating conjunctions*—such as *and, but, for, nor, or, so* and *yet*—are used when the words, phrases or clauses they connect are of equal rank. (A convenient mnemonic device for remembering these conjunctions is the acronym BOY FANS.)

How do we know when the words, phrases and clauses are of equal rank? The rule is that a word equals another word (*wine and roses*); a phrase equals another phrase (*to be or not to be*); an independent clause equals another independent clause (*I'm going, and I'm not coming back*); and a dependent clause equals another dependent clause (*He said school desegregation would follow if the court ruled in the group's favor or if the group won enough seats on the board*).

◯ If a coordinating conjunction connects two independent clauses, put a comma before the conjunction:

The judge said he would open the hearing to the press, but he didn't.

Contrary to the belief of some teachers and editors, there's nothing wrong with starting a sentence with a coordinating conjunction—most often *but*.

By definition, in fact, a coordinating conjunction is one that can start an independent clause, a clause that can stand alone as a separate sentence. The coordinating conjunction is acting as a transition linking the independent clause it starts with a previous one, whether the clauses are written as a compound sentence or separate ones. So, for emphasis, you could write *The judge said she would open the hearing to the press. But she didn't.*

Correlative Conjunctions

○ *Correlative conjunctions* are similar to coordinate conjunctions in that they connect words, phrases or clauses of equal rank. The difference is that correlative conjunctions are used in pairs:

Correlative Conjunctions

as . . . as	not only . . . but also
both . . . and	not so . . . as
either . . . or	since . . . therefore
if . . . then	whether . . . or
neither . . . nor	

Most writers know that *either* and *or* go together, as do *neither* and *nor*. Not many media writers, however, seem to know the following:

○ The negative form of *as . . . as* is *not so . . . as*:

It is *as* long *as* it is wide.

It is *not so* long *as* it is wide.

○ *Not only* must be followed by *but also* or *but* or sometimes by a colon or semicolon:

Not only liberals *but also* some conservatives took issue with parts of the bill.

Not only liberals took issue with parts of the bill; some conservatives did, *also*.
[Journalists would tend to avoid this option because they prefer to avoid semicolons.]

Subordinating Conjunctions

○ *Subordinating conjunctions*—such as *although, as, because, if, since, until, whether* and *while*—connect two unequal parts of a sentence.

Most often, these unequal parts are independent and dependent clauses. Subordinate conjunctions typically introduce dependent clauses that modify the independent clause by explaining cause, contrast, reason or time. (See Pages 30–31.)

○ Don't put a comma before a subordinating conjunction, including *because*.

Generally speaking, don't put a comma before a subordinating conjunction. The main dispute is over *because*. Some books insist that a clause introduced by *because* is always preceded by a comma, but media writers put a comma before a conjunction only in the following cases:

- If it introduces an independent clause. (See Page 181.)
- When the meaning could be confusing without it, as when the conjunction follows a negative statement:

> He said he didn't agree, because he was a libertarian.
> [The reason he didn't agree is that he was a libertarian, so put a comma.]

> He said he didn't agree because he was a libertarian.
> [If he did agree, but not because he was a libertarian, leave the comma out.]

Conjunctive Adverbs

Conjunctive adverbs are good transition words because they show a strong logical relationship between the sentences they connect. They're followed by a comma.

Common Conjunctive Adverbs

accordingly	henceforth	nevertheless
also	however	on the contrary
anyhow	in addition	on the other hand
at the same time	indeed	otherwise
besides	instead	so
consequently	in the first place	still
first, second, etc.	likewise	then
for example	meanwhile	therefore
for this reason	moreover	thus
furthermore	most important	
hence	namely	

Unlike conjunctions, which always come at the beginning of the clauses they introduce, conjunctive adverbs can be placed at the beginning, in the middle or at the end of a clause. Another way conjunctive adverbs differ from conjunctions is that, unlike conjunctions, conjunctive adverbs may be used in a compound sentence after a semicolon and introducing an independent clause: *The battle was over; however, all was not still.* But media writers generally avoid this construction because they prefer to avoid semicolons.

CHAPTER 7

Getting Words in the Right Order

Confused words become must may be, readers in or the order correct.

No, that's not a misprint. We just wanted to illustrate our point:

Words must be in the correct order, or readers may become confused.

Of course, no one would intentionally jumble sentences and hope to be understood, but we sometimes unintentionally jumble parts of them. Even if readers can figure out what we mean, why should they have to work at it? Shouldn't our writing just be straightforward and clear?

Sometimes, our jumbled word order may be clear because it's jumbled in a way people often use in conversation. But as we noted in Chapter 1, the rules of written English sometimes differ from those of conversation. In such cases, we should adjust the word order to the rules of written English.

Misplaced Modifiers

The jumbled word order that causes the biggest confusion for readers is a result of misplaced modifiers.

🔵 **Modifiers should be placed as close as possible to the word they modify. When this doesn't happen, we call the often confusing and sometimes comical result a *misplaced modifier*.**

Sometimes, misplaced modifiers merely require a momentary pause to sort them out. For example, TV talk-show hosts often say something like this to a guest: *As a musician, our viewers are probably wondering why you became interested in this issue.*

As we said, it may take only a moment—if that—to realize the speaker didn't mean that the viewers are musicians. But why shouldn't the speaker say what she means?

Jim Quinn cites this example of a misplaced modifier that probably requires of the reader or listener more of a double take: "Lincoln wrote the

111

Gettysburg Address while riding on a train on the back of an envelope." Because everyone probably understands that the train was not on the back of the envelope, that sentence is more humorous than confusing.

But misplaced modifiers don't just result in momentary pauses to grasp the meaning or laughs at a writer's expense. Readers might genuinely be confused by the following sentence: *Facing an indictment on a tax-evasion charge, the mayor fired the public works director.* Who was facing an indictment? The mayor or the director?

> *The mayor, who was facing an indictment on tax-evasion charges,* fired the public works director. [if it was the mayor]

> The mayor fired *the public works director, who was facing an indictment on tax-evasion charges.* [if it was the public works director]

The *dangling participle* is a kind of misplaced modifier that's so common it has its own name.

○ A *participial phrase* (a group of related words beginning with a participle) should be placed next to the word it's modifying. If not, it's called a *dangling participle*—the participle is left dangling next to the wrong word as though it modified that word instead of the one it should.

In the sentence *Marching down the street, he watched the parade,* the placement of the participial phrase suggests that the person watching the parade was marching down the street. Probably, however, he was standing still, and the parade was moving. Note these further examples of dangling participles:

> *Running down the street,* his hat flew off.
> [Literally, that sentence says his hat was running down the street.]

> *Taking our seats,* the meeting began. [The meeting took our seats?]

○ Don't confuse a dangling participle with a *nominative absolute,* which is a noun or its substitute followed by a participial phrase. A nominative absolute modifies the whole sentence rather than a noun or its substitute, so it acts as a *sentence adverb*:

> *The computer having gone down,* the paper was late.
> [*Computer* is a noun, *having* a participle.]

> The Tigers lost, *poor hitting being to blame.*
> [*Hitting* is a gerund, *being* a participle.]

ONLINE GRAMMAR HELP
bedfordstmartins.com/newscentral

For practice recognizing and avoiding dangling participles, log on to *Exercise Central for AP Style* and go to **No. 10. Misplaced or dangling modifier**.

Unlike dangling participles, nominative absolutes are considered grammatical, but sentences with them might still be better rewritten in a more conversational tone:

The paper was late because the computer went down.

The Tigers lost because of poor hitting.

Adverb Placement

○ Adverbs, like adjectives, should be as close as possible to the words they modify:

UNCLEAR   Donald *just* has *one* car.

CLEAR   Donald has *just one* car.

The word *only* poses a particular problem with placement, not only because it's often misplaced but also because writers are seldom aware of how confusing the result can be. Look at this sentence, for example: *Ostroushko only has one of the handmade instruments.* Does that mean he has *only one* or that *only Ostroushko* has one? The sentence should be rewritten for clarity.

○ It's OK to put an adverb in the middle of a verb phrase.

Some writers and editors believe that an adverb should never be placed in the middle of the parts of a compound-tense verb. For example, they would rewrite *The watch was consistently gaining time* as *The watch consistently was gaining time* or *The watch was gaining time consistently.* But several commentators, including Wilson Follett, whose "Modern American Usage" is one of the most quoted usage guides, say the placement of the adverb in such sentences should normally be between the two parts of the verb. Follett also offers this advice on alternative placement of adverbs:

○ For emphasis, put the adverb at the start of the sentence:

Really, I don't want any.

○ If the adverb is not needed for emphasis, put it in front of a single-word verb, between the helping verb and the main verb, or after the first helping verb if there is more than one:

I *really want* some.

I *don't really want* any.

I *had really been wanting* some.

But we would accept as conversational moving *really* in front of the helping verbs in both of the last two examples.

○ If the adverb modifies the participle part of the verb alone, put it after the helping verbs:

> Smoking *has been positively linked* to higher rates of cancer.

○ If the adverb is a phrase, put it after the whole verb:

> We *have heard again and again* the same thing from the city.

Less Confusing Jumbled Word Orders

○ Most editors prefer you not end a sentence with a preposition unless moving it would make the sentence awkward.

The best-known rule about prepositions is not to end a sentence with one. The rule goes back to the 18th-century English grammar books that based their rules on Latin grammar rather than on how the English language actually works. Because Latin words have different endings depending on the role they play in a sentence, words in Latin sentences can be moved around without the meaning of the sentence being changed. An exception is the rule that a Latin sentence cannot end with a preposition.

As famous as the rule, however, is Winston Churchill's rejoinder: "That is the type of arrant pedantry up with which I will not put." The fact is, English speakers have ended sentences with prepositions for hundreds of years, and some sentences, such as Churchill's, sound awkward when they don't end with a preposition. For example: *What are you waiting for?* It just doesn't sound right to most of us as *For what are you waiting?*

Further, even the most prominent 18th-century grammarian, Robert Lowth, wrote that ending a sentence with a preposition "is an idiom, which our language is strongly inclined to: it prevails in common conversation and suits very well with the familiar style in writing."

Still, it's a good idea to avoid the likely objection of your editor and try to rewrite a sentence that ends with a preposition whenever you can do so in a way that sounds conversational. This is usually easy, although some sentences require more effort. For example, *They're fun to add your own touches to* may be a puzzler at first, but some thought might yield, *It's fun to add your own touches to them.*

○ Try to avoid *split infinitives* (putting an adverb between *to* and the verb following it):

SPLIT INFINITIVE   She would like *to quickly make* her mark.

NONSPLIT INFINITIVE   She would like *to make* her mark *quickly*.
[Note that moving an adverb from the middle of an infinitive often means placing it after an object following an infinitive so that it is actually no longer next to the word it modifies.]

SPLIT INFINITIVE   She wants *to not be* disturbed.

NONSPLIT INFINITIVE   She wants *not to be* disturbed.

Because Latin infinitives are one word, the grammarians who wrote the first English grammars in the 18th century decided that English infinitives should not be split. Most journalists today still follow the rule not to split infinitives. Actually, however, people usually split infinitives in conversation, and split infinitives had long been a feature of the language when grammarians invented the rule.

Sometimes, it's nearly impossible to say what we want without splitting an infinitive. Humorist James Thurber was adamant on this point: "When I split an infinitive, it's going to *damn well stay* split." Many grammarians now agree and allow latitude when the writer can't find an acceptable alternative, wants *to strongly stress* a point or is imitating conversation.

In most instances, a conversational alternative can be found to keep the traditionalists happy. But if not, it's better to break this rule than to create an awkward sentence.

○ Avoid *dangling infinitives*—infinitive phrases not next to the words they modify:

WRONG   *To get ahead in this business, the audience* must be kept in mind.
[The phrase *to get ahead in this business* modifies *the audience,* but no doubt the writer meant it to modify *you,* a word that never appears in the sentence. A reader may be able to figure this out, but a dangling infinitive makes the going tougher.]

RIGHT   *To get ahead in this business, you* must keep the audience in mind.

CHAPTER 8

Usage: Finding the Right Word

Mark Twain said finding the right word is the difference between writing *lightning* and *lightning bug*. You need to use the correct word to convey clearly and accurately what you mean.

The writer best known for finding just the right word was the French novelist Gustave Flaubert, who spoke of the importance of *le mot juste*, or the exact word. Canadian media theorist Marshall McLuhan, punning on Flaubert's French, said *le mot juste* is the word that gives your writing "the most juice."

This chapter looks at *usage*—using the right word in a phrase and making proper distinctions among words that are often confused. Using the right word helps you make your point more clearly so that the reader doesn't have to stop and try to figure out whether you really meant, for example, *killing* rather than *murder*.

Usage is largely a matter of vocabulary and familiarity with idiomatic expressions. People tend to use the wrong word either because they don't really know what the word they're using means or because they're using a word in a phrase that's not what native or educated speakers would normally use.

An example of the first problem would be a person's mistakenly using *bemused* ("confused") when he means "slightly amused." An example of the second problem, a distorted idiom, would be a person's writing *heart-rendering* instead of *heartrending*. She's mistakenly replaced *rending*, a verb meaning "pulling"—as in "pulling at one's heart"—with *rendering*, which refers to melting down animal fat or salvaging other meat-processing byproducts.

Errors such as *heart-rendering* seem clear-cut: A word has a meaning, or a phrase a common wording, that a writer or speaker is violating. But when enough people make such errors, the language can change, and what was once wrong now becomes right. All you have to do is browse through the entries in the Oxford English Dictionary to see what we mean. That dictionary is the best source for the history of how the meanings of words have changed in English usage over time.

For example, when the great architect Christopher Wren finished St. Paul's Cathedral in London, King James II of England is said to have paid him three great compliments, calling the work "amusing, artificial and awful." Don't sound like compliments? Three hundred years ago, when he supposedly said it—although the librarian at St. Paul's has been unable to locate the original source for the quote—*amusing* meant "amazing," *artificial* meant "artistic" and *awful* meant "awe-inspiring." Language changes.

It's also sometimes funny, and more than a little humbling, to see how usage experts of years ago railed against words to which no one now objects. For example, Jonathan Swift in the 18th century thought *communication* and *mob* were horrible new words that should be resisted, just as many editors a few decades ago opposed the use of the term *gay* for "homosexual," a usage that is now preferred by the AP Stylebook.

We think it's fine for people who care about language to resist *neologisms*—newly invented words—or new uses for older words when such changes seem ugly or awkward. So, for example, some people resisted the term *senior citizens* because it seemed to them a euphemistic and wordy replacement for *the elderly*. But now the term finds little opposition, although the AP Stylebook still suggests it be used sparingly. But when language changes, eventually stylebooks need to catch up or our publications lose credibility for sounding behind the times.

Journalism Tip

Conservative Stylebook Rules

That people often ignorantly misuse words is a fact. And sometimes yesterday's error is today's accepted wording. The problem lies in trying to figure out where we are in the process with any given error. It's easy to label an individual's idiosyncratic variations from the norm as mistakes, but most of the errors listed in any stylebook or usage dictionary are variations that are widely practiced, or they wouldn't find their way into the book.

For example, almost no native speaker of English uses *lie* to mean "rest." Instead, people tend to use *lay* in daily conversation. Yet, this is widely pointed out in book after book as an error, even though it is almost universally used except in print, where either writers know to use *lie* or editors correct the error.

When we're confronted by nearly universal "misuse" of certain words and phrases and still the majority of stylebooks and usage guides insist on older rules, the language is in the process of changing or has already changed. We also have to admit that something else is going on: a conservative strain among the arbiters making the policies.

Logical or not, agree with them or not, conservative usage rules are a fact of life we live with when we are told to make our copy conform to a particular stylebook. A wise writer or editor should be informed enough both to know the rules and to see through them. As a newer employee, you may not be able to change them, and, in fact, your job might depend on your following them for now. But when you have decision-making power, make rules that make sense as much as your knowledge permits.

> ### ESL Tip
>
> The main reason the English language is difficult for speakers of other languages to master is English's huge vocabulary. It has a number of *homonyms* (words that sound alike), *synonyms* (words that mean the same thing) and near synonyms (words with different shades of meaning), as well as a wealth of *idioms* that require a particular word in a phrase rather than a synonym. Of course, vocabulary and idioms often pose problems for native speakers of English, as well.

The rest of this chapter lists words and phrases that are often misused. Some items in the list are single entries of words and phrases that many people misunderstand or muddle. Some items consist of multiple-entry listings, primarily pairs of words and phrases but sometimes three or more, that either sound alike or seem enough alike in meaning that people confuse them. The multiple-entry items are listed in groups—the words in each group are listed alphabetically, and each group is listed alphabetically by the first word in the group.

Unfortunately, there's not much we can say by way of overall rules to help you remember all this material. Instead, browse these lists to become familiar with what's here. The more you look over the entries, the more points will stick, and the more you'll think to look something up later when you want to use it. Mark the entries that contain distinctions you didn't know. Then concentrate on learning them, perhaps a few a day.

Also, invent associations that can help you remember one item of every pair. For example, if you want to remember the difference between *premier* and *premiere*, you might associate the one that ends with an *e* with *entertainment*—an opening of a movie or play. If the word needed in a certain passage doesn't have to do with an opening, you know it should be *premier*—the word without the *e* at the end.

Misused and Confused Words and Phrases

A

a while   Use as the object of a preposition: *It's been going on for quite a while.* Also used in expressions *a while ago* and *a while back.*
awhile   the general adverb form: *It's been going on awhile.*

abjure   to renounce
adjure   to entreat earnestly

abrogate   to annul
arrogate   to claim unduly

above   Some editors insist this preposition not be used as an adjective, although the AP Stylebook seems to use it that way sometimes.

WRONG   The *above* statement should appear as a warning.

RIGHT   The plane flew *above* the clouds.

abstruse   hard to understand
obtuse   slow at understanding

accede   to agree reluctantly
exceed   to surpass

accelerate   to speed up
exhilarate   to stimulate

accept   to receive
except   prep., but for; to exclude

access   to enter
assess   to evaluate
excess   surplus

accident   To be an accident, an occurrence must be unforeseen, unexpected and unintended. In a legal sense, it must also be the result of no one's fault or negligence. It is not an accident when, for example, a drunken driver's car hits another vehicle.

acetic   sour; acidic
aesthetic   artistic
ascetic   austere

acquiesce (in, to)   to accept, comply or submit tacitly or passively

act   a single thing that's done
action   something done that's made up of more than one act

acute   critical; intense; crucial
chronic   persistent; recurring; prolonged

ad   advertisement
add   to derive a sum

adapt   to adjust
adopt, approve   to accept. You *adopt* or *approve* a resolution.
pass   to enact. You *pass* an ordinance.

addition   something added on; the arithmetic process of making sums
edition   version of a published work

adherence   support for
adherents   supporters

adventuresome   willing to take risks
adventurous   fond of adventure

adverse   unfavorable. Things are *adverse*.
averse   opposed. People are *averse* to things.

advice   noun
advise   verb

affect v., to influence or produce a change in. Avoid as a noun, except in psychology to describe an emotion.

effect n., result; v., to cause or accomplish

affinity This noun may be followed by the prepositions *between*, *of* and *with* but not *for*. But *penchant for* is correct.

affluence abundance
effluence the process of flowing out
effluents things that have flowed out, especially sewage

after following

WRONG	The driver was killed *after* his car hit a truck. [unless someone went up to him and slayed him following the accident]
RIGHT	The driver was killed *when* his car hit a truck.
RIGHT	The driver *died after* his car hit a truck.

aghast Use only if you mean paralysis of action in addition to being appalled.

aggravate to make worse. Only existing conditions are aggravated.
annoy to bother
irritate to make the skin itch

aggregate collection. If you take things in the aggregate, you look at them collectively as a whole, although you recognize them not to be a single item.

total sum. When separate items are added together into one sum, you have their total.

agree to You *agree to* something.
agree with You *agree with* someone.

aid help
aide an assistant

ail to be sick; to make sick
ale malt beverage

ain't Change to *isn't, aren't* or *am not*.

air gas, atmosphere
e'er ever (poetic)
ere before (poetic)
err to make a mistake
heir an inheritor

aisle row
I'll contraction for *I will* or *I shall*
isle island

alas Avoid this archaic word.

alibi legal defense that one was somewhere else when a crime was committed

excuse   reason put forward to request forgiveness. Except in a legal sense, this is generally the word you want.

all   Don't use this redundantly.

> **WRONG**   Fife, Griffith and Smith were *all* released.
>
> **RIGHT**   Fife, Griffith and Smith were released.

all-around   not *all-round*

allegedly   Never use because the word itself offers little or no legal protection and may actually get you into trouble. Instead, give the charge and identify the person making it.

all-important   An overblown and overused phrase. Whether it's correct depends on the word being modified, but few things, if any, are worthy of it.

all ready   everyone prepared
already   by now

all together   everyone grouped
altogether   thoroughly

all ways   all methods
always   constantly

allowed   permitted
aloud   audibly

allude   not mention directly
elude   evade
refer   mention directly

allusion   casual mention
delusion   mistaken belief, especially one caused by a mental disorder
elusion   an escape
illusion   erroneous perception or belief
reference   specific mention

almost   nearly, as in *almost all*
most   greatest amount, degree or size, as in *most dangerous game* or *most people*

altar   sacred platform in a house of worship
alter   to change

alternate   v., take turns; n., proxy
alternative   n., choice; adj., substitute. Note that this is the only form to use as an adjective.

although   the preferred form at the start of a sentence or clause; the one to use as a subordinating conjunction
though   the only correct form at the end of a sentence; the one to use as a simple adverb with commas on each side of it in the middle of a sentence. Many writers, though, also use it in place of *although*.

alumna   woman who has attended a school. (At some schools, graduation is implied.)
alumnae   women who have attended a school
alumni   men, or men and women, who have attended a school
alumnus   man who has attended a school

amateur   nonprofessional
novice   beginner

amend   to make a formal change
emend   to correct

amid   in the middle of something larger: *amid all that confusion*
among   surrounded by three or more separate things: *among the hungry of the world*
between   relationship involving only two or a number of things compared two at a time

amoral   outside of morality
immoral   in opposition to a moral code

amount   how much (weight or money)
number   how many (individual items)

ancestors, forebears   those from whom you are descended
descendants   those descended from you

anchors aweigh   not *anchors away*

and   Many books tell you not to begin a sentence with *and* or *but*. But technically, either can begin a sentence because both are coordinating conjunctions, which by definition can start a sentence or an independent clause. Journalists often begin sentences with *but* and seldom with *and*, although we would accept either.

anecdote   short, amusing story
antidote   cure for a poison

angel   heavenly being
angle   degree measurement between two lines or planes; a slant

ant   a kind of insect
aunt   sister of mother or father

anticipate   to foresee with the possibility of forestalling
expect   to foresee without necessarily being able to forestall

antiseptic   something that prevents bacteria from growing
disinfectant   something that destroys or neutralizes bacteria

anxious   experiencing desire mixed with dread. One is *anxious about* or *for*.
eager   marked by enthusiasm and impatience. One is *eager to*.

any   used with a choice among more than two
either   used with a choice between two

any more   something additional: *I don't have any more.*
anymore   adv., now, nowadays

any one   any single person or thing
anyone   any person at all

any way   in any manner
anyway   in any event. Note there is no *s* at the end except in colloquial speech.

apparent   appears to be real
evident   evidence makes clear
obvious   unquestionable

appose   to put side by side
oppose   to set against

appraise   to evaluate
apprise   to inform

apt   implies possibility
liable   implies an unpleasant probability; responsible
libel   written slander
likely   implies probability

arbitrate   to judge
mediate   to serve as a person who conciliates or reconciles

arc   a curve; something in that shape
ark   something offering protection

are   v., form of *to be*
hour   n., 60 minutes
our   pron., possessive form of *we*

area   amount of space
aria   operatic song for one singer

aren't I?   Change to *am I not?*

aroma   pleasant smell
stench   foul smell

arouse   to excite or stimulate
rouse   to stir or waken

arrant   notorious
errant   straying

as   conj., introduces clauses
like   prep., introduces words or phrases; noninclusive
such as   prep., conj.; introduces inclusive words, phrases or clauses: *A book like this* means not this one but another; *a book such as this* means this one or one like it.

ascent   climb
assent   agreement

as compared with   See *compare to.*

aside   n., digression; adv., to one side, out of the way, apart from
beside   prep., alongside
besides   in addition to

as if   not *as though* (although some authorities, including AP, now accept either). *As if* is generally preferred when introducing a subjunctive-mood verb.

as to   not *as for. About* or *on* is often preferable to *as to.*

assay   to test
essay   n., short prose composition; v., to try

assert   to state as true
claim   legal right; justified demand

assignation   appointment
assignment   allotted task

assistance   help
assistants   helpers

assume   to hold a hypothesis without proof. You also *assume* a role.
decide upon   You *decide upon* a course.
presume   to believe without proof

assure   to remove worry or uncertainty. People are *assured.*
ensure   to make an outcome inevitable. Events are *ensured.*
insure   to provide insurance. Objects or lives are *insured.*

astride   prep., with a leg on each side
bestride   v., straddle. When you *bestride* a motorcycle, you are sitting *astride* it.

as yet   Change to *yet.*

attendance   number attending; act of attending
attendants   people who attend

attorney   someone who transacts business for you, legal or not; not a profession. A person can have "power of attorney" without being a lawyer.
lawyer   professional attorney in legal matters (member of the bar)

auditions   are heard
trials or tryouts   are watched

auger   tool for boring
augur   to be an omen

aught   n., zero; adv., at all
ought   v., should

aural   pertains to the ear
oral   pertains to the mouth; spoken
verbal   pertains to language, spoken or written

autarchy   totalitarian government
autarky   policy of economic nationalism

avenge   to right a wrong
revenge   retaliation for satisfaction, not justice; to gain vengeance

average, mean   the sum divided by the number of parts: 4 + 9 + 2 = 15; 15/3 = 5 (average)
median   the number with as many scores above as below. In the sequence 2, 7, 13, 16, 21, the median is 13.
range   the highest minus the lowest

avert   to turn yourself away from
avoid   to keep away from
evade   to avoid by cleverness
prevent   to forestall, anticipate or keep from occurring

avocation   hobby
vocation   job; profession

awesome   something evoking awe, an emotion of mingled reverence, wonder and dread. It is often used as slang for lesser feelings.

awful   an adjective. Don't use in place of adverbs such as *very*, *really* and *extremely*.

B

bail   money forfeited to a court if an accused person fails to appear at the trial
bale   bundle, as of hay
bond   bail as a form of bond. To be specific, say someone *posted bail* or *bail was set at* instead of referring to bond.

baited   A hook, witness or bear is *baited*.
bated   Breath is *bated*, meaning "abated."

balance   in accounting, the credits minus the debits
remainder   part left over

ball   sphere
bawl   to cry

baloney   nonsense
bologna   a kind of lunch meat usually pronounced the same as *baloney*

band   musical group; something that encircles and constricts
banned   barred

bankrupt   should not be used to describe a company reorganizing under bankruptcy laws. A person or company is *bankrupt* only if declared to be by a court.

barbell   has adjustable weight
dumbbell   has fixed weight

bare   adj., nude
bear   n., the animal; v., to carry

baron   nobleman
barren   infertile

base   n., foundation, military headquarters, bag in baseball; adj., lacking quality
bass   adj., low-voiced; n., a type of fish; a voice or musical instrument with a low register. The voice or instrument is pronounced the same as *base*; the fish is pronounced like *mass* with a *b* instead of an *m*.

bases   plural of *base* and *basis*. Pronounced *bay-sees*.
basis   main support. Pronounced *base-iss*.

bazaar   marketplace
bizarre   odd

beach   n., sandy area; v., to run aground
beech   a kind of nut tree

beat   n., rhythm; v., to strike
beet   a kind of vegetable

because   preferred word for direct causal relationship
due to   Avoid using to mean *because*. If you do use it, the phrase should follow a form of *to be* and must modify a noun: Instead of *He resigned due to ill health*, write *His resignation was due to ill health*.
since   a temporal relationship

begs the question   This doesn't mean "requires asking" but rather to assume the validity of something being questioned without having any proof.

belittle   Use to mean disparage, not merely ridicule.

bellow   to shout
billow   to surge in waves

bemuse   v., to confuse
bemused   adj., engrossed in thought; doesn't mean amused or slightly confused
confuse   to muddle or stupefy

berry   small fruit
bury   to put under something

berth   place of rest
birth   the emergence of something, especially living

beside   at the side of
besides   in addition to

best   for comparisons of three or more
better   for comparisons of two
bettor   one who gambles

be sure to   not *be sure and*

bi   prefix normally meaning every two: *Biweekly* means every two weeks.
semi   prefix meaning every half: *Semiweekly* means twice a week.

biannual   twice a year
biennial   once in two years

bibulous   given to convivial drinking
bilious   ill-natured; suffering from liver problems

bigger portion   not *bigger half*

bide   v., to stay or wait. You ask someone to *bide* their tongue, not *bite* it.

bight   inward curve in a coast; slack part of a rope loop
bite   v., action involving the teeth; n., wound made by teeth, mouthful
byte   computer term for one group of binary digits

bimonthly   every two months
semimonthly   twice a month; every two weeks

blatant   conspicuous
flagrant   too obvious to ignore

bloc   coalition with a joint purpose or goal
block   cube; obstruction

blond   adjective for either sex; noun for male
blonde   noun for female, although some, male or female, would object to
   being reduced to a hair color

blow   A *blow* is dealt, not administered.

boar   male hog
boor   insensitive person
bore   n., someone who causes boredom; v., to drill

board   v., to get on a ship; n., plank
boarder   lodger who takes meals
bored   v., made a hole in; adj., experiencing ennui (boredom)
border   boundary

boat   small, open vessel. Exception: U-boat, a submarine.
ship   seagoing vessel larger than a boat

bold   fearless
bowled   past tense of *bowl*

bolder   more bold than
boulder   big rock

bole   tree trunk
boll   seedpod

bomb   It's not a *bomb* if it doesn't have an explosive charge. A tear-gas
   canister is, therefore, not a *bomb*.

Usage: Finding the Right Word

born   to have been given birth
borne   to have given birth to; to have put up with; to have carried

borough   walled town
borrow   to be lent something
burro   ass; donkey
burrow   n., hole in the ground; v., to dig. Our favorite stylebook rule, from an old UPI Stylebook, said that a burro is an ass, a burrow is a hole in the ground, and a journalist should know the difference.

bosom   The word is singular in regard to one person: For example, a woman has a *bosom*, not *bosoms*. But it also applies to both sexes: *He clasped the child to his bosom.*

bough   n., branch
bow   n., forward part of a boat, a loop, an archer's weapon; v., to bend in respect

bouillon   broth
bullion   gold or silver ingots

boy   young male
buoy   n., floating marker; v., to lift up

Brahman   Hindu caste; cattle breed
Brahmin   aristocrat

brake   v., to stop; n., stopping mechanism
break   v., to shatter; n., interval

bravery   what someone has within
courage   what someone shows when tested

breach   violation, opening or tear
breech   bottom, rear or back

bread   food
bred   raised

breadth   width
breath   n., air taken into the lungs
breathe   v., to take air into the lungs

briar   pipe
brier   thorned plant; root used for making pipes

bridal   pertains to a bride or marriage ceremony
bridle   what you put on a horse's head to restrain it; rigging on a kite

bring   to carry toward
take   to carry away

Britain   country
Briton   inhabitant

broach   to make a hole; to start a discussion
brooch   ornament

brunet   adjective for male or female; noun for male
brunette   noun for female, although many, male or female, would object to being reduced to a hair color

bunch   a number of inanimate objects
crowd   a number of people

burger   hamburger
burgher   person who lives in a town

burglary   involves entering a building with the intent of committing a crime
robbery   stealing involving violence or the threat of violence
theft   stealing without violence or threat of violence

bus   n., vehicle; v., to move by means of a bus (present participle: *busing*)
buss   kiss (present participle: *bussing*)

C

calendar   chart that records dates
calender   machine for pressing cloth or paper
colander   strainer

calk   cleat
caulk   to make watertight

callous   adj., hardened emotionally
callus   n., hardened skin

Calvary   where Jesus was crucified (near Jerusalem); often part of church names
cavalry   soldiers on horseback

can, could   *could* is the past and conditional form of *can*; is able
may, might   has permission; will possibly. *Might* is the past and conditional form of *may*. Some say *may* implies that uncertainty still persists, while *might* refers to a possibility in the past, but others say *might* is less definite than *may*.

canapé   appetizer
canopy   awning

cannon   gun
canon   church law; body of literature; a type of musical composition

cannot help, can only   not *cannot help but*

canvas   cloth used for tents
canvass   to cover a district to seek support or opinions

capital   city
Capitol   building (note capital letter in all cases)

carat   unit of weight; used with diamonds and other gems
caret   editing mark inserting something

Usage: Finding the Right Word

carrot   vegetable
karat   measure for the purity of gold (24 being pure)
karate   martial art

careen   to sway (especially a boat or ship)
career   v., to move quickly, especially at full speed; n., course or profession
carom   to rebound after striking

carousal   drunken revel
carousel   merry-go-round

cast   n., group of actors; v., to throw
caste   social class

caster   little wheel under furniture
castor   ingredient in perfume; name of a laxative oil: *castor oil*

casual   not formal
causal   pertaining to a cause

celebrant   participant or presiding official in a religious service
celebrator   participant in a nonreligious celebration

celibate   unmarried; abstaining from sexual intercourse
chaste   morally pure; abstaining from sexual intercourse

cement   the powder in concrete
concrete   the rocklike substance of which roads, sidewalks and walls are made

censer   incense burner
censor   n., one who previews things to prevent others from seeing material deemed harmful; v., to preview things to prevent others from seeing potentially harmful items
censure   official reprimand

centenarian   person older than 100
centurion   Roman military commander

centers around   Use *centers on* or *revolves around* because the center is the middle of a circle—the point around which things circle.

ceremonial   formal
ceremonious   overly concerned with formalities

cession   an act of granting, surrendering or transferring something
session   the term of a meeting

chafe   to rub; to wear away by rubbing
chaff   husks

champagne   bubbly wine made only in the Champagne province in France. An imitation of that wine made elsewhere is *sparkling wine*.
Champaign   city in Illinois

champing at the bit   not *chomping at the bit*

chaperon n., a man or woman who accompanies as a guardian; v., to accompany as a guardian

chaperone n., a woman guardian; should be excluded from modern usage

character what a person is
reputation what others think a person is

cheap inexpensive
cheep to chirp

childish immature; pejorative term
childlike maintaining the positive qualities of childhood

choose present tense
chose past tense

choral adj., written for a choir or chorus
chorale n., choral composition or choir
coral n., substance built by sea creatures that forms a reef; adj., reddish pink
corral n., fenced-off area for horses

chord harmonizing musical notes
cord string or rope; unit of wood; part of the body: spinal cord, vocal cord

cite to quote in support
sight something seen; the sense
site a place

citizen one who shares in the political rights of a nation. A person is a *citizen* only of a nation, not of a city, county, region or state.
resident a person who lives in an area

city An area isn't a *city* unless it's incorporated.

civic pertains to a city
civil pertains to polite society, laws other than military or criminal, or internal war

classic n., something of the highest rank; adj., recognized for many years as a model
classical adj., pertaining to a certain historical period, especially ancient Greece and Rome, or to serious music

clew ball of thread or yarn
clue piece of evidence; hint

client person who uses the services of a professional
customer person who buys something

climactic refers to a climax
climatic refers to the weather

Usage: Finding the Right Word

close   to shut; to end
clothes   garments
cloths   fabrics

coarse   rough or crude
course   class; series; division of a meal; field for a sport

collaborate   to work together
collude   to cooperate secretly to deceive
connive   to provide secret help or indulgence

collision   when two moving objects hit
crash   when a moving object hits something else that is mobile or stationary

comic   n., funny person
comical   adj., funny

commandeer   to seize something for use by the government, especially the military. Using it merely to mean to take something by force is colloquial. Using it to mean to take charge of is incorrect.

commensurate   corresponding to
commiserate   to feel sympathy for

common   shared; belonging to jointly
mutual   reciprocal; having the same relationship

compare to   to point out similarities
compare with   to point out similarities and differences
contrast   to point out differences and, perhaps, similarities, as well

complacent   satisfied
complaisant   obliging

complement   v., to complete by supplementing; n., that which supplements and completes
compliment   v., to praise; n., praise

complementary   supplying what's missing in another
complimentary   free; praising

comply with   not *comply to*

compose   to create or put together: *The whole is composed of the parts.* Some editors insist that *compose* be used only in passive voice, but others permit it to be used actively to mean constitute. The AP accepts its use in both voices.
comprise   to contain: *The whole comprises the parts.*
constitute   to form or make up: *The parts constitute the whole.*

comprehensible   understandable
comprehensive   complete

compulsive   obsessive
impulsive   spontaneous; based on whim rather than thought

concerned about   preoccupied
concerned with   engaged in

concert   requires two or more performers
recital   given by one performer

condone   Use to mean excuse, forgive, pardon or overlook. Do not use to mean accept, approve, certify, endorse or sanction.

connotation   implied meaning or emotional flavor of a word or phrase
denotation   actual or literal meaning of a word or phrase

conscience   n., a moral sense
conscious   adj., awake
consciousness   n., awareness

consecutive   one after another without a break
successive   one after another

consequent   following as a natural result; used when the events are related
subsequent   following; used when the events are not related

consul   diplomat
council   deliberative body; assembly of advisers
counsel   n., legal adviser or advice; v., to advise

contact   n., a connection point or someone with whom one communicates. It's best avoided as a verb; use instead words like *call*, *visit* or *write*.

contagious   transmitted by contact
infectious   transmitted by water, air and the like

contemptible   deserving of scorn
contemptuous   showing or feeling scorn

contiguous to   not *contiguous with*

continual   repeated
continuous   uninterrupted

contrast to   not *contrast with*

controversial   Avoid this buzzword. Instead, show why the person or thing is controversial rather than merely labeling it so.

convince   The AP says you *convince that* or *of*; some editors say you convince yourself; The Washington Post Deskbook says convince is "to win over by argument."
persuade   The AP says you *persuade to*; some editors say you persuade others; The Washington Post Deskbook says *persuade* is "to win over by appeal to reason or emotion."

core   center
corps   group of people
corpse   dead body

co-respondent   a person in a divorce suit charged by the complainant with committing adultery with the person from whom the complainant is seeking a divorce
correspondent   one who writes; that which matches with something else

couldn't care less   Do not use *could care less*.
couldn't help   Do not use *couldn't help but*.

council   see *consul*

councilor   member of a council
counselor   adviser; lawyer; aide at an embassy

country   the geographical territory
nation   the political entity

courage   see *bravery*

courteous   kind beyond politeness
polite   having good manners

creak   to squeak
creek   a stream

credible   believable; trustworthy (not merely persuasive)
creditable   worthy of approval, credit or praise

credulity, credulousness   synonyms meaning a tendency to believe too readily
credulous   gullible

crescendo   Because a crescendo is a gradual rise in sound volume or intensity, it is redundant to write "rose to a crescendo."

criteria   plural
criterion   singular

crochet   a kind of knitting
crotchet   an odd fancy

croquet   lawn game
croquette   meat patty

cue   signal; billiard stick
quay   wharf
queue   lineup

currant   n., a kind of berry
current   n., flow; adj., present

customary   set by custom
habitual   set by habit
usual   ordinary

cymbal   percussive musical instrument
symbol   something that stands for something else

cypress   tree
Cyprus   country

D

dais, podium   a platform to stand on while speaking
lectern   the reading desk behind which a speaker stands

damage   harm done to something
damages   compensation a court awards someone for a loss or an injury

damaged   means partially harmed. Don't say *partially damaged* or *completely damaged*.
destroyed   means completely harmed. Don't say *partially destroyed* or *completely destroyed*.

data   usually takes a plural verb: *The data have been gathered* (many separate items); occasionally takes a singular verb: *The data is sound* (viewed as a unit).
datum   singular

debut   n., a first appearance. Do not use as a verb.

decease   to die, to go away
disease   illness

desist   to stop or to abstain from

decide whether   not *decide if*

decimate   The word, originally meaning to kill every tenth person, has come to mean destroy, and most authorities now find that meaning acceptable.

defective   faulty
deficient   lacking

definite   certain, clear or fixed
definitive   thorough; authoritative

defuse   to stop
diffuse   v., to scatter; adj., scattered

déjà vu   Use to refer only to the *illusion* that something has been experienced before. If it actually was experienced, the feeling isn't *déjà vu*.

delude   to deceive
dilute   to water down

democracy   rule by the people directly
republic   rule by representatives of the people. In the strictest sense, the U.S. is a republic rather than a democracy.

demur   v., to raise objections; n., an objection raised
demure   adj., quiet and serious

deny   to say something is false
dispute   v., to argue; n., an argument
rebuff   v., to snub; n., a snub
rebuke   v., to condemn for an offense; n., a reproof
rebut   to argue to the contrary
refute   to prove something is false

depart   *Depart* should be followed by *from* except in the phrase *depart this life.*

depositary   person you entrust with keeping something safe
depository   place where things are kept safe

depraved   corrupted
deprived   underprivileged

deprecate   to disapprove of
depreciate   to belittle or devalue

desert   n., barren region, also used in phrase *just deserts*; v., to abandon
dessert   n., sweet course in a meal. Remember the two *s*'s by this hint, "If it's dessert, I'll take two!"

desert island   not *deserted island. Desert* as an adjective means barren and uninhabited.

detract   to lessen; to take from
distract   to divert attention

devalued   not *devaluated*

device   noun
devise   verb

diagnose   Doctors diagnose a patient's *condition*, not the patient.

dialogue   According to language columnist William Safire (1929–2009), although many insist that the word be used only as a noun to mean a conversation between two people, it may also be used as a verb and as a noun to mean a conversation among more than two people. The word is derived from the Greek *dia*, meaning "across," not from *di*, meaning "two," Safire points out. The use of the word as a verb is not a recent invention but dates back to 1597.

die   to lose life or to cut with a die; forms: *died, has died, is dying* (losing life), *is dieing* (cutting a die)
dye   to change color with a chemical; forms: *dyed, has dyed, is dyeing*

different from   The AP Stylebook says never to write *different than*. But H. W. Fowler, author of a classic usage guide, says that such a rule is a superstition, and the Oxford English Dictionary lists uses of *different than* by the English writers Joseph Addison, Richard Steele, Daniel Defoe, Samuel Taylor Coleridge and William Thackeray. The Washington Post Deskbook probably is correct in stating that either is correct, but *different from* is preferred.

differs from   is different
differs with   disagrees

dilemma   Often misused to mean merely an unpleasant situation or a quandary, the word means a choice between two (and only two) bad alternatives, although it can also mean (but rarely does) a hard choice between two good alternatives. It shouldn't be used to mean a choice between a good alternative and a bad one. Also note that there is no *n* in *dilemma*.

dinghy   boat
dingy   drab

disapprove   to express disfavor
disprove   to show something to be false

disassemble   to take apart
dissemble   to conceal true feelings

disburse   to pay money
dispense   to deal out
disperse   to scatter or vanish

disc   as in *compact disc, disc jockey, Blu-ray Disc*; part of a plow
disk   any round, flat object; computer disk; anatomical structure

discover   to find something that was not seen before
invent   to create something

discredit   to destroy confidence in
disparage   to belittle

discreet   prudent
discrete   separate

disinterested   impartial (may be interested but neutral)
uninterested   indifferent (lacking interest)

dissent from   not *dissent with*

distinct   unmistakable
distinctive   unique
distinguished   excellent

divers   adj., several; n., people who dive in the water. The adjective is pronounced like the word *diverse*, the noun like the word *diver* with a *z* on the end.
diverse   different

dock   large excavated basin used for receiving ships between voyages
pier   platform extending from shore over water
wharf   platform parallel to shore

doff   to take off (a garment)
don   to put on (a garment)

done   past participle of *do*
dun   v., to annoy, as for payment of a debt; adj., grayish brown

dose   amount of medicine
doze   to nap

doubt if   Change to *doubt that* or *doubt whether*, depending on meaning.
doubt that   used in negative statements and questions; *I don't doubt that*
doubt whether   used in positive statements indicating uncertainty as to options; *I doubt whether*

dribble   to bounce a ball
drivel   nonsense

drier   less moist
dryer   device for drying things

drunk   adj., used after the verb *to be*
drunken   adj., used before nouns

dual   composed of two
duel   fight between two people

due to   see *because*

(**E**)

each other   involving two
one another   involving more than two

eclectic   drawing on a variety of sources
electric   operated by electricity: *electric can opener*
electrical   pertains to electricity but not necessarily operated by it: *electrical engineer*
electronic   produced by a flow of electrons in vacuum tubes, transistors or microchips

ecology   the science of the relationship between organisms and environment
environment   surroundings

economic   pertains to finances, especially their management
economical   thrifty
economics   the social science dealing with economic matters such as the production and consumption of wealth

eek   an exclamation
eke   to get with difficulty

effective   having an effect
effectual   true to its purpose
efficacious   produces the desired effect
efficient   competent; productive

egoistic   self-centered
egotistic   boastful

either of the three   Change to *any of the three*.

elder, eldest   used with people
older, oldest   used with things or people

electric   see *eclectic*

elegy   sad song or poem, often written of someone who has died
eulogy   funeral oration

elicit   to draw out
illicit   prohibited

eligible   open to be chosen
illegible   indecipherable

elongated   increased in space
extended   increased in range
prolonged   beyond normal limits
protracted   extended needlessly to the point of boredom

emanate   to emit
eminent   prominent
immanent   inherent in; present throughout the universe
imminent   about to happen

emerge   to come into view
immerge   to plunge into
immerse   to put completely into liquid

emigrant   one who leaves a country
immigrant   one who enters a country

emigrate   to leave a country
immigrate   to enter a country

endemic   native
epidemic   rapidly spread

engine   Large vehicles (ships, airplanes, rockets) have engines.
motor   Small vehicles (including boats) and appliances have motors. A car may be said to have either an engine or a motor.

enormity   great wickedness
enormousness   vastness

entitled   deserving (of); gave a title to (active voice)
entitlement   benefit
titled   designated by a title (passive voice); gave a title to (active voice)
right   just claim; protection from government overreaching

entomology   study of insects
etymology   study of word origins

envelop   to surround; to cover (accent on *vel*)
envelope   container for a letter (accent on *en*)

envisage   to imagine; to visualize
envision   to foresee; to visualize

epigram   concise, clever statement or poem
epigraph   an inscription on a monument or building, or a quotation at the top of a piece of writing

Usage: Finding the Right Word

epitaph   statement or inscription in memory of someone dead
epithet   term characterizing someone or something

epitome   Not merely a high point, an epitome is the ideal embodiment of something.

equable   steady
equitable   fair

equally (as) good as   Change to *as good as*.

equivalent   of equal value
equivocate   to use ambiguous terms to hide the truth

erasable   capable of being erased
irascible   quick-tempered

errant   misbehaving; traveling to seek adventure (see also *arrant*)
erring   sinning; making mistakes

error   a deviation from the truth
lie   an intentional untruth told to deceive; see also *lay*
mistake   an inaccuracy resulting from a misunderstanding or carelessness

erstwhile   means former, not *earnest*

eruption   sudden, violent outbreak
irruption   forcible entry; sudden increase in animal population

eschatology   branch of theology dealing with death and judgment
scatology   obsession with excrement

especially   particularly; notably
specially   for a special purpose or occasion

estimate   Because an estimate is an approximation, it is redundant to follow it with *about*. So, instead of writing "The crowd was *estimated at about 500*," write "The crowd was *estimated at 500*."

ever so often   frequently
every so often   occasionally

every day   adv.: *editing every day*
everyday   adj.: *everyday editing*

every one   each single one
everyone   everybody

evoke   to call up or inspire emotions, memories or responses
invoke   to call for the help of, as in prayer

exalt   to raise in rank; to praise
exult   to rejoice

exceedingly   extremely
excessively   too much

exceptionable   objectionable
exceptional   unusual

excite   to arouse emotionally
incite   to stir to action

exercise   to work out physically
exorcise   to drive out (as in *driving out demons*)

exhume   to dig up a corpse
exude   to radiate

expatiate   to elaborate
expatriate   someone who has left a country to live elsewhere
ex-patriot   former patriot
expiate   to atone for

exploded   Avoid the hyperbolic expression that someone "exploded" when what you mean is that he or she became angry.

extant   still existing
extent   range

extended illness   Change to *long illness*.

extra bases   *A double is only an extra-base hit.*

F

facetious   merely amusing
factious   creating dissent
factitious   not genuine
fictitious   imaginary

faint   adj., weak; v., to swoon
feign   to pretend
feint   fake attack

fair   n., periodical exhibition; adj., just
fare   n., price to travel, passenger or food provided; v., to progress

faker   someone who engages in fraud
fakir   holy man, especially a Muslim or Hindu who performs magic feats

famed   The English writers William Shakespeare and John Dryden used *famed* in place of *famous*, but most editors reject that usage because they consider it journalese.

farther   used for literal distance
further   used for figurative distance

fatal   resulting in death
fateful   deciding the fate of

faze   to disturb
phase   stage of development

feat   deed
feet   appendages on which shoes are worn
fete   lavish party

feel   should be reserved for physical or emotional sensations
think   the proper term to use for mental activity

ferment   to undergo chemical conversion after adding a yeast
foment   to cause trouble

fewer   smaller in number; used for plural items
less   smaller in amount; used for singular items
under   Some editors prefer this be used for spatial comparisons only, such as *under the bridge*, rather than to indicate a smaller amount, such as *under $100*.

figuratively   in a metaphorical sense
literally   actually; often confused with *figuratively*

figurine   representation, up to 2 feet tall, of a person or an animal
sculptor   artist who creates three-dimensional art
sculpture   any three-dimensional work of art
statue   big representation of a person or an animal
statuette   representation, from 1 to 2 feet tall, of a person or an animal
statute   law

filet   net or lace with a pattern of squares; *filet mignon* (other boneless strips of meat may be spelled either as *filet* or *fillet*)
fillet   a narrow strip (as of ribbon or meat); to cut meat or fish so as to create a fillet

find   to discover
fined   penalized

fine   penalty of money
sentence   penalty of time. A convict is *sentenced to five years and fined $5,000*, not *sentenced to five years and a $5,000 fine*.

fir   a kind of evergreen tree
for   preposition
fur   the hair of an animal; garment made from the hair of an animal

fired   A legally dangerous word too often used loosely, *fired* shouldn't be used to describe someone who was laid off from or who quit a job.

first annual   Change to *first*. Something isn't annual until the second time.

fiscal   financial
physical   pertaining to the body

flack   pejorative term for a press agent
flak   anti-aircraft shells; strong criticism

flagrant   glaringly evident
fragrant   having a pleasant smell

flair   talent
flare   n., light; v., to start suddenly

flammable   preferred over *inflammable* by The Washington Post. But many editors consider *flammable* an illiteracy.

inflammable   Use this rather than *flammable* when speaking of temperaments.

inflammation   medical condition

inflammatory   arouses emotions

flaunt   to show off
flout   to defy; to disdain

flea   a kind of insect
flee   to leave

flew   past tense of *fly*
flu   influenza
flue   smoke duct in a chimney

flier   aviator; handbill
Flyer   used in the proper names of some trains and buses

flotsam   wreckage of a ship or its cargo floating at sea
jetsam   things jettisoned from a ship to lighten the load
lagan (ligan)   jetsam attached to a buoy to make recovery easier

flounder   v., to struggle helplessly; n., a fish
founder   to sink or become disabled. *First you flounder, then you founder.*

flour   ground grain
flower   blossom

flowed   past tense of *flow*
flown   past participle of *fly*; often mistakenly used for *flowed*

following   Avoid using as a preposition. Change to *after*.

forbear   to cease; to refrain from
forebear   ancestor

forbid   you *forbid to*
prohibit   you *prohibit from*

forbidding   difficult
foreboding   n., prediction or portent; adj., ominous

forced   compulsory; strained
forceful   effective; full of force
forcible   involves use of brute force

forego   to precede
foregoing   preceding
forgo   to go without; to relinquish
forgoing   giving up; abstaining from

foreword   introduction
forward   onward

formally   in a formal manner
formerly   previously

fort   enclosure for defense
forte   n., strength; adj., loud (Italian)

forth   onward
fourth   place after third

forthcoming   about to take place; willing to give information
forthright   frank

fortuitous   accidental; by chance
fortunate   lucky

foul   adj., rotten
fowl   n., bird

freeze   to form ice
frieze   decorative band

fullness   abundance
fulsome   disgusting; insincerely excessive; do not use to mean full, as in a *fulsome figure*

furl   to roll up

furrow   n., wrinkle, rut in the soil; v., to wrinkle

G

gaff   hook
gaffe   blunder

gait   a way of walking
gate   entrance

gamble   to wager
gambol   to frolic

gantlet   flogging, as in *running a gantlet*
gauntlet   glove, as in *throwing down a gauntlet*

gender   grammatical term for whether a word is masculine, feminine or neuter; sex-based role assigned by society (used when distinction is sociological rather than biological)
sex   describes whether a being is male or female (used when distinction is biological rather than sociological)

genius   Avoid this overused, loosely used word.
genus   class or kind; in biology, the next larger classification than species

genteel   affectedly elegant
gentile   to Jews, anyone not Jewish; to Mormons, anyone not Mormon
gentle   not rough

gibe   to taunt
jibe   to conform; to change course
jive   to kid; to talk in a lingo

gild   to cover with gold
guild   workers' union

glacier   ice field
glazier   person who puts glass in windows

glutinous   like glue
gluttonous   pertaining to overeating

gorilla   ape
guerrilla   fighter

gothic   gloomy or fantastic, as in *gothic novel*
Gothic   all other uses, such as medieval or pertaining to the Goths

gourmand   big eater
gourmet   connoisseur of food

grate   grill for holding wood in a fireplace
great   larger than normal

grill   n., metal bars for cooking meat or fish; v., to broil meat or fish, to
   question harshly
grille   screen or grating, such as on the front of a car

grisly   gruesome
gristly   having cartilage
grizzled   gray-streaked
grizzly   n., brown bear; adj., gray

guarantee   n., pledge to replace the product or refund the money if the
   product doesn't work; v., to make such a pledge
guaranty   n., warranty; pledge to assume someone else's responsibility; a
   financial security

H

hail   v., to greet, to acclaim after the fact; n., ice from the sky
hale   v., to take into court, to drag; adj., healthy

half   see *(in, into) halves*
half a   not *a half*

half brothers, half sisters   children with only one parent in common
stepbrothers, stepsisters   children related by the marriage of parents

half-mast   flags are lowered (not raised) to half-mast on ships and at
   naval stations only
half-staff   flags are lowered (not raised) to half-staff everywhere else

hall   large room
haul   v., to drag forcibly, to carry; n., booty, distance to be traveled

handmade   made by hand
self-made   made by itself. A millionaire may be *self-made*, but an antique is *handmade*.

hangar   aircraft shelter
hanger   someone or something that suspends something else: *paper hanger, coat hanger*

hanged   executed
hung   put up

hapless   unfortunate
hopeless   lacking hope

hardy   bold, rugged. A plant that can survive under unfavorable conditions is *hardy*.
hearty   jovial; nourishing

Harold   name
herald   to announce before the fact

heal   to recover from injury
heel   back of the foot; bottom of the shoe; end piece of bread

healthful   giving health. Foods are *healthful*.
healthy   having health. Living things are *healthy*.

hear   to listen
here   at this place

heard   past tense of *hear*
herd   group of animals

heartrending   not *heart-rendering*

helix   three-dimensional design
spiral   two-dimensional design. Exception: *spiral staircase*.

hero   someone who does something that's brave, not merely someone who dies

heroin   drug
heroine   female hero, although some consider this term a diminutive sexist one and prefer *hero* for either males or females

hew   to chop
hue   color

hike   a walk; don't use as a verb to mean increase.

hippie   a 1960s term for a flower child
hippy   having big hips

hire   to employ; to gain use of
lease   to grant or gain by contract, especially property
let   to grant by contract, especially property

historic having importance in history
historical concerned with history. A *historic* book made history, but a *historical* book is about it.

hoard n., storehouse; v., to store
horde n., swarm

Hobson's choice This is not a dilemma; it means no choice at all.

holey full of holes
holly a kind of plant popular at Christmas
holy sacred
wholly entirely

holocaust A bad fire or accident is not a holocaust unless many people are killed or there is great destruction. Have enough respect for the Holocaust (the mass killing of civilians, especially the genocide of six million Jews, by the Nazis) in World War II not to use this word lightly.

home place where a person or family lives. A *home* cannot be sold.
house building occupied by a person or family. A *house* can be sold.

homicide slaying or killing
manslaughter homicide without premeditation or malice
murder malicious, premeditated homicide (or, in some states, a homicide done while committing another felony). Do not call a killing a *murder* until someone has been convicted.

homogeneous having similar structure: *Mayan and Egyptian pyramids are homogeneous.*
homogenize to make homogeneous
homogenous having similar structure because of common descent: *Mayan and Egyptian pyramids are not thought to be homogenous in that they seem to have developed independently.*

hue and cry not *hew and cry*

human pertaining to people
humane compassionate

hurdle to jump
hurtle to throw

hypercritical too severe
hypocritical pretending to be something you're not

```
I
```

I hope not *I would hope*

ideal model or goal
idle not busy
idol worshipped image
idyll scene, poem or event of rural simplicity; romantic interlude

identical with not *identical to*. Compare to *compare to* versus *compare with*.

Usage: Finding the Right Word

if   introduces a conditional clause: *if a, then b*

weather   atmospheric conditions

whether   introduces a noun clause involving two choices (the *or not* is redundant). Although most authorities say *if* and *whether* may be used interchangeably, many editors still insist on the distinction.

whither   where

wither   to dry up

imaginary   existing only in the imagination

imaginative   showing a high degree of imagination

imbecilic   The word is *imbecile* as either an adjective or a noun, although now its use is considered offensive.

immigrate   see *emigrate*

impassable   not capable of being passed

impassible   incapable of suffering or showing emotion

imperial   pertaining to an empire or emperor

imperious   domineering or proud

impetus   stimulus

impotence   weakness; inability to act; inability to get an erection

imply   to hint. Writers or speakers *imply*.

infer   to deduce. Readers or listeners *infer*.

imposter   one who levies a tax

impostor   one who pretends to be someone else

impracticable   said of a plan that's unworkable or a person who's unmanageable

impractical   said of an unwise plan or a person who can't handle practical matters

impugn   to challenge

impute   to attribute

impulsive   see *compulsive*

in behalf of   in formal support of

on behalf of   in formal representation of

(in, into) halves   not *in half*

in to   in and toward; preposition followed by an infinitive: *She went in to vote.*

into   in and within; preposition only: *She went into the building.*

into [something]   informal. Change to *interested in*.

inapt   inappropriate

inept   incompetent

inasmuch as   in view of the fact that

insofar as   to the degree that

incidence rate at which something occurs
incidents things that occur

incite to arouse; see also *excite*
insight clear understanding

incredible unbelievable
incredulous skeptical

inculcate (in, into) not *inculcate with*

independent of not *independent from*

indeterminable can't be determined
indeterminate not fixed

indict to charge with a crime
indite to put into writing, although we would not recommend using this less-than-common word. Mainly, we note this appears sometimes as a misspelling of *indict*.

indoor adjective
indoors adverb

industrial pertaining to industry
industrious hardworking

inequity unfairness
iniquity wickedness

inert lifeless; lacking motion
innate inborn; inherent; natural

infectious see *contagious*

inflammable see *flammable*

inflict on not *inflict with*

ingenious inventive
ingenuous honest; forthright, perhaps to the point of naïveté

injuries They're *suffered* or *sustained*, not *received*.

insistent demanding
persistent continuing firmly

insoluble can't be dissolved
insolvable can't be solved
insolvent can't pay debts

instill into not *instill with*

instinct nonthinking, automatic response of animals
intuition knowledge gained without conscious reasoning

integrate with not *integrate into*

interment burial
internment detention

interstate   between states
intestate   not having a will
intrastate   within a state

investigation of   not *investigation into*

it's   contraction for *it is* or *it has*.
its   possessive form of *it*

J

jail   where suspects and people convicted of misdemeanors are kept; cities and counties have them
prison   where felons are kept; states and the federal government have them

jam   made from the whole fruit (usually not citrus fruit)
jamb   side of a doorway or window frame
marmalade   made from the pulp and rinds of citrus fruit
preserves   fruit preserved by cooking with sugar

jerry-built   built poorly of cheap materials; compare with *jury-rigged*

judicial   pertaining to a judge or court
judicious   sound in judgment
juridical   pertaining to the administration of justice

juggler   person who juggles
jugular   neck vein

jury-rigged   rigged for temporary use; compare with *jerry-built*

just deserts   not *just desserts*. Here, *deserts* means deserves, not after-dinner treats.

K

killed in a wreck   not *after* (or *following*) *a wreck*

(a) kind of   not *kind of a*

knave   rogue
nave   part of the interior of a church

knead   to mold
kneed   past tense of *knee*
need   to require

knew   past tense of *know*
new   recent

knight   medieval soldier
night   part of the day after the sun has set

knit   to loop yarn to make a fabric
nit   louse

know   to comprehend
no   adj., not any; adv., opposite of yes

L

---

lam   an escape, as in *on the lam*. Because this is slang, journalists should avoid using it except in a quotation from a source, in which case they need to know how to spell it.
lamb   baby sheep

lama   Tibetan monk
llama   animal found in the Andes

languid   weak or sluggish
limpid   clear or calm

last   final. Exceptions: *last week, last month, last year.*
latest   most recent, as in *latest letter* (not the final one)
past   most recent, as in *past three years* (not the final ones)

laudable   praiseworthy
laudatory   expressing praise

lay   transitive v., to set down; principal parts: *lay, laid, have laid, is laying*
lie   intransitive v., to recline; principal parts: *lie, lay, have lain, is lying*
lye   a strong alkaline solution

leach   to separate a solid from its solution by percolation
leech   n., bloodsucker; v., to suck blood

lead   n., metal; v., present tense of *lead*
led   past tense of *lead*

leak   v., to go through an opening; n., hole
leek   n., vegetable related to the onion

lean   to stand diagonally, as in resting against something
lien   the right to take or sell a debtor's property as security or payment on a loan

leased   past tense of *lease*
least   smallest

leave alone   to depart from by oneself; to allow someone to stay by him- or herself
let alone   to allow to be undisturbed

lectern   see *dais, podium*

legendary   Avoid as an overused adjective.

legislator   lawmaker
legislature   body of lawmakers

lend   verb; past tense is *lent*, not *loaned*

loan   noun. Some authorities permit this to be used as a verb if what is lent is money, but you should try to avoid that usage.

lone   adj., by oneself

less   see *fewer*

lessee   tenant

lesser   smaller

lessor   landlord or one who grants a lease

lessen   to make less

lesson   instruction

let's   contraction for *let us*

lets   allows

levee   riverbank

levy   n., an imposed tax; v., to impose a tax

liable   legally responsible; should not be used to mean likely (see *apt*)

libel   v., defame; n., defamation

likely   probable or probably

lichen   funguslike plant that grows on trees and roots

liken   to compare

lightening   making less heavy or dark

lightning   flash of light in the sky

like each other   two are alike

like one another   more than two are alike

linage   number of lines of printed material

lineage   descent from an ancestor

lineament   facial contour

liniment   salve

lion's share   all, not just most. In Aesop's fable, the lion got the whole thing, not just most of it.

liqueur   sweet, flavored alcoholic drink

liquor   distilled alcoholic drink

literal   actual

littoral   pertaining to a shore

literally   see *figuratively*

livid   Use to mean furious or black-and-blue. It is often misused to mean vivid or red.

load   v., to pack; n., a pack

lode   deposit of ore

loath   adj., reluctant; is followed by *to*

loathe   v., to dislike greatly

local   nearby
locale   site

located   set
situated   set on a significant site

loose   v., to unbind; adj., not tight
lose   v., to fail to win; to fail to keep

luxuriant   abundant
luxurious   comfortable or self-indulgent

M

made   past tense of *make*
maid   female servant

magnate   powerful person in business
magnet   metal object that attracts iron

mail   n., letters; v., to post
male   adj., masculine; n., man

majority   more than half
plurality   largest number but less than half

mall   shopping area
maul   to handle roughly

mania   abnormally intense enthusiasm for something
philia   tendency toward, or abnormal attraction to something
phobia   abnormal fear of something

manikin   model of a human body with parts that detach
mannequin   clothes dummy

manner   way; see also *to the manner born*
manor   estate

manslaughter   see *homicide*

mantel   wood or marble structure above a fireplace
mantle   sleeveless cloak; region between Earth's core and crust

margin   the difference between two figures
ratio   the relation between two figures. *If a committee votes 4–2, the margin is two votes and the ratio is 2-to-1.*

marital   pertaining to marriage
marshal   v., to direct; n., title of an official in the military or in a police or fire department; the person leading a parade; sometimes, used capitalized as a name
Marshall   word as name only: *Marshall McLuhan, Marshall Islands*
martial   warlike; pertaining to the military, as in *martial law.*

mask   n., a disguise; v., to disguise
masque   masquerade; amateur musical drama

masseur   man who gives massages; preferred term is *massage therapist*
masseuse   woman who gives massages; preferred term is *massage therapist*

masterful   powerful; fit to command
masterly   expert

material   thing out of which something is made
materiel   supplies of a military force

may, might   see *can, could*
may be   v., as in *it may be late*
maybe   adv., perhaps

meat   flesh of an animal
meet   v., to get together or be introduced; n., a gathering; adj., proper
mete   v., to distribute; n., a measure or boundary

meeting took place   not *meeting occurred*. Planned events take place; unplanned events occur.

medal   award
meddle   to interfere
metal   class of elements, including gold, iron, copper and so on
mettle   character

media   n., plural: *The media are wolves*; adj., as in *media companies*
medium   singular: *The medium is the message.*

meretricious   deceptive; attracting attention in a vulgar or gaudy way; deceptive or insincere
meritorious   deserving merit

might   conditional form of *may*; see *can, could*
mite   small arachnid; small object; small amount

mil   measure of wire
mill   a property tax unit representing $1 per $1,000 of assessed valuation. So, for example, a property tax rate of five mills on a home assessed at $200,000 means the owner would pay five times $200 (1/1000th of $200,000), or $1,000 in property taxes.

militate   to work against
mitigate   to lessen

miner   one who mines
minor   adj., underage, lesser; n., one who is underage

minks   plural for the furry animal
minx   mischievous girl

mislead   present tense of the verb meaning to lead astray
misled   past tense of the verb to lead astray

misnomer   This means an incorrect name for a person or thing, not merely any mistake.

misogamy   hatred of marriage
misogyny   hatred of women

mistake   see *error*

moat   ditch filled with water for protection (around a castle)
mote   speck, as of dust

mold   n., fungus, form; v., to form
molt   to shed

momentary   short-lived
momentous   important
momentarily   Like the adjective *momentary*, this adverb means lasting only a moment. Some usage guides suggest it shouldn't be used to mean in a moment, although most consider that acceptable.

moot   open to argument
mute   speechless

moral   adj., virtuous; n., lesson
morale   confidence or spirits of a person or group

more important   not *more importantly*. The phrase is a shortening of *what is more important*.

more than   used with figures: *more than 60 people*
over   best used in spatial references, but the AP Stylebook allows such constructions as *He is over 40* and *I gave over $100*.

morning   early part of the day
mourning   grieving

motif   main theme or repeated figure
motive   inner drive

motor   see *engine*

mucous   adj., secreting mucus: *mucous membrane*
mucus   n., liquid secreted

murder   see *homicide*

mutual   shared. Because it applies to a relationship between two, this adjective shouldn't be used in the broader sense to mean shared or common, which may refer to a relationship among more than two. Exception: *mutual fund*.
reciprocal   interacting

myriad   a large indefinite number. *Myriad* should be used as an adjective, not a noun: *myriad ways*, not *a myriad of ways*.

Usage: Finding the Right Word

N

nab   Use to mean grab, steal or snatch; don't use if something was earned.

nation   see *country*

nauseated   how you feel when your stomach turns
nauseous   what something is if it makes your stomach turn

naval   pertaining to the navy
navel   n., belly button or depression resembling a belly button, as in *navel orange* (an orange with such a depression)

negligent   careless
negligible   unimportant; small

neither   not either. Alone, *neither* is singular, not plural, so you would write, for example, *neither is*, not *neither are*.
nether   below

new   recent
novel   unusual

nohow   Avoid this, using *instead* or *anyway*.

noisome   offensive
noisy   clamorous

none   not any; not one
nun   female member of a religious order

nor   Some people use *nor* instead of *or* after any negative expression, but most grammarians say this is an overcorrection. *Nor* should be used after *neither* instead of *or*.

notable, noteworthy   worth noting
noted   famous
noticeable   capable of being seen; prominent
notoriety   a bad reputation
notorious   having a bad reputation

O

O   *O* is not followed by a comma and is used in addressing someone: *O Father, I have something to tell you.*
Oh   *Oh* is followed by a comma or an exclamation point and is used for exclamation rather than address: *Oh, my!*

oar   long paddle
o'er   over (poetic)
or   conjunction
ore   mineral deposit

obsequies   funeral rites
obsequious   sickeningly respectful

observance   the act of paying heed to a custom or ritual
observation   the act of viewing

obsolete   Don't use this adjective as a verb.

obtuse   see *abstruse*

ocean   water between continents, the floor of which is made of dense basaltic rock
sea   narrower body of water than an ocean, the floor of which is made of lighter granitic rock of the continent

oculist   may be either an ophthalmologist or an optometrist
ophthalmologist   physician treating illnesses of the eyes
optician   makes eyeglasses (need not be a physician)
optometrist   measures vision (need not be a physician)

ode   lyric poem
owed   past tense of *owe*

odious   hateful
odorous   fragrant

official   authorized
officious   meddlesome

older, oldest   see *elder, eldest*

omnifarious   of all kinds
omnivorous   eating any kind of food

on each side   not *on either side*

once in a while   not *once and awhile*

once removed   First cousins, once removed, are a generation apart; for example, your first cousin's child is your first cousin, once removed; your first cousin's child and your child are second cousins.

one another   see *each other*

ongoing   This adjective usually says nothing because the use of a present-tense verb alone means *still in existence.*

opaque   cannot be seen through
translucent   can be seen through but not clearly; allows light through
transparent   can be seen through clearly

oral   see *aural*

ordinance   law. An ordinance is adopted or approved, not passed.
ordnance   weapons and ammunition

other   adj., *Turn the other cheek. Other* is required in comparisons of the same class: *My car breaks down more than any other car I've owned.* Otherwise, omit.
otherwise   adv., *We should add more reinforcement to the wall, or otherwise it might collapse.*

over　see *more than*

over and over　Avoid this. Instead write *again and again*.

overdo　to do to excess
overdue　tardy

overly　Don't use. *Over* is already an adverb and should be used instead. Say someone is *overqualified*, not *overly qualified*.

own　Often redundant, as in *Do your own thing*.

P

packed　past tense of *pack*
pact　an agreement

paddy　swamp
patty　flat, usually fried, cake

pail　bucket
pale　adj., light

pain　n., hurt; v., to hurt
pane　sheet of glass

pained　receiving pain
painful　giving pain

pair　couple
pare　to trim
pear　a kind of fruit

palate　roof of the mouth
palette　board on which paint is mixed
pallet　small, hard bed; small platform for moving and storing cargo; tool for mixing clay; tool for applying gold leaf

parameter　a constant used for determining the value of variables. Avoid using to mean boundary or factor.
perimeter　the curved, outer boundary of an area

pardon　to release a person from further punishment for a crime
parole　early release of someone imprisoned
probation　the punishment received by one who is sentenced for a crime but not sent to prison

parity　equality
parody　comic imitation

parlay　to increase
parley　to talk

part　piece
portion　allotment

partake of　to share
participate in　to take part in

poorly   Do not use for *badly*.

poplar   a kind of tree
popular   well-liked

populace   the common people
populous   full of people

poring over   looking over
pouring over   emptying a liquid onto

portend   to foreshadow
portent   omen

practicable   describes a thing that's possible
practical   describes a sensible person or thing

practically   This adverb means for all practical purposes. It should not be used to mean almost.

pray   to worship
prey   n., a hunted animal; v., to plunder or hunt

precede   to go before
proceed   to continue

precipitate   to hasten; to bring on ahead of expectations
precipitous   adj., steep

predominant   adj., prevailing
predominate   v., to prevail

premier   n., prime minister; adj., outstanding. The AP Stylebook suggests, though, that you use *prime minister* unless the nation prefers the term *premier*, as in China, or *chancellor*, as in Germany and Austria.
premiere   n., first presentation of a movie or play. Don't use as a verb or an adjective, although many authorities permit it.

prescribe   to order
proscribe   to prohibit or condemn

presence   act of being present; bearing
presents   gifts

presentiment   premonition
presentment   presentation

presently   Despite widespread use to mean now, many editors prefer using it only to mean soon.

presumptive   founded on presumption
presumptuous   taking too many liberties

pretense   false or unsupported claim of distinction
pretext   what is put forward to conceal the truth

prevaricate   Use to mean to evade the truth or stray from it, not necessarily to lie. For example, an equivocation is a *prevarication* because it misleads, even though the statement may be literally true.

primer   elementary textbook; substance used to prepare a surface for painting. In America, the first meaning is pronounced like *primmer*, and the second is pronounced *prime-er*, as both meanings are pronounced in Britain.

primmer   more prim

principal   n., someone or something first in rank; adj., most important
principle   n., basic rule or guide

prodigy   something or someone extraordinary
protégé   someone guided or helped by someone more influential

profit   money made on a transaction
prophet   one who foresees

prohibit   see *forbid*

prone   lying face downward
supine   lying face upward

prophecy   n., a prediction of the future
prophesy   v., to predict the future

proposal   plan offered for acceptance or rejection
proposition   n., assertion set forth for argument, improper proposal; v., to make an improper proposal

prostate   male gland
prostrate   to lie prone

proved   v., past tense of *prove*
proven   adj., tested and found effective

purposefully   aiming at a goal
purposely   intentionally
purposively   psychological term for opposite of aimlessly

put into words   not *put in words*

Q

quarts   plural of quart, the measurement
quartz   a kind of mineral

quash   to annul
squash   n., a fruit related to a gourd; v., to crush

quaver   to be tremulous (said of the voice)
quiver   to shake

quell   to suppress
quench   to satisfy thirst; to douse

queue   see *cue*

quiet   silent

quite   very. Avoid whenever possible. The word means *entirely* or *all the way* and shouldn't be used to mean *considerably, rather* or *somewhat*. It should never be followed by a noun.

quotation   noun; preferred noun form in more formal writing, especially when what's quoted is famous

quote   verb; also acceptable as a noun in informal usage and in referring to quotations in journalism

R

racism   the belief that some races are inferior to others, especially when associated with the idea that "inferior" races should be hated or discriminated against. Although the strict meaning of *racism* would not seem to apply to similar beliefs about ethnic groups, nationalities or religions—such as hatred of Hispanics, Polish people or Muslims—the term is often used those ways for lack of another word. And historically, the term *race* has long been used for ethnicities and nationalities, such as the German race. More problematic is the notion often expressed in academia that disenfranchised minorities cannot be racists because they lack power. But even those without power sometimes believe other races are inferior or to be hated. See Chapter 13.

rack   n., stretching frame used for torture; v., to torture or strain
reek   to give off a strong, bad odor
wrack   damage brought about by violence, as in *wrack and ruin*; best avoided as a verb
wreak   to inflict, as in *wreak havoc* or *wreak vengeance*
wreck   to damage or destroy

rain   precipitation
reign   term of a sovereign's power
reins   straps to control a horse; used in *free rein*, meaning loosened control

raise   transitive v., *raise, raised, has raised*
raze   to destroy
rise   intransitive v., *rise, rose, has risen*

range of actions   not *range of action*

rappel   a descent by a mountain climber
repel   to drive back

rapt in thought   not *(wrapped, wrapt) in thought*

rare   in short supply all the time
scarce   in short supply temporarily

raring to go   not *roaring to go*. Means eager or enthusiastic.

ravage   to destroy
ravish   to rape; to seize and carry away by force; to enrapture

reaction   Don't use in place of *opinion*.

real   adj., *The clock is real.*
really   adv., *She is really tired.*

real good   Grammatically, this idiom should be *really good*. Better still, just say *good*.

reapportion   applies to state legislatures
redistrict   applies to congressional districts

rebound   to spring back
redound   to have a result

reciprocal   see *mutual*

recourse   a resort; that to which one turns for help
resource   a supply

re-cover   to cover again
recover   to regain health or possession

re-create   to create again
recreate   to take leisure

redhead   AP accepts this for a person who has red hair, but many people object to being reduced to a hair color, depending on the context.

refute   Use to mean disprove, merely answer, dispute or rebut.

relaid   laid again
relayed   transmitted

reluctant   unwilling to act
reticent   unwilling to speak

remediable   capable of being fixed
remedial   intended as a remedy

rend   to split apart; to distress
render   to submit; to extract by melting

repairable   usually used with something physical that can be repaired
reparable   usually used with something not physical that can be repaired, such as a mistake

repellent   n., something that repels; adj., repulsive
repulse   to rebuff by discourtesy; to disgust
repulsive   offensive; disgusting

replica   a copy made by the original artist or under that person's supervision
reproduction   a copy made by someone else

reportedly   Use of this word is an excuse for laziness about looking up the facts and a way to try to avoid responsibility for a statement. Avoid it.

re-sign   to sign again
resign   to quit; to give up a job or an office

respectable   worthy of respect
respectful   showing respect
respective   in order

resume   to start again
résumé   a summing up, especially of a career

reverend   This adjective always takes the article *the* in front of it except when directly addressing a member of the clergy. Don't write that someone *is a reverend*.

review   critical examination; scholarly journal
revue   theatrical production with skits, music and dancing

right   correct
rite   religious ceremony
wright   worker, as in *playwright*
write   to put down in words

risk averse   not *risk adverse*

robbery   see *burglary*

role   an assumed part
roll   n., a kind of bread or pastry; v., to tumble

round   single shot
salvo   succession of shots
volley   number of simultaneous shots

rout   overwhelming defeat resulting in confusion
route   a way traveled

rye   a kind of grass; whiskey made from rye
wry   twisted

S

sac   pouch in a plant or an animal
sack   bag for carrying goods

safari   Use for a hunting expedition, not merely a trip.

safe-deposit box   not *safety-deposit box*

salary   fixed compensation for a nonhourly worker
wages   pay to an hourly worker

same thing   not *same difference*

sanguinary   bloody
sanguine   ruddy; cheerful

saving   bargain
savings   money in the bank

sculpture   see *figurine*

seasonable   suitable to the particular time of year
seasonal   occurring during a particular season

sensual   licentious
sensuous   pertaining to the senses

sentence   see *fine*

serf   person in feudal servitude
surf   n., edge of the sea that breaks when it hits shore; v., to ride the waves on a board

serve   v., to work for, to bring food
service   n., employment; v., to have sex with, to maintain in repair

settler   one who settles down
settlor   one who makes a legal property settlement

sewage   human waste
sewerage   system that carries away sewage

sex   see *gender*

shear   to shave or cut
sheer   v., to swerve; adj., steep, transparent or thin

short way   not *short ways*

similar to   not *similar with*

since   see *because*

skew   to distort; to place at an angle
skewer   n., long pin; v., to pierce with a skewer, to make fun of

slatternly   in the manner of a disorderly, unkempt woman
slovenly   in the manner of a disorderly, unkempt person

sleight   skill, especially at deceiving
slight   adj., meager; v., to neglect

sniffle   to sniff repeatedly
snivel   to whine

sociable   enjoying company
social   pertaining to society

solecism   violation of grammar, usage or propriety
solipsism   belief that nothing is real but the self

soldier   generally speaking, one member of the military. But U.S. Marines insist the term should be applied only to members of the Army.
troop   group of soldiers, police, highway patrol officers, scouts, people or animals. But the AP Stylebook also accepts it in the plural in relation to many military personnel, as in *About 40,000 U.S. troops were wounded in Iraq.*
trooper   cavalry soldier, mounted police officer or highway patrol officer
trope   figure of speech

troupe   company of actors, dancers or singers
trouper   member of a theatrical company; veteran performer

solidarity   show of support
solidity   firmness, stability

soluble   capable of being dissolved; capable of being solved
solvable   capable of being solved

some   Don't substitute this adjective for the adverb *rather* or *somewhat*.

sometime   Use to mean *former*, not *occasional*.

sort of   not *sort of a*

spade   shovel
spayed   past tense of *spay*, to sterilize a female animal by removing its ovaries

speak with   not *speak to*

specially   see *especially*

specie   coin
species   the biological term for a grouping more distinct than a genus

specious   deceptive; used to describe abstract things
spurious   counterfeit; used to describe concrete things

stable   n., animal shelter; adj., sturdy
staple   constantly used commodity

staid   sedate
stayed   past tense of *stay*

stake   n., a piece of pointed wood or metal; something bet; a share; v., to mark a location or furnish resources
steak   n., a thick cut of meat or fish; not used as a verb

stamping grounds   not *stomping grounds*

stanch   to restrain, as in *The nurse stanched the bleeding.*
staunch   firm in opinion

stationary   not moving
stationery   writing paper

statue   a kind of sculpture (see *figurine*)
statute   law

stimulant   alcohol, drugs or agents such as caffeine
stimulus   incentive

straight   not crooked
strait   singular. Geographers prefer this term for a narrow passage connecting two bodies of water. But the expression is "strait is the gate" (not "straight is the gate") because here the word means *narrow* rather than *not crooked*.

Usage: Finding the Right Word

straits   plural. This term is accurate when there is more than one strait, as in *Straits of Mackinac*. Note also the expression *dire straits*.

straight-laced   strict; severe

strait-laced   pertaining to confinement, as with a corset. Note also *strait-jacket*.

strikebreaker   someone hired to take the place of a striker, not just anyone who crosses a picket line, such as a manager or a union member who decides to work anyway

successive   see *consecutive*

suit   n., set of clothes, lawsuit; v., to please

suite   set of furniture, rooms or dance pieces

summon   v., to command, as in *Summon him to court.*

summons   a singular noun meaning an order to appear, as in *Give her a summons*; third-person singular verb meaning to order or to call to appear, as in *She summons a cab.*

summonses   plural noun: *Give them summonses.*

superficial   on or near the surface

superfluous   more than is needed

superior to   not *superior than*

supposed to   Note the *d*.

supposedly   not *supposably*

sure   adjective: *He is sure to attend.*

surely   adverb: *Surely she knows better.*

sustain a fatal injury   Avoid this phrase. An injury is not sustained if it is fatal.

systematic   systemlike

systemic   affecting the whole system

(**T**)

tack   course of action

tact   ability to do the kind thing in a delicate situation

talesman   person summoned to fill a jury

talisman   a charm

talk with   not *talk to*

taught   past tense of *teach*

taunt   to mock

taut   tight

tout   to praise or solicit

team   squad

teem   to abound

tempera   a method of painting
tempura   a method of cooking

temperatures   They should be described as *higher* or *lower* but not as *warmer* or *cooler*.

temporal   transitory; worldly
temporary   not permanent

tenant   person who lives in a rented house
tenet   doctrine

terminable   able to be ended
terminal   at the end

terrified   More than simply scared, *terrified* means paralyzed by fear.

that   The AP Stylebook says journalists should use *that* following these verbs: *advocate, assert, contend, declare, estimate, make clear, point out, propose* and *state*. Although *that* can often be cut from a sentence without loss of meaning, for clarity it should be used after *said* when a time element is involved. Also, use *that* rather than *as* after the verbs *feel, know, say* and *think*.

theft   see *burglary*

therefor   for it; for that; for this
therefore   for that reason

there's no admission   Say *There's no admission charge.* Better yet, just say it's free. (*There's no admission* means that nobody will be allowed to attend.)

think   see *feel*

thorough   complete
threw   past tense of *throw*
through   preposition
thru   misspelling of *through* or *threw*

thrash   to beat an opponent. To thrash something out means to settle something with a detailed discussion.
thresh   to beat grain

throne   seat
thrown   past participle of *throw*

thus   Change this conjunctive adverb to *so*, which is less pompous.

tic   twitch
tick   bloodsucking arachnid

til   sesame plant used in India for food and oil
till   prep., preferred shortened form of *until*; v., to plow; n., money tray

tinker's damn   not *tinker's dam*

to the manner born   not *to the manor born. Manner* is the spelling in Shakespeare's First Folio at the Folger Library.

too   Don't use to begin a sentence—instead, use *also*. Don't use as a synonym for *very*. *Too* should be set off by commas, and when used with a past participle it requires an intervening word such as *greatly*, *highly*, *little* or *much*.

toe   one of five appendages on the foot
tow   to pull

toe the line   not *tow the line*

tort   legal name for a wrongful act
torte   a kind of round layer cake

tortuous   twisting; complex; deceitful
torturous   pertaining to torture

transpire   Use to mean leak out or become known, not merely happen.

tread   v., to trample; n., the outer layer of a tire, the sound of someone walking
trod   past tense of *tread*

trek   Don't use as a synonym for *trip* or *journey*. A trek is a slow journey filled with hardships.

troop   see *soldier*

turbid   dense
turgid   bloated

U

under   see *fewer*

under way   Generally used as two words. *Underway* (one word) is correct only in nautical use before a noun, as in *underway convoy*. Often better than the two-word version is to rewrite the sentence using *started* or *began*.

unexceptionable   beyond reproach
unexceptional   common

uninterested   see *disinterested*

unquestionable   indisputable
unquestioned   something that hasn't been questioned

unthawed   There is no such adjective; use *frozen*.

up   Don't use as a verb.

used to   Note the *d*.

V

vain   possessing vanity
vane   device for showing wind direction
vein   blood vessel; streak

valance   short curtain
valence   an atom's capacity to combine

varmint   regional variation of vermin; plural: *varmints*
vermin   disease-carrying pest; plural: *vermin*

venal   corruptible
venerable   worthy of respect
venial   minor

veracious   truthful
voracious   tremendously hungry

verbal   see *aural*
verbiage   excess words
wording   how something is said

vertex   highest point
vortex   whirlpool

very   Cut whenever possible. If you use it with a past participle, it requires an intervening word such as *greatly*, *highly*, *little* or *much*.

vial   small bottle
vile   evil
viol   a kind of stringed instrument

vice   corruption
vise   tool for gripping

viewpoint   *Point of view* is better.

viral   pertaining to a virus
virile   having masculine strength

virtually   Use to mean *in effect*, not *in fact*. In most cases, *almost* or *nearly* is better.

viscose   solution used to make rayon
viscous   resembling a sticky fluid

visible   able to be seen
visual   received through sight

W

waive   to give up or no longer require
waiver   the giving up of a claim
wave   n., a curve of something; v., to move back and forth
waver   to falter

want   n., desire; v., to desire
wont   n., custom; adj., accustomed
won't   contraction for *will not*

wangle   to get by contrivance
wrangle   to bicker

war horse   horse used in battle
warhorse   veteran of battle, either literally or figuratively

warranty   guaranty (see *guarantee*)

way   manner
weigh   to check for weight

weather   see *if*

well-heeled   not *well-healed*

wench   serving girl; peasant girl; wanton woman. The word is an archaic and derogatory term but is still often used with humorous intent.
winch   machine used in hoisting

we're   contraction for *we are*
were   past tense of *to be*
where   adverb. Don't use for *that*. Rewrite "I saw on the news *where* the vice president is coming to town" as "I saw on the news *that* the vice president is coming to town."

wet   v., to moisten; adj., moist; you *wet your whistle* (that is, you moisten your mouth, not stimulate it).
whet   to sharpen, as in *whet your appetite* because you stimulate your appetite, not moisten it

wharf   see *dock*

when   at a particular time. Don't use to mean *by the time that*. For example, rewrite "Most of the house was destroyed *when* firefighters arrived" as "Most of the house was destroyed *by the time* firefighters arrived." Also, clauses introduced by an adverb shouldn't be used in place of a noun or pronoun: Rewrite "In tennis, 'love' is when your score is zero" as "In tennis, 'love' is a score of zero."
whenever   at any time

where   see *we're*

whether   see *if*

while   Some experts say that *while* should be used only to mean *simultaneously*, not *and*, *but*, *though* or *although*. If it's the first word in a sentence and it's meant to show contrast, change it to *although*. If it's meant to show contrast later in the sentence, use *though* or *but*.

who's   contraction for *who is*
whose   possessive of *who*. This should be used only with people or animals, according to some editors. They would rewrite "The door, *whose* lock was broken, had to be replaced" as "The door, the lock *of which* was broken, had to be replaced." But because there is no possessive form of *that* or *which*, we say go ahead and use *whose* if the sentence would be awkward the other way.

worst way   Don't use to mean *very much*.

wrack   see *rack*

wrack and ruin   not *wreak and ruin*

wreak havoc   not *wreck havoc*. Considered by some a cliché, though, so another wording would be preferable.

Y

yet   Some say this word should always have a comma after it, but we say *consider* using a comma—we've seen plenty of places where we wouldn't put one. If *yet* falls at the end of a sentence, put a comma before it.

yoga   a kind of religious and physical discipline
yogi   one who practices yoga

yoke   device or symbol for subjugation
yolk   the yellow part of an egg

yore   long ago
your   possessive of *you*
you're   contraction for *you are*

youth   singular; boy or girl age 13 to 18
youths   plural

Z

zoom   This word refers to upward motion or, in camera work, to moving in closer. Don't use it to mean move speedily, as in *zooming down the highway*.

PART TWO

Mechanics

Quick access to the most commonly looked-up items in this part . . .

CHAPTER 9

Punctuation

Scholars aren't sure when the concept of punctuation began, but the oldest known document to use punctuation is the Mesha Stele, an inscribed stone that dates to the 9th century B.C. What clearly drove the need for punctuation in writing was the invention of moveable type in Europe during the 14th and 15th centuries. Some system of stops, pauses and inflection became necessary, particularly because printed texts, including the Christian Bible, were often read aloud in churches and elsewhere.

According to "The American Printer" of 1885, the importance of punctuation became obvious when recording various sayings for children. For example:

Charles the First walked and talked

Half an hour after his head was cut off.

With a semicolon and a comma added, these lines read:

Charles the First walked and talked;

Half an hour after, his head was cut off.

Some attribute the standardization of punctuation to Aldus Manutius, an Italian printer and publisher. Even today, though, punctuation rules differ from country to country and from language to language. Moreover, even within a single nation, punctuation rules differ among grammar books and stylebooks. Most American journalists accept the AP Stylebook as an arbiter of punctuation. But sometimes, learning the stylebook's rules is one thing, and applying them is another. We've found that a knowledge of phrases, clauses and sentence structure is key to using correct punctuation. It helps you remember and understand the rules and figure out solutions when the stylebook rules don't go far enough.

The two most common sources of punctuation problems are the use of commas and the handling of quotations, so we'll start with those.

Punctuation

ESL Tip

Punctuation differs in different countries. Nonnative speakers of American English should note differences between the rules of punctuation in their countries of origin and the rules followed in the U.S. For example, in France, a dash, rather than quotation marks, is used to indicate a quotation:

—Don't quote me, said Bartlett.

In Britain, single quotation marks are used where Americans would use double ones, and vice versa. Also, commas and periods in Britain are put outside the quotation marks if the quotation is not a complete sentence, rather than inside, as we do in the U.S.:

BRITISH   He called her 'brilliant but wrong'.

AMERICAN He called her "brilliant but wrong."

In Britain, periods aren't used at the end of some common abbreviations:

BRITISH	AMERICAN
Dr	Dr.
Mr	Mr.
Mrs	Mrs.

Commas

Always Use a Comma

○ Use a comma after *said* when introducing a direct quotation that is at least one sentence long:

> Cooper said, "To leave out premarital testing from this bill is like taking a Missouri census and leaving out Kansas City."

○ Use a comma before and after the abbreviation for a state following a city, and before and after a year following a month and date:

> Roberto and Carmen met in Pulaski, Tenn., at the Butter Bowl.
>
> On May 2, 2011, the two giants in the field met.

○ Use a comma after words in a series but not before the conjunction unless the meaning would be unclear. (This rule may be contrary to what you learned in English class for academic writing, but it is the way journalists do it.)

> The new budget proposals would cut spending for student loans, building repairs, road improvements and farm subsidies.

What would be an example of a series that would be unclear without a comma before the conjunction? One in which the same conjunction appears in the series as part of an item:

ONLINE GRAMMAR HELP
bedfordstmartins.com/newscentral

For practice using commas in a series, log on to *Exercise Central for AP Style* and go to **No. 1. Incorrect comma in a series**.

He went to town to buy a can of corn, a can of peas and carrots, and a can of beans.

○ **Use a comma before the abbreviation *etc.* at the end of a series:**

Send us what you've got: the books, the tapes, etc.

○ **Use a comma after introductory clauses, phrases or words:**

Listening to the band, he decided to audition.
[The comma follows an introductory participial phrase.]

In July, Taylor was born.
[The comma follows an introductory prepositional phrase.]

Often, she was without shelter.
[Most writers and editors are inconsistent about using commas after introductory adverbs such as this one. Sometimes, they put them in, but sometimes, they don't, depending on whether they would pause there when saying the sentence. But such a subjective approach wastes time and money because a writer may put in a comma that an editor will take out and a proofreader put back. We suggest always putting a comma after introductory words, phrases or clauses, even when they're only one word long.]

Gee, the rain smells good.
[The comma follows an introductory interjection. For added emphasis, you could use an exclamation point either after the interjection or after *good*. If you put an exclamation point after the interjection, you would capitalize *the*.]

Through the door into the building, the SWAT team charged.
[If there is more than one prepositional phrase at the beginning of a sentence, put a comma after the last one only.]

ONLINE GRAMMAR HELP
bedfordstmartins.com/newscentral

For practice using commas following introductory elements, log on to *Exercise Central for AP Style* and go to **No. 6. Missing comma after an introductory element**.

○ **If a gerund or gerund phrase, or an infinitive or infinitive phrase is the subject of the sentence, it is not considered an introductory word, phrase or clause, so it should not be followed by a comma:**

Jogging is fun. [*Jogging* is a gerund used as the subject.]

Jogging five miles is something she did every morning.
[*Jogging five miles* is a gerund phrase used as the subject.]

To live is to be. [*To live* is an infinitive used as the subject.]

To live well is to live a good life.
[*To live well* is an infinitive phrase used as the subject.]

Compare the previous examples to the following sentences with introductory phrases that would take commas:

Jogging five miles, she tired.
[*Jogging five miles* is a participial phrase, not a gerund phrase. Participial phrases can never be the subject of a sentence and must always be followed by a comma at the start of a sentence.]

To live well, one must eat well.
[*To live well* is an infinitive phrase modifying the subject of the sentence, *one*. *To live well* here is not the subject of the sentence but an introductory phrase requiring a comma.]

○ **Use a comma between two independent clauses joined by a conjunction to form a single sentence. No comma is needed when what follows the conjunction is not an independent clause:**

A dentist and her assistant discussed tooth care with the students, and they used Mr. Gross Mouth to illustrate their points.
[A comma is needed before the conjunction at the start of the second independent clause.]

A dentist and her assistant discussed tooth care with the students and used Mr. Gross Mouth to illustrate their points.
[No comma is used before *and* here because *and used Mr. Gross Mouth to illustrate their points* could not stand alone as a complete sentence—it's the second half of the compound predicate *discussed . . . and used* and is not a clause by itself.]

ONLINE GRAMMAR HELP
bedfordstmartins.com/newscentral

For practice using commas between independent clauses, log on to *Exercise Central for AP Style* and go to **No. 8. Missing comma(s) in compound sentence**.

○ **Use a comma between two imperative clauses linked by a conjunction, such as those often used in recipes:**

Braise the meat for 10 minutes, and then remove it from the pan.
[These are independent clauses because the subject is implied in the imperative.]

○ **Use commas around *nonrestrictive* (nonessential) words, phrases or clauses. (See Pages 31–32.)**

The yellow car, which was in the driveway, belongs to Jim.

○ **Use a comma between *coordinate* adjectives—that is, if you can reverse the adjectives and put *and* between them. (See Pages 100–101.)**

The sleek, spotted cat pounced on the mouse.

○ **Use a comma before the adverbs *also, as well, too* or *yet* at the end of a sentence:**

Roberto Dumas came to the event, too.

○ Use commas to set off a conjunctive adverb (*however, likewise, at the same time, therefore*) from the rest of a single clause or simple sentence. (See Pages 110 and 192.)

> Nitish, however, was early.
>
> However, Nitish was early.
> [In journalism, we change this *however* to *but* and drop the comma.]
>
> Nitish was early, however.

○ Use a comma after a dependent clause at the start of a sentence. Examples would be sentences beginning with *although, because, if* or *since*:

> Although the police were criticized for the arrest, the chief defended it.
>
> Because clouds covered the sky, it was difficult to see the comet last night.

○ Use a comma before *not* when showing contrast:

> She said she thought independent voters preferred Stevens, not Malkowitz.

○ Use a comma to set off a noun of direct address:

> John, could you come help me?

○ Use a comma in a headline in place of the word *and*:

> City Council Rejects Tax Increase, Approves Spending Cuts

But beware of possible unintentional double meanings that might be created:

> Officials Warn Clams, Oysters Can Carry Virus
>
> Louisiana Governor Defends His Wife, Gift From Korean

Never Use a Comma

○ Never use a comma before a dependent clause unless the sentence could be misread without it, such as when it follows a negative statement:

> The game was called because it was raining.
> [*Because it was raining* is a dependent clause at the end of a sentence and can't be misread, so there is no comma in front of it.]

But look at this next sentence punctuated two ways:

> He's not doing that, because he wants to.
>
> He's not doing that because he wants to.
> [This sentence means two different things depending on whether the comma is used. With the comma, the dependent clause is saying the reason he's not

doing it is because he doesn't want to do it. Without the comma, the sentence is saying the reason he's not doing that is not because he wants to but for some other reason.]

○ **Never use a comma between clauses that form part of a compound direct object:**

Bridges said *none of the workers required medical treatment* and *the leak did not pose a danger to public safety.*
[Think of this construction as *He said this and that.* The clauses here are really part of a compound direct object joined by *and.* Putting a comma between them (before *and*) would change the meaning. The sentence would no longer state that Bridges was saying the leak did not pose a danger; rather it would imply that the reporter was editorializing about the leak.]

The poll found *that nine out of 10 people believe smoking should be limited in public* and *that eight out of 10 believe employers should be allowed to limit smoking in workplaces.*
[No comma in this sentence because the poll found both opinions.]

○ **Never use a comma before the conjunction at the end of a series unless the meaning would be confusing without one (see Page 178).**

○ **Never use a comma between compound adjectives—that is, two words that team up as one adjective, with one word describing the main adjective. Use a hyphen instead:**

The sun beat brightly through a *cloud-free* sky the morning of the accident.

(See the discussion of hyphens on Pages 194–95.)

○ **Never use a comma between adjectives when you can't reverse them:**

a new stone wall
[*New* and *stone* are not coordinate adjectives here—you cannot reverse them.]

○ **Never use a comma after a quotation mark. The comma, if needed, goes before the quotation mark:**

"The beverage-container ordinance will probably be supported by the voters," MacDonald said.

○ **Never use a comma after a period, an exclamation point or a question mark in a quotation when the sentence continues past it:**

"Swim!" her father yelled.

⚪ Never use a comma before a paraphrase or partial quotation:

> Feldman said "old-age blues" set in when he turned 30.
> [No comma after *said* because the quotation is not a complete sentence.]

⚪ Never use a comma around the abbreviation *Jr.* or *Sr.* after a name. (This may be contrary to what you learned in English class, but it is the way journalists do it.)

> Martin Luther King Jr. was a civil rights leader.

⚪ Never use a comma around the abbreviation *Inc.* in a company name. (This is another exception to your training in English class.)

> Merck & Company Inc. is a pharmaceuticals company.

Possibly Use a Comma

⚪ You may use a comma to separate a series of three or more short independent clauses:

> "I came, I saw, I conquered."

⚪ You may use a comma to separate the same word used two times consecutively:

> Whatever is, is.

Quotation Marks and Other Problems of Quoting

The handling of quotations is the second most common source of punctuation problems. Because journalists live and die by the quote, this is an especially important matter for them to master. So, the discussion here includes both punctuation and related issues that arise concerning quotations.

What to Quote

⚪ Quote someone's words to add color, detail or authenticity to a news or feature story.

If the words aren't colorful, don't provide important details, or don't help authenticate or back up a point being made, then don't quote them. Consider leaving them out, using a partial quote or paraphrasing them instead:

USELESS QUOTE   She said, "I'm happy to be here."
[This quote provides neither color nor an important detail.]

BETTER   She said she was happy to be here.
[Even though four of these words are an exact quote, they're so common that you need not call attention to them by using quotation marks. In journalism, as opposed to research-paper writing, it is better to drop the quotation marks and simply offer a paraphrase.]

GOOD, COLORFUL QUOTE   Silber said, "It's been so dry around here that the cows are giving powdered milk."

GOOD QUOTE PROVIDING IMPORTANT DETAIL   Christiansen said, "Posicorp is looking to expand into a new market next year with a product line aimed at kids."

GOOD QUOTE BACKING UP A POINT   The grocery's owner charges that the Eversons' lawsuit threatens to drive him out of business. "Since this whole mess began, I've dropped about $150,000 in attorney fees," Mohr said, "and my business has declined 7 percent since all the bad publicity began."

Direct Quotes, Paraphrases and Partial Quotes

		Exact Words a Source Said or Wrote
Direct quote	=	**"The pressure to exploit 845 million users has got to be intense,"** Jesse Kornbluth, former editorial director of AOL Online, wrote of the Facebook IPO in a Wall Street Journal op-ed piece, **"and by changing its definition of 'privacy' so it can share member information with advertisers, Facebook has already disappointed some of its users."**

		Source's Statements Rewritten in Your Own Words
Paraphrase	=	Commenting on Facebook's IPO in an op-ed piece for The Wall Street Journal, AOL Online former editorial director Jesse Kornbluth said **the recent change in the site's privacy guidelines, meant to accommodate advertisers, has caused a negative reaction in some users.**

		Source's Words Integrated Into Your Own Writing
Partial quote	=	Jesse Kornbluth, former editorial director of AOL Online, speculated in a Wall Street Journal op-ed piece that the **"pressure to exploit 845 million users"** of Facebook following the site's IPO must be considerable.

Source: "How AOL—Aka Facebook 1.0—Blew Its Lead," by Jesse Kornbluth, published in The Wall Street Journal, February 8, 2012, p. A15.

◯ Put quotation marks only around the exact words a speaker or writer uses, not around paraphrases:

> The president said the new military aircraft would be built next year. [Do not insert quotation marks here. The word *said* can be properly used with either quotes or paraphrases, so an editor should not assume that the words are a quote. Inserting quotation marks would probably create a mis-quotation because the writer gave no indication that the words were quoted.]

◯ Quotation marks should be a contract with the reader that these are the exact words the source used. Journalists shouldn't normally rewrite a quote and leave it in quotation marks, but public relations writers might be expected to do that in order to maintain a company's image.

If the quote is wordy or grammatically incorrect, consider not using it, paraphrasing it or using a partial quote. If it contains profanity, possibly use hyphens in place of some of the letters of the offending word:

RIGHT   "I don't give a s--- what the president thinks," Stauffer said.

WRONG   "I don't care what the president thinks," Stauffer said. [These are not Stauffer's exact words, so they should not be presented as a quote.]

RIGHT   Stauffer said she didn't care what the president thought. [The statement is paraphrased, so there are no quotation marks.]

◯ Single-word quotations generally don't need quotation marks. At that point, aren't you really paraphrasing? Sometimes, however, a single word may be so colorful that it's worth quoting by itself:

He said he felt fine. [No quotation marks needed around *fine*.]

He said he felt "wondrous."
[The word is unusual enough that it could be quoted.]

◯ Don't draw attention to clichés by putting quotation marks around them:

WRONG   An Ashland, Mo., youth is "sadder but wiser" after a con artist took him for $400 he had saved. [Not only is it unnecessary to quote a cliché, but also, in this case, a reader might mistakenly think the youth is being quoted. It's better to avoid using clichés altogether.]

◯ Don't put quotation marks around the names of musical groups, dance companies or theater troupes:

WRONG   "The Beatles"

RIGHT   The Beatles

○ Don't use a quotation mark in place of the word *inches* or *seconds*:

WRONG   12"

RIGHT   12 inches; 12 seconds

○ Newspapers typically use quotation marks around all titles except those of magazines, newspapers, the Bible and other sacred books, reference books, and descriptive titles of musical works (such as Symphony No. 1 or Opus 23). Actual titles of musical works, such as "Symphonie Fantastique" or "Visage," are set in quotation marks.

This differs from what you learned in English class, where titles of books, films and magazines, for example, are underlined or italicized.

Attribution of Quotations

○ Include attribution (who said it) every time a different source is quoted and thereafter when necessary to remind the reader:

Fire Chief Lawrence Wong estimated damage to the warehouse at "maybe $200,000," but the owner said it could go even higher.

Bill Pendergast, who bought the building last May, said, "I probably lost $200,000 worth of stored equipment alone, not to mention the damage to the warehouse itself."
[The speaker changes, so attribution is required.]

"Unfortunately, the layoffs come at a bad time," said Fred Meyers, an assembly-line worker who escaped this round. "Santa Claus will shortchange lots of kids because Mom or Dad is out of work."
[No attribution needed for the second quoted sentence because it is clear that the same person is speaking.]

○ Include attribution with every paraphrase, or the reader is likely to think the reporter is making the statement:

People shouldn't rush to a solution before the investigation is complete, *Gingrich said.*

○ The first time a quotation is used from a particular person, that person's full name and qualifications are usually cited:

"We condemn all violence," said Muhammad Rashad, leader of an Islamic prayer group.

○ On second reference, the person's last name only is cited:

"Our group supports only peaceful protest," Rashad said.

○ If the person has a title that was used on first reference, such as *the Rev.*, *Dr.*, *Professor* or *Gov.*, that title is dropped on all following references, although sometimes the title—written out and without capital letters—can be used in place of the name on some of the later references:

> The governor said . . .

○ Stick to one tense in attributions—either *said* or *says*— throughout. Use *said* for hard-news stories, *says* for feature stories:

> *said*
> "I'm not happy with the verdict," Teresa Caruso said. She ~~says~~ the jury didn't take into account all the evidence.

○ Don't strain for synonyms for *said* or *says*. Journalists prefer *said* and *says* to other attributions because of the words' brevity and neutrality:

- *Stated* is longer.
- *Claimed* and *according to* can imply doubt. Some editors prefer *according to* when a document is being quoted. *According to* is also correct when you mean "in accordance with rules."
- *Admitted* implies guilt.
- *Refuted* means "successfully answered."
- *Added* means the statement was an afterthought.
- Nobody ever *grinned*, *smiled* or *laughed* a statement. Somebody *said it with a grin*.
- To say someone *believes*, *desires*, *feels*, *hopes*, *thinks* or *wants* something is mind reading unless the person used these words.

> *said he*
> David Wong hopes for the best.

○ If *said* or *says* is followed by a time element and a paraphrase, follow the time element with the word *that*:

> The president said Friday *that* he would send the proposal to Congress.
> [Omitting *that* would create confusion about whether the president gave the speech on Friday or intended to send the proposal to Congress on Friday.]

○ Although some editors prefer that attribution generally be placed after the first sentence of a quote, it can properly appear before or in the middle of the first sentence of a quote, instead:

The senator said, "I won't comment on unfounded accusations."

"The worst thing about the situation," Rep. Maggie Feldman said, "is that we can't find reliable information."

In fact, a more conversational approach, especially useful in broadcast, is to put the attribution before the quote. Also, attribution should not follow a multiple-sentence quote but either precede it, with the attribution followed by a colon, or follow a comma at the end of the first quoted sentence.

- The order of source and attribution verb should usually be *source said*, not *said source*:

  "I can't believe I hit the jackpot," Mary Koch said.

The *source said* order is more conversational because usually the subject precedes the verb in English. However, you may want to use the *said source* order if the source and the *said* would otherwise be separated by a long description, such as a title.

  "This is outrageous," said Marisa Peters, president of a local citizens rights group.

- Put a comma, not a period, between a quotation and its attribution—unless the period is there for an abbreviation. In that case, add a comma:

  WRONG   "We exceeded our fundraising goal by $10,000." She said.

  RIGHT   "We exceeded our fundraising goal by $10,000," she said.

- If the attribution precedes a quote, the punctuation at the end of the attribution should be as follows: nothing in front of a partial quote or paraphrase, a comma in front of a one-sentence quote, a colon in front of a quotation of two sentences or more:

  The airline analyst said airfares from smaller airports stack up well against those from Detroit. [no punctuation in front of a paraphrase]

  The airline analyst said airfares from smaller airports "compare well with those from Detroit." [no punctuation in front of a partial quote]

  The airline analyst said, "Airfares from Toledo, Lansing and Flint compare well with those from Detroit."
  [a comma in front of a one-sentence quote]

  The airline analyst said: "Airfares from Toledo, Lansing and Flint compare well with those from Detroit. It just depends on your destination." [a colon in front of a multiple-sentence quote]

- If the attribution follows a one-sentence quote, partial quote or paraphrase, use a comma at the end of the quote or paraphrase:

"Airfares from Toledo, Lansing and Flint compare well with those from Detroit," the airline analyst said.
[comma following a one-sentence quote]

Airfares from smaller airports "compare well with those from Detroit," the airline analyst said. [comma following a partial quote]

Airfares from smaller airports stack up well against those from Detroit, the airline analyst said. [comma following a paraphrase]

Punctuation

○ Although the AP often uses a comma after a multiple-sentence quote, it is better to move the attribution after the first sentence, following a comma, or in front of the first sentence, followed by a colon:

AVOID   "Airfares from Toledo, Lansing and Flint compare well with those from Detroit. It just depends on your destination," the airline analyst said.

BETTER   "Airfares from Toledo, Lansing and Flint compare well with those from Detroit," the airline analyst said. "It just depends on your destination."

BETTER   The airline analyst said: "Airfares from Toledo, Lansing and Flint compare well with those from Detroit. It just depends on your destination."

Paraphrases

○ If a person is paraphrased as saying two clauses in one sentence, don't separate the clauses with a comma:

Chung said that *the road was icy* and *the other car was speeding.*

○ If a person is paraphrased after the word *said,* many editors insist that the clause following it must be in the same tense to maintain the proper sequence of tenses. But there is some disagreement about this. (See Pages 68–69.)

He said he was [not *is*] going.

Quotations Across Paragraphs

○ Don't put a quotation mark at the end of a *full-sentence quote* if the quote is continued at the start of the next paragraph:

Peters said: "I'm upset by the whole situation.
"I didn't know what I was getting into when I came here."

○ Don't go from a partial quote to a full-sentence quote within the same quotation marks. Instead, add quotation marks at the end of the partial quote and the beginning of the full sentence, starting a new paragraph between them:

WRONG	Jones said he was "happy to be alive. I can't believe it happened."
RIGHT	Jones said he was "happy to be alive." "I can't believe it happened," he said.

Other Issues With Quotes

○ Place periods and commas *inside* closing quotation marks:

"Prohibitions against doctors' advertising are unfortunate," Rhysburg said, "because we end up with uneducated patients."

○ Place semicolons—if you use them—or colons *outside* closing quotation marks:

Nixon said, "I am not a crook"; others weren't so sure.

Fredericks spoke with pride of his "future farmers": his sons, Chris and Sam, and his daughter, Jane.

The AP makes an exception if the semicolon or colon is part of the quoted material, but in practice this exception rarely, if ever, occurs.

○ Place question marks and exclamation points *inside* closing quotation marks if they are part of the quotation, *outside* if they are not:

Have you read Ezra Pound's "Cantos"?
[The question mark is outside the quotation mark because it is not part of the title.]

"Darn it!" she yelled.
[The exclamation point is inside the quotation mark because it is part of the quotation—the person said the statement with strong emotion.]

○ Although the AP permits ellipses (. . .), journalists generally don't use them to indicate words left out of quotations. Instead, we suggest you use paraphrases or partial quotes.

ORIGINAL   He said, "Abraham Lincoln was ahead of his time in opposing slavery, but nonetheless he said he thought that after the slaves were freed, they should be shipped off to Africa."

PREFERRED   He said Abraham Lincoln wanted to free the slaves then ship them to Africa. [using a paraphrase]

PREFERRED   He said Abraham Lincoln was "ahead of his time in opposing slavery," but that he wanted to free the slaves then have them "shipped off to Africa." [using partial quotes]

NOT PREFERRED   He said, "Abraham Lincoln . . . thought that after the slaves were freed, they should be shipped off to Africa."
[Avoid ellipses.]

○ Capitalize the first word of a quotation only when it is a complete sentence directly quoted:

> Thomas said the conditions were "appalling."

> Thomas said, "The conditions are appalling."

○ Use single quotation marks around quotes within a quote or for quotes in headlines. Most publications also use them for quotations in captions or blurbs:

> Houston said, "According to Abraham Lincoln, 'You can't fool all of the people all of the time,' but I disagree."

> Mayor: 'I Won't Resign' [headline]

ONLINE GRAMMAR HELP
bedfordstmartins.com/newscentral

For practice using quotation and attribution, log on to *Exercise Central for AP Style* and go to **No. 24. Quotation/Attribution**.

Semicolons

○ Use a semicolon between items in a series that has commas within the items. Remember to put a semicolon before the final conjunction:

> The American flag is red, white and blue; the Canadian flag is red and white; and the German flag is red, gold and black.

> Their diet consists of juice, toast and coffee for breakfast; fruit with yogurt, cottage cheese or tofu for lunch; and lean meat, vegetables and a starch for dinner.

ONLINE GRAMMAR HELP
bedfordstmartins.com/newscentral

For practice using semicolons in a series, log on to *Exercise Central for AP Style* and go to **No. 9. Missing semicolon(s) between items in a series with internal commas**.

○ A semicolon may be used between independent clauses when a conjunction is absent, but journalists would typically avoid this and instead use something else—a comma followed by a conjunction, or a dash without a conjunction, if the thoughts are closely related. If they're not, a journalist would make them two separate sentences:

> **RIGHT, BUT NOT COMMON IN JOURNALISM**   The Padres are weak this year; they have the worst record in the league.

> **BETTER**   The Padres are weak this year—they have the worst record in the league.

> **BETTER**   The Padres are weak this year. They have the worst record in the league.

○ Use a semicolon in a headline to join two sentences, but make sure the two sentences don't seem as absurd joined into one thought as these two examples:

5½-Foot Boa Caught in Toilet; Woman Relieved

Coach Suspended in Sexual Probe; Players Honored

○ A semicolon can be used before a conjunctive adverb connecting two independent clauses, but journalists would usually rewrite the clauses as two sentences:

RIGHT, BUT NOT COMMON IN JOURNALISM   Frome's lawyer contended he was mentally incompetent; however, the jury decided the evidence was not so clear.

BETTER   Frome's lawyer contended he was mentally incompetent. The jury, however, decided the evidence was not so clear.

Colons

○ Use a colon to introduce a quotation of more than one sentence:

Jimenez said: "As of now, there can't be a merger. We need more cooperation first between the city and county fire departments. We have to work together more."

○ Use a colon to introduce a list of items that begin with bullets or dashes:

In other action, the commission:
—Approved Belle Kaufman's request that she be allowed to build a guesthouse in back of her home.
—Rejected the request by Ralph Kawaski that a parcel of land he owns on Route 1 be rezoned to allow him to build a dog-race track.

○ Use a colon after an independent clause to introduce a single-item summary or an explanation with a dramatic pause:

He said you could summarize Jesus' message in three words: Love your neighbor.

If what follows the colon could stand alone as a complete sentence, as in the preceding example, capitalize it. Otherwise, do not.

○ Use a colon to take the place of *says* in a headline:

Levin: 'I Want to Be Your Mayor'

○ Use a colon to introduce a subtitle:

Theodore Bernstein wrote "The Careful Writer: A Modern Guide to English Usage."

○ Use a colon to show time if it's not an even hour:

7:30 p.m.

○ Use a colon to separate chapter and verse in a Bible citation:

James 2:11

Dashes

○ Use dashes to set off a list or parenthetical material containing commas in the middle of a sentence:

The Jayhawks' defense—the linemen, the linebackers and the defensive backs—was exhausted after being pounded by the Sooners' offense.

○ Use a dash for emphasis when a pause longer than that for a comma is needed:

He said he would do it—later.

Some editors say length of pause is not enough by itself and there also has to be a sharp turn of thought.

○ Use a dash after a dateline or the wire-service credit in a newspaper story:

LONDON—

NEW BEDFORD, Mass. (AP)—

○ Use a dash in front of the attribution in a *blurb* or *pull quote* (material pulled from the text and highlighted in larger type for typographic purposes):

'Let's face it: Hearst started the Spanish-American War.'
—Mayor Jonathan Richardson

Note the use of single quotation marks in such cases. (See Page 191.)

○ A dash is used in many publications as a bullet introducing items in a list:

In other business, the City Council:
—Approved a $525,000 contract with James Bros. Construction Co. to reroof City Hall.

—Refused to rezone a half-acre tract at 202 Trenton Place for construction of a neighborhood market.

—Approved the rezoning of 10 acres at Hinton and Market streets from single-family residential use to multiple-family apartments.

○ Put a space on each side of a dash unless it is used as a bullet item.

This is a wire-service rule, and it also keeps spell-checker programs from flagging words on each side of a dash as one unrecognized word. If your keyboard or software doesn't offer a dash, use two hyphens with no space between them.

Parentheses

○ Although journalists usually avoid parentheses, you may use parentheses to set off an aside, such as nonessential information or words inserted to clarify a quotation. If the aside contains at least one complete sentence, put the period at the end inside the parentheses. If not, put it outside:

She said her favorite movie was "Das Boot" ("The Boat").
[*"The Boat"* is not a complete sentence, so the period comes after the parentheses.]

Her dress was inappropriate for the funeral. (It was bright red.)
[This aside contains a complete sentence, so the period is inside the parentheses.]

Hyphens

○ Use a hyphen between compound modifiers that precede the word they modify, but do not use a hyphen after *very* or an adverb ending in *ly*. (See Pages 101–2.)

high-profile case

very high-profile case

highly publicized case

○ Use a hyphen after some prefixes, especially when, without one, a vowel would be doubled. (See the section on hyphenation in spelling, beginning on Page 208.)

pre-empt

re-elect

○ Use hyphens in suspensive cases involving a modifier that applies to several words:

> She most enjoyed the 3- and 4-year-old children.

○ Use hyphens in place of *to* in odds, ratios, scores and some vote tabulations:

> The odds were 3-2.
>
> She led by a 2-1 ratio.
>
> The Royals beat the Cardinals 11-2 in the exhibition game.
>
> The Senate voted 48-2 in favor of the amendment.

○ Use hyphens when fractions or numbers from 21 to 99 are written out:

> two-thirds
>
> eighty-seven

Apostrophes

Remember, the bottom of the apostrophe always points to the left. If it points to the right, it's not an apostrophe but a single open quotation mark.

○ Use an apostrophe to show possession with nouns:

> the dog's breath
>
> the building's grandeur

○ Use an apostrophe to show that something has been left out in contractions:

> don't [do not]
>
> I'll [I will]
>
> decade of the '90s [decade of the 1990s]
>
> rock 'n' roll [rock and roll]

○ Use an apostrophe to make the plural of a single letter but not of a single numeral:

> A's
>
> 3s

○ Use an apostrophe with a pronoun to form a contraction:

   it's [it is]

   who's [who is]

○ Do not use an apostrophe to form the possessive of any pronoun except those ending in *one* or *body*:

   one's

   anybody's

   theirs

○ Do not use an apostrophe in place of the words *feet* and *minutes*:

   WRONG   10'

   RIGHT   10 feet; 10 minutes

ONLINE GRAMMAR HELP
bedfordstmartins.com/newscentral

For practice using apostrophes, log on to *Exercise Central for AP Style* and go to **No. 12. Missing or misused apostrophe**.

Slashes

○ Use a slash to form a fraction or mixed number if your keyboard does not have a single key for the fraction:

   1/10

   2 1/2

○ Do not use such expressions as *and/or, c/o, either/or* or *his/hers* except in quoted material. It is better to avoid the use of such constructions as *and/or* and *either/or* altogether and to write out *in care of* and *his or hers*.

Periods, Exclamation Points and Question Marks

If only all punctuation were as easy as using these three symbols! Periods, exclamation points and question marks don't give writers much trouble, so we won't go into all their uses. Instead, we'll just note a few frequent problems.

○ Don't shoehorn too many ideas into one sentence.

   Editor Kenn Finkel has said that the main problem journalists have with periods is not getting to them soon enough.

○ Know when to use periods in abbreviations. (See Page 368.)

○ Journalists typically confine the use of exclamation points to quotations in which people express strong emotion or to strong opinions expressed in editorials or personal columns.

In other uses, exclamation points risk making an article sound biased, sensational or gushy. Still, they have their place, as in the first sentence of this section.

○ Never use two exclamation points next to each other or an exclamation point next to a question mark.

Some writers double or triple the exclamation points to show extra emphasis or combine an exclamation point with a question mark to indicate a question asked emotionally. Don't do either. Exclamation points and question marks signal a full stop. Only one is needed or correct.

○ Don't use question marks after indirect quotations:

He said he wondered how it got there?

○ Journalists should avoid putting a question mark in parentheses to suggest dubiousness:

   WRONG   The music (?) consisted of squawks and static.

Such a practice has no place in a news story that readers expect to be free from personal opinion.

CHAPTER 10

Spelling Relief

President Andrew Jackson once said, "It's a damn poor mind that can think of only one way to spell a word!" Good minds or not, professional writers and editors are expected to be able to spell words correctly. And that spell-checker in your word processor makes correct spelling even more important because people assume that you now have no excuse for misspellings.

There are problems, though, with relying too heavily on spell-checkers. Sure, they can be great for helping you catch most typos. But they won't catch *it's* when you mean *its* or *there* when you mean *their*. Publications and the best websites require a consistent spelling of words according to their official stylebooks and dictionaries, but no spell checker will have all the same spellings. The AP Stylebook, for example, occasionally demands exceptions to the suggested spellings of its preferred dictionary, Webster's New World College Dictionary. Because many newspapers, magazines, broadcast stations and websites base style rules on those of the Associated Press and its recommended dictionaries, we follow that protocol in this book.

We begin with a few spelling rules that will save you time by eliminating the need to look up many spellings. A list of often-misspelled words follows. Learn as many of these as possible to reduce the time you spend with a dictionary, or simply use this list as a quick reference. We also have compiled rules of hyphenation and a useful reference list to save you time determining whether something should be one word, two words or hyphenated. Finally, for foreign students who learned British rather than American English, we provide a brief comparison of common spelling differences.

Spelling Rules

Prefixes

A *prefix* is a syllable, group of syllables or word united with or joined to the beginning of a word to alter its meaning or create a new word.

○ Prefixes usually have no effect on the spelling of the root word:

> legal, illegal
> [*Il* is a prefix meaning "not." You don't change the spelling of the root *legal* to add the prefix.]

○ If a word has the prefix *dis* or *mis*, there should be two *s*'s only if the root starts with an *s*:

> disappear, disappoint, disservice, misspell

Suffixes

A *suffix* is a sound, syllable or group of syllables added to the end of a word to change its meaning, give it grammatical function or form a new word. For example, *ish* added to *small* creates *smallish*; *ed* added to *walk* creates *walked*. There are some instances where suffixes change the spelling of words. Here are a few basic rules:

○ Change *y* to *i* before the suffixes *er* and *est*:

> happy, happier, happiest

○ Change a final *y* to *i* before adding a suffix that begins with any vowel other than *i*:

> likelihood, fiftyish

○ The words *mimic*, *panic*, *picnic* and *traffic* add a *k* before the suffixes *ed*, *er* and *ing*:

> mimicked, mimicker, mimicking

○ Words ending in *al* or *ful* form adverbs by adding *ly*:

> minimally, carefully

○ Words ending in *ic* generally form adverbs by adding *ally*:

> basically

An exception to this rule is *publicly*.

Vowels (the letters *a*, *e*, *i*, *o*, *u* and sometimes *y*) and consonants (the other letters of the alphabet) also may affect spelling, depending on where they fall in the word.

○ Double a final consonant before adding a suffix if (1) the suffix starts with a vowel, (2) the root word ends with a consonant, (3) a single vowel precedes the final consonant and (4) either the root word is one syllable or the root word's final syllable is stressed:

> DOUBLED CONSONANT   admitted, beginning, committed, deferred, dropped, forgettable, occurred, preferred, regrettable

SINGLE CONSONANT   benefited, canceled, galloped, happening, traveled, shipment, sadness

Don't double the final consonant for words with two vowels before the final consonant (*eaten, woolen*) or words ending in *x* (*fixing, taxed*). Note also these exceptions: *bused, handicapped, kidnapped, programmed* and *transferred*.

○ To decide whether a word should end in the suffix *able* or *ible*, remember that words ending in *able* generally can stand alone without the suffix and words ending in *ible* generally cannot stand alone without the suffix. Also, if a consonant is doubled immediately before the suffix, then the word is usually spelled with *ible*:

acceptable, adaptable, workable

credible, divisible, tangible

horrible, infallible, permissible, terrible [doubled consonant before *ible*]

○ If a word ends in a single *e*, drop the *e* before adding *able*:

likable, lovable, movable, salable

○ If a word ends in two *e*'s, keep both when adding *able*:

agreeable

○ Add *ible* if the root ends in a soft *c* sound, but first drop the final *e*:

forcible

Exceptions to these rules include *accessible, capable, collectible, durable, flexible, repressible, indispensable* and *responsible*.

Journalism Tip

Spelling and Your Career

If it's not enough to persuade you that a knowledge of spelling is useful because it saves you time and embarrassment, you should know that one of the most common types of tests given to prospective interns and job applicants in the professional writing and editing business is a spelling test. So, even if you're one of those people who think there's no need to learn spelling when there are spell-checkers—even though you need to learn math despite being able to use calculators—it's time to accept the fact that, like it or not, knowing how to spell may be important in getting that job you want.

The Silent *e*

○ A silent *e* on the end of a word usually is kept if the suffix starts with a consonant:

> hopeful

○ A silent *e* is usually dropped if the suffix starts with a vowel:

> hoping

Exceptions to this rule are *European* and *dyeing* (meaning "to color").

○ If the silent *e* follows a *c* or a *g*, the *e* is usually dropped before a suffix that starts with a consonant (*acknowledgment, judgment*) but kept before a suffix that starts with a vowel (*advantageous, enforceable, knowledgeable, manageable, noticeable, outrageous*).

An exception to this rule is *arrangement*.

Other Spelling Rules

○ Form plurals and possessives as described on Pages 44–47.

○ Use *i* before *e* except after *c*. But there are some notable exceptions:

> ancient, aweigh, beige, caffeine, counterfeit, financier, foreign, forfeit, heifer, height, inveigle, leisure, neighbor, neither, protein, science, seize, seizure, sleigh, sleight, sufficient, their, weigh, weight, weird

○ To decide between *ede* and *eed*, remember that one-syllable words typically are spelled with a double *e* but only four words of two syllables are. Other words take *ede*:

> **SINGLE-SYLLABLE WORDS WITH *eed***   bleed, deed, feed, need, peed, seed
>
> **DOUBLE-SYLLABLE WORDS WITH *eed***   exceed, indeed, proceed, succeed
>
> **WORDS WITH *ede***   concede, intercede, precede, recede

Supersede is the only word ending in *sede*.

○ To decide whether a word should be spelled with a *c* or an *s*, remember that nouns usually have a *c*, verbs an *s*:

NOUN	VERB
prophecy	prophesy
advice	advise

Exceptions are *license* and *practice*, which have the same spelling for both noun and verb.

○ Don't subtract letters when words are joined together:

> overrule

> withhold

○ To decide between *ary* and *ery*, remember that only seven common words end in *ery*: *cemetery, confectionery, distillery, millinery, monastery, periphery* and *stationery* (paper). For words other than these, use *ary*.

○ To decide between *efy* and *ify*, remember that only four common words end in *efy*: *liquefy, putrefy, rarefy* and *stupefy*. For words other than these, use *ify*.

○ The AP drops the *s* from words that could end in *ward* or *wards*:

> backward, forward, toward

○ The AP spells most words that could end in *og* or *ogue* with *ogue*, except for *catalog*:

> demagogue

> dialogue

> monologue (according to Webster's New World College Dictionary)

> travelogue

Words Often Misspelled

A		
aberration	acknowledge	aggressor
abet	acknowledgment	alleged
abhorrence	acoustics	allotted
abridgment	acquaintance	all ready (all were ready)
abscess	acquit	all right (not *alright*)
acceptable	acquitted	a lot (meaning much or many, but avoid except in a quote)
accessible	across	
accessory	adherent	
accidentally	admissible	already (previously, by now)
accommodate	adviser	
accumulate	affidavit	Alzheimer's disease
achievement	aficionado	analysis
	afterward	annihilate

anoint
antiquated
appalled
apparent
appearance
appellate
Arctic
argument
arrangement
ascend
asinine
assassin
assistant
athlete
attendance
auxiliary

B

baccalaureate
bachelor
backward
baker's dozen
baker's yeast
ballistic
bankruptcy
barbiturate
barrenness
battalion
beggar
beginning
bellwether
benefited
benefiting
berserk
bicycle
bona fide
bookkeeper
broccoli
Brussels sprouts

burqa
business

C

caffeine
calendar
caliber
campaign
canceled
cancellation
carburetor
caress
Caribbean
catalog
categorically
caterpillar
cemetery
census
centennial
chaise longue (not *lounge*)
changeable
chauffeur
chief
children's play
chitterlings
Cincinnati
circuit
citizens band
coconut
coed
collectible
collector's item
colossal
commemorate
commitment
committal
committee
compact disc

comparable
compatible
competent
conceit
conceive
condemn
confectioners' sugar
confident
congratulations
connoisseur
conquer
conscience
conscientious
conscious
consensus
consistent
controversy
convenient
coolly
corroborate
counterfeit
coup d'etat
courageous
criterion (not *criterium* in AP)
criticism
criticize
cruelly

D

deceit
deductible
defendant
defensible
definitely
deity
demagogue
dependent
derring-do

Spelling Relief

descendant
descent
description
desiccate
desirable
desperately
deteriorate
deterrent
development
dialogue
diaphragm
diarrhea
dietitian
difference
dilapidated
dilemma
dilettante
Diners Club
diphtheria
dirigible
disappear
disappoint
disastrous
discernible
discipline
disc jockey
disillusioned
Disposall (trademark)
dissension
disservice
dissociate
divisive
do's and don'ts
doughnut
Down syndrome
drought
drowned
Dr Pepper (trademark)
drunkenness

duffel bag
duly
dumbbell
dumbfounded
Dumpster (trademark)
durable

E

ebb
ecstasy (capitalize when the drug is meant)
eerie
eighth
elegant
eligible
embarrass
emphysema
employee
endeavor
environment
equipped
erroneous
especially
espresso
exaggerate
exceed
excitable
excusable
exhibition
exhilarating
existence
exorbitant
experience
explanation
extension
extraordinary
exuberant
eyeing

F

facetious
Fahrenheit
familiar
feasible
February
fierce
fiery
financier
firefighter
fluorescent
fluoride
forcible
foreign
forfeit
Formica (trademark)
fortunately
forty
forward
fourth
fraudulent
Frisbee (trademark)
fuchsia
fulfill

G

gaiety
galloped
garish
garrulous
gaudy
gauge
genealogy
glamorous
glamour
goodbye
gorilla
government
grammar

grievance
guarantee
guard
guerrilla

H

handkerchief
harass
hard disk
harebrained
harelip
height
heir
hemorrhage
heroes
hierarchy
hitchhiker
homicide
hygiene
hypocrisy
hysterical

I

ifs and buts
illegibly
illegitimate
immediately
impostor
inadmissible
inadvertent
inaugurate
incidentally
inconvenience
incredible
independent
indispensable
inevitable
inflammation
inherent

innocence
innocuous
innuendo
inoculate
inseparable
insistence
insulation
intercede
Internet
interrupt
irascible
iridescent
irrelevant
irreligious
irresistible
irreverent

J

jeopardy
jewelry
judgment
judicious

K

keenness
khaki
kidnapped
kimono
kindergarten
knowledgeable

L

laboratory
laid
lambaste
laser disc
legerdemain
legionnaire
legitimate

leisure
liability
liaison
license
lieutenant
lightning
likable
likelihood
liquefy
loathsome
loneliness
luscious

M

mah-jongg
maintenance
malarkey
manageable
maneuver
marijuana
marriage
marshal
massacre
mayonnaise
meander
medicine
medieval
Mediterranean
memento
menswear
merited
metallic
millennium,
millennia
millionaire
mimicked
miniature
minuscule
miscellaneous

mischievous
mishap
missile
misspell
mollify
monastery
murmured
mystifying

N

naive
naphtha
necessary
neighbor
newsstand
nickel
niece
ninth
noticeable
nowadays
nuisance

O

oblige
observer
occasion
occurred
occurrence
offense
offered
OK'd
omission
omitted
opossum
opportunity
oppressive
optimistic
ordinarily
original

oscillate
overrule
Oyez

P

paid
papier-mâché
paraffin
parallel
paralyzed
paraphernalia
pari-mutuel
parishioner
parliamentary
particularly
pastime
pavilion
peaceable
peculiarly
penicillin
percent
peremptory
permanent
permissible
perseverance
persistent
Philippines
physician
picnicking
pierce
pigeon
plaque
plausible
playwright
pneumonia
poinsettia
Portuguese
possession
potatoes

practically
precede
predecessor
preferred
preparation
prerogative
presence
presumptuous
pretense
prevalence
preventive
primitive
privilege
procedure
proceed
prodigy
professor
profited
propeller
prosecutor
prurient
publicly
purify
pursue

Q

quandary
quantity
quantum
quarreling
querulous
query
questionnaire
queue
quotient

R

rarefy
rarity

readable
receipt
receive
recommend
reconnaissance
reconnoiter
recur
referee
reference
referred
rehearsal
reign
relevant
religious
reminiscence
renovation
renowned
repetitious
repressible
reservoir
resistance
responsibility
restaurateur
resurrection
retinue
Reye's syndrome
rheumatism
rhyme
rhythm
ridiculous
rock 'n' roll

S

sacrilegious
salable
sanitarium
schedule
scissors
secession

seize
seizure
separate
sergeant
sheriff
short-lived
siege
sieve
signaled
silhouette
similar
sincerely
sizable
skier
skiing
skillful
skulduggery
soldier
solicitor
soliloquy
soluble
soothe
sophomore
sovereign
spiraled
straitjacket
strictly
stupefy
subpoena
subtlety
subtly
succeed
successful
superintendent
supersede
surfeit
surprise
surveillance
susceptible

symmetry
synonymous

T

tariff
teachers college
teenage
temperamental
tendency
tentacles
tepee
theater
thoroughly
till
tinker's damn
tobacco
toboggan
tomatoes
tornadoes
tournament
toward
tranquillity
transferal
transmitter
traveler
travelogue
truly
Tucson
tumultuous
twelfth
tying
typing
tyrannous

U

ukulele
uncontrollable
undoubtedly
upward
usable

Spelling Relief

V		
vacancy	volume	witticism
vacillate	voyageur	women's college
vacuum	voyeur	wondrous
vengeance		woolen
verifiable	**W**	
veterinary	Wednesday	**X**
vicious	weird	X-ray
victuals	wherever	
videodisc	wholly	**Y**
vilify	wield	yield
villain	wiener	
virtually	willful	**Z**
volcanoes	wiry	zany
	withhold	zucchini

Hyphenation as a Spelling Problem

Rules for Hyphenation

Writers and editors often are confused about whether a word is written as one word, as two words or with a hyphen. Here are some rules that may help. The rules are followed by a useful reference list.

- Suffixes are not usually hyphenated unless adding one would result in three *l*'s in a row:

    catlike

    shell-less

- Sometimes, compound adjectives in which the "suffix" is really a separate word are hyphenated, and other times they are not:

    penny-wise

    streetwise

- There's no hyphen before the suffixes *goer* or *wide*:

    churchgoer, filmgoer

    citywide, nationwide

- Many compounds that use a preposition such as *down, in, off, out, over* or *up* are hyphenated, but many other compound words with prepositions at the end have dropped the hyphen:

break-in, carry-over, close-up, fade-out

breakup, fallout, holdover, takeoff

○ These prefixes are generally not hyphenated:

a (not, out)

ante (before)

anti (against)

bi (two)

by (near) — exception: *by-election*

dis (opposite)

full (complete)

hydro (water)

hyper (above, excessive)

infra (below)

inter (among, between)

intra (within)

mid (middle)

mini (small)

multi (many)

non (not)

pan (all)

post (after) — exceptions: *post-bellum, post-mortem, post-obit*

pre (before)

re (again) — exceptions: When two different words would otherwise be spelled the same, hyphenate the one that means "again": *re-cover* (cover again), *re-creation* (a new creation).

semi (partly)

sub (under)

trans (across)

ultra (beyond)

un (not)

under (beneath)

up (above)

○ These prefixes generally are hyphenated:

after (following) — exception: no hyphen if used to form a noun

all (every)

co (with) — exceptions: The AP says to retain the hyphen when forming words that "indicate occupation or status" (*co-author, co-pilot, co-star*) but not to hyphenate other combinations (*coed, coeducation, coequal, coexist, coexistence, cooperate, cooperative, coordinate, coordination*).

ex (former)—exceptions: words that mean "out of," such as *excommunicate, expropriate*

like (similar)—exceptions: *likelihood, likeness, likewise*

odd (unusual)—exception: *oddball*

off (away)—exceptions: *offbeat, offcast, offhand, offload, offprint, offset, offshoot, offshore, offside, offspring, offstage*

one (single)

pro (for)—exceptions: words that do not connote support for something, such as *produce, profile, pronoun*

self—exceptions: *selfish, selfless, selfsame*

well (very)

wide (completely)—exception: *widespread*

○ Words beginning with the prefixes *half* and *pre* are sometimes hyphenated, sometimes not. You'll just have to look them up. If they do not appear in Webster's New World College Dictionary, hyphenate them.

○ The prefix *vice* remains a separate word:

vice president

○ When a prefix is added to a number or to a word that starts with a capital letter, use a hyphen after the prefix:

anti-American, mid-20s, pre-Columbian, trans-Atlantic

○ When a prefix is added to a word that starts with the same letter, use a hyphen after the prefix:

pre-election, pre-eminent, pre-empt, pre-exist, semi-invisible

Exceptions are *cooperate* and *coordinate*.

Looking Up Words for Hyphenation

Compound nouns pose spelling problems because they are so inconsistent. Some are written as two words, some are one word and some are hyphenated. A compound noun generally starts as two words. Then, as the phrase becomes used more often, the two words get shoved together as one, perhaps going through a preliminary hyphenated stage. If you look through the "One Word, Two Words or Hyphenated?" list that follows, you'll see how unpredictable and inconsistent compound nouns can be.

To decide whether a word is one word, two words or hyphenated, here's the procedure for looking it up, according to the AP Stylebook:

1. Check the AP Stylebook.
2. If it's not there, check Webster's New World College Dictionary.

3. If it's not in the New World, check Webster's Third New International Dictionary.
4. If it's not in the Third, we suggest you make the word two words if it's a noun or verb, or hyphenate it if it's an adjective.

Follow these steps in order and do not stop until you either find the word or reach the fourth step. Otherwise, there's a good chance you won't be spelling the word right. For example, it would be possible for the AP to have a certain compound as two words, for Webster's New World to make it hyphenated and for Webster's Third to have it as one word. So, if you thought you'd save time by skipping to Webster's New World or Webster's Third, you'd be spelling the word wrong, according to the AP.

Following these rules, we've put together a list of commonly questioned compound words. You might want to check this list before going through the four-step procedure because if we have the word here, it could save you some time.

One Word, Two Words or Hyphenated?

A

able-bodied
about-face
aboveboard
absent-minded
accident-prone
ad hominem
ad-lib (n., v., adj.)
ad nauseam
A-frame
African-American (n., adj.)
aftereffect
after-hours
afterthought
aide-de-camp, aides-de-camp
air base
air-condition (v.)
air-conditioned
air conditioner
air conditioning
aircraft
airfare

air force base
airline, airlines (but check individual name)
air lock
airmail
airport
air show
airstrip
airtight
airtime
air traffic controller
airwaves
airways
a la carte
a la king
a la mode
all-around (not *all-round*, says AP)
all-clear
all-out
all-purpose
all ready (everyone is ready), already (by now)

all right
allspice
all-star
all time (n.), all-time (adj.)
alma mater
a lot
also-ran (n.)
ambassador-at-large
anal-retentive (adj.)
anchorman, anchorwoman (not *anchor* or *co-anchor*, says AP)
antebellum
anteroom
anti-abortion
anti-aircraft
anti-bias
antibiotic
antibody
anticlimax
antidepressant
antidote
antifreeze

antigen

antihistamine

anti-inflation

anti-intellectual

antiknock

anti-labor

antimatter

antiparticle

antipasto

antiperspirant

antiphony

antiproton

antiseptic

antiserum

anti-social

antithesis

antitoxin

antitrust

antitussive

anti-war

any body (any one person), anybody (any person at all)

any more (something additional: *I don't have any more*), anymore (adv.)

any one (any one person or thing), anyone (any person at all)

any way (in any manner), anyway (in any event)

apron strings

Aqua-Lung (trademark)

archbishop

archdiocese

archenemy

archrival

arm-wrestling

arrowhead

art film

art form

artifact

artwork

ashcan

ashtray

attorney general, attorneys general

autoerotism

automaker

automated teller machine

auto racing

autoworker

awe-struck

a while (noun as object of prep. or in phrases such as *a while ago* or *a while back*), awhile (adv.)

B

baby boomer

baby-sat

baby-sit

baby sitter

baby-sitting

backboard

backcountry

backcourt

backcourtman

back door (n.), backdoor (adj.)

backfield

backfire

backhanded

back porch (n.), back-porch (adj.)

backrest

back road

backroom

back-scratching

back seat (n.), back-seat (adj.)

backspace

backstabbing

backstop

back street (n.), back-street (adj.)

back-to-back

backtrack

back up (v.), backup (n., adj.)

backwater

backwoods

backyard (n., adj.)

badman

bail out (v.), bailout (n.)

baldfaced

ball boy

ball carrier

ballclub

ballgame

ball girl

ballhandler

ballpark

ballplayer

ball point pen

ballroom

Band-Aid (trademark)

bandleader

band saw

band shell

bandwagon

bandwidth

bank robber

bare-bones (adj.)

barefaced

barehanded

bareheaded

barhop

barkeeper

barmaid

bar mitzvah

barrel-chested

barrelhouse

barroom

barstool

baseboard heating

baseline

bas mitzvah

batboy

batgirl

bathtub

bat mitzvah

battle-ax

battlefield

battleground

battleship

battle station

beanbag chair

bedbug

bedclothes

bedpan

bedpost

bedrail

bed rest

bedrock

bedsheet

beekeeper

beeswax

bell-bottom

bellboy

belles-lettres

bellhop

bellwether

belly button

belly dance (n.),
belly-dance (v.)

belly dancer

belly-flop

best-seller

best-selling

biannual (twice a
year), biennial (every
two years)

bifocal

big band (n.),
big-band (adj.)

big-bang theory

big house

Big Three automakers

big-ticket

big time (n.),
big-time (adj.)

bigwig

bikeway

bilingual

bimonthly

biodegradable

biodiversity

bioterrorism

bipartisan

bird dog (n.),
bird-dog (v.)

birdhouse

birdseed

bird's-eye

bird-watching
(n., adj.)

birthmark

birth mother

birthparent

birthplace

birthrate

biweekly

blackboard

blackout

blast off (v.),
blastoff (n., adj.)

blind side (n.),
blindside (v.)

blockbuster

bloodbath

bloodhound

bloodstain (n., v.)

blow-dryer

blow up (v.),
blowup (n.)

blue blood (n.),
blue-blooded (adj.)

blue chip stock

blue collar (n.),
blue-collar (adj.)

blue line

blue-sky (adj.)

boardinghouse

boarding school

boardroom

bobsledding

bodybuilder

body check (n., v.)

body count

bodyguard

boilerplate

boldface

boll weevil

bombproof

bona fide

bonbon

boo-boo

bookcase

bookdealer

bookend

bookmobile

bookshelf

bookshop

bookstore

bookworm

boombox

boomtown

bottom line (n.),
bottom-line (adj.)

bowlegged

bowl game

boxcar

box kite

box office (n.),
box-office (adj.)

box score

boyfriend

brain wave

brand name (n.),
brand-name (adj.)

brand-new (adj.)

breadbox

breadwinner

break dancing (n.),
break-dancing (adj.)

break down (v.),
breakdown (n.)

break in (v.),
break-in (n., adj.)

breakthrough

break up (v.),
breakup (n., adj.)

breast-feed

bricklayer

Bricklayers union

bridegroom

bridesmaid

broad-minded

broadside

broodmare

brother-in-law,
brothers-in-law

brown-nose (v.),
brown-noser (n.)

brownout

brush fire

buckshot

bug boy

build up (v.),
buildup (n., adj.)

bulldozer

bullet hole

bulletproof

bullfight

bullfighter

bullfighting

bullpen

bull's-eye

Bundt cake

bushelbasket

businesslike

businessman

businesswoman

bus line

busload

buy out (v.),
buyout (n.)

by-election

bygone

bylaw

byline

bypass

byproduct

bystreet

C

cabdriver

cabinetmaker

cakewalk

call up (v.),
call-up (n., adj.)

camera-ready (adj.)

candleholder

candlelit

candlemaker

candymaker

cannot

card maker

carefree

caretaker

carmaker

car pool

carport

carry over (v.),
carry-over (n., adj.)

car seat

carsick

carwash

caseload

cashbox

cash cow

cash flow

cast member

catch all (v.),
catchall (n., adj.)

cave in (v.),
cave-in (n., adj.)

CD-ROM

cease fire (v.),
cease-fire (n., adj.)

cellphone

center field

center fielder

centerfold

cha-cha

chain saw

chairman

chairperson

chairwoman

change over (v.),
changeover (n.)

change up (v.),
change-up (n., adj.)

check up (v.),
checkup (n.)

cheese maker

child care

chip-maker (n.),
chip-making (adj.)

chock-full

chowhound

Christmastime

churchgoer

church member

citizens band

city editor

city hall

citywide

claptrap

clean-cut

clean up (v.),
cleanup (n., adj.)

clear-cut

clearinghouse

cloak-and-dagger

clockwise

closed shop

close up (v.),
close-up (n., adj.)

clubhouse

coal mine

coal miners

coastline

coatdress

coattails

co-author

Coca-Cola
(trademark)

co-chairman

coconut

co-defendant

coed (but avoid as
sexist)

coeducation (but
avoid as sexist)

coequal

coexist

coexistence

coffee grinder

coffee maker

coffeepot

coffee table (n.),
coffee-table (adj.)

co-host

coleslaw

colorblind

commander in chief

concertgoer

congressman

congresswoman

con man

consumer price index
(generic), Consumer
Price Index (U.S.)

continentwide

co-op (short form of
cooperative)

cooperate

cooperative

coordinate

coordination

co-owner

co-partner

co-pilot

cop out (v.),
cop-out (n.)

copy desk

copy edit

copy editor

copyright (n., v.,
adv.)

co-respondent (in a
divorce proceeding)

cornstarch

co-signer

co-star

cost-effective

cost of living (n.),
cost-of-living (adj.)

cost-plus

countdown (n.),
count down (v.)

counteract

countercharge

counterintelligence

counterproposal

counterspy

countertop

countryside

countrywide

countywide

courthouse

court-martial (n., v.),
courts-martial

courtroom

cover up (v.),
cover-up (n., adj.)

co-worker

crack up (v.),
crackup (n., adj.)

crawfish (not crayfish,
says AP)

crawl space

crew member

crisscross

Crock-Pot
(trademark)

cropland

cross country (the
sport), cross-country
(other contexts)

cross-examination

cross-examine

cross-eyed (adj., adv.)

crossfire

cross over (v.),
crossover (n., adj.)

cross rate

cross section (n.),
cross-section (v.)

cure-all

curtain raiser

custom-made

cut back (v.),
cutback (n., adj.)

cut off (v.),
cutoff (n., adj.)

cutoffs

cut out (v.),
cutout (n.)

cyberspace

D

damn it

dark horse

databank

database

data processing
(n., adj.)

date line (the international one), dateline
(on a news story)

daughter-in-law,
daughters-in-law

daylight-saving time

daylong

daytime

day to day (adv.),
day-to-day (adj.)

D-Day

dead center

dead end (n.),
dead-end (adj.)

deathbed

decade-long

decision maker

decision making (n.),
decision-making
(adj.)

Deepfreeze (trademark), deep freeze
(postpone)

deep freezer

deep-sea (adj.)

deep water (n.),
deep-water (adj.)

degree-day

derring-do

desktop (n., adj.)

die-hard (n., adj.)

dinner table

disk operating
system

ditchdigger

docudrama

dogcatcher

doghouse

dollhouse

door to door (n.),
door-to-door (adj.)

dot-com

double-barreled
shotgun

double bind

double-check

double-click

double-faced

doubleheader

double-parked
(v., adj.)

double play

downdraft

downgrade

down-home (adj.)

downside

downside risk

down-to-earth

downtown

dressing room

drive in (v.),
drive-in (n., adj.)

driveway

drop out (v.),
dropout (n.)

dump truck

dust storm

Dutch oven

dyed-in-the-wool
(adj.)

E

earmark (v.)

earthquake

easygoing

e-book

e-business

e-commerce

editor in chief,
editors in chief

electrocardiogram

email

empty-handed

end line

end zone

en route

eurodollar

even-steven

every day (adv.),
everyday (adj.)

every one (each individual item), everyone
(all people)

ex-convict

ex-governor

ex-president

extra-base hit

extra-dry (adj.)

extra-large (adj.)

extralegal

extramarital

extra-mild (adj.)

extraterrestrial

extraterritorial

eyesore

eyestrain

eye to eye (adv.),
eye-to-eye (adj.)

eyewitness

F

face-lift

face off (v.),
faceoff (n., adj.)

face to face (adv.),
face-to-face (adj.)

fact-finding (n., adj.)

fade out (v.),
fade-out (n.)

fair ball

fair catch

fairway

fall out (v.),
fallout (n.)

far-fetched

far-flung

farmhouse

farmland

farmworker

far-off (adj.)

far-ranging

farsighted

fastball

father-in-law,
fathers-in-law

feather bedding (mattress), featherbedding
(union practice)

fender bender

Ferris wheel

ferryboat

Fiberglas (trademark), fiberglass
(generic)

field goal

field house

field trip

fieldwork

figure skater

figure skating

filmgoer

filmmaker

filmmaking (n., adj.)

film ratings

fingertip

firearm

fire breather

fire chief

firefighter

fireman

fireproof

firetruck

fire wagon

firewall

first baseman

first-degree (adj.)

firsthand

fistfight

flagpole

flagship

flameout

flare up (v.),
flare-up (n.)

flash flood (n., adj.)

flash flood watch

flea market

flimflam

flip-flop

floodwaters

floor leader

floor-length

floppy disk

flower girl

flyswatter

folk singer

folk song

follow-through

follow up (v.),
follow-up (n., adj.)

foolproof

foot-and-mouth
disease

forebrain

forecast

forefather

foregoing

foreman

fore-topgallant

fore-topmast

fore-topsail

forewoman

fortnight

fortuneteller

fortunetelling

forty-niner *or* '49er

foul ball line

foul line

foul shot

foul tip

foul up (v.),
foul-up (n.)

four-flush

Four-H Club
(4-H Club is
preferred)

4-H'er

fraidy-cat

frame up (v.),
frame-up (n.)

free-for-all

freelance (v., adj.),
freelancer (n.)

free on board

freestanding

free throw

free-throw line

freewheeling

freewill offering

freeze-dried

freeze-dry

freeze-drying

frontcourt

front line (n.),
front-line (adj.)

front page (n.),
front-page (adj.)

front-runner

fruit grower

fullback

full-court press

full-dress

full faith and credit
bond

full-fledged

full house

full-length

full page (n.),
full-page (adj.)

full-scale

full-size (adj.)

full time (n.),
full-time (adj.)

fundraiser

fundraising

<hr>

G

game plan

general obligation
bond

get away (v.),
getaway (n.)

get together (v.),
get-together (n.)

gift wrap (n.),
gift-wrap (v.)

girlfriend

give away (v.),
giveaway (n.)

globe-trotting

go ahead (v.),
go-ahead (n.)

goal line

goal-line stand

goal post

goaltender

goaltending

gobbledygook

go between (v.),
go-between (n.)

godchild

goddaughter

go-go

goodbye

good night

good will (n.),
goodwill (adj.)

goose bumps

granddad

granddaughter

grant-in-aid,
grants-in-aid

greenmail

gross domestic
product

gross national
product

groundbreaking

groundhog

ground-rule double

ground rules

groundskeeper

groundswell

groundwater

ground zero

grown-up (n., adj.)

G-string

guesthouse

gunbattle

gunboat

gunfight

gunfire

gung-ho

gunpoint

gunpowder

<hr>

H

hair dryer

hairsbreadth

hairstyle

hairstyling

hairstylist

halfback

half-baked

half-blood

half brother

half-cocked

half-court press

half dollar

halfhearted

half-hour (n.; adj.)

half-life

half-mast

half-mile pole

half-moon

half note

half sister

half size (n.),
half-size (adj.)

half-staff

half tide

halftime

halftone

halftrack

half-truth

handball

hand-carved

handcrafted

hand-held

handhold

handmade

handoff

hand-painted

hand-picked

hand-set (v.),
handset (n.)

hand-sewn

hands off (n.),
hands-off (adj.)

hand-stitched

hand to hand (n.),
hand-to-hand (adj.)

hand to mouth (n.),
hand-to-mouth (adj.)

hand warmer

handwrought

hangover

hang up (v.),
hang-up (n.)

hanky-panky

hardback

hard-bound

hard copy

hardcover

hard drive

hard line (n.),
hard-line (adj.)

hardworking

harebrained

harelip

has been (v.),
has-been (n.)

H-bomb

headache

headlong

head-on

health care (n., adj.)

health club

heartbeat

heartfelt

heartrending

heartwarming

helter-skelter

heyday

hideaway

hide out (v.),
hide-out (n.)

hi-fi

higher-up (n.)

high jinks

high point

high-rise (n., adj.)

high-step (v.)

high-stepper

high-tech

hit and run (v.),
hit-and-run (n., adj.)

hitchhike

hitchhiker

hit man

hocus-pocus

hodgepodge

ho-hum

hold over (v.),
holdover (n.)

hold up (v.),
holdup (n., adj.)

home-baked

home builder

homebuyer

homefront

homegrown

homemade

homemaker

homeowner

home page

home plate

home run

hometown

hoof-and-mouth
disease

hook shot

hook up (v.),
hookup (n.)

horsepower

horse race

horse racing

horse rider

horse-trader

hotbed

hotheaded

hot line

hot seat

hot spot

hot tub

hourlong

house call

housecleaning

household

househusband

houseplant

hurly-burly

hush-hush

hydroelectric

hydrophobia

hyperactive

hypercritical

I

ice age (n., adj.)

ice storm

ice storm warning

inasmuch

inbound

in-depth

Indochina

indoor (adj.),
indoors (adv.)

industrywide

infield

infighting

infrared

infrastructure

in-group

in-house

in-law

inpatient (n., adj.)

input (n.)

insofar

in spite of

interracial

interstate

intramural

intranet

intrastate

J

jai alai

JavaScript

Jaycees

jerry-built

jetliner

jet plane

job hunting (n.),
job-hunting (adj.)

jukebox

jumbo jet

jump ball

jump shot

jury-rigged

K

keynote

kick off (v.),
kickoff (n., adj.)

kilowatt-hour

kindergarten

kindhearted

Kmart (trademark)

knickknack

knock off (v.),
knock-off (n.)

knock out (v.),
knock-out (n., adj.)

know-how

kowtow

L

lamebrain

lame duck (n.),
lame-duck (adj.)

last-ditch effort

latecomer

lawsuit

layup

left guard

left hand (n.),
left-handed (adj.)

left-hander

left wing (n.),
left-wing (adj.)

left-winger

lengthwise

let up (v.),
letup (n., adj.)

life jacket

lifelike

lifelong

Life Saver (trademark
for candy), lifesaver
(generic)

life-size

life span

lifestyle

lifetime

life vest

lift off (v.),
liftoff (n., adj.)

light bulb

lighthearted

light-year

like-minded

like-natured

likewise

linebacker

line drive

lineman

line up (v.),
lineup (n.)

long distance (n.),
long-distance (adj.,
or in reference to
phone calls)

long-lasting

long-lived

long-range

long run (n.),
long-run (adj.)

long shot (n.),
long-shot (adj.)

long-standing

long term (n.),
long-term (adj.)

long time (n.),
longtime (adj.)

look-alike

lovemaking

low-ball

lowercase

lumberyard

lunchbox

lunch cart

lunchroom

lunchtime

M

machine gun (n.),
machine-gun (adj., v.)

machine-gunner

machine-made

mah-jongg

major league (n., adj.)

major leaguer

makeshift

make up (v.),
makeup (n., adj.)

man-to-man

mapmaker

marketbasket

marketplace

meatball

meatcutter

meatloaf

melt down (v.),
meltdown (n.)

ménage à trois

menswear

merry-go-round

metalwork

mid-America

mid-Atlantic

midcourt

middle class (n.),
middle-class (adj.)

middleman

midnight

midsemester

midshipman

midterm

midwinter

milquetoast

mindset

mine shaft

minibus

miniseries

miniskirt

minivan

minor league
(n., adj.)

mix up (v.),
mix-up (n., adj.)

mock-up (n.)

moneymaker

money-saving

monthlong

mo-ped

mop up (v.),
mop-up (n., adj.)

moral obligation bond

mother-in-law,
mothers-in-law

motorboat

motor home

mountain man

mousehole

moviegoer

movie house

moviemaker

moviemaking

MP3

mudslide

mudslinging

multicolored

multilateral

multimillion

multimillionaire

muscle ache

mutual field

N

nail clippers

name tag

narrow gauge (n.),
narrow-gauge (adj.)

narrow-minded

nationwide

near shore (prep.
phrase), nearshore
(adj.)

nearsighted

neoconservative

neo-Pentecostal

nerve-racking

net asset value

newfangled

newsmagazine

newsroom

newsstand

news writer

news writing

new wave (n.),
new-wave (adj.)

nickname

nightclub

night shift

nightspot

nighttime

nitpicking

nitty-gritty

no man's land

nonaligned

nonchalance

nonchalant

nondescript

nonentity

nonprofit

nonrestrictive

nonsense

nonsensical

nonviolent

no one

O

oceangoing

odd-looking

odd-numbered

oddsmaker

off-Broadway

off-color

off-duty

offhand

officeholder

offline

off-off-Broadway

off-peak

Spelling Relief

off-road

offseason

offset

offshore

offside

off-site

offstage

off-white

oilman

old-fashioned

old-time

old-timer

old times

Old West

Old World

one-fourth

one-half

one-sided

one-third

one time (n.),
one-time (adj.)

ongoing

online

open-minded

outact

outargue

outbluff

outbrag

outclimb

outdated

outdistance

outdrink

outeat

outfield

outfielder

outfight

outfox

outhit

outleap

outmatch

out of bounds (adv.),
out-of-bounds (adj.)

out of court (adv.),
out-of-court (adj.)

outpatient (n., adj.)

outperform

outpitch

outpointed

outpost

outproduce

output

outquote

outrace

outscore

outshout

outsource

outstrip

outswim

outtalk

outwalk

ovenproof

overall

overbuy

overexert

overrate

override

oversize

over the counter
(adv.), over-the-
counter (adj.)

overtime

overview

P

pacemaker

pacesetter

paddy wagon

painkiller

pantheism

pantsuit

pantyhose

Pap (test, smear)

paper bag

paper clip

paper towel

paperwork

Parent Teacher
Association

pari-mutuel

parkland

part time (adv.),
part-time (adj.)

partygoer

passed ball

passer-by, passers-by

patrolman

patrolwoman

paycheck

payday

payload

peacekeeper

peacekeeping

peacemaker

peacemaking

peace offering

peacetime

pell-mell

penalty box

penny-wise

pen pal

percent

pet store

petty officer

pigeonhole (n., v.)

pile up (v.),
pileup (n., adj.)

pillowcase

pinch hit (v.),
pinch-hit (n., adj.)

pinch hitter

Ping-Pong (trade-
mark), pingpong
(generic)

pin up (v.), pinup (n.)

pipeline

pitchout (n.)

pivotman

place kick

place-kicker

place mat

play off (v.), playoff (n., adj.)

pocketbook

pocket watch

point-blank

policyholder

policymaker

policymaking (n., adj.)

pom-pom (weapon), pompom (cheerleader paraphernalia)

pooh-pooh

postcard

postdate

postdoctoral

postelection

postgraduate

post-mortem

post office

postoperative

postscript

postseason

postwar

pothole

potluck

potshot

pound-foolish

powder keg

power line

power play

power-play goal

prearrange

precondition

pre-convention

precook

precut

predate

pre-dawn

predispose

pre-election

pre-eminent

pre-empt

pre-establish

pre-exist

prefix

preflight

preheat

prehistoric

preignition

prejudge

premarital

premenstrual

prenatal

preregister

preschool

preseason

preset

pretax

pretest

pretrial

prewar

prewash

price-earnings ratio

price tag

prima-facie (adj.)

prime rate

prizewinner

prizewinning

pro-business

profit-sharing (n., adj.)

profit taking (n.), profit-taking (adj.)

pro-labor

pro-life

pro-peace

pro-war

pull back (v.), pullback (n.)

pull out (v.), pullout (n.)

punch line

purebred

push-button (n., adj.)

push up (v.), push-up (n., adj.)

put out (v.), putout (n.)

Q

Q-and-A format

quarterback

QE2

question mark

quick-witted

R

racetrack

racquetball

railroad

rainstorm

ranch house

ranchland

rangeland

rank and file (n.), rank-and-file (adj.)

rawhide

razor strop

razzle-dazzle

razzmatazz

ready-made

rearview mirror

recover (regain), re-cover (cover again)

Spelling Relief

red-haired

red-handed
(adj., adv.)

redhead

redheaded

red-hot

red line

redlining

redneck (derogatory
term)

re-elect

re-election

re-emerge

re-employ

re-enact

re-engage

re-enlist

re-enter

re-entry

re-equip

re-establish

re-examine

reform (improve),
re-form (form again)

rendezvous

resign (quit),
re-sign (sign again)

riffraff

right guard

right hand (n.),
right-handed (adj.)

right-hander (n.)

right of way

right-to-work (adj.)

right wing (n.),
right-wing (adj.)

ring bearer

rip off (v.),
rip-off (n., adj.)

riverboat

roadside

rock 'n' roll

role model

roll call (n.),
roll-call (adj.)

roller coaster

roller skate (n.),
roller-skate (v.)

roller skater (n.)

roll over (v.),
rollover (n.)

roly-poly

round table (n.),
round-table (adj.)

round trip (n.),
round-trip (adj.)

round up (v.),
roundup (n.)

rubber band

rubber stamp (n.),
rubber-stamp
(v., adj.)

runback (n.)

run down (v.),
rundown (n.),
run-down (adj.)

runner-up,
runners-up

running back

running mate

rush hour (n.),
rush-hour (adj.)

___

S

safe-deposit box

sales pitch

sandbag

sandstorm

saucepan

savings and loan
association

school bus

schoolteacher

scot-free

screen saver

seat belt (n.),
seat-belt (adj.)

seawater

second guess (n.),
second-guess (v.)

second-guesser

second hand (n.),
secondhand
(adj., adv.)

second-rate

secretary-general

secretary-treasurer

seesaw

self-assured

self-defense

self-esteem

self-governing

self-government

sell out (v.),
sellout (adj., n.)

semiannual

semicolon

semifinal

semi-invalid

semiofficial

semitrailer

semitropical

semiweekly

send off (v.),
send-off (n.)

service mark

set up (v.),
setup (n., adj.)

7-Eleven (trademark)

Seven-Up or 7UP
(trademarks)

sewer line

shake up (v.),
shake-up (n., adj.)

shape up (v.),
shape-up (n., adj.)

Sheetrock
(trademark)

shirt sleeve (n.),
shirt-sleeve (adj.)

shoeshine

shoestring

shoot out (v.),
shootout (n.)

shopworn

shortchange

short-handed

short-lived

shortstop

shotgun

showcase

show off (v.),
showoff (n.)

showroom

showstopper

shut down (v.),
shutdown (n.)

shut in (v.),
shut-in (n.)

shut off (v.),
shut-off (n.)

shut out (v.),
shutout (n., adj.)

side by side (adv.),
side-by-side (adj.)

side dish

side effect

sidestep

side street (n.)

sidetrack

side trip

sightseeing

sightseer

sign up (v.),
sign-up (n., adj.)

single-handed

sister-in-law,
sisters-in-law

sit down (v.),
sit-down (n., adj.)

sit in (v.),
sit-in (n., adj.)

skyrocketing

slantwise

slap shot

sledgehammer

sleight of hand (n.),
sleight-of-hand (adj.)

slide show

slow down (v.),
slowdown (n.)

slumlord

slush fund

small-arms fire

small-business man

smash up (v.),
smashup (n., adj.)

smoke bomb

smoke screen

snow avalanche
bulletin

snowdrift

snowfall

snowflake

snowman

snowplow

snowshoe

snowstorm

snowsuit

so called (adv.),
so-called (adj.)

softcover

soft pedal (n.),
soft-pedal (v.)

soft-spoken

software

songwriter

son-in-law,
sons-in-law

sound barrier

sound bite

sound effects

soundstage

soundtrack (n., adj.)

source code

spacecraft

spaceship

space shuttle

spacewalk

speechmaker

speechmaking

speechwriter

speech writing

speed bump

speed up (v.),
speedup (n., adj.)

spin off (v.),
spinoff (n., adj.)

split end

sports editor

sportswear

sportswriter

sport utility vehicle

spot-check

spotlight

springtime

squeeze play

staff writer

stage fright

stained glass (n.),
stained-glass (adj.)

stand-alone (adj.)

standard-bearer

stand in (v.),
stand-in (n., adj.)

standing room only

stand off (v.),
standoff (n., adj.)

stand out (v.),
standout (n., adj.)

stand up (v.),
stand-up (adj.)

starboard

start up (v.),
startup (n., adj.)

statehouse

states' rights

statewide

station wagon

steady-state theory

stepbrother

stepchild

stepdaughter

stepfamily

stepfather

stepmother

stepparent

steppingstone

stepsister

stepson

stockbroker

stock index futures

stockman

stock market prices

stone carver

stool pigeon

stopgap

stop off (v.),
stop-off (n.)

stop over (v.),
stopover (n.)

storm tide

storyline

storyteller

stove top (n.),
stove-top (adj.)

straight-laced (strict
or severe), strait-laced
(pertaining to con-
finement, as a corset)

straitjacket

street dance

street gang

streetlamp

streetlight

street people

street-smart (adj.)

street smarts (n.)

street sweeper

streetwalker

streetwise

strikebreaker

strike zone

strong-arm (v., adj.)

strong-willed

stylebook

subbasement

subcommittee

subculture

subdivision

submachine gun

suborbital

subtotal

subzero

summertime

sunbathe

sunbather

sunbathing

sundress

sun porch

superagency

supercarrier

supercharge

super collider

superconducting

superhighway

superhuman

superpower

supersonic

supertanker

supragovernmental

supranational

surface-to-air missile

sweatpants

sweatshirt

sweatsuit

T

tablecloth

tablespoon

table talk

table tennis

tag end

tailback

taillight

tailor-made

tailpipe

tailspin

tail wind

take charge (v.),
take-charge (adj.)

take down (v.),
takedown (n., adj.)

take-home pay

take off (v.),
takeoff (n., adj.)

take out (v.),
takeout (n., adj.)

take over (v.),
takeover (n., adj.)

take up (v.),
takeup (n., adj.)

talebearer

talk show

tap dance (n.),
tap-dance (v.)

tap dancer

tape-record (v.)

tape recording (n.)

task force

tattletale

tax-deductible

teachers college

teakettle

teammate

team teaching

tear gas (n.),
tear-gas (adj., v.)

teaspoon

teenage (adj.)

teenager

teeny-weeny

telecommute

teleconference

telecourse

telemarketing

TelePrompTer
(trademark)

telltale

temperature-humidity
index

tenderhearted

tenfold

term paper

terror-stricken

terry cloth

Texas leaguer

thank you (v.),
thank-you (n., adj.)

theatergoer

thermonuclear

Third World

3-D

3M

three R's

threesome

throw away (v.),
throwaway (n., adj.)

thruway

thumbscrew

thumbtack

thunderbolt

thundershower

thunderstorm

thunderstruck

tick-tack-toe

ticktock

tidal wave

tidbit

tiebreaker

tie in (v.),
tie-in (n., adj.)

tie up (v.),
tie-up (n., adj.)

tight end

time-lapse

timeout (n.)

timesaver

timesaving

time share (n.)

time-shared (adj.)

time sharing (n.),
time-sharing (adj.)

timetable

Time Warner Inc.
(trademark)

time zone

tip off (v.),
tipoff (n., adj.)

tiptoe

tiptop

titleholder

tollbooth

tollhouse

Tommy gun
(trademark)

tongue-lashing

top-notch

torch singer

torch song

touchback (n.)

touchdown (n.)

touch up (v.),
touch-up (n., adj.)

town house

townspeople

toy maker

track and field

track lighting

tractor-trailer

trade in (v.),
trade-in (n., adj.)

trademark

trade off (v.),
trade-off (n., adj.)

trade route

trans-Atlantic

transcontinental

transoceanic

trans-Pacific

transsexual

trapshooting

trash can

trendsetter

trigger-happy

triple play

truck driver

truck stop

trustbuster

try out (v.),
tryout (n.)

T-shirt

tune up (v.),
tuneup (n., adj.)

turboprop

turnkey (n., adj.)

turn off (v.),
turnoff (n.)

turnpike

tutti-frutti

24/7

twi-night double
header

two-by-four

twofold

two-on-one break

U

U-boat
ultrahigh frequency
ultraleftist
ultramodern
ultrarightist
ultrasonic
ultraviolet
un-American
unarmed
underclass (n., adj.)
underdog
underfoot (adj., adv.)
undergarment
underground
underhand
undersheriff
undersold
understudy
under way (all senses but nautical), underway (in nautical sense when used as an adj. before a word, as in *underway flotilla*)
unidentified flying object
union shop
unshaven
upbeat
upgrade
uplink
uppercase
upper hand
upside down (adv.), upside-down (adj.)
upstate
upstream
up-tempo
U-turn

V

vacationland
variable interest rate
variable rate
v-chip mortgage
V-E Day
V-8 engine
V8 juice
vice admiral
vice chancellor
vice consul
vice president
vice principal
vice regent
vice secretary
vice versa
videocassette (n., adj.)
videodisc
video game
videophone
videotape (n., v.)
videotext
Vietnam
V-J Day
V-neck
voice mail
voiceprint
voir dire
volleyball
voodoo
vote-getter

W

wagonmaker
wagon master
waistline
walkie-talkie
walk in (v.), walk-in (n., adj.)
walk on (v.), walk-on (n., adj.)
walk out (v.), walkout (n.)
walk up (v.), walk-up (n., adj.)
wallboard
wallcovering
walleye
wall hanging
wallpaper
wall-to-wall
Wal-Mart (trademark)
war chest
war crime
warhead
war horse (horse), warhorse (veteran)
warlike
warlord
warmhearted
warm up (v.), warm-up (n., adj.)
wartime
washcloth
washed up (v.), washed-up (adj.)
wash out (v.), washout (n.)
washstand
wastebasket
wasteland
wastepaper
wastewater
watchband
water bed
watercolor
waterline
waterlogged
watermark

water polo

waterproof

watershed

water ski (n.), water-ski (v.)

water-skier

water skiing

waterspout

water tank

watertight

water wings

wavelength

wax paper

weak-kneed

weakside

weather-beaten

weather forecaster

weatherproof

weatherstripping

weather vane

weedkiller

weekend

weeklong

weeknight

weightlifting

well-being

wellhead

wellspring

well-to-do

well-wisher

westernmost

wet bar

wheelbarrow

wheelchair

wheeler-dealer

whereabouts

wherever

whirlwind

whistle-blower

whistle-stop

white collar (n.), white-collar (adj.)

whiteout (weather condition)

white paper

whitewash (n., v., adj.)

white water (n.), white-water (adj.)

wholehearted

wholesale price index

whole-wheat

wide-angle

wide-awake

wide-brimmed

wide-eyed

wide-open

wide receiver

wide-screen

widespread

wife beater

wild card

wildfire

wildlife

wild pitch

willpower

wind chill index

wind gauge

windmill

window-dress (v.)

window dressing (n.)

windowpane

window seat

window-shop (v.)

window-shopping

wind power

wind shear

wind-swept

wind up (v.), windup (n., adj.)

winemaker

winemaking

wine taster

wingspan

winter storm warning

winter storm watch

wintertime

wire-rimmed

wiretap

wood-burning (as in wood-burning stove), woodburning (as in woodburning kit)

woodcarver

woodcarving

woodcutter

wood heat

woodlot

woodpile

woodsmoke

woodstove (our rule)

woodwork

word-of-mouth (n., adj.)

word processing (n., adj.)

workday

work force

workhorse

working class (n.), working-class (adj.)

workingman

workingwoman

workmanlike

work out (v.), workout (n., adj.)

workplace

workweek

world-weary

worldwide

worn-out

worrywart

worthwhile

wrap around (v.),
wraparound (adj.)

wristwatch

write in (v.),
write-in (n., adj.)

wrongdoing

Y

yard sale

yardstick

yardwork

year-end (adj.)

yearlong

year-round

yellow-bellied

yellow-belly

yesteryear

X

X-ray

---

yo-yo

yuletide

Z

zero-base budgeting

zigzag

ZIP code

Ziploc (trademark)

zoot suit

American Versus British Spelling

American spellings began diverging from British ones in the 19th century when America's most famous dictionary maker, the newspaper editor Noah Webster, decided the U.S. should show its independence by developing its own system of simplified spellings. But his suggested variations didn't go far in making American spelling either simple or logical. If you're used to British spellings, you'll find that American ones generally aren't that different.

A few generalizations will help you recognize many spelling differences.

○ Words that end in *ise* in Britain sometimes end in *ize* in America:

BRITISH	AMERICAN
baptise	baptize
civilise	civilize
criticise	criticize
organise	organize
realise	realize

A common exception to this generalization is that Americans spell *surprise* the same as the British.

○ Words ending in *our* in Britain usually end in *or* in America:

BRITISH	AMERICAN
behaviour	behavior
colour	color
honour	honor

> ## ESL Tip
>
> The playwright George Bernard Shaw once said America and England were two nations separated by a common language. He probably overstated the case, but when it comes to spelling, if you're a foreign student who learned British English or you come from another English-speaking country such as Canada, you'll notice that the preferred American spellings are sometimes different. If you're more familiar with British spellings than American, or if your country's spelling is closer to the British, this section can help you avoid problems.

BRITISH	AMERICAN
labour	labor
neighbour	neighbor

A common exception is that Americans spell *glamour* the same as the British.

⚪ Words that end in *re* in Britain usually end in *er* in America:

BRITISH	AMERICAN
centre	center
litre	liter
metre	meter
theatre	theater

Many American theaters spell their names the British way, however, typically to suggest sophistication.

⚪ Words that contain an *x* in Britain often are spelled with a *ct* in America:

BRITISH	AMERICAN
connexion	connection
inflexion	inflection
reflexion	reflection

A common exception to this generalization is that Americans spell *complexion* the same as the British.

In addition to these generalizations, you should note that a number of other words are spelled differently in the two countries. Here are some common examples:

BRITISH	AMERICAN
aeon	eon
aluminium	aluminum

BRITISH	AMERICAN
burnt	burned
checque	check
diarrhoeia	diarrhea
draught	draft
fulfil	fulfill
gaol	jail
grey	gray
haemorrhage	hemorrhage
judgement	judgment
kerb	curb
manoevre	maneuver
mould	mold
moustache	mustache
oestrogen	estrogen
paediatrician	pediatrician
plough	plow
practise	practice
programme	program
pyjamas	pajamas
sanitorium	sanitarium
skilful	skillful
sulphur	sulfur
sunburnt	sunburned
tyre	tire
vice	vise

You should also note these common vocabulary differences between the two countries:

BRITISH	AMERICAN
afters	dessert
aubergine	eggplant
biscuit barrel	cookie jar
bonnet (of a car)	hood
boot (of a car)	trunk
braces	suspenders
call	formal visit
chips	french fries
closet (or water closet or wc)	bathroom
courgette	zucchini

BRITISH	AMERICAN
crisps	potato chips
cycle	bike
davenport	desk
draughts	checkers
dummy	pacifier
dustman	garbage collector
earthing an electrical line	grounding an electrical line
estate agent	real estate agent
first floor	second floor
flat	apartment
football	soccer
French beans *or* runner beans	green beans *or* string beans
geyser	water heater
greengrocer	vegetable market
ground floor	first floor
to hoover	to vacuum
to be knocked up	to be awakened
ladder	run (in a stocking)
large sofa	davenport
lift	elevator
loo	toilet
lorry	truck
lounge	living room
macintosh	raincoat
mean	stingy
motorcar	automobile
nappy	diaper
nil	nothing *or* zero
noughts-and-crosses	tick-tack-toe
pants	underwear
petrol	gasoline
pitch (athletic grounds)	field
porridge	hot cereal
pram	baby carriage
pullover *or* jumper	sweater
queue	line
rates local	property taxes
ring up	phone

BRITISH	AMERICAN
roundabout *or* circus	traffic circle
scone	biscuit
shares	stocks
silver plate	sterling silver
smalls	underwear
spend a penny	go to the bathroom
stocks	bonds
suspenders	garters
sweet *or* pudding	dessert
sweet shop	candy store
telly	TV
torch	flashlight
treacle	molasses
trousers	pants
vest	undershirt
waistcoat	vest
windscreen	windshield
wing (of a car)	fender

Web Resource

LANGUAGE SKILLS

To hone your language, spelling and editing skills, try the online resources at the following site, which was created to help editing teachers find resources but is open to anyone and has a wonderful collection of exercises.

◯ EditTeach.org
www.editteach.org

PART THREE

Style

Quick access to the most commonly looked-up items in this part . . .

CHAPTER 11

Writing as a Journalist

The night ambulance attendants shuffled down the long, dark corridors at the General Hospital with an inert burden on the stretcher. They turned in at the receiving ward and lifted the unconscious man to the operating table. His hands were calloused, and he was unkempt and ragged, a victim of a street brawl near the city market. No one knew who he was, but a receipt, bearing the name of George Anderson, for $10 paid on a home out in a little Nebraska town served to identify him.

The surgeon opened the swollen eyelids. The eyes were turned to the left. "A fracture on the left side of the skull," he said to the attendants who stood about the table. "Well, George, you're not going to finish paying for that home of yours."

"George" merely lifted a hand as though groping for something. Attendants hurriedly caught hold of him to keep him from rolling from the table. But he scratched his face in a tired, resigned way that seemed almost ridiculous and placed his hand again at his side. Four hours later he died.

—Ernest Hemingway
The Kansas City Star, Jan. 20, 1918

Many people who choose journalism as a career dream of writing the great American novel, as Ernest Hemingway did. In the meantime, becoming a reporter or an editor is a great way to earn a steady paycheck, as Hemingway was doing when he wrote this feature story on a hospital emergency room. Like Hemingway, many great authors get their start in journalism, which gives a budding writer the chance to see all sides of life while learning to write about it.

In addition to Hemingway, those who began as journalists include Ambrose Bierce, Willa Cather, Stephen Crane, Charles Dickens, John Dos Passos, Theodore Dreiser, Paul Laurence Dunbar, Gabriel García Márquez, William Dean Howells, Sinclair Lewis, Jack London, Frank Norris, George Orwell, Katherine Anne Porter, Upton Sinclair, John Steinbeck, Mark Twain, Mario Vargas Llosa, Eudora Welty, Tom Wolfe, Richard Wright and Émile Zola.

More contemporary authors who started as journalists include Amanda Craig, Joan Didion, Gavin Esler, David Gates, Zoë Heller, Carl Hiaasen, Wendy Holden, Rachel Johnson, India Knight, Richard Littlejohn, Jane Moore, Will Self and Susan Sontag.

Many great writers, of course, remain in journalism. Often, their names are not so well-known, but readers appreciate good writing when they see it, whether from Saul Pett, James J. Kilpatrick, Tom Wicker, Edna Buchanan, Jacqui Banaszynski, Simon Rogers, Maria Hinojosa or Tad Bartimus. Those who do stay in journalism are addicted to recording the big stories of our day—the assassination of a president, the first walk on the moon, the pursuit of a cure for cancer, war in the desert, terrorist attacks on New York and Washington or a tsunami in Asia. These events, after all, are human triumphs and tragedies that are compelling partly because of their reality.

Journalistic Writing Versus Fiction Writing

Today's journalism makes liberal use of advanced writing techniques more often associated with novels. Despite the literary license afforded Hemingway in The Kansas City Star almost a century ago, never more than today have journalists enjoyed such immense freedom to strut their stuff—to chronicle the news of the day with compelling prose filled with metaphors, similes and good old-fashioned storytelling. Journalists today often refer to that simply as narrative writing, but it is writing that borrows heavily from the repertoire of the novelist.

Make no mistake, however: Fundamental differences remain between writing news stories and writing novels, just as differences exist between all kinds of writing. The purpose of journalism is to convey information clearly, correctly and concisely. Literary license to invent fictitious scenarios is forbidden in journalism. As one form of nonfiction writing, journalism has much in common with technical writing—writing reports, manuals and instructions—especially in straightforward news stories aimed at conveying information.

Some journalism, of course, such as features, columns, blogs and reviews, has much in common with creative writing, such as novels, short stories, plays and poems. But for those with literary aspirations, here are some differences between journalistic writing and creative writing.

- **Clear, simple writing.** Straight-news reporting stresses the clear, correct and concise statement of facts, rather than an expression of imagination or vision. Creative writers take license with the language for literary effect, and ambiguity is often praised. True, literary critics value writing that is *ambiguous* (which means it has multiple meanings) but usually not writing that is *obscure* (which means readers have no idea what it means). People reading the news, however, want neither obscurity to confuse them nor multiple meanings to puzzle them. Instead, they want the facts, clearly and quickly. Of course, when people read features, columns and reviews, they also expect to be entertained.

- **Quick, efficient writing.** Hard-news journalism, which we see in objective news accounts, is more formulaic than creative writing is. Other than feature writers, reviewers, columnists, and bloggers, journalists place less emphasis on originality of style and more on knowing story formulas that help them write quickly while covering a subject logically and thoroughly. As we'll see in Chapters 14 and 15, however, journalists often use formulas even in soft-news stories.

- **Emphasis on mechanics.** Journalism places greater emphasis on mechanics (grammar, usage, spelling, style and tight writing) than creative writing does because adherence to such rules keeps the news reader from being distracted by irregularities. By contrast, the poet e. e. cummings, for example, avoided capitalization and punctuation in his poems to develop an original style that could sometimes make use of the double meanings that were created when such guideposts were missing. Using correct mechanics also helps maintain a journalist's credibility. If people find mistakes or inconsistencies of any kind in journalism, they start wondering whether they can trust the accuracy of the news presented.

Keys to Good Journalistic Writing

Good, tight journalistic writing demands that the writer and editor:

- Be clear.
- Be correct.
- Be concise.

In this chapter, we look at the first two rules in detail. We shall discuss the third in Chapter 12.

Clarity

If any man were to ask me what I would suppose to be a perfect style or language, I would answer, that in which a man speaking to five hundred people, of all common and various capacities, idiots or lunatics excepted, should be understood by them all, and in the same sense which the speaker intended to be understood.

— Daniel Defoe

Writing as a Journalist

It's especially important for journalistic writing to be clear. News consumers don't want to be confused about what they are reading. Here's a checklist of some key reminders about making your writing clear.

A Clarity Checklist

❑ Make sure all sentences flow from one to another without abruptly changing topics. Make sure all points, details or quotes support the main point.

❑ Write for readability. Don't use less common or bigger words than you need to. Don't write sentences or paragraphs longer than can be easily followed by a reader. (See the Journalism Tip on Page 241 and Chapter 12.)

❑ Make sure all of a reader's likely questions are answered. Explain any jargon or technical terms, or any information with which readers might not be familiar.

❑ Include specific details, making sure to illustrate generalizations with examples. Avoid vague and unsubstantiated statements.

❑ Make sure that any numbers in a story are used to make the meaning clearer for the reader. Readers are often intimidated by numbers, so the writer should tell readers what the numbers mean.

❑ Make sure all pronouns have a clear antecedent (noun they refer back to). (See Pages 92–93.)

❑ Avoid what English teachers call "awkward constructions." Put modifiers next to what they modify. Don't put modifiers between two separate words they potentially could modify. Don't dangle participles. (See Pages 111–13.) Also, express a series of items in parallel structure (similar forms, such as all participles or infinitives). (See Pages 94–95.)

❑ Keep verb tenses as consistent as possible—don't change from past to present tense unless you're speaking about different time periods in the same piece. (See Pages 70–71.)

The first point is common to all nonfiction writing. The last three points are discussed elsewhere in the book. So, for now, we'll look in more detail at the second through fifth points, which are particularly important for journalism.

Write Short Sentences and Paragraphs, and Use Common Words

Journalists try to write at the eighth-grade level, using short, simple sentences. Sometimes, when people hear this, they're shocked. "Why do journalists 'write down' to people?" they ask. The answer is that writing at the eighth-grade level isn't writing down to most people.

Readability tests, such as the Gunning and Flesch indexes, are mathematical formulas for determining how hard it is to read and understand a piece of writing. The tests work by determining how long or unusual the words are and how long the sentences are. A piece written on the post-graduate level would mean the words in it are so long and unusual and the sentences so long that it's likely to be understood mainly by specialists in the field. That's not necessarily good writing. By contrast, something written at the first-grade level could be so basic that it would bore most adult readers. If a piece of writing is judged to be written at the eighth-grade level, that means it should be understandable and engaging to an average student in the eighth grade or to any adult who reads at or above that level.

Don't think that a piece with a high grade-level rating is better written than one with a low grade-level rating. The eighth-grade level—best for a publication aimed at a general audience—does not mean that the content, format and ideas are simplistic. The Wall Street Journal is written at that level, and as magazine consultant Don Ranly says, you'll never hear an MBA complain that the Journal is too easy to read.

Journalism Tip

Writing for Readability

To keep your writing clear and easily understood, follow these tips:

- Keep most paragraphs one or two sentences long.
- Make a quotation that forms a complete sentence into its own paragraph.
- Keep sentences an average of 16 words long.
- Make sure that leads are short and uncomplicated.
- Vary sentence lengths and patterns to provide pacing and to avoid monotony and choppiness.
- Avoid compound sentences, especially ones that use semicolons.
- Cut out words and phrases that don't add meaning.
- Avoid the passive voice, which by its nature is wordy.
- Use short, simple, common words; these are best for journalism.
- Avoid foreign expressions and jargon.
- Explain difficult or technical terms if you need to use them.
- Use adjectives and adverbs only when they are essential.

By the way, the shortest words are usually also the most common, but there are exceptions. Some longer words, such as *important*, are clear to everyone, and some shorter words, such as *fud*, are not. (A *fud* is a rabbit's butt. Remember how Elmer Fudd was often the butt of Bugs Bunny's jokes?) Given the choice between a short uncommon word and a longer common one, choose the more common one. For more on using the right words, see Chapter 12.

Writing as a Journalist

It's not always enough to be brief. Sometimes, it's necessary to say the same thing more clearly in about the same number of words, or even to include additional material. Clarity and completeness go hand in hand.

Anticipate Readers' Questions

Often, a passage is unclear not because the words are confusing but because the passage raises questions in the reader's mind. In such instances, to achieve clarity requires that you *anticipate what questions the reader might have and answer them.*

If you were an editor and a reporter handed in a story with the following passage, what questions would be raised in your mind?

> A sizable crowd turned out to see the Michigan Wolverines play their baseball opener against the Ohio State Buckeyes.

How about these questions: Who won? What was the score? What's a "sizable" crowd? Where was the game played?

Or consider this final paragraph in an auto-accident story:

> Police said the Paris Road and College Avenue intersection is the scene of many traffic accidents.

How many accidents? Why is this intersection dangerous? Is anybody doing anything about it?

Include Specifics

Providing readers with specifics is closely related to the idea of answering likely questions. Occasionally, writers make generalizations that need to be more clearly explained. Once the specifics are supplied, the generalizations sometimes appear patently false, sometimes more persuasively true. In either case, giving specifics helps clarify the issue.

Here are some examples of the most common kinds of general statements and some questions to ask to draw out detail. As an editor, be on guard for these general statements. As a writer, ask yourself these questions about your own statements.

○ When a writer makes an abstract statement, ask "What do you mean by that?" "What's an example of that?"

> Some people can't see the forest for the trees.

> Love makes the world go round.

○ When a writer uses a vague modifier, ask "Compared with what?" "Compared with whom?"

> Democracy is the best form of government.

> He's a great singer.

○ When someone makes a universal statement, one that applies to all members of a group, ask "All?" "Every?" "Never?"

> Women aren't good at science.

> The Irish are hotheads.

○ When someone refers to a large, unspecified group, ask "Who specifically?" "What specifically?" "Which specifically?"

> Scientists say . . .

> Studies show . . .

○ When someone talks about *can't, must, ought* or *should* (or their opposites), ask "Why?" "Who says so?" "What causes that?" "What prevents that?" "What would happen if somebody did?"

> You should drink six glasses of water a day.

> You shouldn't swear.

○ When people say that something does something, ask "How specifically does it do that?" "What makes it do that?" "Why is that true?" "Could it be done in a different way?"

> Using that spray deodorant just hastens the greenhouse effect.

> Opposites attract.

Explain Numbers and Statistics

Numbers should be used in stories to inform and to clarify, but too often they are used in ways that merely confuse people.

Many reporters think they have done their jobs when they pepper their stories with a few figures. But what do those figures mean to readers? Put numbers into a meaningful context—tell readers what they mean.

For example, a business-page story tells readers that the Consumer Price Index rose 1.3 percent in June. If readers don't know enough already to equate that index loosely with the cost of living (that's not exactly what it is), the story probably means nothing to them. Furthermore, is it a good thing or a bad thing for the CPI to have risen 1.3 percent? Readers might automatically think it's a bad thing that prices have risen. But perhaps this was the smallest increase in the CPI in six months.

Big numbers especially tend to lose readers and cease to be real. As the late Sen. Everett Dirksen, R-Ill., once said during a discussion of the federal budget, "A billion here, a billion there, and soon you're talking about real money."

In addition to supplying the raw numbers, try using analogies to help readers grasp the numbers. For example:

If you could pick up a dollar a second, it would take you 32 years to pick up a billion of them.

There's a 1 in 1.5 million chance of being killed in an airplane crash. By contrast, the number of people who die each year of smoking is equivalent to the entire population of Kansas City, Mo.

Because numbers get so fuzzy for many people, they can easily mislead when thrown about unscrupulously. Former British Prime Minister Benjamin Disraeli is quoted as having said, "There are lies, damn lies and statistics."

For example, it is extremely important for journalists to be able to calculate percentages and to understand them. Otherwise, bias tends to creep into stories, either unintentionally or as the result of some interested person's manipulation.

Which of these statements is correct?

1. One percent milk has half the fat of 2 percent milk.
2. One percent milk has 50 percent of the fat of 2 percent milk.
3. Two percent milk has twice the fat of 1 percent milk.
4. Two percent milk has 200 percent of the fat of 1 percent milk.
5. Two percent milk has 100 percent more fat than 1 percent milk.
6. One percent milk has 1 percentage point less fat than 2 percent milk.

Actually, each statement is just a different way of saying the same thing. Some of the statements, however, sound more or less shocking than others. An advocate of 1 percent milk might choose No. 4 because it makes its point dramatically. A journalist should know enough math to see the statement for what it is.

Here's another story problem to mull: A book sold twice as many copies in the U.S. as in Britain, but the U.S. has four times as many people. Which of these statements is correct?

1. The book sold twice as well in the U.S.
2. The book sold half as well in the U.S.

Again, each statement is correct. The choice between the two depends on what is meant by "as well."

Although some journalists might have chosen their career partly to avoid one that entailed math, they can't escape dealing with percentages. Percentages come up in every story involving government budgets, charity fundraising and so on. You need to know how to calculate them.

The formula for calculating percentages is $p = a/b \times 100$, where a is the number you want to find to be what percentage (p) of the number b. To put that in plainer English, divide a by b and then drop the decimal point. For example, 4 is what percentage of 5? Divide 4 by 5. The answer is 0.80. Multiply by 100 to drop the decimal point, and you're left with 80 percent.

Correctness

Different kinds of writing can view "correctness" in different ways. Journalism must be correct in at least four senses, as shown in the checklist that follows.

A Correctness Checklist

❑ Make sure your writing is correct in grammar, usage, spelling and style.
❑ Make sure your writing is appropriate for your audience and your purpose. They are your guides for what to put in and what to leave out of a story.
❑ Use the right story formula for your news story.
❑ Make sure you get the facts right. Your writing must be unbiased and accurate, which is what journalists mean by *objectivity*. Particularly in hard-news stories, don't express your opinions. Don't use words such as *claims* that express a value judgment, in this case, implying disbelief. Report only what you can prove to be true. Present all sides fairly.

Use Correct Grammar, Usage, Spelling and Style

Chapters 1–10 cover grammar, usage and spelling. Style rules, such as those established by the AP, the UPI, or a particular newspaper, magazine or television station, add consistency and therefore clarity. Use Webster's New World College Dictionary or Webster's Third New International Dictionary to check the spelling of words that are not in the stylebook.

Write to Your Audience and Purpose

Your audience and your purpose help you know when to be formal and when to be informal. The style of writing that is proper for The Chronicle of Higher Education might not be right for The New York Daily News. Even in the same newspaper or magazine—print or online—different writing styles are permissible. A feature story may make liberal use of slang, but a more formal news story may not. A blog or review might also include words that convey value judgments, but those words should be edited out of a straight-news story.

Use the Right Story Formula

Story formulas constitute a checklist of what must be included in a story of a particular type and in what order generally. That, in turn, helps you know what could be left out. We present in Chapters 14 and 15 some basic formulas for hard- and soft-news stories for print, online and broadcast

Writing as a Journalist

media. For now, let's just mention as an example the most widely known news formula: *In hard-news stories, use the inverted-pyramid formula—the most important news at the top, the least important at the bottom.*

Maintain Objectivity in Your Writing

Most editors will tell you that accuracy is the most important characteristic of good news writing. The rules of journalistic objectivity are intended to help us achieve accuracy. They also help us take out words and comments from our work that would be inappropriate in a news account.

One of the most cutting epithets the public hurls at journalists is that we are "biased" or "nonobjective." Most journalists try hard to earn public trust by being objective in their coverage. But the public's perception of objectivity and what journalists mean by it are often quite different.

Most people think their own opinions about the world are correct. They think their view of the world is "the way it is." Therefore, if a journalist writes about an issue of concern to them, such as abortion, and the story doesn't, for example, call the pro-choice people "baby killers," the pro-life people may see the story as biased and therefore incorrect. Likewise, if the story doesn't call the pro-life people "anti-women's rights," the pro-choice advocates may object. Many even consider the terms *pro-choice* and *pro-life* to be loaded terms. But many editors would say it's better to use those than even more inflammatory words such as *pro-abortion* and *anti-abortion.*

Never mind that the journalist took pains not to present his or her own opinion but rather tried to present both sides fairly, without biased language. What people often mean when they say news is biased is that it doesn't conform to their own view of the world—it doesn't confirm their prejudices. By contrast, journalists typically see their role as that of a judge in a jury trial. The journalist, like the judge, is a sort of gatekeeper for the jury, or the public. The journalist, like the judge, must be objective—meaning impartial, disinterested and unprejudiced.

Journalists usually don't see their role as that of an attorney for the prosecution or the defense, presenting information to prove one side of a case rather than to get at the truth. Journalists would call playing the attorney's role being "subjective," an activity appropriate for public relations, advertising and editorial columns but not for a presentation of the news.

Rules of Objective Writing

Here are some typical rules journalists follow in their pursuit of objectivity:

○ **Stick to the facts.**

Stick to what you know to be true. Distinguish between fact and opinion. Attribute controversial statements. Don't guess or predict. Don't bend the facts consciously or unconsciously to make a better story.

Be careful to avoid making unwarranted assumptions or writing statements you can't prove. Of course, journalists try to be accurate. But to see how easy it is to make mistakes unintentionally, read the following reporter's notes:

Ricardo Sanchez, 10, is dead. The police have brought in three people for questioning. All three of them are known to have been near the scene of the killing. All three have police records. We've been told by a police representative that Leroi "Fingers" Washington, one of the three, has now been positively cleared of guilt in this incident.

If we assume the notes are accurate and true, which of the following statements are true? Consider a statement true if, from the notes, we know it to be true, false if we know it to be false, and questionable if we cannot be sure on the basis of the given information.

1. Leroi "Fingers" Washington was near the scene of the incident.
2. We don't really know anyone is dead.
3. Leroi "Fingers" Washington is probably black.
4. The other two suspects were also near the scene.
5. Three men have been arrested.
6. Only Leroi "Fingers" Washington has been cleared by the police.
7. This is an especially heinous murder because the victim was a juvenile.

Here are the answers:

1. *True*. Leroi "Fingers" Washington was one of three people near the scene who were brought in for questioning.
2. *False*. The reporter's notes state that Ricardo Sanchez is dead.
3. *Questionable*. Someone may surmise from the name that he is black, but we don't know for sure from this information alone.
4. *Questionable*. The other two people brought in for questioning were near the scene, but we cannot assume they are suspects. One or both of them may merely have been witnesses.
5. *Questionable*. First, we don't know the people brought in were all men. Second, the truth of the statement also depends on what is meant by "arrested." We know of no one who has been arrested in the sense that most people would understand the term. Some attorneys say, however, that true to the root meaning of the word *arrest* — "to stop" — anytime the police stop you against your will, it is an arrest even if you are not taken in and booked.
6. *Questionable*. We know for sure that one of them, Washington, has been cleared. That does not necessarily mean that he is the *only* one and that no one else has been cleared.
7. *Questionable*. We know the person dead is a juvenile, but we don't know this is a murder. Although many would associate the word *killing* with an intent to do violence, perhaps it was meant in the

Writing as a Journalist

sense that Sanchez was "killed," maybe in an accident. Or Sanchez may have been armed, and someone may have acted in self-defense. Or it may have been manslaughter rather than murder. In fact, in a legal sense we don't know it is actually "murder" unless there is a trial and someone is convicted of murder. And to label this "especially heinous," even if it turns out to be murder, is a value judgment. Don't hesitate to quote someone who says that, but don't say it yourself.

◯ **Be neutral. In a news story that's supposed to be objective, keep your own opinions out of it.**

Either keep your opinions to yourself or save them for more personal pieces, such as commentaries, reviews and blogs.

Don't confuse an opinion you believe to be true with journalistic objectivity. Being neutral doesn't permit you to include a statement you believe to be true unless it's also an objective fact not involving a matter of belief or opinion. For example, consider the following statements:

> The U.S. is the best nation on earth.
>
> "Moneyball" is a great movie.

You may believe one or both of these statements to be true. But they are not objective statements in the eyes of a journalist because they involve value judgments, opinions or beliefs. Both, however, could be quoted if someone other than a journalist were making the statement.

Don't use words that express a judgment or an evaluation, such as calling a person *attractive* or a proposal *idiotic*, even when you think most people would agree with them. Some editors might be more permissive about allowing value judgments to go unattributed if they express generally agreed-upon, noncontroversial matters, but they're still nonobjective:

> Mozart was a greater composer than Salieri.
>
> Adolf Hitler was a madman.

Choose your words carefully, making sure they convey no *unintentional* bias. Journalists may unwittingly take sides in a controversy if they are not careful about their choice of words. For example:

- To call an official a *bureaucrat* implies the negative connotation of someone who takes joy in binding helpless victims with red tape.
- To say a candidate *refuted* an opponent's charges does not simply mean the candidate *answered* them but rather that the candidate *successfully answered* them.
- To say that the City Council *still* hasn't taken action on a proposal implies disapproval for taking so long.
- To say national health care would cost *only* a certain amount implies that the cost is insignificant—a value judgment.

- To write *She disagrees with the fact that she is wrong* is to take the side of those who say she is wrong and to contradict her in the same sentence as her denial.

- To use hedging phrases such as *appears to be guilty* or *may be guilty* or *in my opinion, he's guilty* conveys value judgments akin to saying *he's guilty*. Such phrases are not fully neutral.

- To write that a news source *claimed* something implies you don't believe it. Stick with nonjudgmental words of attribution such as *said* or *says*.

- To write *Barbara Alcott—a pretty, blond legal secretary—said she has never been the victim of sexual discrimination* is to subject Alcott to sexual discrimination in print.

Unfortunately, newspapers occasionally make statements such as the last one about women. If you would not say the same of a man, the statement is probably sexist. Besides, such descriptions express value judgments about beauty and have no place in objective news. The following sentence would be neutral: *Legal secretary Barbara Alcott says she has never been the victim of sexual discrimination.* (See Chapter 13.)

In addition to avoiding value judgments and advice, journalists should be careful with the use of adjectives and adverbs in hard-news reporting. Modifiers are one of the most common ways bias creeps into a news story. They also tend to clutter a sentence, making it longer than it needs to be.

Modifiers to Be Avoided

absolutely	disturbing	major
actually	dramatic	most
alleged, allegedly	effectively	mysterious
amazing	evil	obviously
archconservative	exciting	perfectly
archliberal	fittingly	poignant
astounding	frankly	positively
awful	good	predictably
bad	grim	radical (left, right)
best	honestly	really
bizarre	important	reportedly
candid	inevitable	respected
certainly	insurmountable	sadly
complex	interesting	seriously
controversial	ironically	shocking
crucial	least	special
definitely	luckily	spectacular

still	troubling	unprecedented
stunning	ultraconservative	unquestionably
successfully	ultraliberal	unusual
suspected	undoubtedly	very
tragic	unique	worst

○ **Be fair. Present all sides as best you can, giving people a chance to respond to charges or criticism.**

If people refuse to comment when given the chance, say so in the story so that readers will know you tried to be fair.

Choose your words carefully so that they are fair to the people involved. Whenever you write a crime story, for example, write it in a way that does not assume the guilt of the suspect. After all, the charges may be dropped, or he or she may be found not guilty at a trial.

For example, to write *Police said Dave Jones climbed through the window and sexually assaulted the woman* is to convict the man in print before he has stood trial. Instead, write *Police said a man climbed through the window and sexually assaulted the woman. Dave Jones was arrested Monday (on a charge of rape, and charged with rape* or *in connection with the rape).*

Likewise, don't call the suspect an *alleged rapist* or say he *allegedly raped* the woman. Although many journalists don't know it, the words *alleged* and *allegedly* offer little legal protection from later libel action if the person isn't convicted. Who's doing the alleging? You are when you print that statement.

Stories with possible legal consequences are not the only ones that demand fairness to all sides. For example, although prison officials are not likely to sue you, to write *The food is so bad at the prison that inmates have begun a hunger strike* is to agree inadvertently with the inmates. A neutral statement would be *Inmates say the food is so bad that they have begun a hunger strike.*

○ **Be impersonal in a hard-news story. Don't try to sound creative or original or to write in your own "voice" unless you're taking a feature or more opinionated approach to a story.**

We're not trying to stifle your creativity. It's just that such individuality is out of place in most straight-news stories. Feature stories, reviews and commentaries are a different matter.

Web Resources

WRITING HELP

Several websites provide answers to questions about writing. Here are two of the better ones:

○ **The Elements of Style**
www.bartleby.com/141

○ **Online Writing Lab**
owl.english.purdue.edu

CHAPTER 12

Conciseness

Good writing should be precise. That's the single most agreed-upon rule of good writing, whether in journalism, technical writing, business writing or creative writing. In "The Elements of Style," William Strunk Jr. and E. B. White write, "A sentence should contain no unnecessary words, a paragraph no unnecessary sentences, for the same reason that a drawing should have no unnecessary lines and a machine no unnecessary parts."

The mark of the inexperienced writer is to hold every word sacred, as jealously guarded against red-penciling as a drop of holy water against spilling. But novelist Robert Louis Stevenson knew that conciseness is one of the differences between mere scribbling and art. "There is but one art," he wrote: "to omit." He added, "A man who knew how to omit would make an Iliad of a daily paper."

Saving words makes writing clearer and more effective, saves space and saves the reader's time. As the architect Mies van der Rohe said, "Less is more."

Of course, anyone can discard words haphazardly, especially in someone else's writing. What's harder is knowing which words are the dead limbs that need pruning. If you prune too much or the wrong parts, you may kill a plant. Sometimes, beginning writers and editors don't understand this point and try to snip away at everything.

But writers and editors, like gardeners, need to know what they're doing. So let's be more precise than saying brevity is the sole goal. The real virtue is not so much brevity as conciseness, which is a combination of brevity and completeness. Don't use more words than you need to make your point. But don't use fewer words than you need, either.

A story about President Calvin Coolidge, who was known as "Silent Cal," illustrates this point. One Sunday, his wife asked him what the preacher had spoken about at church. He replied, "Sin." When his wife then asked, "Well, what about it?" he answered, "He was against it." That's brevity but not conciseness. Coolidge's report is frustratingly incomplete. So, don't just be brief. Be complete—but as briefly as possible.

How to Tighten Your Writing

Writing tightly means choosing the fewest, shortest, simplest, most exact and, if possible, freshest words to express your thoughts.

Often, beginning writers think they need to use big words and round-about phrasing to impress their audiences. Nothing could be further from the truth. The German poet Johann Wolfgang von Goethe once said a common mistake of young writers is that they try to muddy the waters to make them look deep. But good writing isn't writing that confuses people.

Think about the power of short, common words: In Lincoln's 701-word second inaugural address, 505 of the words have one syllable and 122 have two syllables. Think, too, about the power of simple phrasing: The Lord's Prayer contains 56 words, the King James Version of the 23rd Psalm 118 words and the Gettysburg Address 226. And think about this contrast: A U.S. Department of Agriculture directive on pricing cabbage contained 15,629 words.

Here are some specific suggestions on how to tighten your writing.

Use Fewer Words

Eliminate redundant or irrelevant words, phrases, clauses, sentences, paragraphs, sections or chapters. Get rid of details, examples, quotations, and facts or ideas that don't add anything, and use single words rather than phrases whenever possible.

PHRASE TO AVOID	ALTERNATIVE
a lot	many, much
all of a sudden	suddenly
as a consequence of	because
give consideration to	consider
have a need for	need
put emphasis on	stress

- Get rid of the helping-verb forms of *to be* whenever possible. Often, helping verbs just detract from a more active verb:

WEAK	he is hopeful that
BETTER	he hopes

- Avoid turning verbs into nouns when the simple verb form will suffice:

WEAK	it is my intention
BETTER	I intend

Conciseness

⚪ Forms of the verb *to be* often occur in sentences starting with *there, here* or *it*. When possible, get rid of them:

WEAK   It was Thoreau who said

BETTER   Thoreau said

⚪ Use active voice instead of passive. Passive voice is wordier, less direct and less forceful:

PASSIVE   A 13-year-old boy was shot by police.

ACTIVE   Police shot a 13-year-old boy.

An exception is when the person being acted upon is more important than the person doing the acting: *President Kennedy was shot today by an unknown assailant.* (See Pages 71–76.)

⚪ Avoid vague modifiers, such as *a lot, kind of, perhaps, quite, really, somewhat, sort of* and *very.*

These words are sometimes called "weasel words" because they are favorites of people trying to weasel their way out of taking a clear stand. If you are trying to be honest, using such words appears at worst deceitful, at best wishy-washy.

⚪ Avoid doubled prepositions (*off of* for *off*) or prepositions that aren't needed (the *up* in *heading up*).

In the sentence *She headed up the largest company in town,* the *up* isn't necessary. (But in the following sentence, it is: *They headed up the mountain trail.*) Other examples of verbs that don't need *up* include *count, divide, drink, eat, fold, free, gather, heat, hoist, hurry, polish, raise, rest, rise* and *settle.*

⚪ Avoid whenever possible phrases beginning with *in* or *the* and ending with *of*: (*in*) *the amount of,* (*in*) *the area of,* (*in*) *the case of, the concept of, the factor of,* (*in*) *the field of, the idea of,* (*in*) *the process of, in terms of.*

⚪ Cut the conjunction *that* if it's unnecessary.

If getting rid of *that* doesn't change the meaning of the sentence, then get rid of it:

WEAK   He said that he would

BETTER   He said he would

But *that* is necessary when:

1. A time element, such as a day, comes between the verb and the dependent clause: *He said Tuesday that he would go.*
2. *That* follows one of these verbs: *advocate, assert, contend, declare, estimate, make clear, point out, propose, state.*

3. *That* comes before a dependent clause beginning with one of the following conjunctions: *after, although, because, before, in addition to, until, while.*

○ Cut *which are, which is, who are* and *who is* if they are not needed.

Rewrite *the movie, which is a comedy* as *the movie, a comedy.* Rewrite *the students who are attending* as *the students attending.*

○ Don't tell us what we already know.

In phrases such as *12 noon, personal friend, sad mourners, blue in color, true fact, armed gunman* and *completely destroyed,* one word implies the other, which is therefore unnecessary. Words such as *famed, famous, renowned* and *well-known* likewise are unnecessary if the person or thing described is indeed famed, famous, renowned or well-known.

○ Cut the adjectives *both* and *different* if they add nothing.

What's the difference between *both John and Bill* and *John and Bill?* Between *three different views* and *three views?* But leave *both* in if you think it's needed for emphasis: *She said she liked both Barack Obama and Mitt Romney.*

○ Cut the *or not* after the conjunction *whether.*

Whether includes both possibilities.

Use Simpler Words

○ Use shorter Anglo-Saxon–derived words rather than longer Latin-derived ones whenever possible.

Say, don't *state. Drink,* don't *imbibe.*

○ Avoid vague nouns.

Substitute something more specific for the following words whenever you can: *area, aspect, concept, condition, consideration, factor, indication, infrastructure, parameter, phase, situation, thing.*

○ Avoid *ize* verbs.

Words with *ize* are often no more than pretentious jargon. For example, change *finalize* to *end* or *complete; institutionalize* to *put in an institution* or *make part of the institution; personalize* to *make more personal;* and *utilize* to *use.*

○ Avoid turning verbs into nouns.

Avoid the following: *activation, fabrication, maximization, optimization, rationalization, utilization.*

Conciseness

○ Use verbs rather than noun phrases when you have a choice.

Instead of writing *before the committee investigation*, write *before the committee investigated*.

○ Unless your editor says otherwise, use contractions such as *can't* for *cannot* and *it's* for *it is* or *it has*.

The AP permits the use of contractions, provided they're not overused, and they're generally used for all but the most formal writing. Besides, they sound more conversational and save space.

Use Exact Words

○ Use a specific noun or verb without a modifier rather than a general noun or verb with a modifier:

    WEAK   a small city in Utah

    BETTER   Cedar City, Utah

○ Use specific verbs rather than vague ones.

For example, change *go* or *move* to *walk, run, jump, skip, hop* or *gallop*.

○ Beware of verbs beginning with *re*.

Something is not *reaffirmed, redoubled* or *reshuffled* unless it already has been *affirmed, doubled* or *shuffled*.

○ In hard-news stories, avoid modifiers that could suggest bias.

Pick words that more closely convey the denotation (dictionary meaning) without the connotation (personal viewpoint). (See Pages 246–50.)

○ Avoid *euphemisms*, words that say something in an indirect manner rather than confronting the truth.

Instead of writing *The maintenance engineer met his Maker*, just say *The custodian died*.

Be Fresh, Not Stale

○ Avoid clichés.

Clichés are phrases that have been used so often they've lost their freshness and power, such as *children of all ages* and *crystal clear*. Some clichés are no longer even understood in their literal sense by most people who use them: *by hook or by crook* or *dead as a doornail*.

Others are more recent—the latest fad media phrases. Some of the words and phrases recently repeated endlessly in the media that we've added to our list later in this chapter include *big oil, boots on the ground, cut and run, game changer, hockey mom, man up, obscene profits, perfect storm, shovel-ready, talking points, tax-and-spend liberal, teachable moment, throw [someone] under the bus* and *what went down.*

Still, clichés can sometimes be succinct, and that's why they catch on. In fact, clichés are such a part of everyday conversation that sometimes it's difficult to imagine how you could express certain thoughts without them. How about this solution? Whenever you're about to write an expression you've heard before, take the opportunity to try to express your point in a fresher way.

⬤ **Avoid stale story approaches.**

When journalists approach stories by trying to fit them into a pattern they've seen used many times before, the story not only lacks freshness but also probably misrepresents the truth. Think of these stories as built around clichés of vision. One of the more common stale story approaches is the one that starts, *Christmas came early for* . . . . (See Pages 333–35.)

What to Tighten, A to Z

Here's a list of pompous words and wordy phrases editors typically cut or rewrite. Use the following guidelines to interpret the list:

When a word or phrase can easily be left out without changing the meaning of a sentence, we have indicated to *cut.*

When a word or phrase should be rewritten in a simpler, more straightforward way, we have indicated one or more possible changes.

When a phrase is a cliché, we have labeled it as such, leaving a fresher approach to your own sense of creativity.

We have put parentheses around some words in the list. This indicates different phrases built on the same wording. For example, *absolute (guarantee, perfection)* indicates both the phrases *absolute guarantee* and *absolute perfection.*

The advice in this list should work for most of your writing or editing, but use your own judgment. For example, you shouldn't use any of this advice to rewrite quotations unless you remove the quotation marks to indicate a paraphrase. Also, the suggestions may not work in a particular sentence where the sense of the word or phrase is something other than what we assumed here.

Finally, some of the words we suggest you cut, such as *case* and *character*, are obviously useful in some contexts, but they can usually be cut and the sentence rewritten more directly without them.

Conciseness

A

a distance of   *cut*
a great deal of   much, many
a lot   many, much
a period of   *cut*
abandon   leave
abbreviate   shorten
absolute (guarantee, perfection)   *cut* absolute
absolutely (certain, complete, essential, sure)   *cut* absolutely
accelerate   speed
accidentally stumbled   stumbled
accompany   go with
accomplish   do
accord   grant
achieve   do
acid test   *cliché*
acquire   get
acres of land   land
acted as (chairman, chairwoman)   presided
activation   start
activity   *cut*
actual (experience, fact)   *cut* actual
acute crisis   crisis
add insult to injury   *cliché*
adequate enough   enough
adult in the room   *cliché*
advance (planning, reservations)   *cut* advance
advent   arrival
adverse weather conditions   bad weather
affluent   rich, wealthy
aforementioned   this, that, these, those
after all is said and done   *cliché*
aggregate   total
agree to disagree   *cliché*
aired their differences   *cliché*
albeit   but
all in a day's work   *cliché*
all of   all
all of a sudden   suddenly
all things considered   *cliché*
all things to all people   *cliché*
all throughout   throughout
all too soon   *cliché*
all walks of life   *cliché*
all work and no play   *cliché*
all-time record   record

almighty dollar   *cliché*
amidst   amid
amorphous   formless
analogous   similar
and/or   *rewrite the sentence*
announce the names of   announce, identify
another additional   another
anticipate in advance   anticipate
any and all   any, all
appeared on the scene   appeared
appears   seems
apple of one's eye   *cliché*
appoint to the post of   appoint
appreciate in value   appreciate
apprehend   arrest
approximately   about
the Arab street   *cliché*
ardent admirers   *cliché*
area   *cut*
area of   *cut*
arguably   *cut*
arise   get up
armed gunman   gunman
armed to the teeth   *cliché*
arrive at a decision   decide
as a consequence of   because
as a matter of fact   *cut*
as a result of   because
as already stated   *cut*
as far as the eye could see   *cliché*
as luck would have it   *cliché*
as of this date   *cut*
ascertain   find out
aspect   *cut*
assemble together   assemble
assess a fine   fine
assist   help, aid
assuming that   if
at a loss for words   *cliché*
at a tender age   *cliché*
at an earlier date   previously
at first blush   *cliché*
at long last   *cliché*
at present   now
at the conclusion of   after
at the present time   now

Conciseness

at the time when   when
at this point in time   now
at which time   when
attach together   attach
attempt   try
autopsy to determine the cause of death   autopsy
awkward predicament   predicament

B

back in the saddle   *cliché*
badly decomposed body   body (if long dead)
balanced approach   *cliché*
ball is in (her, his, their) court   *cliché*
ballpark guess   *cliché*
(bare, basic) essentials   essentials
bare naked   naked
basic fundamentals   fundamentals
be acquainted with   know
be associated with   work with
be aware of   know
be cognizant of   know, notice
beat a (dead horse, hasty retreat)   *cliché*
bed of roses   *cliché*
been there, done that   *cliché*
beginning of the end   *cliché*
best thing since sliced bread   *cliché*
best left unsaid   *cliché*
better late than never   *cliché*
between a rock and a hard place   *cliché*
beverage   drink
bewildering array   *cliché*
big government   *cliché*
big in size   big
big oil   *cliché*
biggest ever   biggest
biography of (her, his) life   (her, his) biography
bite the bullet   *cliché*
bitter (end, dispute)   *cliché*
black helicopter crowd   *cliché*
blame it on   blame
blanket of snow   *cliché*
blazing inferno   *cliché*; inferno, blaze
bleeding-heart liberal   *cliché*
blessing in disguise   *cliché*
blissfully ignorant   *cliché*
blood-red   *cliché*

bloodcurdling (scream, sight)   *cliché*
bloody riot   *cliché*
boggles the mind   *cliché*
bolt from the blue   *cliché*
bombshell [announcement]   *cliché*
bond together   bond
bonds of matrimony   *cliché*
bone of contention   *cliché*
boots on the ground   *cliché*
bored to tears   *cliché*
both   *cut except for emphasis*
both alike   alike
bouquet of flowers   bouquet
breakneck speed   *cliché*
breathless anticipation   *cliché*
brief in duration   brief
bring to a conclusion   conclude, end, finish
bring (to a head, up to date)   *cliché*
broad daylight   daylight
brutal (assault, beating, murder, rape, slaying)   *cut* brutal
brute force   *cliché*
budding genius   *cliché*
built-in safeguards   *cliché*
burn the midnight oil   *cliché*
burning (desire, issue, question)   *cliché*
busy as a (beaver, bee)   *cliché*
but one thing is certain   *cliché*
by hook or by crook   *cliché*
by leaps and bounds   *cliché*
by the name of   named
by the same token   likewise

C

calm before the storm   *cliché*
calm down   calm
came to a stop   stopped
can of worms   *cliché*
cancel (each other, out)   cancel
can't see the forest for the trees   *cliché*
case   *cut*
case of   *cut*
champing at the bit   *cliché*
character   *cut*
charmed life   *cliché*
check (into, on, up on)   check
checkered (career, past)   *cliché*

cherished belief   *cliché*
chief protagonist   protagonist
(children, kids) of all ages   *cliché*
chip off the old block   *cliché*
circle around   circle
city of   *cut*
clean slate   *cliché*
clear as a bell   *cliché*
close down   close
close (proximity, scrutiny)   near, scrutiny
closed-door (hearing, meeting)   *cliché*
closed fist   *cliché*
close-up look   *cliché*
coequal   equal
cognizant   aware
cold (as ice, comfort, shoulder)   *cliché*
collaborate together   collaborate
collect together   collect
colorful (display, scene)   *cliché*
combine together   combine
combined total   total
come full circle   *cliché*
come to a head   *cliché*
come to an end   end
come-to-Jesus moment   *cliché*
coming future   future
commence   begin, start
commented to the effect that   said
common accord   accord
communication   letter, memo
commute back and forth between   commute between
competency   competence, ability
competent   able
complete   fill out, finish
complete (chaos, monopoly, overhaul)   *cut* complete
**completely (demolished, destroyed, done, eliminated, empty, finished, full,
    naked, surrounded, true, untrue)**   *cut* completely
comply with   follow, obey
component   part
concept   *cut*; idea
concept of   *cut*
conceptualize   think of
concerning   about
concerted effort   *cliché*
concrete proposals   proposals
condition   *cut*
conduct a poll   poll

conjecture   guess
connect the dots   *cliché*
consensus of opinion   consensus
consequent result   result
consideration   problem
considered opinion   *cliché*
conspicuous by (his, her, its, their) absence   *cliché*
constructive   helpful
consult   ask
consume   eat
consummate   finish
contemplate   think
contingent upon   depends on
continue on   continue
continue to remain   *cliché*
contribute   give
controversial (issue, person)   *cliché*
contusion   bruise
cool as a cucumber   *cliché*
cooperate together   cooperate
costs the sum of   costs
count up   count
countenance   face
country mile   *cliché*
crack of dawn   *cliché*
cradled in luxury   *cliché*
crazy as a loon   *cliché*
crony capitalism   *cliché*
cross to bear   *cliché*
crying (need, shame)   *cliché*
crystal clear   *cliché*
current (temperature, trend)   *cut* current
currently   now
customary   usual
cut and run   *cliché*
cutting edge   *cliché*

D

dangerous weapon   weapon
daring daylight robbery   *cliché*
dark horse   *cliché*
dashed the hopes   *cliché*
dastardly deed   *cliché*
date with destiny   *cliché*
days are numbered   *cliché*
dead as a (doornail, skunk)   *cliché*

dead body　body
deadly earnest　*cliché*
deadly poison　poison
debate about　debate
deceased　dead
decide (about, on)　decide, select
deciding factor　*cliché*
deem　think, believe, judge
deficit　shortage
definite decision　decision
definition of insanity　*cliché*
demonstrate　show
depart　leave
depreciate in value　depreciate
depths of despair　*cliché*
descend down　descend
described as　called
desirable benefits　benefits
desire　wish, want
despite the fact that　despite
determine　find out
devoured by flames　*cliché*; burned
devouring flames　*cliché*
dialogue　talk, talks, negotiations, discussion
diamond in the rough　*cliché*
died of an apparent heart attack　apparently died of a heart attack
died suddenly　died
different　*cut*
dig in (her, his, their) heels　*cliché*
disclose　show
discontinue　stop, quit
disingenuous　*cliché*; insincere
divide up　divide
do it for the children　*cliché*
do your own thing　*cliché*
dog-tired　*cliché*
dotted the landscape　*cliché*
double-check twice　double-check
downright lie　lie
down-to-earth　*cliché*
drastic action　*cliché*
draw a blank　*cliché*
draw first blood　*cliché*
draws to a close　ends
dried up　dried
drink (down, up)　drink
dropped down　dropped

drown your sorrows   *cliché*
drowned to death   drowned
drunk as a skunk   *cliché*
ducks in a row   *cliché*
due to the fact that   because
duly noted   noted
duplicate   copy
during the course of   during
during the time that   while
dwell   live

<hr>

E

each and every   every
earlier on   earlier
early (beginnings, pioneer)   *cut* early
easier said than done   *cliché*
Easter Sunday   Easter
eat, drink and be merry   *cliché*
eat up   eat
edifice   building
educationist, educator   teacher
effectuate   cause
egg on (his, her, their) face(s)   *cliché*
elect   choose, pick
electrocuted to death   electrocuted
eliminate altogether   eliminate, cut
eloquent silence   *cliché*
eminently successful   *cliché*
emotional roller coaster   *cliché*
employment   job
empty out   empty
enable to   let, allow to
enclosed (herein, herewith, within)   here's, enclosed
encounter   meet
end (product, result)   *cut* end
endeavor   try
engage in conversation   *cliché*
enhance   add to, improve
ensuing   following
enter a bid of   bid
enter (in, into)   enter
entirely (complete, new, original, spontaneous)   *cut* entirely
entwined together   entwined
epic struggle   *cliché*
errand of mercy   *cliché*
essentially   *cut*

ever since   since
every fiber of his being   *cliché*
exact (counterpart, duplicate, facsimile, replica, same)   *cut* exact
exactly identical   identical
exceeding the speed limit   speeding
exchanged wedding vows   married
execute   do, sign
exercise in futility   *cliché*
exhibit   show
expedite   speed
experience (n.)   *cut*
experience (v.)   *cut* (Instead of *He said he was experiencing pain*, try
   He said he was in pain.)
experienced veteran   veteran
extensively   greatly
extinguish   put out
eyeball to eyeball   *cliché*
eyesight   sight
eyewitness   witness

F

fabled   *cliché*
fabrication   lie, making, manufacture, product, production
face up to   face
facilitate   ease, help
facilities   buildings, space
factor   *cut*
factor of   *cut*
facts and figures   *cliché*
faded dream   *cliché*
failed to   did not
failed policies of the past   *cliché*
fairly   *cut*
false pretense   pretense
falsely fabricated   fabricated, made up
famed, famous   *cut*
far and wide   *cliché*
far be it from me   *cliché*
far cry   *cliché*
fat chance   *cliché*
fatal (killing, murder, slaying)   *cut* fatal
fate worse than death   *cliché*
favored to win   favored
feasible   possible
feeding frenzy   *cliché*
feel-good movie   *cliché*

fell down   fell
fell on (bad, hard) times   *cliché*
fell on deaf ears   *cliché*
fell through the cracks   *cliché*
festive occasion   *cliché*
few and far between   *cliché*
few in number   few
field   *cut*
field of   *cut*
fiery rebuttal   *cliché*
file a lawsuit against   sue
filled to capacity   filled
final analysis   *cliché*
final (completion, conclusion, ending, outcome, result)   *cut* final
final word   *cliché*
finalize   finish, complete, end
finish up   finish
finishing touch   *cliché*
fire swept through   *cliché*
first (annual, began, commenced, initiated, priority, started)   *cut* first
first time ever   first time
firstly   first
flat as a board   *cliché*
flatly rejected   rejected
fly in the ointment   *cliché*
focus like a laser   *cliché*
fold up   fold
follow after   follow
follow in the footsteps of   *cliché*
food for thought   *cliché*
fools rush in   *cliché*
foot the bill   *cliché*
for all intents and purposes   *cliché*
for openers   *cliché*
for the purpose of   to
for the reason that   because
foregone conclusion   *cliché*
foreseeable future   future
forthwith   *cut*
forward   send
foul play   *cliché*
frame of reference   *cut*
freak accident   *cliché*
free and open to the public   free
free (gift, pass)   *cut* free
free of charge   free
free up   free

freewill offering   offering
frequently   often
fresh (beginning, start)   *cut* fresh
frisky as a (kitten, pup)   *cliché*
from time immemorial   *cliché*
front headlight   headlight
(frown, smile) on (his, her) face   frown, smile
full and complete   complete
fully clothed   clothed
function   act, work
funeral services   services (in obituary; otherwise, *funeral*)
furnish   send, provide
furrowed brow   *cliché*
fused together   fused
future (plans, potential, prospects)   *cut* future

G

gainfully employed   employed, working
gala (event, occasion)   *cliché*
game changer   *cliché*
game plan   *cliché*
gather (together, up)   gather
general (public, rule)   public, rule
generally agreed   agreed
generous to a fault   *cliché*
get this show on the road   *cliché*
getting into full swing   *cliché*
gin up (the base, the voters)   *cliché*
give (a green light, consideration, encouragement, instruction, rise) to   approve, consider, encourage, instruct, cause
give (a, the) nod   approve
give back   *cliché*
given the green light   *cliché*
glass ceiling   *cliché*
glass, half (empty, full)   *cliché*
go   walk, run, jump, skip, hop, gallop
go for broke   *cliché*
go for it   *cliché*
go to the mat   *cliché*
goals and objectives   goals
goes without saying   *cliché*
going nowhere fast   *cliché*
golf-ball–size hail   *cliché*
good (as gold, speed)   *cliché*
good to go   *cliché*
gory details   *cliché*

gradually (waning, wean)   *cut* gradually
grand total   total
grateful thanks   thanks
grave (concern, crisis)   *cliché*
gravitas   *cliché*; serious dignity
great lengths   *cliché*
great majority of   majority of
great minds run in the same (channel, direction, gutter)   *cliché*
great minds think alike   *cliché*
great open spaces   *cliché*
greatly   *cut*
green light (n., v.)   *cliché*; give the go-ahead, approve, OK
green with envy   *cliché*
ground rules   rules
ground to a halt   *cliché*

H

had ought   ought
hail of bullets   *cliché*
hale and hearty   *cliché*
half a hundred   50
hammer out   *cliché*
hand over fist   *cliché*
handsome appearance   handsome
hang up   hang
hanging in there   *cliché*
happy as a lark   *cliché*
happy camper   *cliché*
hard as a rock   *cliché*
hardest hit are (minorities, women)   *cliché*
hardy souls   *cliché*
has got to   has to, must
has the (ability, capability, skill, talent) to   can
hastily summoned   *cliché*
have a (need, preference) for   need, prefer
have an (effect, impact) on   affect
have got   have
have got to   have to, must
have the belief that   believe
head over heels   *cliché*
head up   head
heap coals on the fire   *cliché*
heart (of gold, of the matter)   *cliché*
heartfelt thanks   *cliché*
heart's (content, desire)   *cliché*
hearty meal   *cliché*

Conciseness

heat up   heat
heated argument   *cliché*
heave a sigh of relief   *cliché*
heavens to Betsy   *cliché*
heavy as lead   *cliché*
(He'd, She'd) like to have that one back   *sports cliché*
Herculean effort   *cliché*
hereby   *cut*
herein   *cut*
hereto   *cut*
herewith   *cut*
high as a kite   *cliché*
high (noon, technology)   *cut* high
hit a home run   *cliché in nonbaseball stories*
hit the nail on the head   *cliché*
hobbled by injury   *cliché*
hockey mom   *cliché*
hoist up   hoist
honest truth   truth
hook, line and sinker   *cliché*
hope for the future   *cliché*
hopes and fears   *cliché*
hopping mad   *cliché*
hostile environment   *cliché*
hot (potato, pursuit)   *cliché*
hot-water heater   water heater
hour of noon   noon, noon hour
hungry as (a bear, wolves)   *cliché*
hunker down   *cliché*
hurry up   hurry

┌─────────┐
│   **I**   │
└─────────┘

idea of   *cut*
if and when   if, when
ignorance is bliss   *cliché*
illuminated   lighted
imbibe   drink
immortal bard   *cliché*
implement   do, start, begin
important essentials   essentials
in a very real sense   *cut*
in fact   *can often cut*
in (full swing, high gear, our midst)   *cliché*
in lieu of   instead of
in light of   because of, considering
in my opinion   *cut*

in no uncertain terms   *cliché*
in order to   to
in question   *cut*
in spite of the fact that   although
in terms of   *cut*
in the (aftermath, final analysis, last analysis, nick of time, same boat, wake of)   *cliché*
in the event that   if
in the not-too-distant future   soon
in the shape of   *cut*
in this (day and age, time frame)   *cliché*
in view of the fact that   because
inaugurate   begin, start
include among them   include
inconvenience   trouble
incumbent (governor, president, representative, senator)   *cut* incumbent
incursion   invasion
indeed   *cut*
indicate   show
indication   sign
indignant   upset
individual   person, man or woman
inevitable   sure, certain
inextricably (linked, tied)   *cliché*
infinite capacity   *cliché*
inform   tell
infrastructure   basic institutions of society; power, education, transportation and communication systems
infringe (on, upon)   infringe
initial   first
initiate   begin, start
innocent bystander   *cliché*
input   opinion, suggestion
inquire   ask
institute   start
institutionalize   put into an institution, make part of the institution
insufficient   not enough
interface   connect, talk, meet
interim period between   interim
interrogate   question
inundate   flood
iron out (difficulties, disagreements, troubles)   *cliché*
irons in the fire   *cliché*
irregardless   regardless (*Irregardless* is not a word.)
is going to   will
is hopeful that   (he, she, they) (hopes, hope)
is productive of   produces

is reflective of   reflects
is representative of   represents
issue in question   issue
it appears (seems) that   *cut*
it goes without saying   *cliché*
it is (her, his, their) contention   (she, he, they) (contends, contend)
it is (her, his, their) intention   (she, he, they) (says, say), (she, he, they) (intends, intend)
it is interesting to note   *cut*
it should be noted   *cut*
it stands to reason   *cut*
it takes a village   *cliché*
it would appear that   *cut*

J

Jewish rabbi   rabbi
Joe Sixpack   *cliché*
join (in, together)   join
joint (cooperation, partnership)   *cut* joint
just do it   *cliché*

K

keeled over   *cliché*
keeping (his, her, their) options open   *cut*
kind of   *cut*
knit together   combined, figured out
know about   know

L

labor of love   *cliché*
laceration   cut, gash
lag behind   lag
laid to rest   *cliché*
largest ever   largest
lashed out   *cliché*
last (analysis, but not least, word)   *cliché*
last-ditch effort   *cliché*
later on   later
laundry list (of desired programs, for example)   *cliché*
leaps and bounds   *cliché*
learning experience   experience, something to learn from, educational
leave no stone unturned   *cliché*
leaves much to be desired   *cliché*
left up in the air   *cliché*

legal hairsplitting   *cliché*
legend in (his, her) own (mind, time)   *cliché*
lend a helping hand   *cliché*
level   *cut* (Instead of *She teaches on the college level*, try *She teaches college courses*.)
level playing field   *cliché*
light (as a feather, of day)   *cliché*
like a bolt from the blue   *cliché*
lingered on   lingered
lion's share   *cliché*
local residents   residents, locals
locate   find
lock horns   *cliché*
lock, stock and barrel   *cliché*
lonely (isolation, solitude)   *cut* lonely
long (arm of the law, years)   *cliché*
lose out   lose
low ebb   ebb
loyal (Democrat, Republican, supporter)   *cliché*; Democrat, Republican, supporter
lucky few   *cliché*

M

mad as a hornet   *cliché*
made a motion   moved
made a pretty picture   *cliché*
made a (speech, statement, talk)   spoke
made an escape   escaped
made an inquiry regarding   asked about
made contact with   met, saw
made an escape   escaped
made mention of   mentioned
made the acquaintance of   met
made (up, out) of   made of
main essentials   essentials
maintenance   upkeep
maintenance engineer   janitor, custodian
major breakthrough   breakthrough
make a killing   *cliché*
make a list of   list
make adjustments   adjust
make an approximation   estimate
make hay while the sun shines   *cliché*
makes one's home   lives
man up   *cliché*
mantle of snow   *cliché*

manufacture   make
many and various   *cliché*
many in number   many
marked (contrast, improvement)   *cliché*
married (her husband, his wife)   married
mass exodus   *cliché*
massive   big, large
matinee (performance, show)   matinee
matter of   *cut*
matter of life and death   *cliché*
maximization   best, improvement
maximize   increase as much as possible
maximum possible   maximum
meaningful   big, important
meaningful dialogue   *cliché*
meet head-on   *cliché*
meets the eye   *cliché*
merchandise   goods
merchandize   sell
merge together   merge
mesh together   mesh
met (his, her) Maker   died
method in (his, her, their) madness   *cliché*
might possibly   might
minimize   lessen as much as possible
miraculous escape   *cliché*
mix together   mix
mixed blessing(s)   *cliché*
modicum of   some
moment of truth   *cliché*
momentous (decision, occasion)   *cliché*
monkey (on, off) (his, her, their) back(s)   *cliché*
more preferable   preferable
more than meets the eye   *cliché*
most all   most
most unique   unique
mother of all   *cliché*
motley crew   *cliché*
mourn the loss   *cliché*
move   walk, run, jump, skip, hop, gallop
mutual cooperation   cooperation
mutually beneficial   *cliché*

___N___

name of the game   *cliché*
nanny state   *cliché*

narrow down   narrow, reduce
narrow escape   *cliché*
nature   *cut* (Instead of *He has a serious nature,* try *He is serious.*)
neat as a pin   *cliché*
necessary (requirement, requisite)   *cut necessary*
necessitates   calls for
need my space   *cliché*
needless to say   *cut*
needs no introduction   *cliché*
never a dull moment   *cliché*
never at any time   never
new (addition, baby, beginning, bride, construction, creation, initiative, innovation, normal, record, recruit)   *cut new*
newly created   new
nick of time   *cliché*
night of terror   *cliché*
nipped in the bud   *cliché*
no brainer   *cliché*
no easy answer   *cliché*
no place like home   *cliché*
no sooner said than done   *cliché*
none the worse (for the experience, for wear)   *cliché*
not to be outdone   *cliché*
now comes the hard part   *cliché*
numerous   many

◖   O   ◗

objective   goal
obscene profits   *cliché*
obtain   get
of course   *can often cut*
off of   off
official (capacity, protest)   *cliché*
oftentimes   often
old (adage, cliché, habit, legend, maxim, proverb, tradition, veteran)   *cut old*
old (boy, boys') network   *cliché*
old school   *cliché*
on a few occasions   occasionally
on a roll   *cliché*
on account of   because
on any given day   on any day
on more than one occasion   *cliché*
on the face of it   *cliché*
on the fly   *cliché*
on the grounds that   since, because, as

on the occasion of   when
one and the same   identical
one fell swoop   *cliché*
one of life's little ironies   *cliché*
one of the last remaining   one of the last
ongoing   *cut*
only time will tell   *cliché*
open secret   *cliché*
operative (adj.)   *cut*
opt for   *cliché*; choose
opt out   decline
optimistic   hopeful
optimization   best, improvement
optimum   best
order out of chaos   *cliché*
orient   adjust
orientate   adjust
original source   source
output   production
outside the box   *cliché*
over a period of years   for years
over and above   *cliché*
overview   review, survey
overwhelming (majority, odds)   *cliché*
own home   home
own worst enemy   *cliché*

P

paid the penalty   *cliché*
painted a grim picture   *cliché*
(pair of, two) twins   twins
pale as a ghost   *cliché*
Pandora's box   *cliché*
parameters   limits, boundaries, variables
paramount issue   *cliché*
part and parcel   *cliché*
participate   take part
participate in the decision-making process   have a say
party   person
passed (away, on)   died
passing phase   phase
past (experience, history)   *cut* past
patience of Job   *cliché*
pay (off, out)   pay
paying the piper   *cliché*
peace dividend   *cliché*

penetrate into   penetrate
per   a, according to
perceive   see
perfect storm   *cliché*
perfectly clear   clear
perform a task   do
perhaps   *can often cut*
permanent importance   *cliché*
personal (experience, friend)   *cut* personal
personalize   make more personal
personally (involved, reviewed)   *cut* personally
peruse   read, examine
phase   *cut*
phone is ringing off the hook   *cliché*
physical size   size
physician   doctor
picture of health   *cliché*
picture perfect   *cliché*
pie in the sky   *cliché*
pitched battle   *cliché*
pizza pie   pizza
place   put
place in the sun   *cliché*
plan (ahead, for the future, in advance)   plan
play hardball   *cliché*
play it by ear   *cliché*
play the race card   *cliché*
pleased as punch   *cliché*
pocketbook   purse
point with pride   *cliché*
polemics   arguments
polish up   polish
ponder   consider
populace   people, population
position   job
possess   own, have
poster child   *cliché*
postpone until later   postpone
powder keg (used as a metaphor)   *cliché*
power (lunch, tie, user)   *cliché*
powers that be   *cliché*
preceded in death   died earlier
present a report   report
present incumbent   incumbent
presently   soon
pretty as a picture   *cliché*
primary   first, main

prior history   history
prior to   before
prioritize   rank
problem   *cut*
proceed   go, move ahead
process   *cut*
process of   *cut*
prohibit   forbid
promoted to the rank of   promoted to
proposition   *cut*
protrude out   protrude
provide   give
provided   if
puppy   *cliché in reference to things other than dogs and their relatives*
purchase   buy
pure as the driven snow   *cliché*
purloin   steal
pursuant to   following, in accordance with
pursue   chase
pushing the envelope   *cliché*
put a lid on it   *cliché*
put emphasis on   stress
put into effect   start

```
  Q
```

qualified expert   expert
quality time   *cliché*
question of   *cut*
quick as a wink   *cliché*
quiet as a mouse   *cliché*
quite   *cut*

```
  R
```

radical transformation   transformation
rain (couldn't, didn't) dampen the (spirits, enthusiasm)   *cliché*
raise up   raise
rapprochement   reconciliation
rarely ever   rarely
rat race   *cliché*
rationalization   excuse, reason, explanation
raze to the ground   raze
reading material   books, pamphlets, etc.
really   *cut*
really unique   unique
rear taillight   taillight

reason is because   because
reason why   reason, why
(recall, recede, refer, remand, retreat, revert) back   *cut* back
receive   get
(recur, repeat, resume, restate) again   *cut* again
red-hot   *cliché*
red-letter day   *cliché*
reduce down   reduce
refer back to   refer to
referred to as   called
register approval   approve
register (a complaint, an objection)   *cut* register
register stamp of approval to   approve
regret   are sorry
regular (monthly, weekly) meeting   *cut* regular
reign of terror   *cliché*
reigns supreme   *cliché*
reins of government   *cliché*
reinvent the wheel   *cliché*
reliable sources   sources
relocate   move
remainder   rest
remains to be seen   *cliché*
remark   say
remedy the situation   *cliché*
remunerate   pay
renowned   *cut*
repeated again   repeated
requires   asks for, calls for, needs
reside   live
residence   house, home
resigned her position as   resigned as
resource center   library
respond   answer
rest up   rest
resultant effect   effect
results achieved   results
reveal   show
reverted back   reverted
revise downward   lower
right stuff   *cliché*
ripe old age   *cliché*
rise up   rise
road to recovery   *cliché*
rode roughshod over   *cliché*
root cause   cause
rose to (new, the) heights   *cliché*

rose to the (cause, defense) of   supported, defended
round of applause   *cliché*
rushed to the hospital   *cliché*

```
   S
```

sadder but wiser   *cliché*
safe haven   *cliché*
salt of the earth   *cliché*
scored a gain   gained
sea of (upturned) faces   *cliché*
seal off   seal
seamy side of life   *cliché*
seasoned (journalists, observers, reporters, etc.)   *cliché*
seat of the pants   *cliché*
second to none   *cliché*
secondly   second
seldom ever   seldom
select few   *cliché*
self-admitted   *cliché*
self-confessed   confessed
selling like hot cakes   *cliché*
senseless murder   *cliché*
serious (crisis, danger)   *cut* serious
seriously (consider, inclined)   *cut* seriously
settle up   settle
shared sacrifice   *cliché*
sharp as a tack   *cliché*
shattering effect   *cliché*
sheet of rain   *cliché*
shift into high gear   *cliché*
shopping list (of desired programs, for example)   *cliché*
short (minutes, years)   *cut* short
shot in the arm   *cliché*
shovel-ready   *cliché*
shrouded in mystery   *cliché*
sigh of relief   *cliché*
silhouetted against the sky   *cliché*
simple life   *cliché*
sing "Kumbaya"   *cliché*
single unit   unit
sink down   sink
situated (in, at)   in, at
situation (as in classroom situation, crisis situation)   *cut*
($64, $64,000) question   *cliché*
skirt around   skirt
sky-high   *cliché*

slick as a whistle   *cliché*
slow as molasses   *cliché*
slowly but surely   *cliché*
small in size   small
smart as a whip   *cliché*
smartest guy in the room   *cliché*
smoking gun   *cliché*
smooth as silk   *cliché*
snatched victory from the jaws of defeat   *cliché*
snug as a bug in a rug   *cliché*
soccer mom   *cliché*
social amenities   *cliché*
soiree   party
something fishy   *cliché*
sort of   *cut*
speak volumes   *cliché*
spearheading the campaign   *cliché*
spell out   explain
spirited debate   *cliché*
spliced together   spliced
split apart   split
spotlight the need   *cliché*
spouse   husband, wife
sprung a surprise   surprised
square peg in a round hole   *cliché*
staff of life   *cliché*
stand up   stand
staple together   staple
star-studded   *cliché*
start up   start
started off with   started with
states   says
states the point that   says
staunch supporter   supporter
steaming jungle   *cliché*
stern warning   *cliché*
stick to your guns   *cliché*
sticks out like a sore thumb   *cliché*
still (continues, persists, remains)   *cut* still
stinging rebuke   *cliché*
stolen loot   loot
storm(s) of protest   *cliché*
storm-tossed   *cliché*
straight as an arrow   *cliché*
straight (losses, games, wins) in a row   straight (losses, games, wins)
straight-and-narrow path   *cliché*
strangled to death   strangled

straw that broke the camel's back   *cliché*
stress the point that   stress that
stretches the truth   *cliché*
strife-torn   *cliché*
strong, silent type   *cliché*
stubborn as a mule   *cliché*
submit   send, give
subsequent   later
substantial   big, great, large
substantially   largely
succeed in doing   accomplish, do
such is life   *cliché*
sum and substance   *cliché*
sum total   total
summer (months, season)   summer
summoned to the scene   summoned
sunny South   *cliché*
superhuman effort   *cliché*
supportive   helpful
supreme sacrifice   *cliché*
surrounding circumstances   circumstances
sustain   suffer
sweat of his brow   *cliché*
sweeping changes   *cliché*
sweet 16   *cliché*
swing into high gear   *cliché*
sworn affidavits   affidavits

T

take a deep breath   *cliché*
take into consideration   consider
take place   happen
take the bull by the horns   *cliché*
take them one at a time   *cliché*
talking points   *cliché*
tangled together   tangled
tarnished image   *cliché*
tax-and-spend liberal   *cliché*
teachable moment   *cliché*
team player   *cliché*
telling effect   *cliché*
temblor   earthquake
temporary reprieve   reprieve
temporary respite   respite
tender mercies   *cliché*
tendered her resignation   resigned

terminate   stop, end
textbook example   *cliché*
that   *can often cut*
that dog won't hunt   *cliché*
the above   *cut; repeat the antecedent*
the area of   *cut*
the fact (is, that)   *cut*
the field of   *cut*
the limelight   *cliché*
the month of   *cut*
the truth is   *cut*
therein, thereof, thereon   *cut*
there's the rub   *cliché*
thick as pea soup   *cliché*
think about it   *cliché*
thirdly   third
this day and age   *cliché*
thorn in the side   *cliché*
thorough investigation   *cliché*
threw caution to the wind   *cliché*
through their paces   *cliché*
throughput   *cut*
throw a monkey wrench into   *cliché*
throw [someone] under the bus   *cliché*
throw in the towel   *cliché*
throw support behind   support
thrust   main idea
thunderous applause   *cliché*
tied together   tied
tight as a drum   *cliché*
time (immemorial, of one's life)   *cliché*
tip of the iceberg   *cliché*
to be sure   *cut*
to summarize   *cut*
to the tune of   *cliché*
today's society   *cliché*
ton of bricks   *cliché*
tongue (firmly planted) in cheek   *cliché*
too numerous to mention   *cliché*
took to task   *cliché*
torrent of abuse   *cliché*
total (abstinence, extinction, operating costs)   *cut* total
total strangers   strangers
totally (demolished, destroyed)   *cut* totally
tower of strength   *cliché*
touch base   *cliché*
transport   carry

trapped like rats   *cliché*
trials and tribulations   *cliché*
triggered   *cliché*; prompted
true colors   *cliché*
true fact   fact
tumultuous applause   *cliché*
tuna fish   tuna
turn thumbs down   *cliché*
12 (midnight, noon)   *cut* 12
two alternatives   alternatives, choices
two-way street   *cliché*

U

ultimate   final, last
ultimate (conclusion, end, outcome)   *cut* ultimate
uncharted sea   *cliché*
underground subway   subway
underlying purpose   purpose
undertake a study   study
uneasy (calm, truce)   *cliché*
unexpected surprise   surprise
uniformly consistent   consistent
universal panacea   panacea
unpaid debt   debt
unprecedented situation   *cliché*
untimely end   *cliché*
untiring efforts   *cliché*
up (in arms, the air)   *cliché*
upcoming   coming, impending
updated   current
upset the apple cart   *cliché*
uptight   *cliché*
user-friendly   easy-to-use
usual custom   custom
utilization   use
utilize   use
utterly indestructible   indestructible

V

vanish into thin air   *cliché*
various and sundry   *cliché*
vast expanse   *cliché*
vehicle   car, truck
very   *cut*
viable   workable

viable (alternative, option, solution)   *cut* viable
view with alarm   *cliché*
violence erupted   *cliché*
violent (assault, attack, killing, murder, rape, slaying)   *cut* violent
vitally necessary   necessary
voiced (approval, objections)   *cliché*; approved, objected

W

wait-and-see attitude   *cliché*
walk(s) of life   *cliché*
warm and fuzzy   *cliché*
warm as toast   *cliché*
war-torn   *cliché*
was employed   worked
was in possession of   had
watchful eye   *cliché*
watershed   *cut*
watery grave   *cliché*
wealth of information   *cliché*
wear and tear   *cliché*
wear many hats   *cliché*
wee, small hours   *cliché*
weighty (matter, reason, tome)   *cliché*
well-known   *cut*
wellness   health, prevention
went up in flames   burned
were scheduled to   would
what makes (her, him, them) tick   *cliché*
what went down   *slang cliché for* what happened
where there's smoke, there's fire   *cliché*
whether or not   whether
which are   *can often cut*
which is   *can often cut*
while at the same time   while
whirlwind (courtship, romance, tour)   *cliché*
white (as snow, stuff)   *cliché*
who are   *can often cut*
who is   *can often cut*
who said   said
whole nine yards   *cliché*
wide-open space   *cliché*
widespread anxiety   *cliché*
(widow, widower) *cut* **of the late**   widow, widower
will be a participant in   will participate in
will hold a meeting   will meet
win out   win

Conciseness

winds of change   *cliché*
wipe the slate clean   *cliché*
with bated breath   *cliché*
witness   see
word to the wise   *cliché*
words (can't, fail to) express   *cliché*
world-class   *cliché*
worse for wear   *cliché*
worst ever   worst
wrapped in mystery   *cliché*
write down   write
writing on the wall   *cliché*

Y

you be the judge   *cliché*
you know   *cut*
young juvenile   juvenile

Z

zoo animals   animals (*if context is clear*)

Web Resources

CONCISE WRITING

Several websites can be of use to journalists who need to sharpen their writing and editing skills. Among them are the following:

- Commnet Guide to Grammar and Writing: Concise Sentences
  http://grammar.ccc.commnet.edu/grammar/concise.htm

- Garbl's Writing Center
  http://home.comcast.net/~garbl/stylemanual

CHAPTER 13

Sexism, Racism and Other "isms"

When you are a journalist (interested in presenting facts) or an opinion writer (interested in arguing for your perceptions), nothing is more important than knowing current reality. Being up-to-date on a fast-moving world saves you embarrassment and your loss of credibility. As a journalist, you work to communicate the truth. As an opinion writer, you work to persuade others to perceive facts in a certain way. But, whether you communicate truth or persuasion, your credibility rests on getting basic reality right.

Both journalistic and opinion writing are tougher now than before because in today's globalizing world, what is true keeps changing. This is your challenge: In media serving a world with more than 7 billion inhabitants, global changes require global thinking, writing and editing. To assume the U.S. and European countries are the center of news coverage cuts your audiences off from the reporting they need to shape their own lives. At the beginning of 2012, Internet users in Asia numbered more than 1 billion, or about the same number as those in Europe, North America and Latin America/the Caribbean combined. Worldwide, there are 60 mobile phone subscribers per 100 inhabitants. In this accelerating media world, how do you keep current and choose appropriate language?

Use the three principles of the *Working With Words* Language Triangle—new social change, new language standards and new journalism requirement—as guides in your communications—written, verbal or visual.

As a rule, your best approach in a dynamically changing world is to assume that what you knew—even last year—has changed.

1. **New social change—the new normal.** Language changes to keep in step with power shifts, and, in a globalizing world, power shifts constantly. For clues about how to cope with vast, fast changes in language, look back at social changes in the past few decades in the U.S.

- 1960s—Civil rights legislation recognized that all U.S. citizens had the same rights. One outcome: labeling an adult black man as "boy" or calling an adult woman a "girl" was recognized as disrespectful and wrong.
- 1970s—Only 22 percent of women in the civilian labor force had attended some college or graduated.

- 1980s — As women began attending college in greater numbers, and thus advancing in society overall, describing women as bystanders and men as powerful actors was inaccurate.
- 1980s and 1990s — AIDS epidemic coverage focused disproportionately on homosexual men, bringing the media heavy criticism. Gay and lesbian groups formed in news organizations, demanding fairer treatment in the news.
- Turn of the century — Immediately after the Sept. 11, 2001, terrorist attacks on New York City and Washington, D.C., news organizations scrambled to develop relevant language to avoid racist descriptions of terrorists, Muslims and U.S. citizens born in Middle Eastern countries.
- 2009 — The first African-American U.S. president took the oath of office after winning against a white male opponent in his 70s whose running mate was a white woman and after winning a tough primary race against a white woman. These breakthroughs against racism, ageism and sexism were top topics across the world's media coverage.
- 2011 — "Don't Ask, Don't Tell" in military policy was abandoned. DADT prohibited military personnel from discriminating against or harassing closeted gay or bisexual service members or applicants, while barring openly gay, lesbian or bisexual persons from military service.
- Today — In the U.S., 23 percent of 25-year-old women and 14 percent of 25-year-old men hold a bachelor's degree or higher. Women and minorities own just more than half of U.S. firms. For women under 30, most births occur outside marriage.

Global changes shape us daily, and you — as a journalist — must perceive quickly what has changed and then respond in language that portrays *current reality*, a reality extremely different from when you learned to read and write!

2. **New standards of language — the world of the Internet and entertainment.** The Internet makes audiences global, not just local. More than 2 billion people access the Internet now. With global Internet use through mobile devices just now at 10 percent, huge migrations of users are expected. Also, local is global. For example, one in 8 people in the U.S. is foreign-born. They and their children are probably not U.S.-centric. Reporting, writing, editing and selecting stories now operate worldwide and support a global Web-accessible audience. Therefore, media have a constant struggle to be sophisticated enough in language to serve their diversifying audiences. The current media upheaval comes not just from technology but also from coverage that fails to be current.

The entertainment industry brings many words that used to be forbidden to its audiences — just try to find digital entertainment products that avoid vulgar descriptions of body parts. Kids and teens are bombarded with millions of cruel, coarse, violent and sexual images and words—through online games, music, cable TV, YouTube, Facebook, Twitter, downloads, movies, websites, etc. The U.S. Department of Justice cites child pornography as an epidemic, with 61 Internet Crimes Against Children task forces across the country composed of more than 3,000 federal, state and local law enforcement agencies. *Today's journalist communicates with a public numbed to actual pain and violence because it is confronted with these daily in language and the media.*

3. **New journalism requirements**—"Always on." The world keeps speeding up. You must perform in the two ways journalism is deemed valuable: quickly and accurately.

If you understand what forms today's reality in the Language Triangle, you will be able to deliver words, ideas and information in sync with that reality. In sum, you will be able to produce believable journalistic work.

Accelerating change sometimes looks and feels like chaos. It's your job as a journalist to think through and then communicate change in today's language.

When you pay attention, you'll find even the best of communicators relying on old assumptions that miss new realities. Along with understanding the vast global changes taking place, journalists in the U.S. are forced to be more sophisticated about the power of at least 10 once-invisible groups in their own country:

GROUP	PERCENTAGE OF POPULATION
Women	51
Blacks	13
Hispanics	16
Asian-Americans	5
Native Americans	1
People with disabilities	12
People over 65	13
Gays, lesbians and bisexuals	4
Religious extremists	Unknown
Foreign born	13

To help yourself: Every day examine your work to see if it underplays or trivializes any of these groups. They are about 70 percent of your audience.

Don't Be Ridiculous

Unexamined assumptions can make newspeople appear naive. Here are some 21st-century realities to help you examine your own assumptions.

American does not mean *white*. *American* doesn't even mean *a citizen of the U.S.* Instead, *American* refers to *someone from North or South America.* Period.

Gangs come in all colors. Most teen mothers in the U.S. are white. Since 2005, a majority of adults in the U.S. are *unmarried*. More Muslims than Episcopalians live in the U.S. More than 90 languages are spoken in the Los Angeles public schools. The most populous country in the world is China, followed by India, then by the U.S. By 2050, it is projected that India will be the most populous country.

Language Turns to the Future

Since the 1990 census, when fast multicultural change could be seen in the statistics, journalists and their audiences have been forced to cope with the fastest iteration of change in history. The 2000 census spun out a story of even faster change. Then, the immigration reports after the Sept. 11 terrorist attacks portrayed a leaky-sieve policy, as individuals from every land alit in the U.S. and got lost in the mobile millions of other immigrants. The 2010 census showed differences that require journalists to grasp as audiences are changing. The U.S. population grows at a slower pace than in the 1990s because of an aging population, slowed immigration and low economic growth since 2000. Yet it is still projected that by 2040 the country's majority population will be minority. Infants in the U.S. are already majority minority. Half of all voting-age U.S. citizens are now more than 45 years of age. Real median household income fell for the first time on record. Poverty climbed to 15 percent of the population, the highest level since 1993. In addition, international migrations from developing countries to developed countries reshape the global population and media audiences.

All these changes pose special challenges for journalists. The nation is more racially and ethnically diverse than portrayed in most media, as well as much older. The developed countries have the oldest populations. The developing countries have the youngest. All future world population growth will take place in the developing countries. Here are other projections released by the U.S. Census Bureau:

- Minorities (groups other than non-Hispanic whites) are now one-third of the U.S. population. By 2023, minorities will comprise more than half of all children.

- In 2030, when all the baby boomers will be 65 and older, nearly one in five U.S. residents is expected to be 65 and older.

- Similarly, the 85 and older population is expected to more than triple.

- The non-Hispanic white population is projected to be only slightly larger in 2050 than in 2010. In fact, this group is projected to lose population in the 2030s and 2040s and constitute 46 percent of the total population in 2050, down from 65 percent in 2010.

Futurists tell us: More change has occurred in the past 50 years than in the preceding 100,000. Today's everyday language transformations provide one of the best measures of the driving force of social change.

Many of the spelling, grammar and punctuation rules covered in this book evolved from Latin, a language that is dead. The concepts discussed in this chapter evolved during the past few decades, many in the past few years. The question, then, is: How does a language grounded in Latin cope with such change?

The answer is that Latin may be dead, but English isn't. Like all living languages, English constantly evolves and changes to fit new, uncomfortable realities. In their classic book, "The Elements of Style," William Strunk Jr. and E. B. White state: "The language is perpetually in flux: It is a living stream, shifting, changing, receiving new strength from a thousand tributaries, losing old forms in the backwaters of time."

New Players in the New Millennium

Women and members of racial, ethnic and immigrant groups continue to move from the sidelines to the headlines. Unprecedented numbers reshape the labor force, higher education and public life. *Multiculturalism now defines the U.S.* Meanwhile, the language and media coverage still carry historic assumptions that males of European descent should be considered more important than other people. Accurate journalism in the U.S. lives by updating to accommodate the new multicultural reality.

The driving force of social change is seen by following five "undercovered" groups of your audience and how they have shifted in power, causing language to shift:

1. *Women* make 80 percent of consumer decisions and earn the majority of college degrees.
2. *Young adults* do not neatly fit the label "slackers," "millennials" or "Gen Y." They face a muddy economic future. Young adults are increasingly stuck at home or moving back in with parents. The percentage of the population that moved in 2011 hit 11.6 percent, the lowest percentage since the 1950s.
3. *Racial/ethnic and immigrant groups* are the new entrepreneurs and the future of international business. This will accelerate as "minorities" become the U.S. majority.
4. *People over 50* are lifetime learners and seekers in the developed world. The U.S. is 34th in life expectancy at birth, with females expected to live to 81, males to 76. In Monaco, the peak country, females are expected to live to 93½ years and males 85½ years. From 2008 to 2018, women aged 65 to 74 in the U.S. civilian labor

force will increase more than the number of women in any other age group, while the number of women 16 to 19 and 35 to 54 working is projected to decrease.

5. *Children and teens* are the face of poverty in the U.S., with endless consequences. In 2010, more than 31 million children (42 percent) lived in low-income families, with 15.6 million (22 percent) living in poverty. One in 45 children live on the street, and most childhood poverty is not temporary. A century ago, more elders lived in poverty. Today, 9 percent of those over 65 years live in poverty.

All these shifts remold our society. But change does not happen without comment. As women of all races and men of color have taken on more visible roles in a *society of diminishing paternalism*, there has been a lot of "noise." Much of this comment comes through journalism that resists change and hangs on to what was once the status quo.

For example, hate speech has grown. Why? Because power shifts to "outsiders." As women fill college classrooms and professional jobs, they accrue power. As "minorities" become a larger proportion of U.S. society—and the majority in many communities—they also amass power.

In resistance to the shift in power, more inclusive language is discounted as being "politically correct" by those losing power. In fact, many of the preferred terms listed later in this chapter have been pejoratively labeled "PC." Pay attention. The voices condemning today's reality are usually from segments losing power.

The public notices when sexism, racism or other "isms" are practiced. For instance, in a House of Representatives hearing on the availability of contraception in a health bill, five white males (no women) were called to testify. The lack of women in the policy hearing might have mirrored reality in the 1950s. The lack of balance was "politically incorrect," and the public response was large and swift. For media lack of representativeness, the reaction is less verbal. Media just lose audience when reality is not perceived in its portrayals.

In a world in which we are bombarded by sounds and images, journalism's credibility relies more and more on its ability to see current reality and report it. Fortunately, that credibility can be ensured by living out a basic tenet of good journalism: Get it fast, get it right. Ridding media messages of sexism, racism and other "isms" requires only that journalists report accurately.

Subtle "isms"—the unconscious use of insults, out-of-date terms, biases and assumptions about whole groups of people or individuals in those groups—are harder to eliminate than blatant sexism and racism. Why? Although we may hold nonsexist and nonracist beliefs, we may unconsciously fall into the trap of using dated sexist, racist, ageist and dismissive language.

Today, the world reorganizes. Ethnic, racial and international communities connect globally through the Internet. They create media where their voices can be heard. But to understand what is necessary to embrace (and what is necessary to eradicate) in today's language, we need to examine the past.

A Brief History of "isms"

In Western civilizations, society for centuries dismissed women and children of all races and men of color as peripheral, using those groups as unpaid workers, servants and, sometimes, slaves. Language still displays a bias against women and minorities and reflects a history of inequality.

When the Pilgrims settled in Massachusetts Bay, they brought English common law with them. When Blackstone's Commentaries on the Laws of England was used as the basis of the U.S. legal system, women and children (particularly female children) were legally on a par with the master's cattle, oxen and dogs. And when slavery was institutionalized into the country's laws, black women, men and children were given the same legal status accorded white women and children. All were property belonging to white men.

It can be argued that black men gained citizenship when they got the vote after the Civil War in the 1860s. White women and women of color were elevated to citizen level when they won the vote in 1920. Realistically, men of color and women of all races began to gain equal access to employment, credit and education only in the mid-1960s.

Documents serving as the foundation of this country's government held white males in higher value: "We hold these truths to be self-evident, that all men are created equal."

For those who would argue that *men* was generic then and included everyone, remember that two constitutional amendments were required to bring adults other than white males into the voting process.

Until the civil rights breakthroughs in the 1950s and 1960s, white domination over people of color, as well as male domination over females, was institutionalized and supported in all branches and levels of government. People of color and women were denied their civil rights and opportunities to participate in political, economic and social communities. So, what journalists are faced with in today's usage is centuries of authoritative language diminishing the roles and lives of women and minorities.

But society changes. Accelerating social revolutions are partly about renaming what is. Language must catch up to a world in which the poor, people with disabilities, women, gays and lesbians, blacks, Asian-Americans, Native Americans, Hispanics, Latinos and Chicanos, immigrants, and U.S. citizens who have come from all countries throughout the world demand full citizenship, authority and viable economic power. It helps to remember that mobility of the world's citizens changes audiences, what is newsworthy and your need to update your language. With 264 languages and dialects spoken in Los Angeles, about a third of the population speaks a language other than English. In the Midwest, about 45 languages are spoken, with 10 percent speaking a language other than English.

Dealing With Current Reality

For our work to be respected, we must avoid the following "isms" in specific words, content and images.

Sexism

Sexism is usually thought of as fixed expectations about women's appearance, actions, skills, emotions and "proper" place in society. Sexism also includes sex stereotyping of men.

Instead of adequate and varied portrayals of individual women, five common stereotypes of females emerge in news coverage. They cloud today's reality. In most cases, these dismissive categories are to be avoided.

1. *Mother/nurturer*: woman as caregiver. Examples: grandmother, prostitute with a heart of gold, fairy godmother.
2. *Stepmother/bitch*: woman as non-nurturer. Examples: iron maiden, aggressive woman, aloof executive, boss.
3. *Pet/cheerleader*: woman as appendage to a man or children. Examples: the little lady, soccer mom.
4. *Tempter/seducer*: woman as sexpot (a term used only for women). Examples: gold digger, victim of sex crime who "asked for it."
5. *Victim*: woman as incompetent. Examples: damsel in distress, helpless female, rape victim.

Three stereotypes for men have emerged in language and should also be avoided.

1. *Macho*: man as battler. Examples: financial warrior, political strongman (no parallel word exists for women), master criminal, gang hero.
2. *Wimp/wuss*: man as sensitive. Examples: mama's boy, househusband, caregiver, sissy, single father, metrosexual.
3. *Demon/pervert*: man as "perp." Examples: child molester, rapist, murderer, abuser.

◯ Women are the majority in the U.S. *She* more adequately conveys "everyone" than *he*. Use *man* only when referring to a man or a group of men. When a group includes women and men, or could include men and women, say so. Almost any word ending with the suffix *man* can end with the suffix *woman.*

Racism and Religious Bias

Racism is discrimination against ethnic or racial groups based on the false assumption that one ethnic group is superior to others. Individuals from any racial or ethnic group can be racist. These are common stereotypes to be avoided.

1. *The secondary*: people of little consequence who serve the powerful. Examples: domestic help, migrant farmworkers, service workers, immigrants.
2. *The ignored or invisible*: people whose achievements are trivialized. Examples: slum or reservation residents, the underclass, servants.
3. *Achievers*: exceptions to the "norm." Examples: model minority, credit to one's race.
4. *The despised or feared*: outsiders, criminals, suspects. Examples: welfare cheats, illegal immigrants, drug addicts, "animals."

It appears that racial bias in U.S. crime reporting is increasing, not decreasing. Race is usually played up, not down. Often, those outside the white power framework are portrayed as villains without those human characteristics attributed by default to whites.

In other areas, racial and ethnic groups are overlooked. That is perhaps most vividly apparent in accounts of an event that were corrected decades after the fact. For generations, history books noted that the only survivor of Custer's last stand at the Battle of the Little Bighorn in Montana was a horse, Comanche. Almost a century after the battle, in the 1960s, demonstrating students at the University of Kansas (where the stuffed Comanche resides in a glass case) pointed out that several thousand Sioux and Crow also survived that day.

What major facts are you getting wrong because of your latent prejudices? When members of racial and ethnic groups are made visible, the reference is sometimes gratuitous and fosters old stereotypes: *Police in Minneapolis are searching today for a black man in his 30s who is suspected of taking part in a convenience-store robbery late last night.*

How many black men in their 30s live in Minneapolis? The report is not a description. If height, weight and distinguishing characteristics such as scars or speech patterns were used, enough information would be given on which to base an identification. The gratuitous addition of *black* simply adds a label.

The all-too-common assumption that "minority" issues are the same as "black-white" issues ignores the country's movement from melting pot to mosaic to kaleidoscope. In today's U.S., immigration is and will be an issue worthy of coverage. But it also is an issue that is multilayered, complex and often emotional. This new force for social change can and must be covered without falling back on old, outdated assumptions. To cover it objectively, journalists must face facts.

For instance, almost 20 years ago, in the 1995 Oklahoma City bombing, early media reports pointed to the possibility that international terrorists were responsible, and there were reported sightings of Middle Eastern people who were antagonistic to the U.S. Needless stereotyping distorted media reports. The bomber was a white man, born in the U.S.

Six years later, in September 2001, when Middle Easterners flew U.S. commercial jets into New York's World Trade Center and the Pentagon, and attempted to fly into the White House, killing about 3,000 people, news organizations had to scramble to find ways to describe the groups and individuals involved.

Today, the pressure grows. The number of anti-Muslim hate groups tripled to 30 in 2011, according to the Southern Poverty Law Center, which advocates for civil rights. All hate groups (1,018 active in 2011) have beliefs or practices that attack or malign an entire class of people, typically for their supposedly immutable characteristics.

Here's an example of how the shift on one side of the *Working With Words* Language Triangle led to a scramble to develop relevant language in September 2001. At The Wall Street Journal, a memo containing the following information was sent to all reporters, swiftly responding to the need for sensitive, truthful and appropriate language standards that would avoid racism yet lead to clarity:

al Qaeda   Lowercase the *al* in the name of bin Laden's terrorist network except starting a sentence or a line in a headline.

Arab and Islamic   The terms aren't interchangeable. Many Arabs, particularly in the U.S., are Christian, and a number of Muslim states (including Afghanistan, Iran and Pakistan) are not Arab.

Hamas   The common name for the Islamic Resistance Movement, a militant Islamic group aiming to establish a Palestinian state incorporating Israel and the West Bank.

Hezbollah   The Shiite Muslim militant group opposing Israelis in Lebanon with Iranian support. The name means "Party of God."

Islamic extremists and Islamic militants   These terms are appropriate in referring to zealots involved in terrorist activities, while the term *Islamic fundamentalists* should be avoided. Many Muslims who consider themselves fundamentalists are not supporters of the terrorist acts. For example, the Saudi Arabian government is fundamentalist in the sense that it supports a form of Islamic governance, but it is often portrayed as fighting "Islamic fundamentalists." And some nations and organizations that are suspected of complicity in terrorist acts do not embrace religious fundamentalism. The government of Iraq, for instance, has secular socialist roots, and some radical Palestinian organizations are motivated more by nationalism than by religious zeal.

jihad   The religious struggle or war against nonbelievers in Islam.

Muhammad   Preferred over *Mohammed* for the founder and chief prophet of the Muslim religion, also known as Islam.

Mujahedeen   This is the preferred spelling for the plural noun for those engaged in a jihad, or Muslim holy war.

normalcy Although *normality* has long been considered the preferred noun, this variation seems to have taken over among officials and commentators addressing the nation's attempts to return to the one-time status quo.

Osama bin Laden Lowercase *bin*, meaning "son of," in the name of the terrorist leader, except starting a line in a headline.

Sunni and Shiite Muslims Main branches of Islam. (Most Afghans are Sunnis.)

Taliban The Islamic movement that overran Afghanistan in 1996. The term, literally meaning "students," is construed as plural.

terrorists *Terrorists* attack civilian targets, such as the World Trade Center; *guerrillas* attack military or government establishments.

Ageism

Ageism is discrimination against middle-aged and elderly people.

In U.S. culture, youth has been idealized and age has been posed as an issue for men and women. But the focus on age is usually not necessary and gets in the way of the greater reality, as in these examples:

> The spry 65-year-old salesman works five days a week in the job he's loved for the past 30 years. [The story later says he founded the company.]

> Grandmother Wins Election as Centralia Mayor [headline]

In the first example, *spry* gives the impression that the salesman is unusually active for his age. The assumption is unfair and ageist. In the second example, *grandmother* is both ageist (it focuses unduly on age) and sexist (it focuses on a woman's tie to her family rather than on an appropriate accomplishment—being elected mayor). You're unlikely to see this headline: *Grandfather Wins Election as Centralia Mayor.*

Today, only Japan, Canada, Europe and a few other developed countries have an older average age than the U.S. (median age in the U.S. is 36 and going up). The World War II generation and their children, the baby boomers, form large blocs of society. Both groups continue to be active shapers of new power and won't be dismissed easily in language—even with the advent of the Gen Y and Millennial age cohorts.

The "young old" of the 70- to 85-year-old group continue to retire but also to be employed, form companies and lead communities. For instance, Clint Eastwood at 82 stars in a 2012 Super Bowl commercial, speaks at the Republican Convention and directs major motion pictures. Betty White, at 90, stars in a television series. The "old old," age 85 and older, still vote, subscribe to media sources and invest in the stock market. Some parents and children now live in the same nursing homes.

Other Stereotyping

Stereotyping denies the individuality of people or groups by expecting them to conform to unvarying patterns. For example:

Jones said that after a woman who identified herself only as a "Jewish mother" complained that she and several co-workers were upset because of the lack of day care, the company began making plans to survey employees.

Even when a source uses a stereotype, such as *Jewish mother*, it is not the journalist's job to perpetuate that stereotype. In this example, it would be a simple matter to drop the offensive labeling. It's hard to imagine that the label is in any way necessary to the story.

Such labeling makes it easy for the narrow-minded to engage in discrimination. Perpetuating sexism, racism, ageism and other forms of stereotyping in the language helps contribute to such discrimination against individuals and groups.

Sexist, racist and ageist labels, as well as religious bias, that creep into writing not only are unfair to groups and individuals but also are inaccurate. To repeat the obvious—but obviously neglected, or this chapter would not be necessary—*a journalist's job is to reflect reality.*

The Nonbias Rule

The history of inequality in Western culture has led to language stressing white men as the standard, considering others as substandard. That language is out of date. One rule eliminates most language biases.

◯ Ask, "Would my wording be the same if my subject were an affluent white man?"

Sexist reporting occurs when reporters treat men and women unequally, patronizing women by describing them or their clothing, or labeling women in emotional or reproductive terms. It's reasonable to expect that all media lost credibility as being reliable in the 2008 presidential campaign. Why? All women in the top roles were insulted by sexist coverage, thus insulting the core audience of media.

What male presidential candidate's coverage focused on his attire? What male vice presidential candidate's coverage centered on his abilities as a parent and on his physical attributes? What male spouse of a candidate was critiqued for fashion?

Apply the nonbias rule to test whether you write fairly. When you use a "colorful," "catchy" or "cutesy" phrase, the interpretation may be derogatory. A headline describing Sen. Dianne Feinstein, D-Calif., as "Fiery, Feisty Feinstein" is sexist. Just imagine applying the same adjectives to a male senator. When Jeremy Lin, a Chinese-American basketball player, was covered by ESPN on its mobile website under the headline "chink in the armor," the editor who allowed the headline was fired. The

Asian-American Journalists Association issued a statement to ESPN as to the term being a racial slur. The editor, in coverage later, noted that it never crossed his mind that the headline was offensive. The lesson? Straightforward, factual writing builds credibility. Adjectives and characterizations are always opportunities for derision. Drop as many as possible. Don't label a person as a member of a specific gender, age or racial group.

Symbolic Annihilation

Studies continue to show sources for stories today still are "mainly male, mainly pale." The media do not query individuals from the majority of the population in proportion to their numbers in U.S. society. Audiences deserve a more realistic look at themselves. Multiple and varied sources must be quoted.

As George Gerbner and Gaye Tuchman, sociologists who studied the media, point out, if a group is not represented in media messages and language, that group is not part of the picture we carry around in our heads. When a group is invisible, absent, condemned, trivialized or ignored, people in that group are symbolically "zapped" out of existence.

Although men have always been presidents of this country and chiefs of the FBI, it is unrealistic to assume that the sex, age, race and physical abilities a person holds will neatly fit that person into old stereotypes. Janet Reno was the longest-term U.S. attorney general in the 20th century. Hillary Rodham Clinton narrowly missed being the Democratic Party's candidate for president in 2008. In the 112th Congress, 17 women were serving in the 100-member U.S. Senate, 74 in the 435-member U.S. House of Representatives.

Many blacks are middle class, which runs counter to journalistic reports placing African-Americans in poverty. A record 44 African-Americans serve in the House of Representatives, with none in the Senate. More than half the women in the U.S. are employed outside the home, which runs counter to the out-of-date image of women as the only audience using food information. Mentally disabled people are no longer shut away from participating in the world. People with disabilities may be no more handicapped than the "temporarily abled."

Native Americans are not of one tribe. Citizens of Spanish-speaking ancestry are not a monolithic group: They are Cuban-Americans, Mexican-Americans, Puerto Ricans and others whose roots are in Spain, Latin America and Spanish-speaking Caribbean nations, all with differing cultural backgrounds. Asian-American students are not all stereotypically at the head of the class. Nor are Asian-Americans of one monolithic group: They may be of Japanese, Chinese, Korean, Vietnamese, Thai or other ancestry.

Almost 9 million people in the 2010 census checked off multiple boxes under the category of race, and many of them were young people. Keanu Reeves, Halle Berry and President Barack Obama would fit two or more census categories. This is the shape of things to come. Ignoring the individuality of people does not fit today's reporting.

Dumping Today's Stereotypes

There are terms to avoid (many of them are considered slurs) or to include when writing or editing stories. *Even when preferable terms are suggested, they should not be used except when germane to the story.* Usually, you should identify everyone, or no one, by race, age, sex and so on.

◯ **Ask the source.**

Generally, the best way to determine whether a term is prejudicial is to ask the person(s) it covers. For instance, many members of tribes object to the term *Indian*, although some groups retain it. Many prefer being identified by tribal name; some prefer the term *Native American* or *American Indian*. Ask the person her or his preference. That's the only way to ensure accuracy.

◯ **Eliminate labels.**

Labels stereotype people, annoy audiences and are out of date as language shifts to modernize. Stereotyping all people in a group as acting or being like all others in that group only blinds us to individuals' possibilities and characteristics. Expecting every white male to be like all other white males is just as racist and sexist as expecting all black females to be like all other black females.

◯ **Respect all subjects.**

Be on the lookout for unconscious bias. The most punishing stereotypes are subtle. For instance, medical researchers Michael Lewis, Steven M. Alessandri and Margaret W. Sullivan demonstrate that 3-year-old boys are more encouraged to risk and fail than are 3-year-old girls. Parents, teachers and others reinforce two different expectations without realizing it. This double standard takes a toll on both boys and girls.

◯ **Drop race, sex, age or disability tags.**

Don't provide someone's racial, ethnic or religious background; sex or sexual orientation; or age or disability unless it's relevant to the particular story. The days of the "she's a college professor, but she's black" story were naive because they showed a white-press prejudice. That lack of understanding will push your audience away.

○ Pay attention.

Remember: Fair, objective language cannot be determined solely by popular usage or rules in books that can have the effect of freezing current understanding. Language changes daily as it responds to an increasingly global culture that changes at an accelerating speed.

The constant revision of language is not easy, as seen by arguments over acceptable and unacceptable language in a globally interdependent society. The controversy over what terms are "politically correct" will grow as the world slouches toward multilevel multiculturalism.

Bias-Related Terms

The following list of terms—some preferred and some to be avoided—is controversial. As soon as it is published, some of the entries may be out-of-date. Each time we publish the list, we add and delete terms. The first core set of examples was provided by permission of the Multicultural Management Program at the University of Missouri School of Journalism, which constructed a Dictionary of Offensive Terms with the help of multicultural journalists from across the nation. Other examples are drawn from observation of language in today's media, as well as from a number of resources including those listed at the end of this chapter.

Racism, sexism and other "isms" are unfair, period. Avoid using racist, sexist, ageist and other stereotyping terms, even in quotes. Language changes fast, so keep current with changes by using Web resources. Most media have stylebooks that are in constant revision because of society's need for current language. In some cases, this list may disagree with those stylebooks as well as with The Associated Press Stylebook because this list is based on needs identified by a variety of journalists and professional organizations. *Watch your language.*

A

actor   Not *actress*. Most members of the acting community prefer *actor* for either a man or a woman. Use *actor* unless *actress* is part of a title, such as the Oscar categories "Best Actress" and "Best Supporting Actress."

advertising representative   Not *adman*.

African   Of or pertaining to Africa or its people or languages. Not a synonym for *black* or *African-American*.

African-American   Not necessarily interchangeable with *black*. Ask members of the group in your audience for their preference. Don't use the terms *articulate, intelligent* and *qualified* as modifiers for *African-American*; you would not use those terms to describe whites in the same context.

AIDS victim   Do not use; *person with AIDS* is preferred.

airhead   Do not use; objectionable description, generally aimed at a woman.

alien   Do not use; *illegal immigrant* or *undocumented immigrant* is preferred.

all people are created equal   Use instead of *all men are created equal* unless you need to quote the Declaration of Independence verbatim.

alumnae and alumni   Not *alumni* for a group of men and women who have attended a school. *Alumna* (plural *alumnae*) is correct for a woman (women); *alumnus* (plural *alumni*) for a man (men). The AP Stylebook tells you that *alumni* is the correct term for a group of men and women. But just as *man* does not stand for men and women, *alumni* does not stand for both sexes.

Amazon   Do not use to describe a woman; characterizes women as predators of men; also refers to size.

American   Applies to people from both North and South America. AP style says it may be used to refer to citizens of the U.S.; instead, use *U.S. citizen*.

American Indian   Interchangeable with *Native American*; ask source to determine preference; use correct tribal name if possible. *Wampum, circle the wagons, warpath, warrior, powwow, scalping, tepee, brave, squaw, savage* and other similar terms offend.

anchor   Use *anchor* for all people anchoring the news.

Anglo   Always capitalized. Used interchangeably with *white* primarily in the Southwest regions of the U.S. to denote a white inhabitant of non-Hispanic descent.

Arab   A native of Arabia or any of a Semitic people native to Arabia but now dispersed throughout surrounding lands. Not interchangeable with *Arab-American* or persons from Middle Eastern countries.

"the Arab world"   While 22 countries are in the League of Arab States, this phrase misleads. Some 350 million people inhabit a variety of lands—from North and Northeast Africa to Southwest Asia. Generalizations cannot cover their experiences, religions or politics. Again, name the country instead of making a sweeping generalization that is less specific.

articulate   Offensive when referring to a minority group member and his or her ability to handle the English language; usage suggests that "those people" are not considered well-educated or well-spoken.

artisan   Preferred to *craftsman*.

Asian   Refers specifically to things or people of or from Asia; not interchangeable with *Asian-American*. Some Asians regard *Asiatic* as offensive. Do not use *Oriental* to replace *Asian* when referring to people.

Asian-American   Preferred generic term for U.S. citizens of Asian descent. Be specific when referring to individuals or particular groups: *Filipino-Americans, Japanese-Americans, Chinese-Americans* and so on. *Serene, quiet, shy, reserved* and *smiling* are disparaging stereotypes of Asian-Americans, as are *buck-toothed, delicate, obedient, passive, stoic, mystical, China doll* and *dragon lady*. Also avoid references to the *Asian invasion*, describing Asian immigration.

assembly member Use for all elected to an assembly (also *assembly-woman, assemblyman*).

B

babe Do not use; offensive term referring to a woman.

ball and chain Do not use; offensive phrase that refers sarcastically to a man's loss of freedom because of a woman.

banana Do not use; offensive term for an Asian-American who allegedly has abandoned his or her culture. Just as objectionable are *coconut* for a Mexican-American and *oreo* for an African-American.

bandito Do not use; often applied derisively.

barracuda Do not use; negative generalization of a person without morals or ethical standards or judgments; many times directed at a woman.

bartender Do not use *bar maid*.

basket case Do not use; term began as British army slang for a quadruple amputee who had to be carried in a basket but has come to mean anyone who is incapacitated. When someone says, "I was so drunk, I was a basket case," what is implied is, "I was so drunk, I was as useless as a quadriplegic." Many people consider the term offensive.

bastard Do not use; also do not use *illegitimate*.

beaner Do not use; offensive term referring to someone of Latin descent.

beauty Avoid descriptive terms of beauty when not necessary. For instance, use *blond* and *blue-eyed* for a woman only if you would use the same phrasing for a man.

beefcake Do not use; offensive term referring to male physical attractiveness.

bellhop Not *bellman*.

bi Do not use; offensive term derived from *bisexual*. (See *bisexual*.)

Bible-beater, -thumper, -whacker Do not use; unacceptable terms for evangelical Christians. Acceptable terms are *fundamentalist Christian* or *born-again Christian*; ask source.

Bible Belt Do not use for sections of the U.S., especially in the South and Midwest.

bimbo Do not use; offensive term referring to a woman.

birth name or given name Not *maiden name*.

bisexual Term for a person sexually attracted to members of both sexes; use carefully if at all.

black Ask your source for clarification. Although *African-American* may be preferred by your audience, both terms are considered acceptable usage in the AP Stylebook. Your audience will tell you what is preferred. Do not use the archaic *colored* or *negro* unless the name is used in a title, such as the National Association for the Advancement of Colored People or the United Negro Fund.

blind Adjective to describe a person without sight; nouns are *visually impaired* or *person with low vision*; do not use *the blind*.

blond   Use *blond* for men and women. Do not repeat or refer to jokes where blond-haired people are assumed to be stupid.

blue-haired   Do not use; offensive phrase applied to an older woman.

boy   Insulting when applied to an adult male, especially a man of color.

brave   Do not use as a noun referring to a Native American male.

broad   Do not use; offensive term for a woman.

brotherly and sisterly love   Not *brotherly love.*

brunet   Use only one spelling, *brunet,* for men and women.

buck   Do not use; derogatory word for an African-American or a Native American male.

business professional   Use for all those in business (also *businessman* or *businesswoman*).

buxom   Do not use; offensive reference to a woman's chest size.

C

camera operator   Use for all people operating video cameras.

Canuck   Do not use; derisive term for a Canadian.

career woman   Do not use; offensive. Just report her business title.

Caucasian   Always capitalized. Usually, but not always, interchangeable with *white.* Term appears to be becoming historic as *white non-Hispanic* is the preferred term used for several decades by the U.S. Census.

chairperson, convener, presider, coordinator, chair   Use for all those chairing meetings (also *chairwoman* or *chairman*).

Charlie   Do not use; a derisive term popularized in the Vietnam War by U.S. soldiers to refer to a Vietnamese person.

cheesecake   Do not use; objectionable reference to female physical attractiveness.

Chicano/Chicana   Popular terms in the 1960s and 1970s to refer to Mexican-Americans could be offensive to older Mexican-Americans; check with source.

chick   Do not use; offensive term referring to a woman. Also avoid *chick flick* or *chick lit,* terms that denote movies and literature that feature women.

Chico   First name inappropriately applied to a Mexican or Mexican-American; do not use generically. Also avoid *José, Pancho* and *Julio.*

chief   Offensive when used generically to describe a Native American; use only when title is one given by a tribe.

Chinaman   Do not use; unacceptable racial epithet for an Asian-American or a Chinese person.

Chinatown   Refers to some Asian-American neighborhoods; avoid as a blanket term for all Asian-American communities.

Chink; chink in the armor   Do not use; unacceptable racial epithet for an Asian-American or a Chinese person.

coconut   Do not use; offensive term for a Mexican-American who seemingly has abandoned his or her culture. Just as objectionable are *banana* for an Asian-American and *oreo* for a black.

codger   Do not use; offensive reference to an elderly person.

coed   Do not use; comes from the days when men were the dominant gender in college. Today, women outnumber men in college enrollments and as graduates. Use *student*.

cojones   Do not use; vulgar Spanish word for *testicles*, often used to indicate machismo.

colored   In some societies, including the U.S., the word is considered derogatory and should not be used except when part of an official title, as in *National Association for the Advancement of Colored People*. In some African countries, *colored* denotes individuals of mixed racial ancestry. Whenever the word is used, place it in quotation marks and provide an explanation of its meaning.

common person, average person   Not *common man, average man, average Joe* (*the average person in the U.S. is Jane Doe—women are the majority gender in the U.S.*).

community   Do not use; implies a monolithic culture in which people act, think and vote in the same way, as in *Asian-American, Hispanic, African-American* or *gay community*. Be more specific: *Hispanic residents in a north-side neighborhood*. You are not the judge of whether a group is a community.

congressional representative, member of Congress   Use for a member of Congress (also *congressman* or *congresswoman*).

conjoined twins   Not *Siamese twins*.

coolies   Do not use; refers specifically to a Chinese laborer in the 19th-century U.S.; objectionable then, objectionable now.

coon   Do not use; highly objectionable reference to an African-American.

coot   Do not use; offensive reference to an elderly person.

cougar   Do not use; focuses on women's sexuality and your judgment, not newsworthy.

councilor   Use for a member of a council (also *councilwoman* or *councilman*).

cracker, hillbilly, Okie, redneck   Do not use, even when people refer to themselves this way.

craftsman   Do not use; *artisan* is preferred.

crip   Do not use as a derogatory term for a person with a disability.

cripple, crippled   Do not use; also do not use *handicapped*. *Disabled* is preferred; see *disabled*.

cybergeek   Do not use; derogatory reference to an inventor, a programmer or a technical expert. Also avoid *nerd* and *techie*. Use the person's title.

D

dago   Do not use; derogatory reference to an Italian or Italian-American.

deaf, hearing impaired and speech impaired   Not *deaf and dumb, deaf and mute*. Deaf people are not dumb.

dear   A term of endearment objectionable to some. Usage such as *he was a dear man* or *she is a dear* are personal judgments, which are to be avoided.

deliverer, delivery person   Preferred to *deliveryman*.

dingbat   Do not use; objectionable term referring to a woman.

disabled   A disabling condition may or may not be handicapping. Use *disabled* and *disability* rather than *handicapped* or *handicap*. Don't use *disabled* as a noun. Do not use *crippled, crip* or *invalid*. Use *person (people) with a disability (disabilities)* or check with the individual.

ditz   Do not use; objectionable term implying stupidity.

divorced   Not *divorce* or *divorcee*; say a person is *divorced*. A person's marital status seldom is pertinent to a story. Especially be careful when you start to state a woman's marital status. Women continue to be tagged with marital identifiers more than men.

dizzy   Do not use; offensive adjective for a woman.

door attendant   Not *doorman*.

drafter   Not *draftsman*.

dragon lady   Do not use; objectionable characterization of an Asian-American woman, depicting her as scheming and treacherous.

Dutch treat   Do not use; implies that Dutch people are cheap. Use *separate checks*.

dwarf   Do not use; *little people* is preferred. Also do not use *midget*.

dyke   Do not use; offensive term for a lesbian.

E

English   Not *Englishmen*.

Eskimo   Many people referred to as *Eskimo* prefer *Inuit* (those in Canada) or *Native Alaskan*; ask source for preference.

every person for himself or herself   Not *every man for himself*.

F

factory worker   Not *factory man*.

fag, faggot   Do not use; offensive term for a gay man or lesbian. Do not use even if members of the group refer to themselves by the term.

fairy   Do not use; offensive term for a gay man.

female   Do not use in place of *woman* (the noun). Do not use *woman* or *female* as an adjective. Do not identify by gender unless it is pertinent to the story.

feminine   Can be objectionable to some women.

feminine wiles   Do not use; insulting.

fiance   Language is moving toward one spelling, *fiance*, for all instances. As with the issue of *divorce*, extra care is necessary so that overemphasis is not placed on a woman's marital status.

firefighter   Use instead of *fireman* or *firewoman* for one who puts out fires.

fisher   Not *fisherman*.

flip   Do not use; derogatory term for a Filipino or Filipino-American.

foreman, forewoman   Not *foreman* for both sexes.

foxy Do not use; offensive description of a woman's physical appearance.

fragile Do not use; offensive description of a woman's physical attributes.

French Not *Frenchmen*.

fried chicken Do not use as stereotypical reference to black cuisine. Also avoid *watermelon*.

frigid Derisive when used to stereotype or characterize women; usually applied to women viewed by men as aloof or distant.

fruit Do not use for a gay man or lesbian; offensive.

full-figured Do not use; offensive. Descriptions of a woman's physical appearance are rarely relevant. If you would not describe a man's physical appearance in a story, do not describe a woman's appearance. Physical descriptions are relevant only in a few fields—sports, health, fashion.

G

gabacho Do not use; derogatory Spanish word applied to whites.

gaijin Do not use; exclusionary Japanese term referring to foreigners.

gal Do not use to refer to a woman.

gay Preferred adjective for homosexual men; also acceptable in referring to lesbians. A person's sexual orientation should be identified *only* when pertinent to the story and is rarely relevant. Ask your story subject for preferred descriptor.

gang member Use only when verified. See *wannabe*.

geezer Do not use for an elderly man; objectionable.

geisha Japanese woman trained to provide entertainment, especially for men; offensive stereotype when used as a blanket term or caricature.

gender enders Avoid these terms: *actress, comedienne, executrix, heroine, poetess* and *starlet*. Instead, use gender-neutral terms such as *actor, comedian, executor, hero, poet* and *star*. Also see individual entries for these terms.

ghetto Avoid; stereotype for a poor minority community.

girl Use only when the person is under 18 years of age; insulting when used to refer to a woman. (See *boy*.)

gold digger Do not use; characterizes a woman as a predator of men. Avoid *Amazon, barracuda*.

golden years Avoid; characterizes people's later years as uniformly idyllic.

gook Do not use; unacceptable term for a Vietnamese or other Asian-American.

gorgeous Avoid giving your judgments of the physical attributes of women.

greaser Term used in the 1950s for those with a specific hairstyle and dress; derogatory when applied to Hispanics.

gringo Do not use; derogatory Spanish term applied to whites.

Guido An Italian first name; offensive when used to denote membership in the Mafia or as a description of street punks.

gyp Do not use; offensive term meaning "to cheat"; derived from *gypsy*.

H

handicapped   Do not use; see *disabled.*

handmade, synthetic   Preferred to *man-made.* Also use *manufactured, constructed, fabricated* or *created.*

harebrained   Do not use to characterize people; offensive.

harelip   Avoid; offensive term for *cleft lip.*

harem   Do not use to describe a gathering of women; derisive.

heap big   Do not use; stereotypical phrase denoting size; offensive to Native Americans.

heathens   Do not use; derogatory.

Hebrew   A language. Do not use for *Jew.* Citizens of Israel are Israelis; not all Israelis are Jews.

hero   Use for both men and women; do not use *heroine* for women.

Hiawatha   Character popularized in a Longfellow work. Offensive when applied generically to describe or characterize Native Americans.

high yellow   Do not use; objectionable when used to refer to lighter-colored black persons. Avoid any description of skin color or degrees of color. Also avoid *mulatto* and *half-breed.*

hillbilly   Do not use; term applied to people generally from Appalachia or the Deep South.

Hinduism   Religion in India; adherents are Hindus. Do not confuse *Hindu* with *Hindi,* one of many languages spoken in India.

Hispanic   Term referring generically to those with Latin American or Spanish heritage; not necessarily interchangeable with *Chicano, Latino, Mexican-American* or other specific Hispanic groups. Ask source which term is preferred. Use ethnic background *only* when pertinent to the story. Many Hispanics are second-, third-, fourth- and fifth-generation U.S. citizens, so do not assume a Latino is a recent immigrant.

Holy Roller   Do not use; offensive term used to refer to an evangelical Christian.

homemaker   Preferred to *housewife.*

homosexual   A person's sexual orientation is rarely relevant to a story. *Homosexual* connotes a clinical illness and evokes the pejorative "homo." Preferred terms are *gay* for a homosexual man and *lesbian* for a homosexual woman. *Dyke, fruit, fairy* and *queer* are objectionable. Do not use those terms, even if members of the group refer to themselves by any of these terms. Also, use *sexual orientation* rather than *sexual preference.*

honey   Do not use; objectionable. Also do not use *dear* and *sweetie.*

honorifics   Usually not useful. Women and men are identified on first reference with full name and on second reference, by last name. Use the courtesy title *Mrs.* only if the person prefers it or confusion would result. Otherwise, *Ms.* is the courtesy title preferred for a woman if *Mr.* is used for a man; *Ms.* does not focus on marital status just as *Mr.* does not. Use evenhanded treatment for women and men.

hotblooded Latin   Do not use; derisive stereotype of Latinos as hot tempered and violent.

hours of work   Not *man-hours.*

house worker   Not *maid.*

humanity, humankind, people   Not *mankind.*

hunk   See *"The Myth."*

hymie   Short for Hyman, a man's first name. Do not use as a derogatory term for a person of the Jewish faith. Also avoid other disparaging terms for Jews such as *kike* and *Heeb.*

I

illegal immigrant, undocumented immigrant   Not *illegal alien* or *undocumented worker.* Not all illegal immigrants are from Mexico or Latin America. Immigration from Latin America is declining.

impotent   Clinical term referring to male sexual dysfunction; not appropriate when used to stereotype or characterize males.

Indian   Offensive term to many who call themselves *Native Americans* or who prefer their tribe's individual name. *American Indian* is acceptable unless referring to residents or natives of India.

Indian giver   Do not use; refers to someone who reneges or takes something back once given.

Indochina   Formerly *French Indochina,* now divided into Cambodia, Laos and Vietnam.

Injun   Do not use; derisive term for a Native American.

inscrutable   Adjective carelessly applied to Asian-Americans; avoid all terms that stereotype entire groups.

insurance representative   Not *insurance man.*

invalid   Do not use; see *disabled.*

Irish   Not *Irishmen.*

Islamic   Refers to Islam, the religion. Adherents are Muslims. An *Islamist,* or *Islamic fundamentalist,* believes the Quran should be the basis for religious, political and personal life. See also "Racism and Religious Bias" earlier in this chapter.

Ivan   Do not use; slur for a Russian.

J

JAP   Acronym for *Jewish American princess*; do not use; a stereotype of a young Jewish woman.

Jap   Do not use to refer to a Japanese or Japanese-American; ethnic slur.

Jew   A Jewish person. Always use as a noun, never as a verb or an adjective.

Jew boy   Do not use; offensive to Jewish males of all ages.

Jew down   Slang for negotiating a lower price for services or goods. Do not use; highly offensive.

jive   Do not use; derisively applied to black slang or speech.

jock   Slang applied to both men and women who participate in sports; offensive to some.

john   Do not use; inappropriate term for a man who uses female or male prostitutes.

José   See *Chico.*

joto   Do not use; derisive Spanish term for a gay man or lesbian.

Julio   See *Chico.*

L

lamebrain   Do not use; offensive.

Latin lover   Avoid; stereotype alluding to Latino sexual prowess.

Latino/Latina   Refers specifically to those of Spanish-American ancestry. Use ethnic identifiers for everyone in your story or no one.

layperson   Member of the congregation as distinguished from the clergy (or *layman* or *laywoman*).

lazy   Avoid labels; show what a person does rather than use value judgments. Especially avoid when describing nonwhites, who are commonly and unfairly stereotyped more often than whites.

leader   Use with caution; implies the person has the approval of an entire group of people. Be more specific: *black politician.*

Leroy   Do not use; first name sometimes carelessly used to refer to all males.

lesbian   Preferred term for a homosexual woman; *gay* may also be used. Rarely is a person's sexual orientation relevant to your story.

letter carrier, postal worker   Not *mailman.* Use for a man or woman who works for the U.S. Postal Service.

LGBT   Self-designated initialism since the 1990s which stands for *lesbian, gay, bisexual and transgender;* used to refer to non-heterosexuals. Generally replaces *gay community.* Spell out first occurrence, then abbreviate.

lily-white   Any characterization of skin color should be avoided. Also avoid *paleface* and *redskin.*

limp-wristed   Do not use; dated and derisive description of a gay man.

line repairer   Preferred to *lineman.*

little woman   Do not use to refer to a wife; offensive.

M

Mafia, Mafiosi   Secret society of criminals and its members; do not use as a synonym for *organized crime* or the *underworld.*

maiden name   Avoid. Use *birth name* or *given name.*

mammy   Do not use; antiquated term referring to an older black woman; highly objectionable.

man   Do not use to denote both sexes. Use *humanity, a person* or *an individual.* Avoid *man and wife.* Use either *wife and husband* or *husband and wife; woman and man* or *man and woman.*

"Man, The"   A reference to the white establishment; offensive.

manhole cover   Some have suggested that this term is sexist because women also work in these places. A more neutral term is *utility cover.*

man-made   Better to use *handmade, manufactured* or *synthetic.*

maricón   Do not use; derisive Spanish term for a gay person.

matronly   Do not use for an older woman; offensive.

meter reader   Preferred to *meter man* or *meter maid.*

Mexican   From or of Mexico; not a substitute for *Mexican-American.*

Mexican-American   Preferred term for U.S. residents of Mexican origin.

Mick   Do not use to mean Irishman; offensive. Do not use *Paddy.*

minority/minorities   On its way to becoming out-of-date; use *racial, ethnic* and *immigrant group(s)* instead, or, better yet, drop racial labeling.

"Myth, The" or **"the male myth"**   Avoid any word, description or phrase contributing to the stereotype of black males as strictly athletic, well-proportioned or having a high sexual drive and exaggerated sex organs. Avoid *stallion, stud, hunk, womanizer* and *lady killer.*

N

Native American   Often preferred to *American Indian*; check with source; use correct tribal name if at all possible.

Negress   Do not use; objectionable and antiquated term for a black woman. Use *African-American* or *black*, depending on the source's preference. Check local stylebook for preferred local usage.

Negro   Do not use except when used in a title such as United Negro College Fund. Use *African-American* or *black*, depending on the source's preference. Check local stylebook for preferred local usage.

news carrier   Not *newsboy.*

nigger   Do not use even when people refer to themselves with this term; highly offensive term for a black person.

nip   Do not use; derogatory term for a Japanese or Japanese-American.

nurse   Not *male nurse.*

O

Okie   Do not use; derogatory term for a white person or, more specifically, for a person from a rural area.

old buzzard   Do not use; derogatory term for an elderly person.

old maid   Do not use; archaic term referring to an unmarried woman. Don't refer to a woman's marital status unless you would for a man in the same story. More than half the adults in the U.S. are not married.

old wives' tale   Do not use. Use *superstition* or *tale of wisdom.*

old-timer   Do not use; objectionable term for an elderly person.

operate   Use *operate a machine* rather than *man a machine.* Also use *work, staff* or *serve.*

operational space flight   Not *manned space flight.*

oreo   Do not use; offensive term for a black person who allegedly has abandoned his or her culture; derisively used to mean "black on the outside and white on the inside."

Oriental   Do not use; use *Asian-American, Asian* or a specific term. Sometimes acceptable to describe things, not people, such as *Oriental rug.*

P

paleface   Do not use; objectionable term sometimes used by Native Americans to describe whites.

Pancho   See *Chico.*

peon   A Spanish-American peasant; avoid; sometimes derisively applied to entire groups of Hispanics or others.

people at work   Not *men at work.*

personnel   Not *manpower.* Also use *staff, work force* or *workers.*

person-on-the-street interview   Not *man-on-the-street interview.*

pert   Do not use; offensive; adjective describing a female characteristic.

petite   Do not use; can be offensive in reference to a woman's body size.

pickaninny   Do not use; offensive term for a black child.

pimp   Use only as a man who profits off prostitutes; highly objectionable stereotype of African-American or other men.

poet   Not *poetess.*

Polack   Do not use; derogatory term for a Polish person.

police officer   Not *policeman.*

Pop   Do not use; offensive reference to an elderly person.

postal worker   Not *postman.* Also use *letter carrier* or *mail carrier.*

powwow   Do not use; see *American Indian.*

PR   Do not use; offensive acronym for *Puerto Rican.*

project   Do not use, as in *public housing project;* has come to be a racial code word, as in *people in the projects.* Use *public housing* or *subsidized housing.*

proper names   Do not make wordplays on people's given names; see, for example, *Chico, Hiawatha, Ivan* and *Leroy.*

prosthesis, artificial limb   Not *peg leg.* Also avoid *hook.*

Q

qualified minorities   Do not use; unnecessary description that implies members of racial, ethnic and immigrant groups are generally unqualified.

queer   Do not use to describe a gay or lesbian even if members of the group describe themselves with the term.

R

redneck   Do not use; offensive term for poor, uneducated white farmers.

redskin   Do not use; objectionable description of a Native American. Avoid any reference to skin color.

refugee   Do not use for people who are settled in the U.S. and no longer have refugee status. Use only to describe people who flee to find refuge from oppression or persecution while they have refugee status. Also, a person who flees a hurricane-devastated area is an *evacuee*, not a refugee.

retarded   Do not use; refer to a specific medical condition. Also avoid *stupid* and *ignorant*.

rubbing noses   Do not use; stereotypically, an "Eskimo kiss." However, Eskimos (many of whom prefer *Inuit* or *Native Alaskan*) do not rub noses, and many object to the characterization.

Russian   Use only to refer to people who are from Russia or of Russian descent and to the language spoken in the region. If a label is necessary, refer to country of origin.

S

sales representative   Preferred to *salesman*.

samurai   As a term or caricature, can be offensively stereotypical; avoid unless referring specifically to the historical Japanese warrior class.

sanitation worker, trash collector   Preferred to *garbage man*.

savages   Do not use; offensive when applied to Native Americans or other native cultures. Also avoid *heathen*.

senile   Do not use to refer to older people; offensive. *Dementia* is the correct term for the mental or physical deterioration of old age.

senior citizen   Avoid. In general, give ages only when relevant. Do not describe people as *senile, matronly* or *well preserved*. Do not use *dirty old man, codger, coot, geezer, silver fox, old-timer, Pop, old buzzard* or *blue-haired*. Do not identify people as grandparents unless it is relevant to the story. Many people object to the term *senior citizens* as "an unsavory euphemism"; alternatives are *the aged, the old, the elderly* and *the retired*.

shiftless   Do not use; highly objectionable as a description of the poor.

shine   Do not use; objectionable reference to a black person.

shrew   Do not use; derogatory characterization of a woman who competes in the workplace or whose behavior is seen as nagging.

siesta   A Latin tradition of a midday nap; use advisedly. Do not use to denote laziness.

silver fox   Do not use; objectionable term referring to an elderly person.

skirt   Do not use; dated and offensive term referring to a woman or girl.

"Some of my best friends are . . ."   Hackneyed phrase usually used by someone accused of racial bias or wanting to appear unbiased, as in *Some of my best friends are Hispanic*.

soulful   Objectionable adjective when applied strictly to blacks.

spade   Garden tool or card suit. Do not use in reference to an African-American; highly insulting.

Spanish   The language or a person from Spain; not interchangeable with *Mexican, Latino/Latina* or *Hispanic*.

spastic   Do not use as an adjective describing those with muscular dysfunctions, tics or jerky physical movements. Also do not use *spaz*. Use the correct medical condition: *has cerebral palsy*.

sped, spec ed　Do not use; offensive reference to a child in a special education class.

spic　Do not use; unacceptable term for *Hispanic*.

spokesperson　Not *spokesman*.

spry　Do not use; cliché describing the elderly that assumes most older people are decrepit.

squaw　Do not use; offensive term for a Native American woman.

stallion　Do not use; offensive sexual term for a man.

statuesque　Do not use; avoid referring to a woman's appearance.

stud　Do not use; offensive sexual term for a man.

stunning　Do not use; avoid referring to a woman's appearance.

suffers from　Do not use. A person has a disease, such as *has leukemia* or *a person with AIDS*.

swarthy　Do not use; objectionable reference to skin color. Other objectionable terms are *paleface*, *redskin* and *lily-white*.

sweet young thing　Do not use; highly objectionable phrase that reduces a woman to a sex object.

sweetie　Do not use; objectionable term of endearment. Also avoid *dear* and *honey*.

T

taco　Do not use; objectionable reference to a Mexican.

telephone worker　Not *telephone man*.

tepee　See *American Indian*.

those people　Do not use; objectionable phrase used by one group to refer to another group. Also avoid *you people*.

timber nigger　Do not use; offensive term used by sporting enthusiasts and those in the tourist industry to describe a Native American involved in the fishing and hunting rights debate.

token　Do not use; refers to someone hired solely because of race, ethnicity or gender; implies the person was not qualified for the job.

Tonto　Do not use; unacceptable characterization of a Native American.

trades worker　Not *tradesman*. Be specific if possible: *construction worker*.

transgender　General term for individuals, groups and behaviors that vary from conventional gender roles. Self-identification as woman, man, neither or both. Not a noun. Do not use *transvestite*, *transgendered* or *tranny*. Ask the subject what personal pronoun (*he* or *she*) is to be used.

U

ugh　Do not use; highly offensive sound used to mimic the speech of Native Americans.

Uncle Tom　Do not use; derogatory term used to refer to a black person who has abandoned his or her culture by becoming subservient to whites; objectionable because no person or group can claim exclusive power to define what it is to be black in the U.S.

V

vegetable Do not use to describe someone in a comatose state or a person incapable of caring for himself or herself. *Persistent vegetative state* is the medical terminology, if applicable.

W

wampum See *American Indian*.

wannabe Refers to someone who mimics a style or behavior of another group or wants to be a member of another group; use advisedly. For instance, a person dressed in red or blue isn't necessarily a *wannabe Blood or Crip gang member*; nor is the person necessarily a gang member. Also use the term *gang member* advisedly for the same reasons.

warpath See *American Indian*.

WASP Acronym for *white Anglo-Saxon Protestant*; offensive to some.

watermelon See *fried chicken*.

welch, welsh Do not use; offensive term meaning to break an agreement.

well-preserved Do not use; offensive term applied to women and elders.

wetback Do not use; derisive term for an illegal immigrant, specifically a Mexican who has crossed the Rio Grande.

wheelchair Do not use *wheelchair-bound* or *confined to a wheelchair*. Preferred expression is *uses a wheelchair*.

white trash Do not use; derogatory term for poor whites.

white-bread Do not use; term denoting blandness; can have a racial connotation.

whore/"ho" Do not use; derogatory. A man's sexual status has no commensurate descriptor. Also avoid *trollop, tart, loose woman* and *hussy*. A person paid for sex is a *prostitute*, whether male or female.

wild Indian Do not use to denote unruly behavior; offensive to Native Americans.

without rhythm Do not use; a stereotype of whites; implies that other races have rhythm, also a stereotype.

woman Preferred term for a female adult; *girl* is appropriate only for those under age 18. Do not use *gal* or *lady*. Avoid derogatory terms for women, such as *babe, ball and chain, bimbo, broad, chick, little woman* and *skirt*. Do not use adjectives describing female physical attributes or mannerisms, such as *buxom, cougar, feminine, foxy, fragile, full-figured, gorgeous, pert, petite, statuesque* and *stunning*.

wop Do not use; derogatory reference to an Italian.

worker Preferred to *workingman* or *workman*.

workers' compensation Not *workmen's compensation*. Close to 50 percent of the work force is female.

X

Xmas Do not use; offensive to many Christians.

> **Y**

yanqui   Do not use; derogatory Spanish term for a North American white. Also avoid *gringo*.

yellow   Do not use; offensive term referring to skin color; also a derogatory term meaning "coward."

yellow peril   Do not use; offensive term used in the U.S. in the 19th and early 20th centuries to elicit fear of Chinese or Asian immigrants.

you people   Do not use; objectionable phrase used by one group to refer to another group. Also avoid *those people*.

Web Resources

COMPETENT LANGUAGE

These websites conduct studies, publish research and provide continuing updates.

- Arab and Middle Eastern Journalism Association of Journalists
  www.ameja.org

- Asian American Journalists Association
  www.aaja.org

- Gay and Lesbian Alliance Against Defamation
  www.glaad.org

- Geena Davis Institute on Gender in Media
  www.seejane.org

- International Women's Media Foundation
  www.iwmf.org

- Journalism and Women Symposium
  www.jaws.org

- Maynard Institute
  www.mije.org

- Muslim American Journalists Association
  www.muslimamericanjournalists.org

- Name It. Change It.
  www.nameitchangeit.org

- National Association of Black Journalists
  www.nabj.org

- National Association of Hispanic Journalists
  www.nahj.org

- National Association for Multi-Ethnicity in Communications
  www.namic.com

○ National Center on Disability and Journalism
www.ncdj.org

○ National Lesbian and Gay Journalists Association
www.nlgja.org

○ Native American Journalists Association
www.naja.com

○ The Poynter Institute's Diversity Digest
www.poynter.org/category/how-tos/newsgathering-storytelling/
diversity-at-work/

○ Religion Newswriters Association
www.religionstylebook.com

○ Society of Professional Journalists
www.spj.org

○ UNITY Journalists of Color
www.unityjournalists.org

○ Women in Media and News
www.wimnonline.org

○ Women's Media Center
www.womensmediacenter.com

PART FOUR

Writing Methods for Different Media

(continued)

CHAPTER 14

Writing News That's Fit for Print

Newspaper and magazine writing does not have to be boring. Nor does it have to be written in a rigid, formulaic style devoid of flair. Consider how Mark Twain did it while reporting for the San Francisco Daily Morning Call on June 7, 1864:

BURGLAR ARRESTED

John Richardson, whose taste for a cigar must be inordinate, gratified it on Saturday night last by forcing his way into a tobacconist's on Broadway, near Kearny street, and helping himself to fourteen hundred "smokes." In his hurry, however, he did not select the best, as the stolen tobacco was only valued at fifty dollars. He was congratulating himself last evening in a saloon on Dupont street, in having secured weeds for himself and all his friends, when lo! a Rose bloomed before his eyes, and he wilted. The scent of that flower of detectives was too strong even for the aroma of the stolen cigars. Richardson was conveyed to the station-house, where a kit of neat burglar's tools was found on his person. He is now reposing his limbs on an asphaltum floor — a bed hard as the ways of unrighteousness.

Twain's flowery, personalized writing style offers opinion and therefore differs dramatically from what today's editors want. It's much more like grandpa's storytelling than something you might read in The New York Times or Time magazine. Still, it illustrates quite dramatically just how readable a story can be. Perhaps sadly for readers, though Twain's style would be frowned upon by most newspapers and magazines today, it's hard to deny how wonderfully entertaining it is.

More than likely, the same story today would be written in a standardized format, probably using the traditional inverted pyramid — storytelling in which the most important facts are presented first and the least important last. Standardized writing is not necessarily bad. Indeed, an understanding of journalistic formulas will help a writer produce lots of stories in a brief period of time. It's a terrific way of delivering the news. Just as a knowledge of grammar — the structure of language — lets us write and edit sentences better, so, too, does a knowledge of news-writing formulas allow us to write and edit stories more efficiently.

Talk of formulas inevitably ignites fears that someone is trying to take away the writer's creativity or turn the writer into a hack. That's not our purpose in discussing the most common newspaper-writing formulas in this chapter. We would never suggest that stories should be written like a paint-by-number picture. We simply note that the experience of thousands of journalists over the years has resulted in typical ways of doing things. You don't have to imitate slavishly these typical methods, but you should understand them as a starting point. Most likely, the sweet spot in journalistic writing falls somewhere between Twain's flowery prose and the traditional approach of the inverted pyramid.

To be sure, if you were assigned to the police beat, after covering several accidents you'd figure out there are certain things that always need to be included in that kind of story. You'd also learn there is a typical order of importance—deaths ahead of injuries, injuries ahead of damages unless the injuries were slight and the damages large. And you'd learn that certain pitfalls need to be avoided, such as not assigning someone guilt for an accident if that person hasn't yet been convicted of a crime.

That doesn't mean every accident story should be written as a fill-in-the-blank report. Details will vary, and those details could require writing the story in an atypical way. But understanding what typically needs to be included and in what order will help you make sure that the most important elements are covered, you write or edit more quickly and efficiently, and you know the difference between creative variations that grow organically from the material and variations that are merely the result of ignorance or inexperience.

In other words, news formulas, like the standard chord changes in a blues song, can actually free your writing to be more creative in ways that work.

Pick the Best Angle

Sometimes, journalists have trouble writing a story because they can't figure out what *angle* to take. That is, they're looking for the best overall approach—the best way to focus the story. Once you decide what angle to take, the rest usually comes easily. You can make this decision in several ways.

- Use the "Hey, did you hear about . . . ?" approach, in which you simply ask yourself what you would tell a friend about the event.

What you would say after "Hey, did you hear about . . . ?" is the angle to take. Broadcasters strongly recommend this approach, but print journalists use it, too.

- Focus on basic news values.

Focusing on basic news values works for print, radio and television, and online stories alike, and it includes the following news values:

Audience: who your audience is and what news it needs or wants from you.

Impact: the number of people involved, the number affected or the depth of emotion people are likely to feel.

Timeliness: how up-to-the-minute the information is.

Proximity: how nearby the story took place.

Prominence: how rich, famous or powerful the people involved are.

Novelty or oddity: how unusual the news item is.

Conflict or drama: how exciting the news is; the more conflict involved, the more dramatic the news is.

With this method, you ask yourself which of these values is appropriate to the story and lead with it. If there's more than one appropriate value, rank them. Then bring them up in the order of their importance.

○ **Stress the angle you think would most affect or interest your audience.**

The strongest angle is always to tell readers, listeners or viewers about something that has a direct effect on them. Look for how this information will have an impact on people, and tell them that. For example, will their taxes be raised, will people be laid off, will the price of meat go down or will the streets be safer? If the story doesn't contain information that directly affects the audience, the next best lead is what would most interest them. Don't bury the most interesting parts where people are less likely to see or hear them. Move them toward the top of the story, where they'll attract more attention.

If a story has neither impact nor interest, you might ask why run it at all. Who cares? Often, however, if the story appears at first to fail these tests, it will pass if you rewrite it to stress people doing things rather than the things themselves. Words about a thing typically contain less built-in interest than words about a person. News is people and what they do or what happens to them. An encyclopedia article about gastropods is not news.

Once you've picked an angle, decide whether to write the story as hard news or soft news. Different formulas define the usual order of details. Depending on the story, you'll choose a hard-news or soft-news lead and story structure.

Types of News Leads

No matter what medium they work in, news writers share the idea that each story should start with a good introduction, or *lead*. They also agree that there are two basic approaches: Either get to the bottom line or dramatically grab the reader's attention.

Leads that stress summarizing the story and telling the reader the bottom line are called *hard-news leads* because they're typically used for hard-news stories such as crimes, accidents, government meetings, and political and economic news. They're also called *straight-news leads*, and the object is to get straight to the point of the story.

Leads that stress attracting the reader's attention by using a dramatic grabber are called *soft-news leads* because they're typically used for soft-news stories such as personality profiles, sports, reviews, entertainment and lifestyle features, and columns.

What complicates these definitions today is that soft-news leads are increasingly used on stories that once demanded hard-news leads. Newspapers and online sites, in particular, have begun to use soft-news leads as a way of enticing readers into a hard-news story. Still, it's important to understand the differences in these types of leads.

Hard-News Leads

Hard-news leads are found more often in newspapers and online than in magazines. They get to the bottom line, as people in business say. That is, they tell you in the first sentence the essence of the news. If you read no further—and many readers won't—you'll still have the gist of the story.

It's a myth that the lead needs to tell the reader *who, what, when, where, why* and *how*. A lead with all that information would probably be too long and hard to read. (A lead should be only a sentence or two long, a maximum of 20 to 30 words.)

Many hard-news stories leave out the *why* and *how* because those elements are often more speculative and less objective. Only when *why* or *how* can be discussed objectively are they likely to appear. (Soft-news leads, as you'll see, stress drama more than information and may leave out even some of the basic four details—the *who, what, when* and *where*.)

"The Five W's and an H" are worth remembering, however, because the order in which people typically recite them—*who, what, when, where, why* and *how*—is almost always their order of importance in a story. That means it's also the order in which details typically should appear in a lead.

For example, the two most important details in a story are usually *who* did *what*, in that order. In some stories, the *what* may come first if what happened or was said is more important than the person involved. Next most important are *when* and *where*. *Why* and *how* come last in "The Five W's and an H" and are almost never found in the lead.

We suggest you think of the basic formula for the hard-news lead as *who, what, time, day or date,* and *place*—in that order. This corresponds to the well-known *who, what, when, where, why* and *how*, leaving out the *why* and *how* and breaking *when* into *time* and *day or date*. *Place*, of course, is the same as *where*. *Time, day or date,* and *place* are rarely if ever the most important part of a story, so they should not start the lead. They often come not in the lead itself but in later paragraphs, and, in some stories, one or more of these three elements may not appear at all if unimportant.

There's been a tendency over the past 25 years to use a soft-news lead on some hard-news stories that have special drama. Take a look at the figure below to see how a news story might be structured with a hard-news (inverted pyramid) lead as opposed to a soft-news (feature) lead. So, again we say: Don't slavishly imitate the following formula. Understand it and appreciate it, but use your discretion—and don't be afraid to try something different when you have a valid reason for doing so. And be aware that some types of hard-news stories often use variations on the formula described here. For example, an obituary should begin with the person's name, not just an identifying label, even if the deceased was not famous, and the *place*, the deceased's address, is often given only as a town to eliminate the risk of a burglary during the funeral.

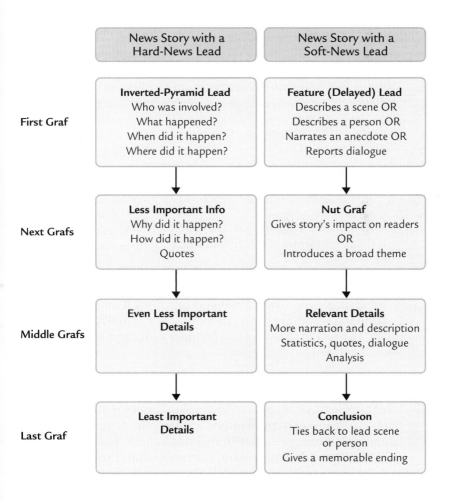

	News Story with a Hard-News Lead	**News Story with a Soft-News Lead**
First Graf	**Inverted-Pyramid Lead** Who was involved? What happened? When did it happen? Where did it happen?	**Feature (Delayed) Lead** Describes a scene OR Describes a person OR Narrates an anecdote OR Reports dialogue
Next Grafs	**Less Important Info** Why did it happen? How did it happen? Quotes	**Nut Graf** Gives story's impact on readers OR Introduces a broad theme
Middle Grafs	**Even Less Important Details**	**Relevant Details** More narration and description Statistics, quotes, dialogue Analysis
Last Graf	**Least Important Details**	**Conclusion** Ties back to lead scene or person Gives a memorable ending

Writing News That's Fit for Print

Here's the formula and how to use it.

Who Was Involved?

○ Use an *immediate-ID who* if the person is well-known to your audience. If the person should be well-known to your readers by name, simply begin with the person's name:

> Madonna sang to a full stadium.

○ Use a title with the name if the person should be well-known to readers of your newspaper but still could benefit from identification. Place a short title in front of the name or a longer title following it:

> Johnson City Mayor Anne Williams said . . .

> Shaun Donovan, secretary of Housing and Urban Development, said . . .

Note that official titles in front of a name are capitalized, but those following a name are not.

○ Use a *delayed-ID who* if the person isn't well-known to your audience. In the lead, write down a label for the *who*:

> An Ypsilanti man . . .

> An area plumber . . .

After you finish the lead sentence using the delayed ID, start the second paragraph with the name of the person represented by the label in the first sentence:

> *A Petersburg man died* in a two-car accident Thursday on U.S. 23. *Wilbur Jeffers* was southbound when . . .

What Happened?

○ Use the *single-element what* if only one thing happened or is the focus of the story. That way, there's no problem figuring out the *what*. The rest of the story will be filled with extra details about what happened:

> Slain police officer Enrique Montez will be remembered today.

○ Use the *most-important-element what* if more than one thing happened but one is more important than the others. This situation is often the case with meeting stories. The rest of the story is filled with details about the main *what*, then a listing of and details about the other *what*s:

Police have arrested a suspect in last month's kidnapping of a Spring-field girl.

The story may then update the audience on how the girl is doing a month after the ordeal and provide other information, but the focus in the lead is on the arrest.

○ Use the *multiple-elements what* if more than one thing happened and the events are unrelated and all roughly of equal importance. You're going to have to list them all in the lead before you turn to details about any of them.

The list can be in the first sentence if it doesn't make the sentence too long and unwieldy. Or you may have to list each *what* in separate sentences. Remember to maintain parallel structure:

The City Council approved Monday night the widening of Main Street but rejected a proposal that would have required city employees to live in town.

In listing the separate elements, try to give them in the order of most impact or interest to your audience, even though, of course, they're all important.

○ Use the *summary what* if more than one thing happened and all the events are of equal importance and have enough in common that they can be summarized without having to list all of them separately. You can summarize all the *what*s in one sentence in the lead:

Most economic indicators rose in the third quarter.

○ Consider whether to reverse the *who* and the *what*.

Sometimes, the *what* seems more important than the *who*—as is often the case in a crime story—and the *who* and *what* are reversed in the lead:

First National Bank in downtown Springfield was robbed this morning by two hooded gunmen who got away with more than $200,000 in cash.

If the *what* involves what someone said—such as in the coverage of a speech, a meeting or an interview—many newspaper writers start with the *what*, then go to the *who*:

Mesa County needs to spend $1.5 million this year to repair roads and bridges, the public works director told the County Commission at Monday night's meeting.

In beginning with the *what*, however, reporters should avoid presenting a misleading lead that begins with a startling statement that sounds as though it's being presented as a fact, then attributing it in the next paragraph:

> **AVOID**   Odofile Guinn is guilty of killing his wife, Judith Dandridge, and her friend Joseph Goldfarb.
>   That's what Prosecuting Attorney Elaine Chu told a jury in Los Angeles today.

○ State the summary as a thesis, not as a mere topic, in a story where the *what* summarizes a speech, a meeting or an interview.

The lead should make a definite statement, as a headline does, not just be a word or phrase, like the title of a term paper. One of the worst leads for such a story would be one that tells only that someone spoke without giving a clue as to what the person said.

> **NO TOPIC MENTIONED**   A researcher from the University of Kansas spoke Tuesday night to an audience of local health care providers.

> **ONLY A TOPIC**   A researcher from the University of Kansas spoke Tuesday night to an audience of local health care providers about new developments in cancer treatments.

> **THESIS**   A researcher from the University of Kansas told an audience of local health care providers Tuesday night that there are many exciting new developments in cancer treatments.

If you have trouble telling a topic from a thesis, here's a hint: *Anytime you've written that somebody <u>discussed</u> something, <u>spoke on</u> something or <u>spoke about</u> something, what follows is probably a topic, not a thesis. If, instead, you force yourself to write that someone <u>said</u> something, it's almost impossible to follow that with a mere topic instead of a thesis.*

When Did It Happen?

○ *Time*, wherever it appears, should precede *day* or *date*. Remember to avoid redundancy in expressing the time element in a story. You could write *6 p.m.* or *6 this evening* but not *6 p.m. this evening.*

○ Never use both the day and the date except in a calendar item if local style permits it there.

○ For an event happening on the day of publication, you may write *this morning, this afternoon, this evening, today* or *tonight*, as appropriate. But the wire services say never to write *yesterday* or *tomorrow*, but rather to use the day of the week instead.

○ Use the *day of the week* if the *what* will take place (or has taken place) within a week forward (or backward) of the publication

Journalism Tip
Words to Avoid in Attributing Information

Good reporters follow the dictum that simple forms of attribution are the best. Almost always, that means sticking to *said* or *says*. Failing to do so almost invariably gets reporters in trouble because they seem to lose their objectivity. Here are some words to avoid when attributing information:

- Words that imply the reporter is a mind reader: *believes, feels, hopes, thinks*. How do you know the source believes, feels, hopes or thinks something unless he or she said so?

- Words that suggest the reporter's opinion: *admitted* or *conceded* (imply the person confessed or made a concession), *claimed* (expresses disbelief), *refuted* (expresses agreement with the person answering another's charges), *alleged* (can sound to a reader like disbelief and to an attorney as if the reporter is making the allegation).

date. Use the *date* if the event will take place (or has taken place) further ahead or back than one week. If the event happened exactly a week ago or will happen exactly a week away, you may use the date or a phrase such as *next Wednesday* or *last Thursday*.

○ In some stories, you might mention a general time frame in the lead, with the specifics coming later in the story. For example, a lead might say a fair will be held *this weekend*, with the exact times further down in the story.

○ If the *what* involved what someone said or reported, or what a governing body did, the *when* (either the time or day or date) is often moved up in the sentence immediately following the verb:

> Ben Bernanke, chairman of the Federal Reserve Board, said today . . .

> The Board of Governors voted Wednesday . . .

Where Did It Happen?

○ Use a significant identifier for the *where*. The *place* may be the name of a street, a building, an institution, a neighborhood, a town or another location, as appropriate:

> The campus chapter of Women in Communication will meet at 7 p.m. Monday in Room 120 of the Shichtman Student Union.

Notice that this example uses the order of elements recommended for the lead of a story and that the order is based on what's typically most to least important among these five elements.

Problems With Hard-News Leads

○ Don't make the lead too complicated. Don't load it with too many names, figures or details. Keep the lead sentence short—never more than 30 words and closer to 15 to 20 if possible:

TOO MANY NAMES   Gus Gish, manager of Springfield's Downtown Development Fund, said today at a Chamber of Commerce luncheon in Fairfield Village that this year's drive will be co-chaired by Carla Zim, Springfield National Bank vice president, and David Roche, Elmdorf Electronics Corp. general manager.

TO THE POINT   The Springfield Downtown Development Fund has named two people to co-chair this year's drive.
    Gus Gish, the fund's manager, said . . .

TOO MANY NUMBERS   The Springfield Board of Education voted 5–4 Tuesday night to place on the November ballot a proposed property-tax increase of two mills, or $2 for every $1,000 of assessed valuation, up from the 10 mills property owners currently pay, to help cover the school district's budget of $13.2 million, which itself is $350,000 more than last year's.

TO THE POINT   Springfield voters will have to consider in November whether to raise their property taxes to pay for schools.
    The Board of Education voted 5–4 Monday night to . . .

TOO MANY DETAILS   Pete's Brewing—maker of the brown, malty Pete's Wicked Ale—raised about $40 million in its initial public offering Tuesday, as well as an additional $12.5 million for its owners, a total of around 56 times its estimated earnings for next year, as it became the second specialty beer company this year, behind Redhook Ale Brewery of Seattle, to offer its stock to investors.

TO THE POINT   Pete's Brewing has become the second specialty beer company to go public this year.
    The maker of Pete's Wicked Ale . . .

○ Don't begin with the *time*, *day or date*, or *place*.

Time, *day or date*, or *place* is less important than the *who* and *what*. Hint: If your lead starts with a prepositional phrase, it's probably starting with *time*, *day or date*, or *place* and should be rewritten.

> **WRONG**   At 11 a.m. this Thursday, the County Commission will hold a public hearing on allowing fireworks within the county limits.

> **RIGHT**   The County Commission plans to hold a public hearing this week on allowing fireworks within the county limits. The meeting will be at 11 a.m. Thursday.

○ Don't begin with an empty, say-nothing expression or a generality that fails to distinguish this news from other news:

EMPTY	In a report released today . . .
	[Someone] spoke. . .
	[Somebody] held a meeting.
GENERALITY	Voters elected a mayor and six council members Tuesday.
	Sen. Paul Hogan spoke to the Booster Club here last night.
	The Student Council acted on four of its most pressing problems Tuesday.

○ Don't begin with a question if the question is answered in the story:

What does Ralph Nader have in common with Venus Williams?

The question lead is one of many cliché leads seen too often in print and heard too often in broadcast. In the preceding example, it's better just to tell us what the two have in common—that would be startling in itself.

○ Don't begin with a direct quote if it's a full sentence or longer. Such quotes should first appear in the second or third paragraph of most stories:

WRONG	"This is the happiest day of my life," said the man honored as Chelsea's Man of the Year.
RIGHT	A man who rescued a family of four from a burning home was honored Tuesday night as Chelsea's Man of the Year.
	"This is the happiest day of my life," said Fred Winston. . . .

Partial quotes in the first sentence are sometimes permissible, especially when a colorful phrase that aptly summarizes the theme can be excerpted from a speech:

Senate candidate Fred Hawkins told a Springfield Auditorium audience last night that "feminazis, compassion fascists and environmental wackos" are on the retreat as more Americans "see them for what they are."

○ Don't use a form of the verb *to be* in the lead, if you can avoid it:

WEAK	The County Commission was unanimous in approving . . .
BETTER	The County Commission unanimously approved . . .

○ Don't overstate the news in the lead, making it more dramatic than it really is:

OVERSTATED	A Springfield woman may have averted a holocaust today when she used her fire extinguisher to put out an inferno in a family's SUV engine. [The words *holocaust* and *inferno* overstate the situation.]
REALISTIC	A family of four has a Springfield woman to thank for putting out the engine fire in an SUV this morning. [When the lead is thus reduced to reality, we might ask whether this is even worth a news item.]

For your lead, either state the "bottom line"—what it all boils down to—or use a grabber that dramatically attracts the reader's attention. Anything else, such as a long history of the problem, won't work.

What Comes After the Hard-News Lead?

A hard-news story is often written in the inverted-pyramid form.

○ After the hard-news lead, give additional details in descending order of importance.

The advantage of this style to readers is that if pressed for time, they can read only the headline and lead and still get the main information. The advantage of this style to reporters and editors is that it gives them a mutual understanding of what should be cut from a story first when it's too long to fit. Because the reporter puts the information he or she thinks is most important at the top, editors can make quick cuts on deadline by chopping from the end without fear of "butchering" the story.

○ Any detail that would be of particular interest to the audience should be moved toward the top of a story if it's not there already.

The main mistake reporters make with story structure is simply not putting the items in the best possible order. For example, if a plane crashed and among the passengers was a local family, that detail should be part of the lead, not buried further down.

To take another example, a wire-service story about a man who one day went to a restaurant and shot 21 people included a detail near the bottom that should have been moved up. The man's wife told police her husband had called a local suicide hot line that morning but had been told to call back later. Because of funding cuts, there were not enough people on duty to answer all the lines.

That detail deserved to be near the top of the newspaper version of the story—although, as we will see in Chapter 15, it could have made a terrific ending for a broadcast version of the story.

Soft-News Leads

Soft-news leads introduce the story dramatically. As mentioned before, in addition to using them for soft-news stories, journalists are increasingly using soft-news leads with certain hard-news stories.

Soft-news leads are also sometimes called *delayed leads* or *feature leads*. They take a storyteller's approach by setting the scene, describing a person, starting with dialogue or relating an anecdote before telling the main point. In soft-news leads, it is acceptable to use an *immediate-ID who* even though the *who* may not be well-known.

> The young man in the Coast Guard uniform slumped forward.
> His forehead hit the microphone in front of him, sending an amplified "thunk" ringing through the still air of the hearing room. His slim body was racked with sobs as he buried his face in his hands.
> Patrick Lucas, 23, was reliving the night his ship sank and 23 of his friends died.

Soft-News Clichés

Don't confuse story types with clichés. Many stories fit into a recognized genre, but that doesn't mean all stories of a given kind should have the same lead.

Clichéd leads usually begin life as something creative that someone has done—maybe taking a clever, soft-news-lead approach to a story. The problem arises when other reporters steal the idea and repeat it often and automatically. After you've heard it a few times, it's no longer clever—just annoying.

Here are some examples of the most common, most annoying leads.

○ **Avoid the one-word lead, especially when followed by an exclamation point:**

> Tired. That's how John Smith felt after winning his first marathon at the age of 56.

> Sex! Now that I have your attention, let's talk about birth control.

○ **Avoid the question lead:**

> How hot was it Sunday? So hot that Dieter Mann required hospital treatment after walking barefoot on a downtown sidewalk.

> What do Bean Blossom, Ind., and Bill Monroe, the father of bluegrass music, have in common?

Notice that in each of these examples, the question lead is phony—the reporter is merely rhetorically asking a question he or she intends to answer. The one time a question lead isn't phony and clichéd is when the question isn't answered in the story—that is, when the news is that there's an unanswered question:

> What happened to the night clerk at Fred's QuikMart on Friday?
> That's what police investigators are asking this morning.
> When the early-morning-shift clerk arrived, night clerk Terry Schmidt, 22, was missing, along with all the money from the safe. Police are uncertain whether this is an inside job or a case of robbery and abduction.

In short, don't lead with a question that's answered in the story.

○ **Avoid the dictionary lead:**

> Webster's Dictionary defines freedom as . . . . But to Denny Davison, freedom means . . .

○ **Avoid the "good and bad news" lead:**

> First the good news, then the bad.

○ **Avoid the lead that labels what kind of story this is or isn't:**

> This is not another story about street people.
>
> This is a story about people who have survived.

○ **Avoid the "something came early" lead:**

> Thanksgiving came early for Diego Ramirez this year.

○ **Avoid the "you might think" lead:**

> You might think to look at the Victorian-style house that it's someone's comfortable home, perhaps filled with antiques. But you'd be wrong. The house actually is home to one of the city's high-tech software firms.

○ **Avoid the "one thing's different" lead:**

> Like most kids his age, Billy Small goes to school, likes baseball and enjoys ice-cream cones. But one thing about him is different: He's quadriplegic.

○ **Avoid the "what a difference" lead:**

> What a difference a day makes. Friday, the Red Sox were in first place. Now, with a loss to the Angels, they've fallen to second behind the Yankees in the American League East.

○ Avoid the "rain couldn't dampen" lead:

> Rain couldn't dampen the spirits of a capacity crowd at Comerica Park Saturday as Detroit won its season opener against Oakland 5–3.

○ Avoid the "all in the family" lead:

> To Brian and Betsy Feintab and their three children, flying is all in the family. Each of them has a pilot's license.

○ Avoid the recipe lead:

> Take one dash of love, sprinkle in a dash of excitement, and mix with a lifetime of commitment. That's the recipe for a 50-year marriage, say Ted and Ethel Peck, who celebrated their 50th anniversary today.

○ Avoid the "official" lead:

> It's official: The Florida Gators are the No. 1–rated football team in the nation, according to the latest Associated Press sports-writers poll.

○ Avoid the "funny thing" lead:

> A funny thing happened to Hillary Clinton on her way to the presidency.

○ Avoid the "not just for . . . anymore" lead:

> Country music isn't just for country folk anymore. It's become the fastest-growing segment of the recording industry.

○ Avoid the "little did she know" lead:

> When Betty Smith walked up to the ATM at Seventh and Main streets to take out money for lunch, little did she know that a man waiting nearby in his car would force her at gunpoint to withdraw all her money and give it to him.

○ Avoid the truism lead:

> Everybody has to eat.

○ Avoid the Snoopy lead:

> It was a dark and stormy night.

○ And one final chestnut we'd like to roast:

> Yes, Virginia, there is a Santa Claus.

What Comes After the Soft-News Lead?

Features, commentaries, analysis pieces and other soft-news stories are not written in inverted-pyramid form. Soft-news stories don't follow the order of most to least important. Instead, they simply try to attract attention in the lead; supply details, analysis or opinion in the middle; and end with a memorable conclusion. For that reason, editors should never shorten a soft-news story by cutting from the end, as they would with a hard-news story.

The Wall Street Journal is excellent at taking abstract subjects such as the economy and personalizing them—showing how they actually affect people. The Wall Street Journal *formula* begins with a person who is affected by the topic under discussion. The lead shows how the topic affects that person.

Then, a *nut graf*—a paragraph that explains why the reader should care about the information in a story—makes a general statement, perhaps about the extent of the problem. Following the nut graf, which typically can be found in the first six or seven paragraphs of the story, The Journal presents facts, figures and analysis about the topic in general and then returns in the end to the person with whom it started.

Take a look at a few of The Wall Street Journal's front-page pieces, in print or online, for examples. Notice this construction, and see how effectively it enlivens what could have been a dull abstraction.

Using Paraphrases and Transitions to Build a Story

◯ **Paraphrases must be clearly attributed.**

The second sentence in the following example sounds like a gratuitous opinion offered by the reporter. Always make sure paraphrases are attributed to someone so that the reader doesn't think you are editorializing.

> Perez says more than 55 percent of American homes have a computer. But someone needs to worry about those too poor to join the information revolution.

By contrast, if a reporter quotes someone in one sentence, it's often clear that the same person is being quoted in the following one, even without the attribution:

> "We don't see any compelling reason to change our product line this year," Kurlak said. "Our current models are exceeding our expectations."

⚫ Use clear transitions to connect your points.

Don't be afraid to start a sentence with *but* to show contrast. *And* can also be useful at the start of a sentence to introduce something additional. *Meanwhile* and *however*, though, are objectionable to many editors, the first for being overused, the second for being longer and more pompous than *but*. Also, watch for transitions like *as a matter of fact* and *undoubtedly*, which violate journalistic objectivity.

Web Resources

JOURNALISM REVIEWS

The best-known national reviews that cover and critique the practice of American print journalism are the Columbia Journalism Review and American Journalism Review. The Quill, the magazine of the Society of Professional Journalists, does similar work, as does The American Editor, a publication of the American Society of News Editors.

⚫ The American Editor
http://tae.asne.org

⚫ American Journalism Review
www.ajr.org

⚫ Columbia Journalism Review
www.cjr.org

⚫ Quill
www.spj.org/quill

Writing News That's Fit for Print

CHAPTER 15

Writing News for Radio and Television

Print, online, and radio and television journalism don't always organize sentences and stories alike. We speak differently with friends than with teachers, bosses or parents, and we write differently for a newspaper or website than for radio or television. Whether we're speaking with different people or writing for different media, we use the same language but different dialects.

Some of the differences are apparent. Newspapers and magazines stress the written word but may contain illustrations and photographs. Radio stresses the spoken word and has no pictures at all other than the mental ones it stimulates through sound portraits. Television stresses moving pictures and the sound of the spoken word.

Less obvious to casual readers, listeners and watchers is that different media require news stories to be worded differently. A sentence that reads well in a newspaper or magazine or online might be hard to understand when read aloud on the radio. Likewise, something that might be conversational on radio or television could look wordy in print or on a smartphone.

Print-journalism students who have received news most of their lives mainly through television and radio often have to learn to adjust to the different wording of print. Radio and television students, meanwhile, have to learn how to write for the ear and not for the page, which differs from the more formal, less conversational style they learned while writing term papers in school. Online journalists have to adjust to the reality that news presented in that medium may well have audio and video as well as text and graphics.

Sometimes, when students take classes in print, radio and television, and online journalism, they get confused by differing advice they hear in their classes, not realizing that the discrepancies may stem from differences in the natures of the media. Underneath it all, print, radio and television, and online news writing have much in common: They all report news that's relevant to their audiences in a manner that's timely and interesting.

Some journalism students choose to learn about writing for other media as a way to expand their job opportunities. Some journalists do it in search of tips from a related field that they may be able to apply to what they're already doing. And many of us are finding we have to learn skills outside our own fields, as online journalism with its ability to offer multimedia content becomes more important and as technology continues to change.

Print and Online Versus Radio and TV News

Print news is written for the eye and is typically longer than radio and television news, which is written for the ear. Online news stories aren't typically as long as print stories, but they also are designed to appeal to readers. When you pop the hoods, though, you find that the three vehicles for news have more in common than they have differences. That shouldn't come as too big a surprise, given that radio and television news writing was pioneered by print journalists who moved to the radio and television media as new opportunities arose, just as many today are moving to online.

Radio and television writing requires less knowledge of style rules and editing symbols than do print and online journalism, so people who are considering careers in journalism should hold themselves to meeting the greater demands of the written media in these areas. But that doesn't mean writing for radio and television isn't as demanding. It can be just as — or even more — demanding of a journalist's knowledge and skills.

For example, radio and television journalists need to pay more attention to how words sound. They must be even more concise and more conversational in their writing. They also need to know in what order the details should be presented to be understood best by someone listening — someone who doesn't have the luxury of being able to look back to the previous sentence or paragraph if something important slipped by unheard. Of course, the time constraints of radio and television news, as well as the need to match words with audio and video, place additional demands on radio and television writers.

Even journalism and communications students who are not primarily studying radio and television journalism should take a class or two in the field and perhaps even volunteer to write news at the campus radio or TV station. They'll have the opportunity to hear additional journalists' viewpoints; get practical news experience; acquire audio and video editing skills; and learn to write more conversationally, focus their angle on people, tighten their writing and, when necessary, cut stories quickly while keeping them focused on the main points.

Here are some major guidelines for writing for radio and television.

Use a Conversational Style

Radio and television news must be written for the ear. When it's read over the air, it should sound conversational, not stilted. Keep the sentences short—around an average of 15 words, rarely more than 25. Keep the sentence structure as simple as possible, and use active-voice verbs whenever you can. Read your copy aloud (or at least faintly mumbling to yourself) to make sure it doesn't sound awkward or artificial.

Radio and television news should sound informal, not stuffy. The following suggestions are especially useful for those in radio and television, although there is nothing wrong with using most of them in print or online, too — except in the most formal situations.

Note that the examples in this chapter are written in radio and television style, which is summarized on Pages 348–52. Look for the differences in mechanics, such as the treatment of abbreviations and numbers, from the style used for print and online stories, which appears in the appendix.

○ Try to keep sentences only one thought long. It's usually better not to tack on additional thoughts:

> NOT CONVERSATIONAL   A local student, Latisha Green, who is one of only 10 students selected nationally, will get to shake hands with the president today.

> CONVERSATIONAL   A local student will get to shake hands with the president today. Latisha Green is one of only 10 students selected nationally.

○ Avoid vocabulary or wording that people don't usually use in conversation:

> PRINT WORDING   The three youths . . .
> [Does anyone actually say *youths*? Wouldn't somebody instead say *teenagers* or something similar?]

> PRINT WORDING   Judith Cushing, 33, said . . .
> [Again, no one would say this. It's just the way newspaper reporters write. People would say something more like *Judith Cushing is 33*. But ages are seldom used in radio and television news, anyway, except in describing children.]

> NOT CONVERSATIONAL   One should use caution today when driving on Interstate 94 near downtown.

> CONVERSATIONAL   Drivers should use caution today when driving on I-94 near downtown.

> CONVERSATIONAL   You should use caution today when driving on I-94 near downtown.

○ Use contractions — that's how people talk:

> TOO FORMAL   The president says he cannot attend.

> RADIO AND TELEVISION STYLE   The president says he can't attend.

○ It's OK to start a sentence with *And* or *But*:

> And that was just in the first game.

> But economists are saying next year could be worse.

○ It's OK to use dashes for dramatic pauses:

> CNN reports that since the verdict, ratings have dropped 80 per-
> cent—from a rating of three-point-five down to zero-point-seven.

Personalize the News

The faces and voices of radio and television reporters and anchors are
familiar to their audience, and part of their success or failure can be attributed to how the audience relates to them personally. By contrast, print and
online journalists usually establish far less personal rapport unless they're
columnists, bloggers, or highly skilled feature writers or sports writers.

As a result, a radio or television audience may put pressure on the
newscaster to be personally likable. This can result in more emphasis on
personality in reporting, which can lead to a subtle blurring between news
and commentary.

For instance, look under the second rule in the previous section at
the examples suggesting that drivers should use caution on a particular
highway. Those sentences aren't really objective because they are personal
expressions offering advice. (See Pages 246–50.)

By contrast, here's a more objective statement, one that might follow
such sentences in a radio or television story:

> Road work has reduced traffic to one lane in both directions.
> [No value judgment or advice is offered.]

But radio and television news generally allows more leeway for
expressing personal judgments—especially ones that would get little disagreement, such as suggesting that drivers use caution. And such statements have increasingly found their way into print and online news, as
well.

Make It Easy to Understand

Radio and television news has to be written in an order that lets the audience catch the news in one hearing. We'll go into more detail later about
the order of information in a radio and television lead, but here are four
general suggestions to help you write news for the listener's ear.

○ Get to the main point at the start of the sentence, not at the end.

Don't begin the sentence with a dependent clause, prepositional
phrase or participial phrase that introduces details before we know the
subject.

> **CONFUSING WHEN HEARD**   Because of reports from the National
> Weather Service that a thunderstorm is on the way, you may want to
> take an umbrella along if you're going to the White Sox game.
> [The dependent clause at the beginning makes this sentence difficult for a
> listener to follow.]

CLEARER WHEN HEARD   You may want to take an umbrella along if you're going to the White Sox game. The National Weather Service reports a thunderstorm on the way.

CONFUSING WHEN HEARD   In Ohio this weekend for a national meeting of law-enforcement officials, Sheriff Everette Watson is being honored by his peers.
[The extended prepositional phrase requires the listener to remember details before he or she knows what's being discussed.]

CLEARER WHEN HEARD   Sheriff Everette Watson is being honored by fellow law-enforcement officials this weekend at a national meeting in Ohio.

Avoiding such details before the subject of the sentence is introduced also fixes the problem of lack of attribution that sometimes creeps in when writers begin with a participial phrase:

NO ATTRIBUTION   Believing that Governor Sam Wilson is vulnerable because of his abortion-rights stand, a second candidate has announced she'll run in the Republican primary.
[The reporter is not a mind reader, presumably, but the sentence never attributes how she or he knows what the candidate believes. Similar words that evade attribution are *thinking* and *feeling*.]

SUBJECT FIRST AND STATEMENT ATTRIBUTED   A second candidate has announced for the Republican primary. Jill Xavier says she thinks most voters disagree with Governor Sam Wilson's abortion-rights stand.
[Notice that this wording also lets the reporter more easily expand on what before had been the dependent clause.]

○ **Start with a general statement to attract the audience's attention, putting listeners on alert for what's to come:**

Area motorists are having trouble getting home tonight. Chicago police are reporting 33 fender benders already as the blizzard reduces visibility and makes roadways slick.

Most newspaper editors would cut the first sentence of a lead like that (even if a newspaper could report events as they were happening) as would online editors. In print, that sentence seems to be a delay and, perhaps even more, a comment rather than an objective observation. For most print journalists, the second sentence contains the real lead.

○ **Repeat key information for someone who has just tuned in or who may have caught part of a longer story but missed an essential element.**

Especially in a longer or particularly important story, the newscaster may repeat *who* was involved, *what* happened (such as a key sports score) or *where* the event occurred.

● Rewrite phrases containing a word that has a *homonym* (a word that sounds like another word) that a listener could reasonably confuse with the intended word:

> *comity* of nations [Or was it *comedy* of nations?]

> steel *magnate* [Or was it steel *magnet*?]

Keep It Short

Print, online, and radio and television media all stress tight, concise writing, although radio and television leads are often more general than print and online leads.

The sentences and paragraphs in newspaper, online, and radio and television writing are shorter than those in magazine and book prose. Those in radio and television are even a little shorter than those in newspapers and on websites, especially the sentences.

Newspaper, online, and radio and television stories also tend to be shorter than those in magazines, and radio and television stories average the shortest. Most radio and television stories are told in 20 to 30 seconds. Rarely does a radio or television story go more than two minutes except on noncommercial public radio or commercial all-news television stations.

Keep It Timely

News delivered electronically can be more up-to-the-minute than news that's been set in print and delivered by carriers. As a result, newscasters use different conventions of news writing from what print journalists do when it comes to time elements.

● Radio and television journalists write even hard-news stories in the present tense.

Radio and television journalists tend to write about news happening this day, this hour, even this minute. Print news, especially in this age of morning newspaper dominance, is often a day old.

● Radio and television journalists also are less likely to report news of events happening days or weeks away than newspapers are.

For this reason, getting verb tenses and time elements straight tends to be easier in radio and television than in print.

Make It Clear

Many entries in the wire-service stylebooks are devoted to getting things right that could appear wrong when a reader looks at them. Radio and

Writing News for Radio and TV

television style involves making things *look* clear to the newscaster, who must then make them *sound* clear to the listeners.

Students taking classes in both print and radio and television should note that in some cases, the style rules differ between the two fields. See the appendix and Pages 348–52 for summaries of the most common rules for each.

Radio and Television Journalists Must Know Grammar

Don't let the fact that radio and television news is more conversational than print or online news fool you into thinking that the rules of grammar can be ignored.

If they want to improve their writing for radio and television, radio and television students should watch their usage and check their subject-verb agreement and pronoun-antecedent agreement. Newscasts demand that the news be written in clear, simple sentences that avoid dependent clauses and that adjectives and adverbs be cut as much as possible. To follow such advice, newscasters must know grammar.

One of the best books we've seen on improving radio and television news copy is "Rewriting Network News" by Mervin Block, a former staff writer for the ABC and CBS evening news shows. His book looks at examples from 345 television and radio news scripts and demonstrates how they could be improved by closer attention to grammar, usage, tightening and order of details. The lessons are useful for print and online journalists, as well.

Good writing means knowing how to put the best words in the best order, and that's what grammar and usage are all about.

Radio and Television Hard-News Leads

Radio and television hard-news leads typically present the same five main elements in the same order as do print leads, but the wording of these elements often differs. As with a newspaper lead, the first two items, *who* and *what*, are the most essential. *Time, day* and *place* may appear later or even not at all, depending on the nature of the story.

Start With the *Who*

◯ If there's any identification or title with the name, put the ID or title before the name.

> **PRINT STYLE**   Dennis Archer, former mayor of Detroit, will speak to the Legion of Black Collegians . . .
>
> **RADIO AND TELEVISION STYLE**   Former Detroit Mayor Dennis Archer will speak to the Legion of Black Collegians . . .

Although many print and online reporters would also write that sentence in the radio and television style, the second example would be clearly preferred in radio and television.

⚪ **Always put the attribution at the beginning of the sentence and before the verb.**

> **PRINT STYLE**   Home sales rose in September to the highest level since the housing-market collapse of 2008, according to a report Wednesday from the National Association of Realtors.
>
> **RADIO AND TELEVISION STYLE**   The National Association of Realtors reports home sales rose in September. They were up to the highest level since the housing-market collapse of 2008.

⚪ **If the *who* involves a number of people, don't start the lead with the number because the reader has not yet heard what subject the number modifies.**

For example, a newspaper or website lead might read like this:

> **PRINT STYLE**   Five people died and 15 more were injured when an Amtrak train left the tracks near St. Louis this morning.

That lead conforms to the injunction in newspaper journalism that you should lead with what's most important—in this case, that five people died and 15 were injured, not that a train had left the tracks. But newscasters would typically write something like this:

> **RADIO AND TELEVISION STYLE**   An Amtrak train left the tracks near Saint Louis this morning. Five people were killed, and another 15 were hurt.

What Happened?

⚪ **Use the present tense or present progressive as much as possible, as opposed to the past tense or present-perfect tense used in newspaper and magazine hard-news stories.**

> **PRINT STYLE**   The Republicans *have called* for Medicare cuts.
>
> **RADIO AND TELEVISION STYLE**   The Republicans *are calling* for Medicare cuts.

In this regard, radio and television news is like a print soft-news story. This style point also stresses an advantage radio and television news has over print news: Radio and television can be more timely and up-to-the-minute.

When attributing quotes, don't write someone *said* but someone *says*:

PRINT STYLE   Columbia Mayor Bob McDavid said . . .

RADIO AND TELEVISION STYLE   Columbia Mayor Bob McDavid says . . .

○ If the past tense must be used in the lead, include the time element after it:

Speaker of the House John Boehner said last night . . .

○ Put a verb in the lead, as in any other sentence.

Some news directors won't allow any fragments in news copy at their stations. Some permit an occasional fragment if it sounds conversational, but most object to fragments being overused.

For example, some newscasters have overreacted to the common advice that they should avoid the verb *to be* in leads whenever possible and end up with nongrammatical leads like this:

Owners selling the Los Angeles Dodgers.

Without the *are* in front of *selling*, that sentence has just a participle, not a verb. Try this instead:

Owners say they want to sell the Los Angeles Dodgers.

Granted, some newscasters occasionally leave out the verb *to be* for some punch:

Another victory in progress at Fenway Park.

But couldn't that fragment have just as much punch if it were recast into a sentence?

It looks as if the Red Sox can chalk up another victory.

Other Points to Remember

○ Don't say *today* if you can avoid it.

Stress timeliness, and give the story the most up-to-the-minute news peg you can. Say *this morning, this afternoon* or *this evening*.

○ If the news comes from a previous day, it's probably not news in radio and television. An upcoming event more than a week off would probably not be in today's radio and television newscast.

Most references to other days are likely to be within the upcoming week and will simply be referred to as *Thursday, Saturday* and so on. An event further off would most likely be referred to as *next week*, in *three weeks, next month* and so on.

● Street addresses of people or businesses in the news are not used in radio and television in the routine way they are in print.

Radio and Television Story Structure

Radio and television news is typically written to an assigned length of time, often 20 to 30 seconds. This means the journalist writes the average number of words that could be read in the time allotted.

After the lead come the most important and interesting details—as many as will fit conversationally in the time slot. Radio and television stories are like feature stories in print in that they need not only a strong beginning but also a strong ending. In radio and television, the last sentence is called the *snapper*, and, as the name implies, it must have some snap to it.

The snapper may be the punch line for a humorous story, a simple restatement of the main point, a statement putting the story in context or telling the audience what it means, a line quoting a different side of a dispute or a subject stating "no comment" in a controversial story. The one requirement is that the snapper give the listener a definite sense of closure—that it sound like an ending. Consider these types of snappers.

Punch-line snapper:

Next time, she says, she'll take the bus.

Restatement snapper:

Once again, Toledo's mayor says he won't run for re-election.

"What it means" snapper:

That would mean property taxes on an average 220-thousand-dollar home would go up 220-dollars a year.

"Other side" snapper:

Pettit says he'll appeal.

"No comment" snapper:

We asked the commissioner to respond to the allegations, but he said he had no comment.

Some snappers have been done so often, they're as stale as the cliché leads we discussed in Chapter 14 (Pages 333–35). Here are a few canned snappers we'd like to see tossed.

Writing News for Radio and TV

The "one thing is certain" ending:

> The election results are a week away, but one thing is certain: The winner will be left-handed.

The "only time will tell" ending:

> So will it be global warming or global cooling? Only time will tell.

The "riding the elephant" ending:

> At the zoo, this is Bill Gahan for Eyewitness News.
> [The camera pulls back to reveal the reporter is riding an elephant.]

The late Charles Kuralt, famous for his "On the Road" series, once said this last ending was one of the biggest clichés he noticed in local TV news as he traveled the country. That was years ago, but it's still the case that reporters too often think it is clever for the final shot of a feature story to show them good-naturedly participating in an event they are covering, especially if it shows them doing something ridiculous.

Radio and Television Style Summary

Preparing Your Manuscript for Radio

Here are a few guidelines on manuscript preparation at radio stations:

- Most stations want you to triple-space your news copy, although some say double-space.
- Many stations want you to write in all capital letters. We think this is harder to read, but follow your station's conventions on this and other matters.
- In the upper-left corner, type the following information in this order:

  Story's slug (identification) on the first line.

  Time of the newscast.

  Date of the newscast.

  Reporter's name.

  Also at the top, or at the bottom at some stations, you should put a colon followed by the time in seconds it takes to read the story (for example, *:18*), and then circle the time.

- The copy should be typed 70 characters per line—some stations say 60. For the purpose of timing, figure that the newscaster will read aloud about 15 lines a minute on average.
- The story should start 2 to 3 inches from the top of the page and stop at least an inch or two from the bottom. If the story is longer

than that, put the word *MORE* in parentheses at the bottom center of the page. At the top of the next page, as the last line of the heading, type *FIRST ADD, SECOND ADD* and so on, or *PAGE ONE OF THREE, PAGE TWO OF THREE* and so on. Type *ENDS* or three hash marks (# # #) at the bottom of the last page of a story.

- Don't split words at the end of a line, and don't split sentences across pages.

Preparing Your Manuscript for Television

- As with radio, most stations want you to triple-space your news copy, although some say double-space.
- Again, as with radio, many stations want you to write in all capital letters. We think this is harder to read, but follow your station's conventions on this and other matters.
- Across the top, on one line, write the time of the newscast, the date, the story slug and the reporter's name.
- Set the copy at 40 characters per line in a column on the right side of the page. It should take the newscaster a minute to read about 25 lines.
- To the left of the news copy, type in all capital letters a description of the video and audio, the timed length and any instructions, such as whether the sound should be turned off or a title superimposed.
- If the story goes more than one page, type *MORE* in parentheses at the bottom center of the page. At the top of the next page, under the slug, type *FIRST ADD, SECOND ADD* and so on, or *PAGE ONE OF THREE, PAGE TWO OF THREE* and so on. Type *ENDS* or three hash marks (# # #) at the bottom of the last page of a story.
- Don't split words at the end of a line, and don't split sentences across pages.

Editing and Other Symbols

○ For the most part, newscasters don't use the traditional copy-editing symbols used in the print media.

Instead, they simply mark a line through an error and write the correction above it. If a passage has several errors close together, it's better to cross out and rewrite that whole section rather than make the reader's eyes go up and down between errors.

○ Some of the few copy-editing symbols that have carried over from print to radio and television are those for deleting and inserting, closing spaces, and separating and connecting paragraphs.

○ Newscasters don't use the ¢ symbol for *cents*, $ for *dollars* or %
for *percent*. They write out the word after the number and use a
hyphen between them:

> three-cents
>
> 25-dollars
>
> 13-percent

Pronunciation

○ Write the pronunciation of any difficult names phonetically in
parentheses after the name:

> Dmitri Shostakovich (duh-ME-tree shaw-stuh-KO-vich)

○ To make words easier to pronounce, many news writers add
hyphens to words that don't have them in the dictionary:

> hydro-electric
>
> wood-stove

○ To indicate that a word should be stressed in a sentence, either
underline it or write it in all caps:

> What do you think about <u>that</u>?
>
> Despite the rain, the parade WILL go on.

Abbreviations

○ In most cases, writers should avoid abbreviations in radio and
television copy.

That includes no abbreviations for states, days of the week, months,
military titles or countries other than the United States.

○ Some abbreviations are acceptable:

> C-I-A, F-B-I, F-C-C, G-O-P, N-double-A-C-P, U-S
> [Note the use of hyphens.]
>
> a.m., p.m., Dr., Mr., Mrs., Ms.

○ When abbreviations form acronyms pronounced as one word,
no hyphens or periods are used:

> NATO

○ Interstate highways are almost always called by their
abbreviated form in radio and television, even on first reference:

> I-94

Numbers

As is generally the case with newspaper style, write out single-digit numbers. In addition, write out *eleven*, which sometimes poses problems when written as *11*. The numbers *10* and *12* through *999* should be written as numerals. For larger numbers, use a numeral up to three digits long followed by a hyphen and the word *thousand, million, billion* or *trillion*:

> 6-thousand
>
> 160-billion

● Write sports scores and stock index numbers as numerals even if they are in single digits:

> score of 6 to 4
>
> The Dow Jones index is down 110 points.

● Write out fractions in words:

> one-half
>
> two-and-three-eighths

● Write out decimal numbers in words:

> twenty-point-six
>
> one-point-five-trillion

● Break street addresses and years into pronounceable units of numerals:

> 13-0-1 East William Street
>
> the year 20-10

● Add *nd, rd, st* or *th* to the end of numerals whenever the number would be pronounced that way:

> July 20th
>
> 14th Amendment

Punctuation

The only punctuation marks newscasters typically use are the comma, hyphen, dash, period and question mark.

● Newscasters use a dash in place of parentheses, a colon or a semicolon.

● Because radio and television copy is written to be performed, it often makes sense to put in dashes or ellipses for longer, dramatic pauses:

At stores like this one, you can buy anything from special hiking shoes . . . to backpacks . . . to canoes. But most sales are of items like sleeping bags and down jackets—items that are practical even for those who only faintly hear the call of the wild.

○ Most newscasters don't use quotations in their copy because it's awkward to convey in words where a quote begins and ends.

Saying "quote" at the beginning and "unquote" at the end of a quotation sounds too awkward and formal, although some newscasters will say "quote" without the "unquote" or use a phrase such as "to quote the mayor." It's better to paraphrase a quote to avoid the problem or, when the exact words are required, to write something like "what he termed," "as she put it" or "in his words" to alert the newscaster that it's a quote.

○ Use a hyphen between a numeral and the word *cent* or *cents*, *dollar* or *dollars*, *percent*, *thousand*, *million*, *billion* or *trillion*:

20-dollars

three-percent

105-thousand

six-million

Names

○ Unlike in print style, it's not always necessary to give famous names in their entirety on first reference:

President Obama

Governor Cuomo

○ Unlike in newspapers, middle initials should be used only to distinguish someone with a name similar to that of another, and a nickname should be used only with the last name, not following the first name:

George W. Bush
[to distinguish him from his father, George H. W. Bush]

Sly Stallone [not Sylvester "Sly" Stallone]

Spelling

Why worry about spelling when your audience will never know whether the words they hear read were spelled the way the dictionary says? Because misspelled words may cause the newscaster to stumble, pause or mispronounce the word. Even if the spellings are recognizable, misspellings will lower the respect your colleagues in the newsroom have for you.

Web Resources

RADIO AND TELEVISION

The professional association for radio and television journalists is the National Association of Broadcasters. Another leading industry group is the Radio Television Digital News Association.

- **National Association of Broadcasters**
  www.nab.org

- **Radio Television Digital News Association**
  www.rtdna.org

CHAPTER 16

Writing for Online Media

When a man went on a shooting rampage and killed four people at a Jewish school in southwest France in 2008, the story became one of worldwide interest. That sparked the British Broadcasting Corporation to pull out all the stops in covering the tragedy—not only for its traditional radio and television audiences but also for its industry-leading website.

Quickly, French police linked the killing to another the week before in which three French soldiers of North African descent had been killed. Authorities feared they were dealing with either hate crimes or a madman and ordered the country's first-ever "scarlet alert." According to the BBC, the alert condition allowed officials to implement sweeping security measures, including mixed police-military patrols, and powers to suspend public transport and close schools.

To be sure, the BBC gave plenty of attention to the story on radio and television, but its mammoth effort on the BBC website showed the growing importance of the Web in its media mix. There were a photo gallery, an analysis of possible motives, an easy-to-read compilation of what happened in the previous attack, an examination of the links between the two attacks, an extended report on restrictions imposed in a scarlet alert, videos, audio clips and maps.

That Herculean effort shows how traditional media companies have begun to adjust to the growing importance of the Web in news dissemination. But for every news organization like the BBC, there are three or four still stuck in the past. Those still simply place on the Web the same stories used in traditional media and make little effort to add value by taking advantage of the Web's ability to offer not only text and photos but also audio, video, maps, database access and even interactive graphics.

Slowly, though, even newspapers—among the most traditional media outlets—are investing more and more time and effort into making the Web a special place to visit for the latest news. Among the leaders in that industry is The New York Times, a publication often seen as stodgy in its print incarnation. Its website, however, is the home to some of the best journalism practiced on the Web. The Times' graphics department has become the national leader in producing marvelous interactive graphics that engage readers in ways other media cannot. Occasionally, readers are even allowed access to databases of interest.

Newspapers also are adjusting to the fact that they now need to be Web-first operations that embrace the use of social-media sites like Twitter and Facebook to drive traffic to their sites.

All this is changing not only the way news and feature information is presented but also how it is written. In this chapter, we look at current best practices in writing for online media. But first, let's review the advantages of using online media over those of the traditional media:

- Distribution is instantaneous, like radio and television but unlike newspapers and magazines.

- Information is often thorough and detailed, as in newspapers and magazines and unlike radio and television.

- Users not only partake of what editors offer but also sift through original information themselves.

- The Web is nonlinear. That is, the consumer doesn't have to take the story from top to bottom or start to finish. He or she can jump around to bits and pieces of the story or related material as desired.

- Databases and the capability of delivering animation, audio and video offer a combination possible in no other medium, including radio and television. Television simply cannot deliver database material.

- Readers often skim rather than read, so headlines and leads are even more critical in online media than they are in print, and short articles are much preferred.

There are, however, a couple of significant problems with using online media:

- Writers and editors are still determining the best ways to write for it.

- In a medium in which anyone can become a publisher, there are significant concerns about how to evaluate the reliability of the information being offered.

Let's examine online media in more detail.

Online Media Are Unique

When radio and television came along, the first newscasters simply read news over the air just as it was written for newspapers. That often was the medium from which they came, and they understood the art of crafting a news story for print.

It soon became obvious, however, that the writing formula had to change for radio, and even more for television. The way we speak is not the way we write, and broadcast journalism had to make those adjustments. For the most part, they weren't dramatic differences but subtle ones. The tone had to be more conversational, and tough-to-pronounce phrases had to become more casual. When television arrived, the words and pictures had to be melded to tell a story. But through it all, the basics of good journalism—articulated in Chapters 11 and 12—remained: Be clear. Be correct. Be concise.

And just as the arrival of radio and television required journalists to rethink the way news was presented, so, too, has the arrival of the Web.

Clarity on the Web is the same as in print journalism. It's particularly important for Web stories to be complete—journalists need to anticipate and answer all the questions a reader might ask so that readers don't turn elsewhere for information.

Correctness leads to credibility, and on the Web, where there are so many contradictory sources of information, credibility is one of the keys to success. If a source is consistently or even often wrong, its credibility wanes. Credibility keeps people coming back for more. Correct use of language, grammar and style also tell readers that a site has high professional standards.

Conciseness is a major virtue on the Web, where hooking a reader must be accomplished in one computer screen of information. Links beyond that page provide volumes of depth, or what those who write for the Web call *layering*. But if the reader isn't hooked on Page One, he or she will never get to the rest of the story, no matter how good it may be.

Let's examine each of these issues in more detail.

Be Clear

In the traditional media, clarity refers to conveying the message in ways that are not contradictory. Lack of clarity creeps into a news report when we spell a person's name one way in the first part of the story and another way at the end. It also results when numbers don't add up within a story or when we say one thing in the main story and another in a sidebar.

All the guidelines for writing clearly in print (see Chapter 11) apply to writing for online media too. Because of the 24/7 news cycle on the Web, though, writers need to be particularly careful to explain emerging details as clearly as possible with each new version of a story and to anticipate readers' questions and responses.

Be Correct (and Credible)

The Web is full of false information or information provided by people with a cause to promote. Sorting fact from opinion can be difficult. If the source is a respected organization such as The New York Times or The Washington Post, most journalists would consider the information to be trustworthy. But if it is published by an organization promoting a cause, there is ample reason to be wary.

Online journalists can go wrong in two ways. First, they can use information from unreliable sources. Second, they can provide Web links to unreliable sources. Stan Ketterer, a journalist and journalism educator, suggests that journalists evaluate information on the Web by following the same journalistic practices they use for assessing the credibility and accuracy of any other information. He developed these guidelines.

○ **Before using information from a Web page in a story, verify it with a source.**

The exceptions to this rule include taking information from a highly credible government site, such as the Census Bureau, or not being able to contact the source on a breaking story because of time constraints. An editor must clear all exceptions.

○ **In most cases, information taken from the Web and used in a story must be attributed.**

If you have verified the information on a home page with a source, you can use the organization in the attribution—for example, "according to the EPA" or "EPA figures show." If you cannot verify the information after trying repeatedly, attribute unverified information to the Web page—for example, "according to the Voice of America's website." Consult your editor before using unverified information.

○ **If you have doubts about the accuracy of the information and you cannot reach the source, get it from another source, such as a book or a contact person. When in doubt, omit the information.**

○ **Check the extension on the site's Web address for clues as to the nature of the organization and the likely slant of the information.**

The most common extensions used in the U.S. are *.gov* (government), *.edu* (education), *.com* (commercial), *.mil* (military), *.org* (not-for-profit organization) and *.net* (Internet administration). Most government and military sites have credible and accurate information. In many cases, you can take the information directly from the site and attribute it to the organization. But consult your editor until you get to know these sites.

○ **Follow accepted standards of evaluating Web information.**

If college and university sites have source documents, such as the Constitution, attribute the information to the source document. But beware. Personal home pages of students often have *.edu* extensions, and the information on them is not always credible. Do not use information from a personal home page without contacting the person and without the permission of your editor.

Writing for Online Media

○ Verify and attribute all information found on the home pages of commercial and not-for-profit organizations.

○ Don't assume information you find on blogs is accurate. Blogs contain plenty of erroneous information.

○ Check the date when the page was last updated. If no date appears, if the site has not been updated for a while or if it was created some time ago, do not use the information unless you verify it with a source.

The date generally appears at the top or bottom of the first page of the site. Although a recent date does not ensure the information is current, it does indicate the organization is paying close attention to the site.

Using the Web as a source of information is no riskier than using books, magazines or other printed material, provided you use common sense. Remember, too, that material on the Web is subject to copyright laws. Taking care to use only credible sources and to abide by copyright laws will enhance your own credibility.

Be Concise

In addition to making sure their writing is tight, Web journalists use a technique called layering to give readers just as much information as they want, without forcing them to read what they don't want.

Typically, the first layer is roughly equivalent to the newspaper headline or magazine article title plus a lead. Often, there is a secondary headline or sentence that gives the consumer more information as a tease to read the complete story. If the reader is hooked, he or she will click on the headline to get to the next layer of information, usually a complete newspaper-length story. Then another layer may consist of internal links to earlier stories or stories on the same subject and external links to source material. Links to audio, video, graphics or animations that complete the story may constitute another layer. The reader decides how far into the story to go.

Writing and Presenting News Online

When it comes to the actual composition of Web stories, writers and editors for digital media often work with storyboards, computerized templates that help them format content for the Web. The template organizes the story's layers, for example:

1. Headline or title.
2. One-sentence tease, or lead.
3. First page or quick summary of what happened, not unlike a short radio or television story.
4. Accompanying visuals, usually photos or graphics.

5. Accompanying audio and video, if any.
6. Depth report, perhaps further layered.
7. Links—both internal and external.

At a newspaper, magazine, or radio or television station, the work of assembling those items traditionally was parceled out to reporters, graphic artists, photographers, videographers and editors. In a contemporary newsroom, one person may well handle most or all of those functions. That's because today's journalist is expected to be adept in handling all aspects of multimedia journalism.

There is no one way to produce a story for the Web. A short, quick story may lend itself to the classic newspaper inverted-pyramid writing style. A more complex one may require links to audio, video and still photos, with multiple layers of text. Major projects may require even more complex forms of storytelling. Almost without exception, the best way to tell any story on the Web is with a combination of media.

The toughest part of preparing such a site is knowing how to prepare the text. Researchers John Morkes and Jakob Nielsen studied just that by taking a website's content and rewriting it. They found that Web users prefer writing that is concise, easy to scan and objective rather than promotional.

We've discussed conciseness in this chapter and in Chapter 12, and we covered objectivity in Chapter 11. But what makes a story scannable? Morkes and Nielsen found that readers don't *read* a Web page—they *scan* it. Readers online are surfers or scanners, much more so than readers of print—perhaps because it takes 25 percent longer to read online than it does in print. Online expert Shel Holtz says you want readers to dive, not to surf or scan. Surfing is what frustrated readers do. Here are some suggestions for writing on the Web and for making divers of surfers—at least for holding their attention long enough to get your message across.

○ **Write concisely.**

Use a fraction of the amount of text you would have used in print, perhaps as much as 50 percent less. Web users seldom read extended amounts of text, so make it easy for them by condensing.

○ **Write in chunks.**

Break longer stories into chunks that most often do not exceed what will fit on one screen. The chunks can be connected with hypertext links to make it easy for the readers to find and read the related chunk or chunks of most interest.

○ **Make the story easy to scan.**

In most cases, the inverted-pyramid writing style is best for the Web because it gets to the gist of the news quickly. Adding links and graphics will also help to attract readers and perhaps cause them to stop and read.

● **Save readers' time.**

The best way to save readers' time is to be clear. Choose simple words and verbs in the active voice; vary the length of sentences, but keep them short; write short paragraphs. Emphasize keywords by highlighting them or by putting them in color.

● **Write as if immediacy is a key issue.**

It is, of course. Writing online is like writing for the wire services. Everyone on the Web now consumes information the way a wire-service subscriber does. Keeping readers with you means keeping them informed up-to-the-minute. Update breaking stories quickly and add depth when it is available.

● **Help the reader navigate.**

Provide a table of contents, clear headings and useful links for additional information on a topic. Have clear entrances and exits; layer information in such a way that readers can choose the amount of information they need. Creating internal hyperlinks allows readers to click on information elsewhere on your site or find past stories on the same subject. External links lead readers to background information. To find appropriate external hyperlinks, you need to know how to use search engines such as Yahoo! (www.yahoo.com) and Google (www.google.com).

● **Use lots of lists and bullets.**

Often you can cut copy by putting information into lists. Whenever you can make a list, do so. Lists get more attention and allow for better comprehension and more retention than ordinary sentences and paragraphs.

● **Think visually.**

In the past, writers for print thought little about how their stories were going to appear. Television news writers know that they must write to the pictures. Good television has good video; a visual medium tries to show rather than tell. Similarly, an online journalist must *think* both verbally and visually. This includes thinking not only about the organization of the page but also about ways to use graphics and icons online; how to make a site interactive; and how to use other online tools like animation and video, the use of which is growing exponentially on websites throughout the world. A great example may be found at newsy.com, which compares the coverage of news from various traditional media outlets.

● **Give readers a chance to talk back.**

Web readers want a chance to respond, and a big part of being interactive is allowing them to do just that. It's the journalist's job to make sure the readers have the opportunity to give feedback. This can be achieved in a number of ways. You can give readers a chance to write directly to you, to your website or to the writer of a piece by including an email address, which is often part of the byline of newspapers like the Miami Herald. Many radio and television stations, newspapers and magazines also allow readers to respond directly to stories on their websites. Readers also can comment on blogs or engage with others in chat rooms devoted to specific sites or interests.

It's important to remember that news increasingly is consumed not on desktop and laptop computers but on smartphones and tablet computers. Many websites now have the ability to transform stories for easy readability on such devices. Software does the trick. But brevity is important when stories are delivered on such devices. Short stories with links to more information are ideal.

You may take readers down one path that branches into several others. Some call this technique "threading." Sports fans, for example, can enjoy seeing a whole gallery of shots from Saturday's championship game after reading about their team's win. They can read interviews from all the stars of the victory—or the defeat. In another example, the story of a plane crash can lead to various threads—the airline and its record of crashes, the plane itself and the record of that type of plane, the place of the accident, the people involved and more.

SEO: Writing With Search Engines in Mind

It's almost impossible to overemphasize one additional consideration in writing for online media: If your online story cannot be found, it won't be read. That's why editors of websites place great emphasis on *search-engine optimization*, the process of making sure your story will be found when someone searches for its topic on sites such as Google or Yahoo!

Newspapers and magazines are notorious for writing baseball stories that never mention the word *baseball* and hockey stories that never use the word *hockey*. That's fine if the story contains metadata that include that search term. It matters not at all, though, if the user searches for the team name, such as Texas Rangers. That user will find your story even if the word *baseball* is not included. But what if the user searches for "baseball"? Your story will not be found without that word in the metadata. Understanding that is the key to making sure that possible search terms appear either in the metadata accompanying the story or in the story itself.

Many websites have protocols for ensuring that the proper terms are used, and several companies now offer services that ensure content is maximized for search engines. That can be a wise investment for the website looking to grow readership.

Writing for International Audiences

Few U.S. media companies operate websites that are bilingual or multilingual, but many users do not speak English, Spanish or French as a first language. Ideally, websites would be multilingual, but providing staff for extensive translation is cost-prohibitive. Fortunately for the English-speaking world, English has become the most commonly used language in international commerce and interaction, so if a site must have only one language, English is usually the best choice.

Still, it's important to remember that the Web is a worldwide medium, not a local one. At the least, plain language in writing and the avoidance of colloquialisms allow users throughout the world to better understand content. Simple writing also allows international users to more accurately run a story through online translation programs, such as Google Translate, and make sense of it.

Writing for Blogs

Blogs are an increasingly popular means of connecting with readers, and many traditional media operations have embraced them. If your job—whether as a reporter or an editor—requires you to write and maintain a blog, it's important to remember the difference between writing for traditional media and writing for a blog.

- Traditional journalism is formal, but blogging is informal.
- Traditional journalism is dispassionate, but much of blogging is passionate.
- Traditional journalism is written in the third person ("he," "she," "they"), but much of blogging is written in the first person ("I," "we").
- And while most traditional writing is vetted by multiple editors, much of blogging goes straight from the writer to the reader.

Not all blogs are written by journalists, of course, but when blogs are sponsored by a newspaper, magazine, or radio or television station, certain standards will apply. Each company sets its own standards, so if you are asked to blog, be sure to understand those limits. There are likely to be constraints on foul language, insults to readers and the like. None of that, however, should limit your ability to connect with readers.

David O'Brien, for example, is the Atlanta Journal-Constitution's beat writer who covers the Atlanta Braves. His stories for the newspaper are traditional, but in his blog he writes in first person, shares inside information about the team and even shares with readers his thoughts on the latest trends in music. Those notes on music close each of his blogs. It's a totally informal approach that allows him to connect with readers—almost all of whom are Atlanta Braves fans.

Reading blogs of this type is not unlike participating in a discussion while seated around a large table at a country store or while watching a game at a watering hole in Boston. People air their opinions freely, discuss what O'Brien has written and even get into passionate arguments about the virtues—or lack thereof—of the newest pitcher in the Braves' bullpen. O'Brien's blog is so popular that he has to write a new one every few days so readers are not overwhelmed with thousands of comments.

Journalism Tip

Editing Your Own Copy

One casualty of the rise of Web-based journalism is quality editing. Increasingly, writers are asked to place tweets or blog posts on a website without that material being reviewed by an editor.

That's a scary prospect when one considers that a longtime axiom of journalism is this: Everyone needs a good editor. The publication of unedited copy increases the risk of grammatical and spelling errors, libel, slander and all sorts of related disasters.

Most editors would prefer that all such material go through the traditional editing process, but with cutbacks in newsrooms there simply aren't enough editors to make that feasible. Also, in an era where speed to the Web is important, delays in getting the news online are unacceptable.

So, the publication of unedited copy is inevitable today. Here are some tips for disciplining yourself to engage in self-editing:

○ Read through a tweet, a blog entry or a Facebook post at least three times before posting it. All of us miss things the first time or two around. Repeated reading of the item before it is posted can help prevent errors or embarrassment.

○ Be sure you are using your word processor's grammar- and spell-checker features. Those aren't perfect, but they help.

○ Team with a colleague to read each other's material before it is posted. He or she may spot something you missed.

○ Ask readers to help you spot errors in items you post, particularly in blogs. You'll find readers eager to do so, and you can even make a game of it.

○ Correct mistakes as soon as they are pointed out to you. Remember that being correct is the key to maintaining your credibility.

So, the best blogs are conversational, full of information and engaging to readers in ways that are fun, provoke discussion and even start arguments. Remember, though, that while some Internet writers do not distinguish between fact and fiction, professional journalists must be meticulous about the facts in their blogs.

Promoting News on Facebook and Twitter

Most journalists today are asked to promote their stories on Facebook or Twitter or both. When a writer's article goes live on the website, he or she posts a Twitter message with a link to the piece. That helps to drive traffic to the news organization's website. News organizations charge for advertising on their websites by determining how many unique visitors go to their sites each month and how many of those people click on the news stories offered. Driving traffic to those sites has become part of the job for both reporters and editors.

Facebook is used in a similar way. Many newspapers, magazines, and radio and television stations have Facebook sites on which reporters post links to their stories and readers comment on them. Most, of course, allow such comments on their own websites, too.

Facebook Subscribe is a subservice of Facebook that allows readers to subscribe to the public updates of journalists on Facebook without having to add that journalist as a friend. Both The New York Times and The Washington Post are heavy users of that service.

Journalists use Twitter primarily to promote their stories, according to a PEW Research Center study, in much the same way that television anchors use teases before they break for commercials: "After the break, we'll find out when the snowstorm will arrive." A good tease gives enough information to pique the reader's interest but not give away the key elements of the story.

Journalists also use Twitter to solicit reader suggestions, to talk about the process of news gathering and to break news before they are able to write even a short story for the Web.

Because tweets don't go through the editing process, it is important that you read and edit your own tweet before sending it. Journalists who send tweets with spelling, grammar and fact errors are sending damaging messages.

Writing at Poynter.org, Jeff Sonderman reported on research by Dan Zarrella, who studied thousands of tweets to determine what led to the highest click-thru rates. Zarrella's advice:

- Write between 120 and 130 characters.
- Pace links about a quarter of the way through the tweet (not always at the end).
- Tweet only once or twice an hour.

Zarrella also confirmed earlier research that advised using more verbs and determined that tweets are more effective at night or on weekends.

Legal and Ethical Concerns

As a Web journalist, you must be aware that you have the same legal and ethical concerns and responsibilities as other journalists. Libel is still libel, and plagiarism is still plagiarism. Just because you are not "in print" doesn't mean you can destroy someone's reputation or distort the truth.

You also must always be aware that what is on the Web is not all yours, even though the very design of it allows you to easily download words and images. If you use someone else's words, you must put quotation marks around them and cite the source.

Failure to credit a source can have legal repercussions. The Web makes it easy to catch someone who has plagiarized. Already there have been several cases where Web readers of local columnists or reviewers have turned in a writer for stealing others' work. But plagiarism is not the only danger. The following subjects have stirred up ethical concerns, and some continue to remain difficult for online journalists to solve: privacy, advertising, manipulating photos and concealing your identity.

Privacy. Websites exist that have files and personal information on nearly everyone. Some sites allow you to see what anyone has ever posted in a chat room. What may journalists use, and what might constitute an invasion of privacy? It's often tough to tell. Most everyone agrees that private email is off limits. But what about material sent to corporate intranets? The experts are divided on that question, and there's really no sure answer.

Advertising. Newspapers and magazines generally try to label advertising as advertising, and they have rules that require ads to use typefaces different from those the publication uses for news and other articles. They also have guidelines about the placement of ads. However, online ads regularly break up the copy of news stories or pop up over news stories. There is little separation of ads from editorial content, which can lead to reader confusion as to what is what. Why don't the rules that apply to print apply online? The code of the American Society of Magazine Editors says they should. According to ASME's website, the detailed list in its Guidelines for Editors and Publishers "can still be summarized in one sentence: The reader should always be able to tell the difference between edit and ads."

> The dynamic technology of electronic pages and hypertext links creates a high potential for reader confusion. Permitting such confusion betrays reader trust and undermines the credibility not only of the offending online publication or editorial product, but also of the publisher itself. It is therefore the responsibility of each online publication to make clear to its readers which online content is editorial and which is advertising, and to prevent any juxtaposition that gives the impression that editorial material was created for—or influenced by—advertisers.

Others agree that it is the job of the publication to make the distinction between editorial and advertising content for the reader. For example, the code of the American Society of Business Press Editors says the difference "may involve typefaces, layout/design, labeling and juxtaposition of the editorial materials and the advertisement." The ASBPE code adds this important point: "Editors should directly supervise and control all links that appear with the editorial portion of the site."

Manipulating Photos. The Web makes it easy to digitally alter or manipulate photos, so how can readers tell what is original and what has been changed? How can readers trust what they see? New York Times photographer Fred Ritchin proposed using an icon to flag a digitally altered photo. Most editors prefer to ban the practice altogether. In news photography, there is no place for alteration.

Concealing Your Identity. It's easy to conceal your identity as a reporter on the Web, but usually the time to reveal yourself as a reporter is at the outset of your questioning people online. People have a right to know they are talking with a reporter, and failure to disclose your identity can be a serious ethical violation unless there is good reason to conceal your identity. What's a good reason? Most editors would say that doing so is acceptable only while doing an investigative report and then only if there is no other way to get the information.

Corrections

What happens when a news site makes a mistake? Some act as if they never do; they simply post new stories with updated information. However, the best journalistic practice is to tell readers that the story has changed or has been updated with new information and how that was done so that the readers are fully informed. For example, Forbes.com erroneously quoted former Disney Chairman Michael Eisner as saying he didn't think his company's network, ABC, would be operating "in four to five years." In the update to the story, the changed headline read, "Clarification: Eisner Discusses the ABC Brand and Other Brands."

In addition to correcting the story, Forbes.com put asterisks next to the changed sentences and included explanations at the bottom of the story, such as this: "The original version of this story incorrectly stated that Eisner did not see the third-ranked network being around in four to five years." In his column in The Washington Post, Howard Kurtz reported that Forbes.com editor Paul Maidment said his reporter had "extrapolated" without the "broader context." Unfortunately, such notice of correction or updating will not be done unless the news site has a clear policy requiring it.

Web Resources

ONLINE MEDIA

The Web is revolutionizing the way journalists research and write stories, and it is affecting the way readers access them. The following three general sites are dedicated to online journalism:

- **Internet Press Guild**
  www.netpress.org

- **Online Journalism Review**
  www.ojr.org

- **Online News Association**
  www.journalists.org

Writing for Online Media

Wire-Service Print and Web Style Summary

Most publications adhere to rules of style to avoid annoying inconsistencies. Without a stylebook to provide guidance in such matters, writers would not know whether the word *president* should be capitalized when preceding or following a name, whether the correct spelling is *employee* or *employe* (dictionaries list both), or whether a street name should be *Twelfth* or *12th*.

Newspapers, magazines, and radio and television stations and their online sites use the wire-service stylebooks to provide such guidance. For consistency, most newspapers and many magazines follow rules in the AP Stylebook, and radio and television stations often use a version of the AP guidelines modified to account for the spoken word. Many also publish their own lists of exceptions to AP style. There often are good reasons for local exceptions. For example, AP style calls for spelling out *First Street* through *Ninth Street* but using numerals for *10th Street* and above. But if a city has only 10 numbered streets, for consistency it might make sense to use *Tenth Street*.

This section is an abbreviated summary of the primary rules of wire-service style. (For more punctuation rules, see Chapter 9. For rules on radio and television style, see Chapter 15.) This summary should be helpful even for those without a stylebook, but we provide it assuming that most users of this book have one. Why? Because this section includes only the rules used most often, arranged by topic to make them easier to learn. Only about 10 percent of the rules in a stylebook account for 90 percent of the wire-service print and Web style you will use regularly. You will use the rest of the rules about 10 percent of the time. It makes sense, therefore, to learn first those rules you will use most often.

Abbreviations and Acronyms

Punctuation

○ In general, abbreviations of two letters or fewer have periods:

   600 B.C., A.D. 1066

   8 a.m., 7 p.m.

   U.N., U.S., R.I., N.Y.

   8151 Yosemite St.

Exceptions include *AM radio, FM radio, 35 mm camera, the AP Stylebook, D-Mass., R-Kan., IQ* and *TV*.

○ In general, abbreviations of three letters or more do not have periods:

   CIA, FBI, NATO, mpg, mph

One exception is *c.o.d.* (preferred in all references to *cash on delivery* or *collect on delivery*).

Symbols

○ Always write out % as *percent* in a story, but you may use the symbol in a headline.

○ Always write out *&* as *and* unless it is part of a company's formal name.

○ Always write out ¢ as *cent* or *cents*.

○ Always use the symbol *$* rather than the word *dollars* with any figure, and put the symbol before the figure. Write out *dollar* only if you are speaking of, say, the value of the dollar on the world market.

Dates

○ Don't abbreviate days of the week except in a table.

○ Don't abbreviate a month unless it has a date of the month with it: *December 2012*; *Dec. 7*; *Dec. 7, 2012*.

○ Don't abbreviate the five months spelled with five or fewer letters except in a table: *March, April, May, June, July*.

○ Never abbreviate *Christmas* as *Xmas*, even in a headline.

○ *Fourth of July* or *July Fourth* is written out when the holiday is meant.

○ Use *Sept. 11* or *9/11* to refer to the attacks on the U.S. on that date.

People and Titles

A few publications still use courtesy titles (*Mr., Mrs., Ms., Miss*) on second reference in stories. Many publications use them only in quotations from sources. Others use them only in obituaries and editorials, or on second reference in stories mentioning a husband and wife. In the last case, some newspapers prefer to repeat the person's whole name or, especially in features, use the person's first name. The Associated Press suggests using a courtesy title only in direct quotations or when a woman requests a specific title.

○ Use the abbreviations *Dr., Gov., Lt. Gov., Rep., Sen.* and *the Rev.*, as well as abbreviations of military titles, on first reference, but then drop the title on subsequent references.

   Some titles you might expect to see abbreviated before a name are not abbreviated in AP style: *Attorney General, District Attorney, President, Superintendent.*

○ Use the abbreviations *Jr.* and *Sr.* after a name on first reference if appropriate, but do not set them off with commas.

Organizations

○ Write out the first reference to most organizations in full rather than using an abbreviation:

   National Organization for Women

Exceptions include *CIA* and *FBI*. The abbreviation for these may be used on the first reference. *GOP* is acceptable on second reference when referring to the Republican Party.

○ You may use well-known abbreviations such as *FCC* and *NOW* in a headline even though the abbreviations would not be acceptable on first reference in the story.

○ Do not put the abbreviation of an organization in parentheses after the full name on first reference. If the abbreviation is that confusing, don't use it at all but rather call the organization something like "the gay rights group" or "the bureau" on second reference.

○ Use the abbreviations *Co., Cos., Corp., Inc.* and *Ltd.* at the end of a company's name even if the company spells out the word. Do not abbreviate these words if they are followed by other words such as "of America." The abbreviations *Co.*, *Cos.* and *Corp.* are used, however, if followed by *Inc.* or *Ltd.* (and, by the way, *Inc.* and *Ltd.* are not set off by commas even if the company uses them).

○ Abbreviate political affiliations after a name in the following way:

Sen. Claire McCaskill, D-Mo., said . . .

○ Never abbreviate the word *association*, even as part of a name.

Places

○ Don't abbreviate a state name unless it follows the name of a city in that state:

Nevada

Wurtland, Ky.

○ Never abbreviate the six states spelled with five or fewer letters or the two noncontiguous states: *Alaska, Hawaii, Idaho, Iowa, Maine, Ohio, Texas, Utah.*

○ Use the traditional state abbreviations, not the Postal Service's two-letter ones: *Miss.*, not *MS.*

Exception: Use the two-letter postal abbreviations when a full address is given that includes a ZIP code: *217 Ridgecrest St., Westminster, MA 01473.* Here are the abbreviations used in normal copy:

Ala.	Fla.	Md.	Neb.	N.D.	Tenn.
Ariz.	Ga.	Mass.	Nev.	Okla.	Vt.
Ark.	Ill.	Mich.	N.H.	Ore.	Va.
Calif.	Ind.	Minn.	N.J.	Pa.	Wash.
Colo.	Kan.	Miss.	N.M.	R.I.	W.Va.
Conn.	Ky.	Mo.	N.Y.	S.C.	Wis.
Del.	La.	Mont.	N.C.	S.D.	Wyo.

Note: *D.C.* for *District of Columbia* is not normally used in AP style because *Washington* stands alone in a dateline or within a story.

○ Use state abbreviations with U.S. towns and cities except those that appear in the wire-service dateline list of cities that stand alone.

Many publications add to the wire-service list their own lists of towns well-known in the state or region. Use nations' full names with foreign towns and cities unless they appear in the wire-service dateline list of cities that stand alone. Once a state or nation has been identified in a story, it is unnecessary to repeat the name unless clarity demands this.

The lists of cities in the U.S. and the rest of the world that the wire-service style says may stand alone without a state abbreviation or nation are too lengthy to include here. Consult the appropriate stylebook. A handy rule of thumb is if it's an American city and has a major sports franchise, it probably stands alone. Likewise, if it's a foreign city most people have heard of, it probably stands alone.

○ Don't abbreviate the names of thoroughfares if there is no street address with them:

> Main Street
>
> West Boulevard

○ If the thoroughfare's name has the word *avenue, boulevard, street* or any of the directions on a map, such as *north* or *southeast*, abbreviate those words with a street address:

> 1044 W. Maple St.
>
> 1424 Lee Blvd. S.
>
> 999 Jackson Ave.

○ In a highway's name, always abbreviate *U.S.*, but never abbreviate a state. In the case of an interstate highway, the name is written in full on first reference, abbreviated on subsequent ones:

> U.S. Route 63 or U.S. Highway 63
>
> Massachusetts Route 2
>
> Interstate 70 [first reference], I-70 [second reference]

○ Never abbreviate *Fort* or *Mount.*

○ Use the abbreviation *St.* for *Saint* in place names.

Exceptions include *Saint John* in New Brunswick, *Ste. Genevieve* in Missouri and *Sault Ste. Marie* in Michigan and Ontario.

○ You may abbreviate *U.S.* and *U.N.* for *United States* and *United Nations* whether used as a noun or an adjective.

Miscellaneous

○ Use the abbreviation *IQ* (no periods) in all references to *intelligence quotient.*

○ Abbreviate and capitalize the word *number* when followed by a numeral: *No. 1.*

○ Use the abbreviation *TV* (no periods) in headlines and as an abbreviated form for *television*, whether a noun or an adjective.

ONLINE GRAMMAR HELP
bedfordstmartins.com/newscentral

For practice using abbreviations, log on to *Exercise Central for AP Style* and go to **No. 21. Abbreviations**.

○ Use the abbreviation *UFO* in all references to an unidentified flying object.

○ Write out *versus* or abbreviate it as *vs.* except in the name of court cases, which use *v.*

Capitalization

Proper Nouns

○ Proper nouns are capitalized; common nouns are not.

Unfortunately, this rule is not always easy to apply when the noun is the name of an animal, a plant or a food or when it is a trademark that has become so well-known that people mistakenly use it generically. (See Chapter 3.)

○ When two or more compound proper nouns are combined to share a word in common made plural, the shared plural is lowercased:

> Missouri and Mississippi rivers
>
> Chrisman and Truman high schools

Geographic Regions

○ Regions are capitalized; directions are not:

> We drove *east* two miles to catch the interstate to the *West*.

○ Adjectives and nouns pertaining to a region are capitalized:

> Southern accent, Western movie, a Southerner, a Western

○ A region combined with a country's name is not capitalized unless the region is part of the name of a divided country:

> eastern U.S., North Korea

○ A region combined with a state name is capitalized only if it is famous:

> Southern California, southern Colorado

Government and College Terms

Government and college terms are not always consistent.

○ College departments follow the animal, plant and food rule: Capitalize only words that are already proper nouns in themselves:

Spanish department, sociology department

○ By contrast, always capitalize a specific government department, even without the city, state or federal designator, and even if it's turned around with *of* deleted:

Police Department, Fire Department, State Department, Department of Commerce

○ College and government committees are capitalized if the formal noun is given rather than a shorter, descriptive designation:

Special Senate Select Committee to Investigate Improper Labor-Management Practices

rackets committee

○ Academic degrees are spelled out and lowercased:

bachelor of arts degree

master's degree

Avoid the abbreviations *Ph.D.*, *M.A.*, *B.A.*, and the like, except in lists.

○ Always capitalize (unless plural or generic) *City Council* and *County Commission* (but alone, *council* and *commission* are lowercased). *Cabinet* is capitalized when referring to advisers. *Legislature* is capitalized even if the state's body is not formally named that. States such as Missouri, which has a *General Assembly*, are an exception; lowercase *legislature* if a story uses it in a subsequent reference to a body identified as a general assembly. *Capitol*, the building, is capitalized, but *capital*, the city, is not. Capitalize *City Hall* even without the city name but not *county courthouse* without the name of the county.

○ Never capitalize *board of directors* or *board of trustees* (but *Board of Curators* and *Board of Education* are capitalized). *Federal*, *government* and *administration* are not capitalized unless part of a formal name such as *Federal Communications Commission*. *Federal court* is not a formal name and should not be capitalized. Better yet, use the correct name of the court. *President* and *vice president* are capitalized only before a name and only when not set off with a comma:

> President Barack Obama
>
> Vice President Joe Biden
>
> the president, Barack Obama,

- Military titles (*Sgt.*, *Maj.*, *Chief Warrant Officer*) are capitalized before a name, as are *Air Force*, *Army*, *Marines* and *Navy* if referring to U.S. forces.

- Political parties are capitalized, including the word *party*:

> Democratic Party, Socialist Party

Be sure, however, to capitalize words such as *communist*, *democratic*, *fascist* and *socialist* only if they refer to a formal party rather than a philosophy.

Religious Terms

Religious terms are variously capitalized and lowercased. (See Chapter 13 for additional examples.)

- *Pope* is lowercased except before a name:

> the pope
>
> Pope Benedict XVI

- Pronouns for *God* and *Jesus* are lowercased.

- *Bible* is capitalized when meaning the Holy Scriptures and lowercased when referring to another book:

> a hunter's bible

- *Mass* is always capitalized. Sacraments are capitalized if they commemorate the life of Jesus or signify his presence, not if they do not:

> Holy Communion, baptism

- Capitalize the names of religious and secular holidays:

> Christmas Eve, Ramadan, Hanukkah, Martin Luther King Jr. Day, Veterans Day

- *Quran*, rather than *Koran*, is the preferred spelling for the Muslim holy book.

Titles

○ Formal titles of people are capitalized before a name, but occupational titles are not:

> President Barack Obama, Mayor Kenneth V. Cockrel Jr., Dean Jaime Lopez

> astronaut Mary Gardner, journalist Fred Francis, plumber Phil Sanders, pharmacist Roger Wheaton

But if a comma is used to set off a title in front of a name, do not capitalize the title: *the president, Barack Obama.* Some titles, such as *managing editor* and *chief executive officer,* are not easy to tell apart. When in doubt, put the title behind the name, set it off with commas, and use lowercase.

○ Formal titles that are capitalized before a name are lowercased after a name:

> Barack Obama, president of the U.S., said . . .

> Dave Bing, mayor of Detroit, said . . .

> Jaime Lopez, dean of students, said . . .

○ Formal titles that are abbreviated before a name are written out and lowercased if they follow a name:

> Gov. Jay Nixon; Jay Nixon, governor of Missouri, said . . .

> Rep. Lindsey Graham of South Carolina; Lindsey Graham, representative from South Carolina, said . . .

Miscellaneous

○ Actual names of races, ethnicities and nationalities are capitalized, but color descriptions are not (also see Chapter 13):

> African-American, American Indian, Asian (do not use *Oriental* in reference to people), Caucasian, Hispanic, white, black

○ Use *Negro* and *Colored* only in the official titles of organizations and in quotations.

○ The first word in a direct quotation is capitalized only if the quote meets all these criteria:

- It is a complete sentence. (Don't capitalize a partial quote.)

- It stands alone as a separate sentence or paragraph, or it is set off from its source by a comma or colon.

- It is a direct quotation (in quotation marks).

ONLINE GRAMMAR HELP
bedfordstmartins.com/newscentral

For practice using capitalization, log on to *Exercise Central for AP Style* and go to **No. 22. Capitalization**.

○ A question within a sentence is capitalized:

My only question is, When do we start?

Numbers

Cardinal Numbers

○ Use cardinal numbers, or numerals, in the following cases:

- Addresses. Always use numerals for building numbers in street addresses: *7 Fifth Ave., 1322 N. Main St.*
- Ages. Always use numerals, even for days or months: *3 days old*; *John Burnside, 56.*
- Aircraft and spacecraft: *F-4, DC-10, Apollo 11.* Exception: *Air Force One.*
- Clothing sizes: *size 6.*
- Dates. Always use the numeral alone—no *nd, rd, st* or *th* after it: *March 20.*
- Decades: *the 1990s, the '90s, the early 2000s* (or *first decade of the 21st century*).
- Dimensions, heights: *the bedroom is 8 feet by 12 feet, the 8-by-12 bedroom*; *the 5-foot-6-inch guard* (but no hyphen when the word modified is one associated with size: *3 feet tall, 10 feet long*).
- Distances. Use figures for *10* and above; spell out one through nine: *She walked six miles*; *they walked 16 miles.*
- Highways: *U.S. 63.*
- Millions, billions and trillions: *1.2 billion, 6 million.*
- Money. Always use numerals, but starting with a million, write amounts like this: *$1.4 million.*
- Numbers: *No. 1, No. 2.*
- Percentages. Use numerals except at the beginning of a sentence: *4 percent.*
- Proportions. Always use figures: *2 parts water to 3 parts powder.*
- Ratios. Use figures and hyphens: *the ratio was 2-to-1, a 2-1 ratio.*
- Recipes. All numbers for amounts take numerals: *2 teaspoons.*
- Speeds: *55 mph, 4 knots.*
- Sports. Use numerals for just about everything: *8-6 score, 2 yards, 3 under par, 2 strokes.*

- Temperatures. Use numerals for all except zero. Below zero, spell out minus: *minus 6* (except in tabular data).
- Times: *4 a.m.*, *6:32 p.m.*, *noon, midnight, five minutes, 16 hours.* Note that *12:00 noon* and *12 a.m.* are incorrect usages.
- Weights: *7 pounds, 11 ounces.*
- Years. Use numerals without commas. A year is the only numeral that can start a sentence: *2007 was a good year.*

Numerals With Suffixes

Use numerals with the suffixes *nd, rd, st* and *th* in these instances:

- Political divisions (precincts, wards, districts): *3rd Congressional District.*
- Military sequences: *1st Lt., 2nd Division, 7th Fleet.*
- Courts: *2nd District Court; 10th U.S. Circuit Court of Appeals.*
- Streets. For *First* through *Ninth*, use words: *Fifth Avenue, 13th Street.*
- Amendments to the Constitution. For *First* through *Ninth*, use words: *First Amendment, 16th Amendment.*

Numbers as Words

Write out numbers in the following cases:

- Numbers less than 10, with the exceptions noted earlier in this section: *five people, four rules.*
- Any number at the start of a sentence except for a year: Sixteen years ago . . .
- Casual numbers: *a hundred or so.*
- Fractions less than one: *one-half.*

> **ONLINE GRAMMAR HELP**
> bedfordstmartins.com/newscentral
>
> For practice using numbers, log on to *Exercise Central for AP Style* and go to **No. 23. Numbers**.

Other Rules for Numbers

Use mixed numerals for fractions greater than one:

$1\frac{1}{2}$

Use Roman numerals for a man who is the third or later in his family to bear a name and for a king, queen, pope or world war:

John D. Rockefeller III, Queen Elizabeth II, Pope Benedict XVI, World War I

Social Media and Computer Terms

○ Refer to the following list for the preferred spellings of selected terms:

blog, blog post, blog entry

BlackBerry(s)

Bluetooth

Blu-ray Disc

cellphone

chat rooms

click-thru(s)

crowdsourcing

email (n., v.) (but *e-book, e-business, e-commerce, e-reader*)

home page

IM (acceptable on second reference for *instant message*); IMing, IMed

Internet

iPad, iPhone, iPod (*IPad, IPhone, IPod* at the start of a sentence or headline)

retweet (n., v.)

smartphone

social media (n., adj.)

teleprompter

website (but *the Web, Web feed, Web page*)

Wi-Fi

Web Resource

ASSOCIATED PRESS STYLE

The Associated Press provides both printed and online editions of its stylebook, considered the journalist's bible.

○ **The Associated Press Stylebook**
http://apstylebook.com

Web Resources

Additional Sources

In addition to the websites listed at the end of several chapters, many other resources for media writers and editors are available on the Internet. This list contains some of our favorites, grouped by topic.

REFERENCE MATERIALS

- Bartlett's Familiar Quotations   www.bartleby.com/100
- Merriam-Webster Dictionary   www.merriam-webster.com
- Thesaurus   www.thesaurus.com

PROFESSIONAL DEVELOPMENT

- American Press Institute   www.americanpressinstitute.org
- Poynter Institute   www.poynter.org

NEWS PROVIDERS

- ABYZ News Links   www.abyznewslinks.com
- NewsLink   http://newslink.org

PHOTOJOURNALISM

- National Press Photographers Association   www.nppa.org
- Pictures of the Year International   www.poyi.org

MAGAZINES

- MPA – The Association of Magazine Media   www.magazine.org
- Media Finder   www.mediafinder.com

COPY EDITING

- American Copy Editors Society   www.copydesk.org
- Copyediting   www.copyediting.com
- The Slot: A Spot for Copy Editors   www.theslot.com

CLASSIC TEXTS ONLINE

- Project Gutenberg   www.gutenberg.org

Bibliography

Agnes, Michael, ed. *Webster's New World College Dictionary*. 4th ed. Cleveland: Wiley, 2004.

American Heritage Editors. *The American Heritage Dictionary of the English Language*. 5th ed. Boston: Houghton Mifflin, 2011.

Bass, Frank. *The Associated Press Guide to Internet Research and Reporting*. Cambridge, Mass.: Perseus Books, 2002.

Batko, Ann. *When Bad Grammar Happens to Good People*. Ed. Edward Rosenheim. Franklin Lakes, N.J.: Career Press, 2008.

Bendell, John, and Jason Ward. *National Lampoon Presents True Facts: The Big Book*. Chicago: Contemporary Books, 1995.

Bernstein, Theodore M. *The Careful Writer*. New York: Free Press, 1995.

———. *Dos, Don'ts and Maybes of English Usage*. New York: Random House, 1999.

Bremner, John B. *Words on Words*. New York: Fine Communications, 1998.

Brooks, Brian S., George Kennedy, Daryl R. Moen and Don Ranly. *News Reporting and Writing*. 10th ed. New York: Bedford/St. Martin's, 2011.

Brooks, Brian S., James L. Pinson and Jack Z. Sissors. *The Art of Editing*. 9th ed. Boston: Allyn and Bacon, 2009.

Bruder, Mary Newton. *Dear Grammar Lady*. New York: Hyperion, 2009.

Cappon, Rene J. *The Associated Press Guide to News Writing*. 3rd ed. Englewood Cliffs, N.J.: Prentice-Hall, 1999.

———. *The Associated Press Guide to Punctuation*. Cambridge, Mass.: Perseus Books, 2003.

Cazort, Douglas. *Under the Grammar Hammer*. New York: Barnes & Noble, 2002.

Celce-Murcie, Mariane, and Diane Larsen-Freeman. *The Grammar Book: An ESL/EFL Teacher's Course*. 2nd ed. Boston: Heinle & Heinle, 1998.

Chalker, Sylvia, and Edmund Weiner. *The Oxford Dictionary of English Grammar*. Oxford: Oxford University Press, 1998.

Clark, Roy Peter. *The Glamour of Grammar: A Guide to the Magic and Mystery of Practical English*. New York: Little, Brown, 2010.

Cohn, Victor, Lewis Cope and Deborah Cohn Runkle. *News and Numbers: A Writer's Guide to Statistics*. Hoboken, N.J.: Wiley-Blackwell, 2011.

Cooper, Gloria, and Columbia Journalism Review, eds. *Red Tape Holds Up New Bridge and More Flubs From the Nation's Press*. New York: Perigee Books, 1987.

———. *Squad Helps Dog Bite Victim: And Other Flubs From the Nation's Press*. Garden City, N.Y.: Dolphin Books, 1980.

Copperud, Roy H. *American Usage and Style: The Consensus*. New York: Hawthorn Books, 1982.

Dunlap, Karen Brown, and Jane T. Harrigan. *The Editorial Eye*. 2nd ed. New York: Bedford/St. Martin's, 2003.

Flesch, Rudolf. *ABC of Style: A Guide to Plain English*. New York: HarperCollins, 1980.

Fogarty, Mignon. *Grammar Girl's Quick and Dirty Tips for Better Writing*. New York: Holt Paperbacks, 2008.

Follett, Wilson. *Modern American Usage: A Guide*. Ed. and completed by Erik Wensberg. New York: Hill & Wang, 1998.

Fowler, H.W. *Fowler's Modern English Usage*. New York: Oxford University Press, 2004.

Frank, Steven. *The Pen Commandments: A Guide for the Beginning Writer*. New York: Pantheon, 2004.

Garner, Bryan A. *Garner's Modern American Usage*. New York: Oxford University Press, 2009.

———. *The Oxford Dictionary of American Usage and Style*. New York: Berkley Books, 2000.

Goldsberry, Steven Taylor. *The Writer's Book of Wisdom: 101 Rules for Mastering Your Craft*. Cincinnati, Ohio: Writer's Digest Books, 2007.

Goldstein, Norm, ed. *The Associated Press Stylebook and Briefing on Media Law 2012*. New York: Basic Books, 2012.

Hale, Constance, and Jessie Scanlan. *Wired Style: Principles of English Usage in the Digital Age*. New York: Broadway Books, 1999.

Holley, Frederick S. *Los Angeles Times Stylebook*. New York: New American Library, 1981.

Horowitz, Franklin E., Robert J. Connors and Andrea Lunsford. *The St. Martin's Handbook*. 7th ed. New York: Bedford/St. Martin's, 2011.

Kalbfeld, Brad. *AP Broadcast News Handbook: A Manual of Techniques & Practices*. New York: McGraw-Hill, 2000.

Kilpatrick, James J. *The Writer's Art*. Kansas City, Mo.: Andrews, McMeel & Parker, 1985.

Leno, Jay. *Headlines IV: The Next Generation*. New York: Warner Books, 1992.

———. *Jay Leno's Real But Ridiculous Headlines From America's Newspapers*. New York: Wings Books, 1992.

Lewis, Norman. *The New American Dictionary of Good English*. New York: Signet Books, 1987.

Liljeblad, Fredrik. *Berlitz English Grammar Handbook*. Springfield, N.J.: Berlitz, 2011.

Lippman, Thomas W. *The Washington Post Deskbook on Style*. 2nd ed. New York: McGraw-Hill, 1989.

Manhard, Stephen J. *The Goof-Proofer*. New York: Simon & Schuster, 1998.

Merriam-Webster Dictionary of English Usage, The. Springfield, Mass.: Merriam-Webster, 1994.

Miller, Casey, and Kate Swift. *Handbook of Nonsexist Writing*. 2nd ed. New York: iUniverse, 2001.

———. *Words and Women*. New York: iUniverse, 2001.

Mitchell, Richard. *Less Than Words Can Say*. Boston: Akadine Press, 2004.

Morris, William, and Mary Morris. *Harper Dictionary of Contemporary Usage*. 2nd ed. New York: HarperCollins, 1992.

O'Conner, Patricia T. *Woe Is I: The Grammarphobe's Guide to Better English in Plain English*. New York: Riverhead Books, 2009.

———. *Words Fail Me*. New York: Harcourt Brace, 2000.

Ogden, James R., and Research and Education Association Staff. *REA's Handbook of English Grammar, Style, and Writing*. Rev. ed. Piscataway, N.J.: Research and Education Association, 1998.

Paulos, John Allen. *A Mathematician Reads the Newspaper*. New York: First Anchor Books, 1996.

———. *Beyond Numeracy*. New York: Vintage, 1992.

Pinckert, Robert C. *Pinckert's Practical Grammar*. Cincinnati, Ohio: F&W Publications, 1991.

Quinn, Jim. *American Tongue and Cheek*. New York: Pantheon, 1982.

Randall, Bernice. *Webster's New World Guide to Current American Usage*. New York: Webster's New World, 1988.

Ranly, Don, and Jennifer Moeller. *Publication Editing*. 3rd ed. Dubuque, Iowa: Kendall/Hunt, 2001.

Ross-Larson, Bruce. *Edit Yourself: A Manual for Everyone Who Works With Words*. New York: Barnes & Noble, 2003.

Safire, William. *The Right Word in the Right Place at the Right Time*. New York: Simon & Schuster, 2004.

Schwartz, Jane. *Kaplan Grammar Power*. New York: Kaplan Books, 2003.

Shertzer, Margaret. *The Elements of Grammar*. New York: Barnes & Noble, 2001.

Siegal, Allan M., and William G. Connolly. *The New York Times Manual of Style and Usage*. Rev. and expanded ed. New York: Times Books, 2002.

Smith, Ken. *Junk English*. New York: Blast Books, 2001.

———. *Junk English 2*. New York: Blast Books, 2004.

Strunk, William, Jr., and Chris Hong, editor. *The Elements of Style: 2011 Revised Edition*. New York: Macmillan, 2011.

United Press International. *UPI Stylebook and Guide to Newswriting*. Sterling, Va.: Capital Books, 2004.

Walsh, Bill. *Lapsing Into a Comma*. Lincolnwood, Ill.: Contemporary Books, 2000.

———. *The Elephants of Style: A Trunkload of Tips on the Big Issues and Gray Areas of Contemporary American English*. New York: McGraw-Hill, 2004.

Webster's Third New International Dictionary. Springfield, Mass.: Merriam-Webster, 2000.

Wilson, Kenneth G. *The Columbia Guide to Standard American English*. New York: Fine Communications, 1998.

Zinsser, William. *On Writing Well, 30th Anniversary: The Classic Guide to Writing Nonfiction*. New York: HarperResource, 2006.

Index

separating advertising content in, 365
story-layer format for, 356, 358–59, 360
verifying sources, 356–58
visual thinking for, 360
Web resources for, 366
writing and presenting news, 358–66
writing style for, 10, 359, 360
See also Internet
only, 113
only one of those . . . who, 91
"only time will tell" ending, 348
opinions, 246, 248–49
or, 85
organizations
abbreviations for, 369–70
punctuating *Inc.*, 183, 369–70
websites for, 357, 358
"other side" snapper, 347
ought, 58
overstatement, in news leads, 332
Oxford English Dictionary, 116

paragraphs, in journalistic writing, 240–41
parallel structure, 15, 16, 84
for prepositions, 107
for series of items, 94–95, 240
for series of verbs, 95
paraphrasing
attributions for, 186, 336
in broadcast writing, 352
guidelines for, 184, 189, 190
punctuation for, 183, 185, 188–89
verb tense and, 68–69, 189
parentheses, 31, 32, 194
parenthetical elements, 25, 31–32. *See also*
nonrestrictive elements
participial phrases
at beginning of sentence, 180, 341
as modifiers, 29, 112
in nominative absolutes, 112
participles, 14
as adjectives, 97, 105
confusing with gerunds, 55
dangling, 17, 112, 240
defined, 82, 97
objective pronouns with, 55
object of, 41, 50
as prepositions, 105, 107
verb tenses and, 97, 105
parts of speech
defined, 14–15
words that change form, 14, 18–21
See also specific parts of speech
pass/adopt, 21, 119
passive voice, 71–76
confusing with other verb forms, 73–74
consistency in using, 95
defined, 20, 71–72
guidelines for spotting, 73
in journalistic writing, 75
reasons for avoiding, 72–73, 241, 254
verb *to be* in, 72, 73, 74

past-participle forms
of irregular verbs, 65–67
passive voice and, 73, 75, 76
past-perfect progressive tense, 63, 67
past-perfect tense, 62, 67
past-progressive tense, 63, 68
past tense, 61, 67
of irregular verbs, 65–67
of regular verbs, 64–65
sequence of, 67–68
of subjunctive mood, 79
people. *See* names and titles
percentages
strategies for using, 244
style rules for, 350, 352, 368, 376
verb agreement with, 88–89
perfect, 99
perfect tense, 61–63
periods
with abbreviations, 178, 197, 368
common problems with, 196–97
with quotation marks, 26, 190
person, of verb, 60–61
person agreement, of pronouns, 16, 47,
93
personal communications, informal style
for, 9, 10
personal home pages, credibility of, 357
personalizing
in broadcast writing, 341
in soft-news leads, 336
persuade to, 17, 133
PEW Research Center, 364
photo manipulation, online media and,
365
phrases, 14
as connecting words, 30
defined, 28
editing wordy, 253, 257–86
misused and commonly confused,
16–17, 118–73
as modifiers, 29
as nouns, 38–39
restrictive and nonrestrictive, 31–32
as subjects and objects, 29
as verbs, 29
place
abbreviations for, 370–71
in broadcast writing, 344, 347
capitalizing, 372
in news leads, 324–25, 329, 330
plagiarism, 364–65
plant names, 44
plurality, 88, 89, 153
plural nouns, 26
rules for, 44–45
verb agreement with, 88
plural pronouns, 18, 47, 89–90
political affiliations, 370, 374
"politically correct" language, 292
population, changing U.S., 290–92, 300
possession, prepositions indicating, 107

Copy-Editing Marks

Below are the most commonly used manuscript markings. Keep this list handy when editing or reading an edited or proofread manuscript.

⌐Indent for new paragraph

(no)¶ No paragraph (in margin)

Run in or bring⁀copy together

Join words: week‿end

Insert a⌃word or phrase

Insert a mis⌃ing letter

Take out an extra letter

Transpose (words⌐two)

Transpose t(ow) letters

Make ⁄etter lowercase

Capitalize columbia

Indicate *italic* letters

Indicate small capitals

Indicate **bold face type**

Abbreviate (January) 30

Spell out (abbrev.)

Spell out number (9)

Make figures of (thirteen)

Separate run⌐together words

Join letters in a w⌒ord

Insert period⨀

Insert comma ⋏

Insert quotation marks ⱽ ⱽ

Take out ~~some~~ word

Don't make ~~this~~ correction *stet*

Mark ⌉centering⌊ like this

Indent copy from both sides by using these marks

Indent copy on left

Spell name [Smyth] as written

or

Spell name Smyth as written (l.c.)

There's more story: (MORE)

This ends story: # (30)

Do not obliterate copy; mark it out ~~with a thin line~~ so it can be compared with editing.

Mark in hyphen: =

Mark in dash: ⊢⊣